The Exploration of Ideas

'Allamah Muhammad Taqi Ja'fari

A Collection of
Interviews and Dialogues Conducted by
Global Scholars on Religion, Mysticism, Literature,
Culture, Aesthetics, Philosophy, Human Sciences
with Allameh M. T. Ja'fari

Translated by
Beytollah Naderlew

Edited by
Shahriar Fassih

Top Ten Award International Network
Vancouver, BC
Canada

Published by: Top Ten Award International Network Inc.

Vancouver, BC **CANADA**
Email: Info@TopTenAward.Net
www.toptenaward.net

Ordering Information:
Quantity sales. Special discounts are available on quantity purchases by universities, schools, corporations, associations, and others. For details, contact the "Sales Department" at the above mentioned email address.

The Exploration of Ideas, 'Allamah Muhammad Taqi Ja'fari
ISBN: 978-1-990451-89-8   Paperback

In The Name Of Allah,
the most Beneficent, the
most Gracious, the most
Merciful!

Contents

Contents \ 11

Introduction

We should see the exchange of ideas and opinions as a path towards the beyond which, according to theosophers, starts from the "invisible", stretches into other existential orders and finally touches the "Mystery of Mysteries". In fact, thoughts, in their essence and structure, besides having a clear sign of depths, are continuously in search of depths and sometimes even in search of the depths of depths.

The first thing to which one can ascribe this excavation of depths is undoubtedly the essence of thought itself. The search for springheads and the reclamation of beginnings are counted among the most fundamental aspects of thought. Thus, one cannot find any thought indisposed of depth in at all. It is also to be mentioned that the thinking faculty is illimitable due to its springy and resilient nature. It is this very quality of thinking that has induced thinkers to consider it the moving immovable; indeed, how can one envisage it otherwise while thinking is the mother of every idea, perception, discovery, achievement and all spiritual and corporeal realities?

History itself has proven that human identity is indeed built upon thinking as such. Consciousness and wisdom, which are two cornerstones of a conscious life for all nations, represent only two reflective extensions of this primordial quality of humanity. Thinking is an integrated process which begins with the simplest of matters and continues through the most sophisticated psychological and existential realities of human beings and ends up in an eternal synthesis of past, present and future.

Thus, no one would ever cast any doubt over this part of the identity of thinking. These remarks bring us to the point which is worthy to be touched in this prologue, i.e. the enrichment and amendment of ideas under the auspices of debates and dialogues. A renowned Arabic proverb says that the truth is the daughter of debate. Those who believe in the idea which has been articulated in this proverb are well aware that discussion heightens the flames of thought, which is enough to eradicate the darkness of ignorance and ambiguity.

It is not an exaggeration to say that nothing has ever been more illuminative than debate and dialogue in the history of ideas. Had people not engaged in dialogue with each other, life would have been confined only to misunderstandings and every possibility for an intellectual consensus, which is a prerequisite of both social and individual life, would have vanished. As a result, it must be reiterated time and again that dialogue has been among the first steps taken by man to find his way to the land of knowledge. Despite the impressive changes that human epistemic structures have gone through since the dawn of modernity, dialogue is still being seen as a unique path that can lead the wayfarers of knowledge to the kingdom of truth.

The significance which is attached here to dialogue has its origin in the fact that in dialogue, a single mind does not undertake the issue; rather, at least two minds along with their specific presuppositions, backgrounds and methods engage in a debate to shed light on the dark sides of the issue at hand. This has to be elaborated more in its due place. In the second half of the twentieth century, two scholars have been the pioneers of religious dialogues and debates in Iran – though from different perspectives and in their own particular manners: Allameh Muhammad Hussein Tabatabaei and Allameh Muhammad Taghi Ja'fari. Allameh Tabatabaei's intellectual engagements were typically focused on the traditions of Iranian wisdom and philosophy, as reflected in his groundbreaking dialogues with Professor Henry Corbin. On the other hand, Allameh Ja'fari's debates and dialogues with world-leading thinkers and scholars covered a wider range of issues and areas of knowledge.

The publication of Ja'fari's intellectual engagements with Eastern and Western scholars and academics on theology, philosophy, culture and almost all fields of human sciences in the early 80's in his native country revealed for Persian readers another constructive and serious face of the philosopher's thought. Now the work is being published to be presented to the global audience.

It should be noted that most of these interviews and dialogs took place in Jafari's home library, while some others took place in Switzerland, Greece and several other different countries.

This work would have not seen the light of the day if some generous people had not assisted the AJI. We would like to offer our wholehearted thanks to Dr. Beytollah Naderlew, who passionately translated this voluminous work into English. We are also obliged by a number of people who kindly assisted the Institute in the preparation of original draft of the book in Persian: Ali Rafei, Shahram Taghizadeh Ansari, Mohsen Sahraiyan and Narges Sadat Butorabi. The AJI hopes that the reader will find a way beyond by excavation of the depths of these dialogues and interviews.

We hereby feel obliged to thank Mr. Shahriyar Fassih as the editor, Prof. S. M. A. Boutorabi and Mr. Mahmood Ahmadirad for their cooperation in the compilation of this book. We would also like to thank Mrs. Roya Azizi Mousavi for setting the computer layout and Mr. Saeed Ajami for designing the cover of this book.

The Allameh Jafari Institute
March, 2015

About the Author

Muhammad Taghi Ja'fari (born 1923, Tabriz, Iran, and died 1998) was a contemporary sage and an expert in philosophy and Islamic knowledge. Ja'fari was familiar with Western culture and also with the needs of modern human being and the contemporary culture. He was indeed an original and innovative thinker.

One of the most important innovations of this honorable master was that he, like Allameh Tabatabaei and Sayyed Muhammad Bagher Sadr, used the methodology of comparative studies for introducing Islamic knowledge to a generation who was thirsty for truth. Indeed, Ja'fari has left us a collection of invaluable works on Islamic teachings, philosophy of arts, aesthetics, literature, mysticism, the study of the *Nahjulbalaghah*, psychology, human rights and pedagogy.

In addition to being an expert in philosophy, in Islamic mysticism and in *Fiqh* (jurisprudence), Ja'fari was familiar with the works and the ideas of classical Western philosophers such as Socrates, Plato, and Aristotle. He was also versed in the works of modern philosophers including Descartes, Leibniz, Hume, Kant, Hegel, and contemporary philosophers such as Balzac, Dostoevsky, Tolstoy, Hugo, and modern-day physicists including Max Planck, and Einstein.

Ja'fari's epistemic geometry comprises of the knowledge of the mind, the revelation and the heart, tradition and modernity, physics and metaphysics, law and aesthetics. While the first three sources were the main pillars of his thinking, the expressions of his thoughts were nonetheless the result of dialogues made on the different bases of this epistemic geometry, which – due to their up-to-date nature – made his works novel and attentive to the debates on the difficulties of the "modern human" and the "modern life".

Ja'fari's 15-volume *Rumi: the Man and His Ideas, an Interpretation, Criticism and Analysis of Rumi's Masnavi* and his 27-volume *Translation and Interpretation of the Nahjulbalaghah* have a distinct place in his body of work. In terms of the clergies' principles, attending to Rumi's *Masnavi* was a heresy, or disliked to say the least. Moreover, writing commentaries on the *Nahjulbalaghah* was considered as a virtue, not a science. Scholarship was, and still is seen as footnoting on important books on *fiqh* (jurisprudence). It was in such an environment that the honorable master instilled *Masnavi* back in the minds of students and academicians. By comparing Rumi's sublime and amorous assertions with those of French and Russian thinkers and scholars, with whom Iranian intellectuals are more familiar, he once again took Rumi's *Masnavi* back into Iranian homes, in which households were more acquainted with Western culture. Afterwards, by writing an exegesis on the *Nahjulbalaghah*, entitled "A Manifesto on Wisdom, Mysticism and Politics," he familiarized the younger generation with an Islam devoid of superstition, factionalism and backwardness, an Islam based on the mind, revelation, justice and love. We can consider Ja'fari as the vanguard in writing commentaries on Rumi's *Masnavi* and the *Nahjulbalaghah* in the contemporary era, to whom all the later commentators are indebted.

According to Allameh Ja'fari, love and the mind are the two wings that make humans fly towards the absolute truth. The mind and revelation, science and religion, the mind and *shari'a* (Islamic law) are all compatible and do not contradict one another. Of course, the mind is the solid pillar of knowing (episteme). In his thoughts on the political principles of Islam, he saw justice, compassion, mercy, tolerance, serving the people, and reliance on consultation (*Shura*) and also on people's decisions as the basis of Islamic governance.

In terms of personal character and ethical manner, despite his high stature, Ja'fari was humble and modest. Unlike some learned scholars, he did not consider himself as someone who knew everything; there was no trace of arrogance and contemptuousness in him. Throughout his productive life, he preferred the trappings of science by devoting himself wholeheartedly to the cultivation of intellectual life.

He passed away on 15 November, 1998 suffering from a cancer disease in London. He was buried in Dar-Al-Zohd, by Imam Reza's Holy Shrine in Mashhad.

The Allameh Jafari Institute

The Persian Editor's Note

From 1961 to 1998, a large number of great men of science and knowledge conducted interviews and dialogues with Allameh Muhammad Taghi Ja'fari in fields involving human sciences, theology, philosophy, mysticism and the foundations of sciences. These interviews and dialogues show that there are so many common constructive principles in the domain of human knowledge that the ruining conflicts between the nations could in fact be adjusted into constructive competitions and scholars from different cultural backgrounds can sincerely compete and challenge each other on religious culture, worldview and social and moral management in an atmosphere far away from egotisms and inhumane incentives.

By reviewing the factors influential in human developments throughout history, one may come to the conclusion that these factors had been consequences of constructive challenges and competitions of various cultures of human society. Thus, if we are supposed to contribute to the human progress which is vital for human survival in this part of history, which could be considered a turning point in human history, we should engage in the aforementioned competitions rather than in the critique of destructive cultures.

To reach this end,which is also reflected in the dialogues conducted by Ja'fari, I asked him to edit this collection and prepare it for publication. I was lucky enough to take on the task and accomplish it.

This book provides promising reading for those who wish to see a world ruled by goodness and wisdom, and at the same time it is a dependable source for those scholars and researchers who seek to know man in genuine sense and Islam as well as Islam in its pure form.

I should like to point out the life-long untiring efforts of Ja'fari, who has sincerely offered human society brilliant ideas and novel innovations in philosophy, humanities and religious studies resulting in a bulk of 127 volumes of his collected works, only 95 volumes of which have been published so far.

The following remarks embody my strategy in editing and preparing this work for the publication:

1- All interviews and dialogues contain the answers provided by

Allameh Ja'fari exactly as he articulated them, without additional adjustments.

2- I have added explanations as footnotes to the book wherever I felt it necessary to expand Ja'fari's arguments.

3- In some cases, I've asked Allameh Ja'fari to elaborate his points; these sections have been interpolated into the text after three asterisks (*).

4- The ordinary marginal events which happen in every dialogue and interview, like greetings and compliments, have been cleared off the text as unnecessary.

For example, in 1971, Ja'fari held a dialogue with a group of thinkers and scholars from the Soviet Union in his personal library. When the guests lined up so as to be introduced to him by the translator person to person, Ja'fari asked the guests to avoid this ceremony, arguing, "There is no need for such ceremonies as your host is a seminarian. Please come in and have a seat!" This remark of Ja'fari's created an atmosphere of friendship and sincerity which governed this two hour-long session with the Russian scientists and scholars.

5- As the intellectual readers will see for themselves, these dialogues and interviews have been held in an intellectual and scientific atmosphere.

6- In 1974, a conference was held in the Islamic Society of Philosophy and Wisdom on Islam and Christianity, which hosted a number of German scholars. It was in this symposium where Ja'fari broached his innovative idea of Abrahamic Primordial Religion as the common ground of all revealed religions. This novel idea of Ja'fari's was warmly received by native and foreign (Moslem and Christian) participants. Then, Ja'fari elaborated this idea in a lengthy article which appeared in the 17th volume of his seminal 27-volume Translation and Interpretation of the Nahjulbalaghah.[1] Moreover, after Professor Koroda's interview with the Allameh on the unity of the Islamic community, Ja'fari wrote a relatively lengthy essay on this issue, which has been published in the 22th volume of his Interpretation of the Nahjulbalaghah. I've included these essays after their respective interviews as I thought it would be much

---

1- Upon the editor's permission, this article – which has been included in the 17th volume if the Ja'fari's treatise on the *Nahjulbalaghah* entitled "The History of Monotheism Is Tantamount to the History of Humanity" – was removed from the present work. (AJI).

easier for the reader to see these articles in the present work.

7- The names of the interviewers have been indicated in the opening of each chapter along with their nationalities and professional majors.

8- In some cases, after answering the questions presented by the interviewer, he would ask, "Any questions?" and the interviewer would reply, "No, I have no question, continue please". Thus, some relevant remarks have been added to the answers.

I would like to express my gratitude to all colleagues and friends who assisted us in the preparation of this work and ask the Lord to compensate their sincere contributions and efforts.

Ali Rafei

Author's Preface

During the long course of the history of human life, whenever the occasion arose for the emergence and progression of civilizations, sciences, exalted ideas and cultures, dialogues between civilizations and the exchange of truth-seeking researches and ideas between peoples and nations from various ethnic and cultural backgrounds have played a really indispensible role. The fruitfulness of these dialogues and intellectual exchanges are contingent upon some conditions, the most significant of which are as follows:

↓ A sound knowledge of, accompanied with a well articulated understanding of, the ideas, opinions, principles and related issues shared by those who have engaged themselves in the process of dialogue and intellectual exchange – i.e., the men of ideas who seek to clear a room for dialogue need to have at least an unblemished knowledge of their posited thoughts. It is needless to say that the deeper and broader the knowledge and scholarship of the posited ideas for dialogue are, the better the expected outputs will be. It is also beyond all doubts that dialogical mediums, specifically those local and international mass media in charge of the presentation of ideas, opinions and cultures, have an unrivalled role in this respect, as these mediums could seek their own purported goals through intellectual exchanges.

↓ Enough tolerance for giving one's ears to and the acceptance of any truth that is posed and keeping oneself in safe distance from the prejudice for and the defense of a wrong situation that one finds oneself stuck in. Indeed, as Rumi has put it:

> Severity and prejudice is equivalent to being crude and raw;
> As long as you are an embryo, all you do is suck blood...[1]

↓ Intellectual sincerity in the expression of facts, principles and issues that one stands for along with an equal openness for the acquaintance with ideas and problems posed by others without surrendering oneself to the lusts of egotism that may bring unmanageable havoc upon the edifice of human knowledge.

1- Rumi's *Masnavi*, Book 3.

↓ Turning a brown eye to this condition could trigger numerous maddening conflicts and dilapidating clashes instead of tiling the path for constructive intellectual dialogues and engagements as one can easily provide countless historical evidences for it; not to mention the possible scientific and cultural disorders that could deprive innumerable citizens.

↓ When an idea, principle or issue already has been established as a matter of certainty, the inquirer must devote himself to a sincere defense of it as far as he can, since any negligence in the expression and defense of realities eventually results in scientific and cultural backwardness.

What has frequently proven its primordial veracity to me during the past thirty years is the fact that if unscientific, utilitarian and despotic issues and orientations keep their noses away from truth-seeking inquiries, human sympathies on the highest principles of material and spiritual life are so extensive and deep-seated that there remains almost no room for injustice and ruining conflicts.

***

Since 1961, I have had various debates, dialogues and interviews with a number of distinguished and gifted men of ideas both from the East and the West over religious, literary, philosophical, mystical, scientific, aesthetic, ethical and legal issues, and records of these talks have been kept in my collection of library notes. In 1991, Mr. Ali Rafei resolved to edit them. I would like to express my heartfelt gratitude to Mr. Rafei, whose sincere efforts have made it possible for this work to see the light of day.[1]

M. T. Ja'fari
Summer 1993

1- It is also necessary to mention that this volume has been thoroughly revised by the editorial body of the AJI in 2009. Some of the Ja'fari's unpublished dialogues before his decease in 1998 have been added.

1

Prof. Rosenthal

Subject: Ownership, Ransom and the Penalty of Larceny
Nationality: German / Area of Expertise: Law
Dialogue Date: 1961

Allameh Ja'fari's dialogues with Western and Eastern scientific and philosophical dignitaries and scholars began in 1961.

In this year, two gifted Western professors, Professor Rosenthal, a German jurist, and Professor Young, an American literary Orientalist, conducted some interviews and dialogues with Ja'fari. Moreover, an American Ph. D. student in philosophy, who was planning to write his dissertation on Fakhr-e Razi,[1] started his discussions – which would continue over the next two years – with him in the same year.

Professor Rosenthal was the first Western scholar who engaged in a dialogue with Ja'fari. He was a celebrated and courteous thinker and would always pose his questions very politely. Kenneth Allan Luther, a Ph.D. student in Eastern philosophy, was his companion in the interviews. These interviews were conducted during the period Ja'fari was residing in the Pachenar district in Tehran. Professor Rosenthal posed some questions regarding ownership, ransom and the penalty for larceny.

1- Also known as Imam Fakhr al-Din al-Razi (1148-1210), he was an Iranian medieval Asharite theologian who launched a series of remorseless objections on philosophical ideas, specifically those that Avicenna has inscribed in his *Al-Isharat wa-'l-tanbihat ("Remarks and Admonitions")*. (Translator).

Rosenthal: In your view, is ownership a genuine and substantial phenomenon in human societies or a mentally posited phenomenon that is brought about by contextual issues?

Ja'fari: On ownership, we can pose two questions:

1. Does this phenomenon have its origin in the actual realities of man and the world? Or, to pose the question differently, does ownership have a true basis in reality as a globally appreciated social phenomenon that has extensively been debated by scholars from various schools of thought?

2. Does ownership represent a mentally posited idea that originates in marginal issues of life and is indeed an epiphenomenon?

For example, marriage owes its essentiality first of all to the indispensability of reproduction. This necessity is immediately followed by the issue of sexual desires; in fact, God has guaranteed the reproduction process by means of an ever-growing pleasure to secure the Divine Command of creation.

Now we should ask whether ownership has the same essentiality that is found in marriage or not. It seems that ownership is a substantial phenomenon, but as to whether it has the same degree of essentiality that one finds in marriage and wedlock, we shall need to pursue a different line of research.

Although some have understood it in purely mental terms, ownership not only is not an imaginary epiphenomenon, but it in fact represents a deep-seated phenomenon. One underlying reason for this latter claim lies in the fact that whenever man soundly gains something without crossing any line drawn by social institutions and human conscience, he will seek to make it his own alone and in an absolute fashion.

When someone has legitimately gained something, no one could nullify his ownership of that thing. But the quantity and quality of this ownership, however, is ultimately decided by religions, legal systems and definite norms. To put the matter otherwise, ownership as an essential phenomenon which has been loaded with many covenantal conditions such as limitedness, legitimacy, and last but not least, the condition that Islam puts the ultimate stress on, i.e. that ownership must be seen as a means, not an end in itself. In other words, ownership should not be turned into the heart of life. This condition would by no means hollow ownership from its substantiality; as a matter of fact, it seeks to relocate it in an intelligible fashion. Like many other human phenomena, ownership owes its essentiality to life and thus secures its continuity.

Ownership guarantees that everyone shall reach what he deserves according to his work. We exhaust our energies and time to keep the pot boiling. Now some guarantee is needed to warrant everyone's rights.

Some individuals or schools might reduce ownership to allocation so as to save themselves from the former's binding implications. However, this does not work appropriately. Both as a rule and a right, ownership must be understood in terms of its functions not as an end per se. This is a pedagogical matter in the sense that it should be internalized in citizens that such notions as ownership only keep the harmony of life and never should be approached in the spirit of a telos, for that would uproot all clashes and conflicts from the society.

On the other hand, we need take this fact into earnest consideration that ownership is a limited – rather than unlimited – phenomenon. This condition is to be met via conscientious legislations. In other words, no one is allowed to exercise his ownership right through such diabolic businesses as drug trafficking, which ruin the society and family.

Thus, ownership is limited and you cannot, for example, corner it. Otherwise, authorities will be allowed to confiscate your cornered property and put it up for auction. Of course, you are the owner of your properties, but this ownership is valid insofar as you have not crossed the drawn lines or trespassed on other citizens' rights. In that case, ownership is limited by certain measures that are taken by authorities in order to protect private and social rights.

Rosenthal: What sanctions this limited exercise of ownership right? How could we tell citizens that they are allowed to own their properties to this settled point?

Ja'fari: This issue is to be handled by the legal acts and religious codes of the society – whether the latter has a religious origin, like Islamic countries, or is of a secular nature, like many Western states, which legislate and articulate these acts and codes. To begin with, these acts and codes need to be secured upon the right philosophical ground – i.e., ownership is not the end in itself. When it is taught and dictated in our academic centers that ownership is limited and should be considered as a means not an end, the society will be prepared to take an appropriate legal approach.

On the other hand, they may argue that you cannot make use of your capital in a way that would have damaging consequences for the society. Besides the occasional reasons for the prohibition of illegitimate exercise of the ownership right that harms the society, such as the ban of cornering and drug trafficking, we have a series of reasons that is not merely determining in particular cases but speaks for the life-centeredness of laws. The law forbids every practice that is harmful for the society – *do not inflict injury nor repay one injury with another.*

The above-mentioned law states that we are not allowed to act and make use of our properties in a way that may harm the society. This prophetic tradition is authentic and immune to all jurisprudential doubts. In doing so, we can both limit ownership and determine the quality of its application. This is the most significant sanction warranting the limited ownership.

This sense of ownership has its roots in the economy fathomed within the parameters of Islam – an orthodox economy. The latter, on the other hand, is indeed an alternative to the liberal economy which breaks its monopoly. In an orthodox economy, the economical processes are continuously watched over by the experts lest they would result in capital accumulation that could lead to economical downturn and the abundance of private ownerships that harm the society. This is the very essence of an orthodox economy.

Rosenthal: In Islam, usury has been strongly prohibited, while today if usury or loan interest were to be removed from banks across the globe and other financial institutions, the global economy would certainly collapse. Having said these, are you still in favor of the ban on usury?

Ja'fari: It is not only Islam that has taken such a tough stance against usury, as it has also been severely banned in Judaism. Jewish jurisprudence explicitly suggests if a Jew lends money to his fellow Jew for the sake of its interest, both the lender and the one who is loaned to must be expelled from the Jewish nation.[1]

As it is needless to say, before Islam and Christianity, Judaism has already prohibited usury in the toughest terms. Even after Moses, we have Aristotle, who has declared usury as unlawful:

> As we have already mentioned, production is the principle of trade. Therefore, commerce and business are of secondary importance. As a result, among all forms of money-making, usury is the one most

---

1- Muhammad Hafez Sabri, *Between Judaism and Islam: A Jurisprudential Encounter.*

against nature. As the well-known saying in Athens goes, 'Fathers are not to bear babies'.[1]

This Aristotelian musing is truly thoughtful. He argues that money is merely the index of values and a means of exchange (labor for labor, labor for commodity, commodity for labor and commodity for commodity), since it does not feature a commodity and it is only commodity and labor that have applicative value. Except for two metals – gold and silver – which have also a relative applicative value, most of the units of currency used in trades worldwide have only exchange value and are no more than mere credit.

Of course, we must have in mind that Christian jurisprudence has also its origin in Jewish jurisprudence and besides religious schools, such philosophers as Aristotle have severely banned usury mainly because the money, which is merely a means and the index of values and only in the second place it stands for – surely if it is acceptable – the reserved wealth, should not reproduce itself by itself. This idea can serve as a strong argument for the prohibition of usury.

Rosenthal: Regarding the fact that at the end of the day we need to find some way to circulate the money, particularly in a case in which someone has money and wants to use it while he does not have ability to get involved in economical situations, then what should be done?

Ja'fari: This situation can be addressed by such economical procedures as the bailment of a capital or limited partnership. If the latter procedure, for example, were to be done correctly, then money would be circulated and at the same time, the interest would come from commodity and labor rather than from money itself.

Rosenthal: Once, in France, the authorities turned to limited partnership, but it did not result in a sound commerce. Do you suggest that this kind of business association could lead the money flow in human society toward a logical direction?

Ja'fari: Yes, if limited partnership is approached and implemented in real terms, in a way that the money itself is exposed to damage as the main reason for the ban on usury ban is the claim that money is immune to all harms and frictions which work force is continuously exposed to and expects to be added even when the business financed by it goes bankrupt. Everything is always exposed to loss and tort, except for the money lent for usury, which has been inoculated against

---

1- Aristotle, *Politics*.

all damages like an eternal monster! I think this is indeed in conflict with a socially-grounded economy. Human life must be replaced by jobbery. In doing so, money would find itself exposed to the same damages and dangers that work force is always entangled with.

Rosenthal: Of course, no one would accept to have his own money's buying power decreased, for the currency is always exposed to downfall. Now if someone lends money without getting anything by the end of year in the face of possible losses of capital bailment, then he has certainly suffered a loss.

Ja'fari: This is the most important question which is being posed about usury, and we will once again answer it by referring to a socially-grounded economy. As if the individual himself were able to use up his own money, he would be exposed to fiscal damages, by the same token, there is equally the possibility of damage and profit in the limited partnership as well. Thus, we should always consider these two possibilities. However, if you want to legally put the money into circulation, you would suffer losses; likewise, you might obtain inconceivable gains.

Power is also exposed to damage. Let us say that I might dig hundreds of wells and yet not even a single one of them ends up in water. Now how could money expect just to increase? Is it intelligible to think that among various works, commodities, intellectual and physical energies, only money can have the privilege not to suffer any losses? So if the damage is intolerable for individual investor, then what is the purpose for having a government? Social insurances have to deal with such situations. This is to say, at last, money should not vouch for my illegal life. As springtime does not last forever, energies are exhausted, credits decline and all of these are exposed to damage and exhaustion, money cannot remain the same, either. As a result, it must be correctly put into circulation, say, in the form of commodities and works so that if the latter suffered any losses, the money will also suffer equal losses.

Of course, the value of currency is perpetually on the decline and no one can help it in this regard, as you can't preserve the energy in your body organs. This energy must be expended and changed into beneficial work, and the society is also incumbent to pay you in exchange for your services, either in cash or by commodities. You know that your physical or mental energy cannot be preserved for a moment in future, since if you don't use it now, it shall be exhausted and depleted by tomorrow. If I do not use my muscles in youth, their power shall be drained with time. Money must have the same quality, and this quality is not reached through putting the money into circulation. Let us not, however, leave this fact unsaid that the society and state have to be responsible for the damages done to money invested like those of the work force and commodities.

Rosenthal: What should, in your view, be done by world banks?

Ja'fari: We have our own standing on this issue as well. We do not say that banks can be reformed by means of banning usury, as once it was thought impossible to uproot slavery from human societies, since it had penetrated through all dimensions and aspects of human life. Slavery had so immensely permeated into morality, religion and all cultures that man couldn't even imagine in his dreams that one day slavery would be entirely removed, but it in fact turned into reality by man. Islam entered through different paths and by various methods and extirpated slavery. As for usury, we have to bring home to people its pernicious effects both for the individual and the community so as to discredit it. The only issue which needs to be addressed is whether we could substantiate this for the laity or not. We should answer: yes, it can be substantiated, but the investor does not want to suffer any losses *right against the current!* Why should all energies and powers be exposed to exhaustion and depletion but allow money to remain an exception?

Rosenthal: Doesn't this appear to be much more than a Herculean task?

Ja'fari: Yes, but we need to remember that we once had such an estimation of slavery too, since it had already underpinned itself as a social institution. Today, usury has such a status.

Rosenthal: I would like to ask how limited partnership should be operationalized exactly.

Ja'fari: Limited partnership is in fact an association between the investor and the enterpriser. The one who takes the initiative to put the money into circulation through his business enterprise must act under the supervision of the state and along the lines drawn by it. The oriented nature of economy in Islam makes such things much easier for us. Nevertheless, we do not mean by this a governmental economy that is controlled by state leviathans in all its aspects, since human beings are free in choosing their desired undertakings, aims and means, of course, within the legitimate limits. We need a higher authority to guarantee the justness of contracts.

Rosenthal: It has been recorded that when Muslims conquered a land, they did impose a decided amount of tax upon the inhabitants called ransom. Isn't ransom like the toll always forced upon the oppressed throughout history by oppressors after having defeated them?

Ja'fari: No, ransom had never been a matter of imposition; rather, when Islam subdued other countries, particularly those which populated by the people of the Scripture who accepted to live under Islamic government, Islam charged them with a just sum of tax like other citizens. Thus, ransom had been a type of tax, not the toll forced upon the oppressed by bullies along the history.

When we study accounts of history, we see that one reason for Islam's progression has been this very just system of taxation. As Gustav Le Bon expressly argues:

> The prudence of Rightly-Guided Caliphs in state affairs was beyond corps arrangement and martial and military techniques which they had learnt in a short time. At first, they came in contact with peoples who had been quelled by the oppressions of tyrant oppressors and treated cruelly for long years. These oppressed proletariats willingly embraced the reign of new rulers, because they found themselves with perfect security and freedom from which they had been deprived in the past. The way these defeated people should be treated has already been determined in clear terms, and Moslem Caliphs, particularly in virtue of their good politics, never attempted to publicize religion through the bayonet. In fact, instead of exercising their influence in the dissemination of religiosity, as it is on the tongues of men, they openly stated that they would venerate all traditions, rituals and religions of defeated nations, and in lieu of the freedom they gave to these peoples, they received a small tribute as ransom, the amount of which had been inconsiderable as compared to the heavy taxes imposed to them by previous tyrants.

> Before mobilizing their troops toward a particular spot, these warriors proposed the peace conditions by special envoys and these conditions, as it has been quoted by Abul Mahasin, are basically the same conditions that Amru As proposed to Gaza residents, who were under siege, in the year 17 A.H. and were also suggested to Iran and Egypt too. They read as follows:

> "Our ruler has ordered us to fight you if you do not accept Islamic Shari'ah. Then come to us and be our brothers and partners in all interests. Beware! From now on, no damage or injury from us shall inflict you. If you are not satisfied with these conditions, you need to

pay us annually a determined amount as tribute (ransom) in return of which we pledge to battle with those who try to hurt you or are hostile toward you. We shall never breach the contract that we sign with you, and if you reject this too, then nothing will judge between us but the sword, and we shall fight you until the command of Allah is fulfilled."

The behavior of the Second Caliph in the conquest of Jerusalem exemplifies the manner of the Moslem conquerors when it came to dealing with defeated nations, but in contrast to this good manner, some centuries later, the crusaders treated people in a manner that is terribly shocking. Omar — the Second Caliph — entered the city with few companions and mannerly asked Sophronius to help them visit sacred dignities. At the same time, he ordered the announcer to state, "We are obligated to preserve this city's properties and holy places; even Moslems are not allowed to pray in churches."

The way Amru As treated the Egyptians was by no means lesser than this manner. He ordained them to be free in their religion and rituals, the law and justice to be equally implemented among them, the actions taken about their properties and tenements to be according to the rules of ownership and instead of the huge sums that were imposed upon them by the monarchs of Constantinople. In fact, he ordered everyone to pay a paltry sum — amounted to 15 franc — as ransom annually.

The peasants from environs and outlying areas prized this contract so much that they embraced it fast, gathered the peace price and consigned it as ransom.

The agents of the Islamic administration were so unflinching in their pact and treated the people so graciously that they chose Islam and Arabic with open arms. I should reiterate once again that such achievements cannot be ever obtained by the force of the sword, and the conquerors that entered Egypt never could have scored such successes.

There is a point in Arab conquests that is not found in other conquerors. In fact, other nations — like Barbarians who conquered Rome and gained illustrious victories — could not establish a civilization; rather, they sought to plunder the properties of the defeated nation. On the contrary, Moslem conquerors laid the foundations of a new civilization in a short time, and prepared the people of the conquered lands to imbibe all of the elements of this new civilization, even its religion and language.

The ancient nations of Egypt and India accepted the language, costumes and etiquettes of these conquerors through the companionship that we earlier spoke of. In addition, they even adopted their architectural style. Of course, other nations had conquered these lands before and ruled them for a while, but the influence exerted by the teachings of the Prophet Muhammad (SAW) on these countries still remains unchanged.

In all African and Asian lands, from Morocco to India, wherever an impression has remained from Moslem warriors, the impression proves itself to be unchanging. Even the conquerors that have entered these countries could not obliterate the imprint of their religion and language. Among all these nations, it is only Andalusia that has delivered itself from the bondage of Islamo-Arabic civilization, but, as we shall demonstrate in the near future, this land accelerated its decline by means of this deliverance.[1]

To substantiate this claim, I shall now provide you with two arguments, the first of which is supported by an authentic historical book which reads:

Abu Hafaz of Damascus quotes Saeed Ibn Abdulaziz to have said, "It has been reported through Yemen that when Heraclius gathered his troops for battling the Moslems, and the Moslems were informed that the troops dispatched by Heraclius have been prepared for the Yarmuk battle, they returned the taxes they had received from the people of Hamas and told them, 'Now we cannot take on your protection. You should run and defend yourselves, since we are too busy dealing with the critical situation on our hands.'

The people of Hamas said, 'Your administration and justice is better for us than our former situation, when we lived under the pressures and tortures of oppressors. We will drive Heraclius' troops out of the city under your leadership.' Then the Jews also rose and said, 'Swear to Torah! The commander of Heraclius' troops shall not enter the city unless we make our best and yet to be defeated.'

The people of Hamas closed the gates of the city. The residents of other cities, whether Christians or Jews, who had signed a peace pact with the Moslems, did the same thing the people of Hamas had done. They said, "If the Romans overcome the Moslems, we shall return to the

---

1- Gustav Le Bon, *La Civilization d'Islam et Arab.*

state we were formerly in, and if they do not, we shall remain faithful to our pact with the Moslems to our last breath."

When God vanquished the pagans and helped the believers to overcome their enemies, the Jews and Christians opened the gates for the Moslem troops, welcomed them with open arms and paid them their tributes.[1]

Therefore, ransom was never an imposition. This issue had a jurisprudential basis; in fact, although the tax is supposed to be consumed for coexistence and running collective life, whenever the governing body fails to fulfill its commitments, it is not both legally and canonically allowed to impose ransom.

The Second Argument: Some jurisprudents, including Muhaqiq Helli, the author of *Shari'ah*, have stated that when a man from the People of the Book who have signed a pact of coexistence with us commits felonious homicide, such as when a Jew kills a Christian unintentionally, or if a Christian or a Jew murders a Moslem by accident, since the murder is unintentional the verdict will not be reprisal. In such a case, the convict is initially asked whether he can pay the blood price himself or not. If he is not able to pay it, it must be paid from the Islamic state treasury. Since people have paid their taxes, the Islamic state treasury is committed to pay their debts.[2]

Rosenthal: Isn't hand-chopping a cruel punishment for theft? This punishment is not working, and temporal goods is not something in return of which a member of human body to be chopped off. Moreover, the one who loses his hand cannot easily pull himself together and seek a respectful life in the society.

Ja'fari: I agree that it seems cruel to cut off one's hand for temporal goods. The laws of Islamic Shariah are seemingly cruel, like the Code of Hammurabi[3] on the surface, but this is in fact not true. According to our researches, the execution of such punishment requires more than twenty conditions to be fulfilled. One of these conditions, for instance, is that the thief should not be in a state of emergency in all its forms such as inflation, recession, famine and even economic insecurity. One of the reasons for the stipulation of a non-emergency state as a

---

1- Abu al-Abbas Ahmad Ibni Yahya Ibni Jaberi(Balazori), *Futuh ul-Buldan*,Vol. 1.
2- Prof. Rosenthal insisted that the Allameh to publish these key ideas as the lawyers and sociologists need to read them.
3-A code consisting of 282 laws established by King Hammurabi of Babylonia during the 18th century BC. (Translator).

condition of the realization of theft is the exposition provided by Imam Reza (PBUH)' that has been related in a narration:

> *A thief had been arrested and Mamun wanted to punish him. "I have not thieved voluntarily," the thief argued, "in fact, it was you who deprived me from my right! Firstly execute your own penalty then punish others," and the Imam (PBUH) detailed the audience of this argument.*[1]

In the same gathering, Mamun al-Rashid said, "I shall not abandon the Lord's laws for this nonsense." At this time Imam Reza (PBUH) stated, "The thief has raised his own argument and you must respond to it. Social conditions have enforced him to commit this sin." This caused Mamun to harbor a grudge against Imam Reza (AS).

For example, if an object or some money is dropped in an alley and someone comes and picks it and leaves, he has not committed theft, but such an act is regarded as usurpation. It can be taken back and returned to its owner, and no hand will be chopped off. Or if someone picks one's pocket and leaves, this is not theft and no hand is hewn, for it is in fact regarded as aggressive domination. Among others are the conditions that the individual should be conscious of the subject and its penalty, or that the individual should not have stolen from a property of which he is a beneficiary. In addition, it should not be from the Islamic state treasury, since he has his own share there, as well as other conditions that amount to twenty articles.[2]

The Conditions of the Realization of Theft and the Execution of a Penalty

Some conditions are needed to be gathered for the realization of theft in a form that causes penalty the absence of even one of which leads to penalty decline although not to the elapse of punishment in general. Now we turn to articulate these conditions:

1- Property-ness

The stolen object must have property-ness – regarded as a legitimate property according to Shari'ah Law to be owned by someone – thus, stealing something like wine which is not canonically declared a

---

1- See *Uyuni Akhbar al-Reza (PBUH)*, Chapter 58.

2-These twenty conditions of the realization of theft in Islam have been subsequently articulated for the reader. For more information on the subject, see Ja'fari, M. T., *The Message of Reason*, 2000. (Originally in Persian).

property does not lead to penalty.

2- Limit
The property should have reached the limit that is one fourth or fifth of a Dinar.

3- Not being a beneficiary of the property
Stealing from something like the Public Treasury of which the thief is himself a beneficiary is not a theft unless he overreaches his right. Stealing a property of which the theft is a beneficiary is of two kinds:

I)   The robber is not able to reach his own right through legal routes and inevitably acquires his right by theft. In such a case, not only the committed action is not theft and is naturally without penalty. Rather, it is not basically a crime and does not lead to arbitrary punishment.

II)   The thief is not deprived from legal proceedings to obtain his right, no matter what kind of theft he commits. In this case, although the penalty is not valid, the criminal is punished for trespassing public treasury.

4- Not being participated in property
Stealing from a property that is shared by a number of people including the thief is not theft, and if the property is a trust, then it is an abuse of confidence.

5- Not to be a trust
If someone steals from a property held by him as a trust, his action is not theft but it is a breach of confidence.

6- Safekeeping
The property should be kept safely in a place that could not be easily reached. This condition depends on common sense understanding.

7- Furtive stealing
The property should have been stolen furtively and the existence of exterior force and dominance causes the penalty to be thwarted, although the robber is punished for aggressive domination.

8- Complete involvement
The thief should have been completely involved in the crime in the

sense that the thief must have done everything needed for the theft by himself, such as breaking the lock, taking the property and so on.

9- The absence of deception
Stealing something by deceiving its owner is not regarded as theft, but it is an example of other criminal designation.

10- The absence of paternal relationships
A father's stealing from his child's property does not cause penalty, although not vice versa.

11- Knowledge of the subject and judgment
The thief should be informed of the judgment and the subject of the theft. Thus, if he steals something on the supposition that it is not theft or he understands the concept of theft but is not knowledgeable of its judgment, the penalty is declined.

Note: This is a point of supremacy of the legal system of Islam against many schools of law that "do not see the ignorance of law a reason for thwarting the punishment." Of course, the ignorance that shuffles off the responsibility should not be rooted in individual delinquency; to put it otherwise, it must be an effect of the cultural and social situation that needs to be recognized by the ruler.

12- The Material Realization of Theft
What renders the execution of penalty possible is the material realization of theft. Accordingly, if a convict proceeds to steal a property with the intention of theft, while some conditions are absent, the penalty shall be declined.

Note: This is one of the conditions versus other two elements of the fulfillment of crime (spiritual and legal elements), not in general.

Complementary Note: On the intention of theft and its commitment with regards to the very action that is done, two issues are necessary to be taken into account:

I) If someone intentionally steals a property that is not safe-kept, though the penalty shall be removed from him, he will be punished for such crimes as usurpation and the like.

II) If someone intentionally steals a property and then it is revealed to him that the stolen object had been his own, not only is the penalty removed from him, but punishment is also baseless, since the committed action is basically allowed. What is important here is that the intention of theft is essentially repulsive and the legal authority in charge can punish the convict for reformative purposes.

13- Age of Maturity

The thief should have already entered the age of maturity – which is 16 for men and 10 in women.

Note: If the thief has not yet reached the age of maturity, he will be punished after reaching that age, provided he has consciousness and recognition -- unless he is evaluated as absolutely free from all forms of punishment.

14- Psychological Balance

Committing theft following psychosis or other psychic disorders that blur the person's behavior leads to a removal from penalty. In such cases, it is up to the ruler to take proper actions for ensuring security.

15- Free Will

The theft is to have happened at the thief's own will. Thus,

I) If the theft has been committed by reluctance, the penalty shall be declined. Reluctance consists of the repression of one's will by other people or a group's wills.

II) If the theft has been committed under pressure and compulsion, the penalty shall be dismissed. Compulsion consists of one's being removed from his will when he commits the crime.

16- The Absence of Public Emergency

Public emergency may be documented to one of the following triple factors:

I) Natural hazards such as drought, famine, earthquake, pandemic diseases and the like.

II) Economic crises

III) Political turbulences

17- Ownership

If it is proven that the thief owns the stolen property, he will be removed from the penalty.

18- Repentance

If the thief expresses his repentance from the crime he has committed, the penalty is dismissed.

Note: Needless to say that this repentance should not be formal and the criterion of its formality is the repetition of crime.

19- Confession and Repentance

In this case, the consequent punishment after the decline of the penalty is decided by the ruler.

20- Intimidation

Intimidation of the act of theft during the process of investigations that causes the stolen object to be returned leads to penalty dismissal.

21- Crime Demonstration

The demonstration of crime and penalty execution needs the thief to confess twice.

22- Eye-witness

This article states that the demonstration of crime needs two just witnesses to attest with the same narratives against the thief.

23- The owner

The execution of the penalty depends on the decision of the stolen object's owner, and he can decide to spare the thief.

24- Preventing the convicts from expressive confession

The ruler can prevent the convict from expressive confession by dictating to him, "Were you in a state of emergency? Did you know the penalty of theft?" and other questions like this so as to inflame the sense of repentance in the convict and save him from the doomed penalty.

25- Doubt thwarts the penalty

As soon as doubt is raised about one of the constituent elements of theft, the penalty is removed. This is based on a jurisprudential principle that reads: "doubt thwarts the penalties".

26- There are also other secondary conditions that can be found in jurisprudential books on the subject.

Conclusion

The conclusion that is drawn from this brief discussion is that chopping off the thief's hand as the penalty of theft is more similar to actions that are called "deterrent punishments" in modern law rather than the penalties that are necessarily executed.

This penalty is like an unsheathed sword in the hands of the blindfolded angel of justice that had not chopped off any hand for a long time. If social and individual education finds a logical configuration, it is quite likely that generations will come after one another without any hand hewn with this unsheathed sword.[1]

In fact, this penalty is for protecting people's properties that sometimes cost innocent blood. Someone's property might be stolen, and although it may seem worthless in price, it can nevertheless be vital for that person's whole life and cause unbelievable troubles. Accordingly, in the early days of Islam, we see that some penalties were executed. We read these 26 conditions for prominent lawyers and they were convinced, stating that with all these conditions, the thief is a real threat to a nation. These 26 conditions are like 26 red lights that are being passed by an individual, and such an individual could jeopardize a nation for his selfishness.

1- We must once again emphasize and reiterate that penalty suspension here does not mean the absolute suspension of punishment; in fact, it refers to paler forms of discipline.

2

Dr. Kenneth Allan Luther

Subject: Islamic Philosophy and Theology
Nationality: American/ Major: Eastern Philosophy and Theology
Dialogue Date: 1961

> *Luther's dissertation was about Fakhr-e Razi's[1] philosophy and theology. For almost one year, every Tuesday and Thursday, he came to Allameh Ja'fari's house and studied Fakhr-e Razi's 'Arbaein' [which translates as 'Forty'] with him. During these sessions, several questions were asked by Luther of Razi's book, and Ja'fari answered them. Hereunder, a significant number of these questions have been quoted:*

Luther: What is the definition of philosophy and theology from Eastern and Western point of views?

Ja'fari: Various definitions have been suggested of philosophy in the past and even in our time, both in the East and the West. Nevertheless, the most comprehensive and exhaustive definition of philosophy is what we have been handed down by Sadrulmuta'allehin Shirazi[2], who in the articulation of which has extremely benefited from his

---

1- See the translator's footnote on first page of Chapter 1.

2- Muhammad Ibn Ibrahim Ibn Yahya al-Qawami al-Shirazi (1571–1640), also known as Mulla Sadra and Sadrulmuta'allehin ("the Foremost of Theosophers") is the founder of transcendent theosophy ("al-Hikmat al-Muta'alyah") in the history of Islamic philosophy. This new philosophical school is a synthesis of three intellectual perspectives, i.e. reason, gnosis and the Qura'n, whose fusion, in Sadra's view, can lead a philosopher to his primordial destination – the truth. Sadra's magnum opus is *al-Hikmat al-Mutaalyah fi al-Asfar al-Arbati al-Aqlyah* ("Transcendent Theosophy Concerning Four Intellectual Journeys") in nine volumes that serves the reader as an encyclopedia in Islamic Philosophy which deals with the perennial problems of philosophy in an active dialogue with other Islamic schools of philosophy – majorly peripateticism and illuminationism – and mysticism. (Translator).

predecessors. He states:

> *Philosophy is the knowledge of the reality of things within man's possibility.*

As you can see, the condition "within man's possibility" forestalls a serious challenge concerning this definition, since with our limited mental and perceptual tools, as well as the other cognitive apparatuses available to us, we cannot reach the reality of things "as they are". Thus, "within man's possibility" guarantees the intelligibility of this definition and reflects the true human ideal, i.e. reaching the reality of things.

In fact, it is a human ideal to touch the reality of things and be an honest beholder of it, but it is difficult to say how successful he has been in fulfilling this ideal. Thus, a considerable number of philosophers – of course, mostly in West – have stated that now that we cannot find any determinate subject-matter and a precise definition for philosophy, let us devote ourselves to those matters that should definitely be addressed by philosophy, such as the definition of matter, knowing the truth of motion, time, place, will, law, motive power of history and the like. Regardless of the definition that is proposed of philosophy, these are indisputable philosophical issues that have occupied many brilliant minds throughout history.

Luther: What is the basic cause of our inability to know the reality of things in your view?

Ja'fari: The other issue that I was about to address is the same thing you just mentioned. In defining and knowing things, we do not know the *real differentia* without which the definition will not be possible in perfect form. Real differentia is what essentially distinguishes one reality from other similar realities and allows us to say, for example, this is how an identity called water is defined. We do not have yet access to the real differentia of time and motion to distinguish them from other realities. As a result, whatever we make out of these matters is all based on logical differentia, the basis of which is usually assumed by thinkers in their intellectual pursuits. Notwithstanding, the real differentia is not merely contractual, but it is truly discerning.

For example, if we say "Man is a thinking animal", we are actually differentiating man from other living creatures that are by no means a thinking being. But is this quality called thinking the real differentia? Or when we, for instance, say that "Man is a social animal", have we in fact managed to discover the reality of man by knowing this differentia (thought or sociality)? Those thinkers, who are almost not one-sided, will give a negative answer to this question. Therefore, we accept Sadrulmuta'allehin's definition for philosophy with the condition "within human possibility."

Of course, the problem-oriented method[1] has its own advantages in philosophy, including the fact that it helps philosophers not become bogged down in fruitless abstractions. The debate of time, space, contingency and the eternity of the world and so on and so forth, for example, has its privileges, say it does not leave man in ambiguity concerning the basic principles of issues. However, these debates are not honestly whole and systematic; as a matter of fact, they are incoherent and such a philosophical form of knowledge is not satisfactory for humanity indeed.

In fact, as we aforementioned, the analytic method in philosophy[2] has the advantage that by its application, man is allowed to encounter a limited range of problems, but this approach turns a deaf ear to the synthetic nature of reality. To state the matter otherwise, it deprives us from the synthetic knowledge[3] of those particulars that constitute the universe as a whole.

There is no doubt that this method is also a human desire, particularly the desired method of sublime thoughts. It is not indeed unlikely that someone with a shallow knowledge is contented with this method, but for those individuals who are in possession of enlightened minds and seek to behold the universe from a broader aspect, these issues and also the problem-oriented method shall not prove to be satisfying.

Luther: Which one of these two methods is more significant in your final analysis?

Ja'fari: Both methods have their own respective values. The analytic

---

1- The problem-oriented method is a minimalistic view of philosophy that is grounded in the belief that if we cannot reach a perfect definition of philosophy as an independent discipline and epistemic enterprise, at least we can pursue it through problems. Allameh Ja'fari's views on this method have been elaborated in one of his works, *A Survey of the Philosophy of Science* (2007).

2- The analytic method in philosophy refers to a methodology upon which universal notions are being reduced into particular concepts through analytic methods until no more particular notion would be reached anymore, and with these basic particular notions, a proposition is constructed.

3- Synthetic knowledge stands at the heart of a research program in which the thinker appraises his propositional understanding of relations of natural facts in a broader context.

method helps the human mind to penetrate deep into the constitutive elements of existence as far as possible and present the propositions abstracted from them to the scientific community. On the other hand, the synthetic method allows man to reach an integrated vision of existence. In this latter method, science, knowledge and even life are not insulated phenomena cut off from principles and foundations. Some may argue that our portrayal of analytic and synthetic methods is the very method of holism,[1] but they must take it into earnest consideration that it is the spirit of authentic Oriental philosophy that tries to deal with existence in its wholeness, both with respect to its creator and personal identity as well as with regard to its relationship with "ego", in the same way that it addresses particular analytic issues of philosophy.

Thus conceived, philosophy no longer has any condition, and being unconditional is indeed a peculiarity of philosophy now. To put it differently, philosophy does not submit to the pre-established principles of humanly made schools of thought and cultures and precipitated epistemic factors. This is to say, the philosopher is alone with his thoughts, even though his mind-set has been shaped within the horizon of scientific issues. The philosopher struggles to understand by his own self and does not rely on anything else but his speculations. Has such a philosophy ever been crafted so far? Could one indeed create a convincing systematic well-made weltanschauung which has all philosophical issues in view without resorting to pre-established principles? This needs an excessive deal of good opinion to believe it.

It has been claimed that in philosophy, everything should be sketched and understood by the individual himself. Has the history of mankind ever witnessed such a thing? Have human beings not developed preordained principles under the influence of their cultures? Do human orientations in life not wield a delicate and intangible impact on their worldviews? And aren't men influenced by these cultural principles? I do not give negative answers to these queries. Said otherwise, it is quite unlikely that the human brain may get itself involved in abstraction to such an extent that not to be touched by any predetermined principle. Thus, it is a wholly wrong belief that theology is inferior to philosophy just because it relies on the words of prophets or religious leaders! This mind-set needs to be revised. Now

---

1- The theory that entities are complete units and should be related to as such and not separated into parts. (Translator).

let us see what the definition of theology or *Kalam* is.

Kalam consists of the knowledge of religious beliefs through affording arguments and clearing doubts. This is exactly what has been said by Abdulrrazaq Kashi and others in the definition of this discipline.

Theologians have repeated this latter definition with a few modifications and differences, but it seems that theology and theological debates have been more extensive than this. We need to cast a closer look on Khajeh Nasiruddin Tusi's *Tajrid al-Eteqad* ["The Purification of Belief"] along with the glosses that have been written on it, e.g. Allameh Helli's *Kashf ul-Murad* ["The Point Discovered"] and *Sharhi Tajrid* by Mulla Ali Qushchi, to see whether they only speak about religious truths or of the general principles of ontology as well. These are definitely issues that philosophers are concerned with and discuss them as philosophical issues. Khajeh Nasiruddin Tusi, who is not a theologian proper but theology only features an aspect of his multifaceted thought, argues:

> *The first chapter on existence and non-existence and defining them as immovable reality (existence) and movable reality (non-existence), or defining them as something that can be reported on (existence) and what cannot be reported, and other definitions that are all circular regress (these definitions are not real).*

These issues belong to the domain of the philosophical universe of discourse, like the debate over existence and non-existence, quiddity, cause and effect and others, and all of these are discussed in theology. Therefore, it is unfair to limit theology to the argumentative discussion of religious beliefs and the clarification of doubts. Had theologians from sects such as Imamyah, Asharites and Mutazilites not discussed atomic particles? There is a book entitled *Madhab al-dhurra inda al-muslimīn wa alāqatuhu bi-madhāhib al-Yūnān wa al-Hunūd : wa-maahu falsafa Muhammad ibn Zakarīyā al-Rāzī ("Muslim Takes of Atomism and Its Relationship with Greek and Hindu Schools of Thought along with the Philosophy of Zakariya-ye Razi")* by Dr. S. Pines that has been translated by an Egyptian called Abdulhadi. This book has garnered the ideas and positions of more than a hundred theologians of atoms. In those days, these were not discussed physically, but it was disputed that whether physical objects can ultimately be reduced to indivisible atoms or not. It is far more evident that this issue is not directly relevant to theology in its proper sense. Moreover, they have dealt with time, space and causality as well as many other significant issues that certainly could have been interesting and of avail for philosophers if they dared to leave their ivory tower and take a look upon them.

Thus, it is a peculiarity of theology that seeks to understand its problems based on traditions and transmitted prophetic wisdom. These traditions have a hundred percent authenticity there.

It needs also to be mentioned that it is a big mistake to give the upper hand to philosophy on the pretext that the authority of tradition and narration in theology has broken the monopoly of reason. The science of Kalam is primarily concerned with the articles of faith that must be grounded in reason without appealing to emulation in any form. When you decide to expand the debate over the pillars of belief, you will have to turn to philosophical principles. In other words, since religious beliefs, say resurrection, are established upon reason, it is in fact a philosophical and rational issue.

> The world, galaxy and stars would be a plaything
>
> If this long day of the terrestrial had no tomorrow. (Nasir Khosrow)

It might be said that many philosophical issues do not have an argument of such strength and power. As persons who are in search of the lawfulness and order of majesties and values, the sense of obligation, philanthropy, services and beauties in this world, you need to know that if a "tomorrow" is not accepted for this life, no single one of these latter categories will have any foundation. How could you want a more powerful argument than this? Thus, we must be completely careful in distinguishing between theology and philosophy.

Accordingly, the basic difference existing between these epistemic disciplines lies in the fact that in theological knowledge, besides reason, religious resources are also approached as the means of the clarification of hidden aspects of reason and backstage activities of intellection, while the philosopher resorts to standard methods of reason – which are based on senses and other perceptual devices – and does not see it necessary at all to incorporate concealed rational factors into his arguments.

For example, in Islam, physical resurrection is supposed to be one of the articles of faith, but the philosopher may see himself unable to accept it due to a number of issues like "non-existence is impossible to be restituted" and content himself with spiritual resurrection, while in Kalam, intellection gets intensified and substantiates the rationality of physical resurrection in light of the station of lordship and based on the law of similarity that states that two similar objects share the same sentence.

Luther's dissertation on Islamic philosophy and Fakhr-e Razi was appreciated as a brilliant study. He published it and sent a copy of it to Ja'fari. Many people helped him collect his required works and documents, among whom late Hajj Sheikh Abdulhussein Ibnuddin was also helpful for Luther when it came to addressing many theoretical problems.

3

Prof. Young

Subject: Poetry and Poets in the East and the West
Nationality: American/ Major: Oriental Literature
Dialogue Date: 1961

Young was an American professor of Persian literature who visited Allameh Ja'fari in 1961 along with Dr. Luther and held comparative dialogues with him about poetry and poets in the East and the West as well as the ecological peculiarities of these poets. After long debates, it was concluded that Persian literature, with its formal delicacies and emotive subtleties, has many excellences over other forms of poetry. Of course, this is not to turn a brown eye to other poets and forms of poetry, particularly Arab poets like Abu Farras, Mutanabbi, Mahyar Deylami, Sharif Razi and others. Ja'fari also spoke of their innovative themes and methods.

Ja'fari: If we say that Persian poetry in all cases is merely a form of literature written in a rhythmical style which reveals the poet's sentiments and imaginations, we will be quite mistaken, for Persian poetry is fraught with wisdom, psychology, sociology and transcendent points of religion. To put the matter otherwise, we have poems in Persian that can be taken as the foundations of a philosophical school. These poems are not few in number either, so we cannot claim that the existing ones are only exceptions. I have frequently reminded academic friends that we need some graduate theses and PhD dissertations to be written on the relevance of wisdom, morality, mysticism, philosophy, psychology, sociology, culture and other issues with Persian literature. To fulfill this task, on the other hand, we require a group of truly well-versed researchers. Moreover, there are more than hundred oeuvres that have to be critically edited.

The easiest way to get this done is for departments of Persian literature have students work on these oeuvres. However, when the opus is lengthy and sophisticated like those of Hafez and Rumi, the project must be managed by a team. This is a very significant issue that should be taken into serious consideration, as Persian literature is a rich treasure.

> *Professor Young visited Allameh Ja'fari for the second time at the home of Professor Mahmoud Hessaby.[1] Proffessor Young asked Ja'fari about the currency of nom de plume in Persian literature and why Persian poets use their pen names instead of their own names? In response to this question, the attendees, many of whom were scholars and academics, set forth some points among which was an analysis proposed by a professor of literature. He said, "For example, when a nightingale perched on a flower begins to sing and the beauty of flower haunts her senses, she sees herself a privileged creature since she is in the company of the flower. By the same token, when poets use particular pen names, they in fact seek to highlight their distinctive status conferred upon them by the Lord."*
>
> *Although many accounts were proposed of this issue, they were not convincing. One among the audience said, "Poets used a nom de plume in dread of possible acts of plagiarism." This idea was, however, severely criticized as it allegedly defames a society due to one's inability of finding the underlying motive of using pen names. This is not the right way to answer this question.*

Young: Why do Persian poets commonly use some pseudonyms instead of their real names in their poems?

Ja'fari: In most of the cases where pseudonyms have been used, you

---

1- Sayyed Mahmoud Hessaby (born February 23, 1903, in Tehran, Iran, and died September 3, 1992 in Geneva, Switzerland) was an Iranian scientist, researcher and professor of the University of Tehran. He was a man of a scientific mind, however, and continued his research in physics at the Sorbonne University and obtained his Ph.D. in Physics from that University at the age of twenty-five. He continued lecturing at the University of Tehran for three working generations, teaching seven generations of students and professors. He was buried, at his own request, in his hometown Tafresh. (Translator).

can easily replace them with the phrase "O' Man" without betraying the meaning. For example, in works of poetry by Hafez[1], one reads:

> *Every cup of felicity the Lord offered Hafez*
>
> *was the reward of night orisons and morning prayers.*

This means, "O' Hafez! It was because of these pains and toils that God honored you the ability to offer intellectual services to the society." If we replace the word Hafez with "Man" in the above poem it changes as follows: O' People! If you want to reach the lofty position of serving society, you must take pains and also have patience in the face of throes and hardships. This works in most of the poems which include pseudonyms.

For instance, Sa'di[2] says:

> *O' Sa'di! If the deluge of extinction debases the mansion of life,*
>
> *Keep your heart strong as the foundation of eternity is stronger than that.*

If we replace Sa'di in this poem with "O' Man", it will once again not make any difference.[3]

We have many common notions and principles in poetry. Said differently, poetry is a human medium through which man expresses his own sentiments and feelings, seeks to pour the beauties of nature into words and finally to articulate the universal oughts and values which address humanity as a family. Thus, Oriental and occidental poetry are not surely separated from each other in this respect. The difference occurs when they endeavor to appraise and reorganize these descriptions according to their particular cultural and ecological elements. They may sound different in such a case. Every one of us humans has a special culture of his own that represents the ecological, historical and religious peculiarities of the society that he belongs to, but this is not in contrast with the universal ethos we share.

If we purify these universal principles from all cultural, geographical, historical, legal and political attachments, we could understand why

---

1- Iranian lyric poet and mystic. (Translator).

2- Sa'di is an Iranian poet of the thirteenth century and the author of *Gulistan* ("The Orchard") completed in 1257 and *Bustan* ("The Rose Garden") in 1258 (Translator).

3- This explanation proved to be convincing for Professor Young. Having dealt with oriental poets and poetry, now the Allameh turns to poetry in the Occident.

the German literate Goethe[1] feels such deep empathy with Hafez and tries to introduce him to Europe in the same way that we enjoy reading poems by Victor Hugo[2] and introduce him to our people. Now if we come across differences, they are local differences that belong to a particular geographical area. We take the same pleasure from reading the thoughtful verses of de Lamartine[3] as they [Europeans] enjoy reading them. To put it otherwise, there is no difference between Sa'di's poems and the works of ancient Chinese poets in the point of view of universal human sentiments and magnificence.

Another account that we can afford of the philosophy of the application of pseudonyms is that in doing so, poets sought to say to their society that we ought to be like that. When I assess myself, the poet is saying, I see that I should be thus and act upon these truths and realities. I also realize that I stand before a universe that has these features and peculiarities. I see people this way and I have particular expectations from people, my personal stance toward these realities is this and I seek to be so. Such be the case, others may follow the poet in universal principles and try to actualize them in themselves. If they see these realities, they shall be fond of them.

1- Johann Wolfgang Von Goethe (1749-1832), German poet novelist, dramatist, and author of "Faust" (Translator).
2- Victor Hugo (1802-1885), 19th century French poet, and the author of "The Hunchback of Notre Dame" and "Les Miserables". (Translator).
3- Alphonse Marie Louis de Prat de Lamartine (1790-1869) French poet, intellectual, politician, and the author of "Jocelyn" (1836) and : Méditations Poétiques' (1820). (Translator).

4*

Dr. Bedford

Subject: A Comparison of Islamic Knowledge
of the Soul and Contemporary Psychology
Nationality: German/ Major: Psychology/ Dialogue Date: 1961

Bedford: Is it necessary to find a unique definition for the "soul" [as a substantial entity] and study it as the subject matter of a field called psychology? Or will it suffice to examine our internal activities as psychic states and persuade students to pursue their studies and research in this platform?

Ja'fari: This is a very good question. It has been debated for a long time whether we should understand the soul or not in order to ground a well-formed psychological system. Some believe that unless we understand our subject and figure out what we are going to research on, our issues will remain indeterminate; thus, we will approach themes about the base of which we have no idea.

On the other hand, as it is needless to say, the understanding of the reality of soul, or the psyche, has been and still is confronted with difficulties. Most contemporary psychologists have readily chosen the second stance and utterly pronounced that we do not need to grasp the nature of the "soul" and "ego"! It would merely suffice to know that there is an organizing factor inside man that is expressed by such words as soul, ego, self, personality, essence and others, terms which are applied by psychologists and we are not obliged to know its truth at all. But this is not the case indeed. To state the matter otherwise, if we do not know the reality of this organizing factor called the soul, and if we do not understand the meaning of internal management, then we cannot pursue psychological research in a *sapiential* fashion. This is what we term as retrogression in science, which has contaminated psychology due to the irrationality of some shallow-minded researchers. This has been recognized by Erich Fromm when he argued:

The metamorphosis of the intellectual and emotional atmosphere has wielded a deep influence on the development of psychology as a science. Despite such figures as Nietzsche and Kierkegaard, the tradition of studying the human soul in the light of moral integrity and happiness has been abandoned in psychology. The academic psychology that sought to follow the footsteps of natural sciences and experimental methods of measurement dealt with everything but soul. Moreover, it struggled to unearth some aspects of human existence that can be studied in the laboratory and argued that conscience, the judgment of values and the recognition of good and evil are metaphysical notions and stand outside the domain of psychology. It always dealt with trivial issues that more fitted in an allegedly scientific method rather than the invention of fresh methods for the study of major problems humanity is concerned with. Thus, psychology changed into a science without its main subject-matter, i.e. the human soul. This psychology was merely interested in mechanisms, reactions and instincts, and paid no attention to very special human phenomena such as love, logic, conscience and values.[1]

Rumi has spoken in the same spirit, saying that:

If we should fail to hit a detailed and punctual acquaintance with a reality, we can continue our research through discussing its peculiarities and coordinates; then, we may one day reach the truth. However, we should not stop the quest on the pretext of not having access to the truth.

He has another analogy akin to the latter:

If we find a stuff whose reality is unknown to us, we drop it into water and see whether it is soluble or not. Then we argue that whatever it may be, one thing is for sure about it, i.e. it is not soluble in water. Now we strike it with a stone and see that it is striking-resistant; thus, we conclude that this unknown object resists blows from stones. Then we check it again and see that it reflects our image and infer that it is reflexive material. This way we continue our quest for understanding the nature of the unknown entity at issue and deepen our knowledge of it and are hopeful to hit its truth.

This method is based on a principle that we always apply:

1- Fromm, Erich, *Religion and Psychoanalysis*.

We should not wholly abandon whatever we cannot wholly understand.[1]

We move forward as far as possible until our knowledge becomes whole! It has to be taken into consideration that in doing so we are not wholly deprived from the quest for the truth. Everything here is dependent on our mental and intellectual maturation and the increase of our love and interest in truth. Although the truth, in its highness, must be seen as *one* both as to the world and man, since we reside within temporal events and realities, there seems to be no objection toward us advancing relative truths for ourselves and garnering factual data about them that can both be effective in our practical life and also satisfy our sense of realism and keep doing this until we succeed in gaining our share of absolute truth. Therefore, if we do not touch the reality of the soul, there would be no objection to engaging ourselves in serious researches of our mental activities, phenomena, actions and reactions and ground our life upon enlightenment both – intellectually and practically.[2]

This causes some contemporary psychologists to deny the very existence of the soul – while it is impossible to do so, as there are many proofs that demonstrate the reality goes otherwise – they indeed seek to cover their inability! When we are not able to know something, why should we renounce it? If we have no path ahead along which to progress and know the soul, we should not at least cast doubts on its existence and pursue our task.

Some scholars have proposed more than sixty proofs on the existence of soul. It is somewhat irrational to think that sixty proofs have all been thought out for nothing.

Bedford: In Western psychology, we do not have any independent research done of the existence of the soul and its immateriality. If Islamic knowledge of the soul contains proofs in this regard, would you please outline them for us?

Ja'fari: One of the proofs that substantiate the existence of the soul is the argument arising from the perception of universals. The perception of universals has neither quality nor quantity, and is not measurable

---

1- Also known as the "Rule of All Things Simple."

2- Both peripatetic and illuminationist philosophers were clever enough to confess that we have no access to the real differentia of objects and it is irrational to expect to have a comprehensive knowledge of reality; as a matter of fact, our knowledge of reality is based on logical differentia.

by mental apparatuses, either; in fact, it is an immaterial reality. Accordingly, what it indwells or what structures it certainly must be other than neural and mental stuffs, because our brain cannot represent the universal, as the latter does not have any form to be depicted.

The second proof developed by philosophers is the argument concerned with the soul's superintendence over the matter and material objects, since had the soul been part of nervous system of the brain, it could not manage the material, while we find it to be in fact a reality inside man that has a tight grip on his situation and manages it.

Amongst the rest, there is a third proof that seems to be more telling and easy to understand, which reads as follows: as we regard our limbs, such as our arm, our foot, as well as our ear, our eye, our hair, our head and other parts as belonging to "I", in the same way we attribute such internal parts as reason, emotions, sentiments, thought and will to an "I". Moreover, we have also a sense of the "I". This is the so-called presential knowledge that is known as *self-consciousness* in modern psychology. It seems that almost all scholars in the field of psychology around the globe endorse the very existence of knowledge-by-presence or self-awareness. Thus, the reality that is conceived by man is doubtlessly not a mere delusion, but it is an "I" that inspects all aspects of human existence. The demonstration of this reality is simultaneously a proof for its incorporeality; who has ever seen the vision of eye by the eye?[1]

In presential knowledge, it seems as if the eye wants to see itself, while the eye cannot see itself unless its picture has already been reflected somewhere.

The other proof is an argument from human internal sense of judgment. For example, are my emotions prior to my thoughts? Or, to put it otherwise, are my thoughts more effective in my life or my sensations? Are all my internal activities and abilities in tune with each other? Who is in charge of judging these latter cases and others like them? We would assign this task to a still unknown part of brain. But if we come across doubts concerning the judgments of the brain, then

---

1- *Nothingness is the mirror, the universe is the picture, and man*
   Is like the eye of that picture in which the individual is hidden.
   You are the eye of the picture, and he is the light of eye;
   Who has ever seen the vision of eye by the eye!
   The universe became man and so man a universe;
   There is no other cleverer exposition than this. (Sheikh Mahmoud Shabestari)

we shall have to find another reference. This justice is "I", which stands above all sensations, feelings, emotions, thoughts and intellections.

Bedford: As you know, some thinkers have a melancholic vision of humanity and believe that man is, by nature, a cannibal based on the principle of struggle for existence. On the other hand, all moral and religious principles seem to be very pale in the face of the selfish nature of humanity as it can be easily verified by such human cruelties as those done in Auschwitz and Dachau. What is your idea of human nature? Is it good or bad?

Ja'fari: The picture you just depicted is only the case where men act only under their natural self which, according to Thomas Hobbes, is the platform of hedonism, egotism and selfishness. However, education can change this brute natural situation. The evidence to this claim is many examples of sacrifices that have been made for human freedom and happiness. History is fraught with martyrs of the path of humanity. Needless to say, neglecting these is tantamount to the negligence of truth.

5 & 6

Ibrahim Suleyman and Sharif Sahimat

Subject: Shi'ite Kalam
Nationality: Jordanian/ Major: Theology
Dialogue Date: 1964

In 1964 two students from Jordan called Ibrahim Suleyman and Sharift Sahimat visited Allameh Ja'fari and asked some questions regarding Kalam[1] and held discussions with him. They also studied parts of the Nahjulbalaghah with Ja'fari for two years.

Jordanian Students: What does Ash'arite acquisition mean regarding the issue of compulsion versus volition?

Ja'fari: We have at least sixteen theories in regard to whether all human actions are compulsory or some are by compulsion while some others are volitional. Of course it needs to be noted that if man is to live a conscious life in the context of human culture, he should address these issues and seek to find their respective answers.

Sunnite scholars have discrepant interpretations of Ash'arite acquisition. Some of them construe this acquisition almost in a deterministic fashion. For example, they argue that it is as if the sun's ray were to be reflected through a light reflecting mirror on a wall. Divine effusion is like a sun that shines on man, causing him to perform "actions". That is to say, since all power and authority belong

---

1- *Kalam* (which literally means "the science of discourse") is a branch of Islamic Sciences that deals with the rational bases of articles of faith and religious creeds. In doing so, it seeks to defend the consistency of system of beliefs and practices offered by Islam through rational means in a logical fashion. For more details, see Professor Harry Austryn Wolfson's seminal work *Philosophy of Kalam* (1976, Harvard University Press) and the third volume of *An Anthology of Philosophy in Persia* edited by S. H. Nasr and M. Aminrazavi entitled *Philosophical Theology in Middle Ages and Beyond* (2010, I. B. Tauris & Co. Ltd.) (Translator).

to God, then action is a divine privilege as well. Man is merely the locus of emergence of action while he has all these from God. Man acquires it and concretizes the action he has been conferred upon by the Lord through his mental and physical organs. Thus, as you can see, if this issue is not interpreted in a correct fashion, it may end up in determinism.

Tamhid, written by Abu Bakr Baqlani, contains a more intelligible Sunnite interpretation concerning Asharite acquisition that is not totally alien to Shi'ite "Golden Mean or Middle Ground". If this issue is explained correctly, it shall be embraced by all Islamic denominations. Consequently, it will not be so removed from the correct understanding of Ash'arite acquisition.

Jordanian Students: Why do Asharites not accept divine justice?

Ja'fari: Since justice is subsidiary to law, they argue, then some law needs to be envisaged may God be considered just upon His acting according to it. If this is not the case, then God is not just.

On the other hand, justice, whether in the sense of placing everything in its appropriate position or as acting and behaving according to the law, is not a pertinent notion to be applied to Divine Essence as God stands above all laws. Man cannot impose any obligation to God to act according to the law. Moreover, justice as "placing everything in its appropriate position" suggests that a situation has been spotted in the absence of Divine Will to which Providence needs to fall so as God could be just. Thus conceived, justice by no means can be applied to God.

The Asharites' claim is sensible, but as Rumi states, "*I am not the Judge; I just relate*". We are not to order and say that God must be obliged to act justly, but rather we relate of an Omnipotent, Omniscient and All-Beneficent God who has created the world without having any attachment whatsoever to it. Thus, if He does not act in justice, then what should He do? Injustice is resulted from need, ignorance or the like which have nothing to do with Divine Essence. Hence, God is purely just according to rational reasoning. However, the scriptural reasoning endorses it as well; as stated in the Holy Quran:

> **And the word of your Lord has been accomplished truly and justly; there is none who can change His words.**

> (The Cattle 6: 115)

In the above verse, "word" means Divine Providence. Of course, divine practice, providence and wisdom have been grounded in justice and nothing can change that. It is quite unlikely that Asharites may have not acknowledged the truth revealed through divine words like the aforementioned verse. However, what they have broached and is also acceptable by us is the idea that "the norms enacted for just behavior are not outside divine providence".

Thus, even if we do not fathom the truth of justice, the All-Richness of God requires Him to rule existence according to His Wisdom, as He has primordially set the world in order, and to observe the terms of justice in His relations with human beings as well as in their relations with each other and the like. In addition, this does not indicate the imposition of any obligation to God, but rather, as Rumi argues, we are relating about a just Lord the meaning of whose justice is moving according to His transcendent wisdom, and we do not determine the law upon which God must act. There is certainly such a law, but it is beyond our wills and perceptions.

Jordanian Students: Where do the doctrinal differences between Shi'ism and Sunnism lie in your view?

Ja'fari: To answer this question we need to draw out their respective ideas from their own books and compare them so as to see what shared features and differences exist between these two denominations! I strongly recommend that you should not ground your knowledge of these great schools only upon non-Muslim researchers and historians. For example, if a Shi'ite Muslim seeks to know something concerning Sunnism, he must refer to the books written by Sunnite theologians and thinkers. When we have access to original sources, why should we turn to second-hand translations that even might have been written without enough acquaintance with language, problems and ordinances? Of course, this method requires that one be accompanied with the spirit of impartiality. Those Sunnite researchers and intellectuals who may intend to gain knowledge of some determinate aspects of Shi'ism should also tread in the same lines. Unfortunately, in recent times, we have seen some figures who have based their judgments and assessments of Sunnism and Shi'ism upon second-hand material written by Orientalists. We are not happy with this approach, and it should not be accepted by Sunnite scholars.

As to the differences existing between these two groups, however, to begin with, we shall need to take into consideration the fact that discord on the details of Islamic articles of faith and knowledge is not merely restricted to Shi'ism and Sunnism, since there are other intra-sectarian disagreements concerning doctrinal and jurisprudential issues within both denominations. As a matter of fact, these discords and discrepancies among Islamic schools show the intellectual capacity of Islam for development one way or another. However, as to the differences of these Islamic schools, we can briefly allude to the following points:

1- In Shi'ism, all decrees that have been dictated by the Prophet Muhammad (PBUH) are based on revelation, and even what is known as prophetic tradition is also considered to be an expression of divine inspirations due to the Prophet's inner purity and candor. Of course, the Prophet was not like an ordinary man who obtains jurisprudential authority [*Ijtihad*] through studying and education, while many Sunnite scholars consider Prophet Muhammad as a *mujtahid* [an authorized interpreter of Shari'ah Law]. In his commentary of *The Book of Catharsis* Mullah Ali Qushchi has described the Second Caliph's disagreements with the Prophet in following words:

> *Surely a mujtahid's disagreement with another mujtahid on jurisprudential issues is not an example of unorthodoxy.*

2- Sunnite scholars believe that *innocentia* is an exclusive requirement of prophecy and the successors of Prophet have another requirement to fulfill, i.e. justice.[1]

3- On the issue of caliphate, these two schools propose their own respective arrangements as follows:

Sunnism: 1. Abu Bakr, 2. Omar, 3. Othman, and 4. Ali (AS).

Shi'ism : Ali (PBUH) is the first successor of the Prophet (PBUH) and is followed by the other 11 Imams, all of whom are his sons according to authorized texts and sources.

Jordanian Students: How can one bring about unity between Shi'ites and Sunnites and generally among all Islamic denominations?

Ja'fari: This is the ultimate ideal of both Shi'ites and Sunnites. However, it needs to be taken into account that unity here does not denote a general and absolute unity in beliefs, branches, judgments and details. Not only has such a unity never been recommended, but it is also in fact rather unintelligible, for as we know, there is sizable

---

1- However, there are different opinions concerning the condition of Imamate in various Shi'ite sub-sects. Amongst the others is the major Shi'ite school of Imamiyah, which sees innocentia as the necessary precondition of Imamate and considers Ali and his progeny as the true successors of the Holy Prophet Muhammad (PBUH).

difference of opinion among Shi'ite as well as Sunnite scholars themselves. This difference is concerned with the interpretation of the Qur'an and the details regarding articles of faith and jurisprudential issues. If this difference expresses itself in the form of a constructive competition, not only is it not harmful, but it shall also lead to the blossoming of a primordial school of Islam. The number of jurists, thus, should not be narrowed down to some determinate individuals, since the door of jurisprudential reasoning is always open and intellectual differences cannot do any damage to the integral unity of Islam. Constructive competition is our constant wish as it helps us to reach higher realities.

In this regard, there are some extra-Shi'ite-and-Sunnite prejudices that are not happy with such constructive competitions and efforts. It must be taken in earnest consideration that the Holy Qur'an, as a book adored by all Islamic denominations, which is according to Divine Words the light of guidance and healing, cannot give rise to fatal and prejudicial discords. As a result, we need to devote ourselves for many years to the study and discussion of our commonalities and differences; may our children in future benefit from the outcomes of these debates and researches. Having done these, we can reach to an intelligible unity among Shi'ism and Sunnism and other Islamic schools and create a rational *mitsein*. Those who think that there is no harmony whatsoever between these schools, they are either truly ignorant or biased. Our major articles of faith, the *qiblah* [the direction a Muslim is to face when saying his prayers], the Holy Book and *Sunnah* are all the same. Therefore, the Shi'ite and Sunnite unity, as some set it forth, is not a far-fetched ideal. We need only to put marginal, unscientific and irreligious matters aside so as to settle these disagreements like other problems. As it is needless to say, due to the common context these sects share with each other, such a unity is not so difficult to be reached.

7

Bertrand Russell

Subject: Philosophical and Scientific Issues
Nationality: British/ Major: Philosophy and Sciences
Correspondences Took Place in: 1963-1964

*During the years 1963 and 1964, some correspondences
were exchanged between Mr. Ja'fari and Sir Bertrand
Russell (1872-1970), the renowned British philosopher.
Due to the importance of these correspondences, we
shall cite here some of these letters together with an
introduction by Ja'fari on Russell's intellectual career
and significance.*

Introduction

Undoubtedly, Russell is a thinker with a sharp, dynamic mind and
memory, an extraordinary capability of the simplification of difficult
philosophical issues and notions as well as a tenuous sense of irony
and a prodigious scientific outlook. He is an unrivalled pioneer of
mathematical logic and has an understandable interpretation of
Einstein's theory of relativity. Generally speaking, he represents one of
the first-rate contemporary intellectuals of the Occident whose works
are not so unfamiliar to Eastern nations including Moslem societies.
The ideas and personality of Sir Russell in some points are so
enchanting that have triggered diametrically opposing estimations.
Despite having these aforementioned privileges, Sir Bertrand Russell
has not offered a systematic philosophy that devotes itself to the
explanation and analysis of quadruple issues concerning the
ontological relationships of humanity (i.e. human relationships with
man himself, God, the world of existence and his fellowmen, "as they
are" and "as they ought to be"). Having said these, it is due to relate
some of my replies to questions that posed about the philosophical and
scientific aspects of the personality of Sir Bertrand Russell.
The following interview has been published in two successive issues of

Etela'at Daily (13116-13117) on Monday and Tuesday, February 9 and 10, 1970, a few days after Russell's death.

Q1: How did you find Bertrand Russell's philosophical perspective?

Ja'fari: It is not an easy task to mark off the boundaries of the Russellian notion of philosophy as he has offered various definitions of the discipline in his works. In *Bertrand Russell Speaks His Mind*, he has depicted philosophy as the body of theoretical researches of issues which are not yet possible to have an exact knowledge of. In the same book, when Woodrow Wyatt asks him to which group of philosophers he belongs, Russell replies, 'I have not had any label; the only label that I have is "logical atomist".'[1]

In his *A History of Western Philosophy* (1964), Russell puts philosophy somewhere between science and theology as "middle term". As you see, Russell has understood philosophy almost in three ways:

I. In his first definition, he has conceptualized the notion in such a broad manner that it even includes those scientific issues that are not possible to have an exact knowledge of for the time being. To put it otherwise, this notion contains every scientific discipline's theoretical part like theoretical physics, theoretical chemistry, theoretical mathematics and theoretical law and so on and so forth, which do not have a purely scientific character when they are being researched and studied.

II. In the second definition, the notion is somewhat clearer, as philosophy has been depicted as a middle zone between science and theology. Russell does not provide enough explanation in this regard for us to presume the existence of such a third realm. Are the principial reasons that will be utilized in this regard in fact issues between science and theology? If these reasons have neither a scientific nor a metaphysical origin in theological sense, then what kind of reasons are these?

III. On the other hand, as to Russell's third designation of his philosophical career as "logical atomism", we must say that this only can serve as a delineation of part of Russellian methodology in philosophical investigations and cannot shed light on the essence of

---

1- Here it needs to be taken into earnest consideration that whether Russell wishes or not, he has coined many theories in philosophy. Having elaborated these theories, Russell has became part of the very fabric of twentieth century philosophy, as it should have been so, since his philosophical theories are by no means lesser than other philosophers' theses in the West.

them as a whole as compared to other philosophic enterprises.

Q2: Would you please explain why the method of Logical Atomism can stand for a genuine philosophical school?

Ja'fari: Of course, you know that great ideas on the cosmological scene mark different ways of intellectual activity. Some of them are unconcerned with their deposited units of information and are only to construct a system of philosophy by their own data. These philosophers represent a group whose method is synthetic.

The second group hosts those philosophers who start their intellectual movement from cosmological units – which in their turn are sets of subunits – and push their way forward through gradual analysis. And, as Sir Russell states in his book, this analysis must be kept until we reach some point that there would not be units smaller than those reached.

Needless to say, besides the fact that the analytic method as such does not feature a particular kind of philosophical system, it cannot provide an enlightened mind with a philosophical outlook that offers an integrated view of the universe, as there is no doubt that the synthetic method is as much important in philosophy as analytic method is. To state the matter in more telling words, these two methods are like two necessary wings for flying in the air of particular and universal knowledge which are integrative.

Q3: What is your idea about Russell's genius?

Ja'fari: It is beyond all doubts that this thinker has enjoyed a marvelous genius. His genius, as we mentioned earlier, has clearly shown itself in the huge amount of experiences that his memory has recorded through the long span of his life. Moreover, he has easily put this splendid memory into work. The third manifestation of Bertrand Russell's genius is his wondrous power of exemplification, insofar as we can say that his talent for exemplifying as well as the mental activity that he makes on particular events to compare universals is uncommon in our age. However, as to his scientific genius, Russell's creative ideas in modern logic and mathematics are so clear for scholars to comprehend that they do not need any extra elaboration.

Q4: What is Russell's role in contemporary philosophies in your view?

Ja'fari: I think we should analyze this question into two issues and then address each one independently. If you mean by the impression Russell's philosophy has had on contemporary philosophies, as well as the influence that his intellectual method has exerted on contemporary ideas, we undoubtedly must designate a certain share for him in contemporary philosophy as a whole. Here I mean the influence that Russellian liberal musings have had on some issues concerning man and the universe, which need to be approached in keeping with their own respective rules and principles. The consequence that has been accrued to contemporary worldviews through the application of this method is a considerable amount of information along with horrible paradoxes and gaps that have struck the contemporary body of knowledge. Of course, by Russell's intellectual method, here we are referring to the methods he has applied in philosophy rather than those that he has used in scientific researches.

However, if you mean that Russell has founded a systematic school of philosophy that influenced other philosophers, of course the answer is no, for if we gather all Sir Russell's works together and seek to break down their paradoxes and gaps and derive a systematic school of philosophy out of them as an effort to offer to the world, we shall end up in an utter failure. Accordingly, many groups of thinkers consider Russell as an intellectual man of genius, but they do not regard him among the philosophers who have had a school of philosophy their own.

Q5: Would you please brief us about a number of his philosophical paradoxes?

Ja'fari: I have recognized countless philosophical paradoxes through reading his philosophical works. Here, as an example, I shall refer to those cases that are easy for the reader to spot in Russell's works:

I.   Sir Russell denies "subjective freedom" and the category of "free will," and regards it in contradiction with dynamical rules. In this spirit, he argues:

> For free will, I think the argument was not a valid one, and I don't any longer think it is still conclusive. But I thought that because of the motions of matter are determined by the laws of dynamics, the motion of a man's lips when he speaks must be so determined, so that he can have no control over what he's going to say. I don't think that was a valid argument, but it convinced me at the time.[1]

This represents Russell's negative view of human free will. Now if we align this deterministic perspective of Russell's with his indefatigable efforts in defense of humanity, freedom and peace to

---

1- Ja'fari, M. T., *An Analytic Exposition of the Russell-Wyatt Dialogues*, 4th impression, 2008. (Originally in Persian).

which he might owe much of his global fame, the paradox will unmask itself. These two lines of ideas (the denial of freedom and the defense of humanity, freedom and peace), considering the denial of the fundamental reality of conscience – from which love in humanity, freedom and peace originates – cannot be compatible with each other, because the denial of subjective freedom requires the refusal of conscience by the rejection of which the love in humanity, freedom and peace becomes meaningless.

In regard to this critical issue, I wrote a letter to Sir Russell in 1961; unfortunately, however, he did not respond. Then in August 18, 1963, I asked him to explicate a phrase in his dialogue with Woodrow Wyatt. 5 days later, Russell sent me a letter that still did not address the freedom and determinism dilemma, but nonetheless merely provided an expression of a kind of leniency before the argument that I had outlined, as the reader can see it:

From: The Earl Russell, O.M.,F.R.S..
23 August 1963

Dear Mr. Ja'fari,

 Thank you very much for your letter. Quantum theory introduces certain doubts about the complete predictability of behaviour in theory; the admission of doubt, however, does not imply adherence to the opposite of that doubted.

 Yours sincerely,

 Bertrand Russell

 Bertrand Russell.

 E.g. It is not certain that it will rain tomorrow, but this doesnot imply that it is certain it will not rain.

Dear Mr. Ja'fari:

Thank you very much for your letter. Quantum theory introduces certain doubts about the complete predictability of behavior in theory; the admission of doubt, however, does not imply adherence to the opposite of that doubted.   **Bertrand Russell**

After signing the letter, Sir Russell added the following example:

 For example, the fact that it is not for sure that it will rain tomorrow does not imply that it definitely will not rain tomorrow.

As you see, the problem of freedom and determinism has remained in limbo in Russell's words, and his argument does not prove any of the two theories.

To state the matter otherwise, if freedom is to be denied, then conscience – particularly moral conscience – should also be declined; thus, by no means shall we be able to demonstrate the right of life, right of dignity and the modality of committed freedom for mankind. This is to say, we have no longer any reason to defend humanity and its values as well as for rising up for the oppressed. This is the very sore consequence that Alfred North Whitehead – who in my view is the greatest Western philosopher in the twentieth century – has underlined in his *Adventures of Ideas* (Chapter 3, Part 2). There, he manifestly argues:

> *Although Hume and Huxley both denounce slavery, they still deny the existence of any independent dignity for man who makes humanity a worthy object of love.*

This is the consequence that has been engendered by Russell's paradoxical method of thinking. As I mentioned earlier, I reminded Russell of this statement of Whitehead's, but he had no answer for it.

II. The other striking point is that of the problem of God's existence. Regarding the whole corpus of Russell's works, he is not the denier of God's existence. In other words, Russell is not an atheist, since he explicitly says:

> *I don't think that there is definitely nothing as God, although those reasons proposed by the proponents of the God hypothesis are all disputable.*

It should be said that man may be able to dispute even the most evident principles including his own existence, in the same way that Sophists did, but impartial and unbiased thinking cannot cast any doubt upon Divine Existence, as indicated by prominent Western and Eastern theosophists.

Russell argues:

> *Their method is that of justification-based logic, in which the pretension is firstly presumed demonstrated and then some proof is being provided for its veracity.*

This theory of Russell's is itself a justification for the necessity of doubt about God's existence, a point of view Russell has already taken.

In *Bertrand Russell Speaks His Mind*, Russell introduces three sources for fondness for God:

> - *Fear of nature's destructive factors.*

- *Fear of human beings themselves who destroy each other by warfare.*

- *The regrets that strike man after committing carnal activities.*

There is no doubt that fear of destructive factors in nature can be a reason for some people to turn to God and religion, in the same way that a superb work of art can be a mere means of gain for an avaricious person without having even thought about its deep aesthetical and intellectual implications for the beholder! But as to human beings' fear of each other due to their potentiality for destroying their fellowmen, it should be mentioned that this is also correct by way of the particular proposition, however this fear cannot be the universal factor for fondness for God and religion, because history as a whole is fraught with brave resistances before the oppressions of power-drunks and even brilliant victories have been achieved through this path; at the same time, those who strugglerd were people of God and true adherents of religion.

On the other hand, there are people who have abandoned their faiths in God and religion due to such phenomena as fear of destructive elements of nature, oppressors and grievances and hardships. To have a dependable judgment in this case, then, we need to examine the character of those who are exposed to these factors. Moreover, Sir Russell has forgotten the factors of human primordial craving for perfection, morality, sense of majesty in existence, love, heavenly endowed nature and transcendental sense of commitment, and at the same time has not mentioned the fact that there had been a huge number of people throughout history who have wholeheartedly turned to God and religion as a result of the same mentioned factors and elements. Furthermore, Sir Russell must have understood a la Max Planck[1] – who is one of the renowned physicists that have revolutionized modern physics – the necessity of a deeper and broader insight into religion as a vital aspect of human life through the prism of which other aspects of *menschenleben* become reflected.

Let us read the following words by Max Planck:

> *There can never be any real opposition between religion and science, for one is the complement of the other. Every serious and reflective person realizes, I think, that the religious element in his nature must be recognized and cultivated if all the powers of the human soul are to*

1- Max Karl Ernst Ludwig Planck (1858-1947), German physicist, father of quantum physics, and the winner of the 1918 Nobel prize for physics (Translator).

act together in perfect balance and harmony. And indeed it was not by any accident that the greatest thinkers of all ages were also deeply religious souls, even though they made no public show of their religious feelings. It is from the cooperation of understanding with the will that the finest fruit of philosophy has arisen, namely, the ethical fruit. Science enhances the moral values of life, because it furthers a love of truth and reverence – a love of the truth displaying itself in the constant endeavor to achieve a more exact knowledge of the world of mind and matter around us, and reverence, because every advance in knowledge brings us face to face with the mystery of our own being.[1]

We will not go into further details on this issue anymore,[2] because I intended here only to expose Russell's paradoxical stance on the issue of human fondness for God and religion.

Then Wyatt asks, "Couldn't man dedicate himself to the search for the causes of faith, some of which stand outside him and seem to be greater than the human individual? Does he not search for this being not just due to any fear or existential dependence but rather in order to fulfill some tasks merely for the sake of him being him?"

Russell answers:

There are indeed many things that are greater than man himself; I mean family, and the nation and finally the humanity in general, all of whom are greater and larger than the individual and are adequately enough for satisfying any sense of generosity inside human beings.

As you see, Sir Russell has implicitly admitted the existence of a primordial sense of search for a superior being although he suggests that:

We satisfy this sense by family, nation or humanity at large.

This is an unacceptable paradox from a philosopher of such stature as Sir Bertrand Russell, who on one hand ascribes theism and religiosity to fear and human weakness, and accepts the existence of a sense of search for perfection inside man on the other. Accordingly, on September 11, 1963, I wrote a letter to Russell and asked for an answer for this paradox. Sir Russell replied to me in the following words:

1- Plank, Max (1932): *Where Is Science Going?*
2- For more details, see: Ja'fari, M. T., (2008): *An Analytic Exposition of the Russell-Wyatt Dialogues.*

The "search for perfection" is rather vague but, in any event,
lofty impulses such as the "search for perfection" are not as common as you
suggest.   Yours sincerely,

Bertrand Russell

Bertrand Russell.

The "Search for Perfection" is rather vague but, in any event, lofty impulses such as the search for perfection are not as common as you suggest.   **Bertrand Russell**

It is noteworthy that in Sir Russell's abovementioned words, the existence of an independent drive for a "search for perfection" – that I had broached in my letter – has not been wholly rejected; as a matter of fact, he says, "I don't see this alleged universal sense in all human individuals". Having narrowed down the engendering factors of theism and religiosity to the three previously stated ones, however, Russell should not have accepted this universal impulse (search for perfection) even in this general form as it has been already proved in logic that *a general negation does not imply the generality of that negation.*

To state the matter differently, if you say, the members of the whole audience taking part in this forum are not graduated, it is not as if to say that not even a single person among the audience attending the forum is graduated. Moreover, it is a baseless instilment to introduce the love for family, nation and humanity as extensions of the gratification of the primordial sense of search for perfection, while if Sir Russell had bothered to dig into the depths of human existence, he would have asserted that not only is there no contradiction between theism and religiosity, on the one hand, and devoting oneself to one's family, nation and humanity, on the other. In fact, the love that the authentic theism and religiosity cultivates inside man as to his family, nation and humanity in general, is deeper and more reliable than those humanistic instilled sentiments that have done nothing for humanity but created an agitated melancholia.

One of the issues that Sir Russell deals with in an obscure and paradoxical fashion is religion. In some of his renowned books, Russell has frequently said, "Religion has always had grave consequences." As we have mentioned previously, he has introduced ignorance, weakness and compulsion as the factors of fondness for religion; in fact, a 19th century stereotype view of the matter. In any event, Russell has two ideas that make his take on religion more obscure and paradoxical.

To begin with, in his dialogues with Wyatt, Russell argues:

> But the founders of religions, I mean all religions, have the least contact with the ideas of their followers; this is indeed the case in reality, too.

To make his readers' minds clear on the subject matter, shouldn't Sir Russell have first introduced them into the nature of such a serious phenomenon as religion and then sought to determine the basic intention of its founders, and only after having done these, proceeded to critique the intellectual dependence of religious people on the ideas of the establishers of religion?

Secondly, in *History of Western Philosophy*, Russell has argued:

> In the sphere of thought, sober civilization is roughly synonymous with science. But science, unadulterated, is not satisfying; men need passion, art and religion as well.[1]

Q6: What result would we reach in your view through comparing Bertrand Russell with other [Western] philosophers like Descartes, Kant, Hegel, and such Eastern philosophers as Avicenna and Mullasadra?

Ja'fari: I guess I have already made such comparisons by way of indication and in a succinct fashion. Nonetheless, let us broach some other themes in this regard here. Russell abstains from expressing his conclusive take on many philosophical issues as well as numerous issues pertaining *Geisteswissenschaften*, save those of political sciences. In many cases, at least the intellectual readers of Russell's work cannot determine his final stance on, say, a particular scientific and philosophical issue having the whole Russellian corpus in view. Moreover, comparing Russell with other philosophers whether from the West like Hegel and Kant or from the East such as Avicenna and Sadrulmutalehin, is in one respect like comparing a thinking style with a thinking product, since other philosophers have systematically offered the products of their philosophizations in the form of a school to humanity while Russell's philosophy is being featured by its analytic and critical style of thinking.

If we claim that Russell was a man of philosophy, this is to say that he

---

1- Russell, Bertrand (1945): *A History of Western Philosophy*.

has engaged himself in the contemplation of a considerable amount of knowledge accumulated around the man and universe and made sizable efforts – that have surely been pleasurable for him – to determine the degree of the reliability of principles and means of philosophical speculations. However, he has not laid down a whole philosophical edifice of his own that can host other philosophers and thinkers within.

Having said this, we can think of comparing Russell with other thinkers and philosophers like Socrates, though with total awareness of the differences between him and other philosophers.

The committed conscience offered the cup of hemlock to Socrates so as to show by drinking it a practical proof for the sacrifices he had made in the path of wisdom and the progression of human noble morals, whereas Russell does not precisely maintain any human value for moral conscience and lofty ethical principles and does not show any positive take on God, either. As a result, his efforts and activities in the path of humanity and "transcendental" commitment require more convincing proofs that neither he has demonstrated in his works nor can the external act substantiate. Of course, we know that he has tirelessly toiled for the establishment of a foundation for peace, which we hope will prove to be effective for humanity.

Q7: What is in your view Russell's stance on metaphysical issues?

Ja'fari: Three points can be outlined in this regard:

1- In a number of cases, Russell clearly acknowledges the existence of metaphysics; for example, in *Mysticism and Logic*, where he argues:

> A truer image of the world, I think, is obtained by picturing things as entering into the stream of time from the eternal world outside, rather than from a view which regards time as the devouring tyrant of all that is. Both in thought and feeling, even though time is real, to realize the unimportance of time is the gate of wisdom.[1]

Moreover, the stone-deaf example that Russell relates in *ABC of Relativity* – and we have quoted previously– also substantiates the existence of metaphysics.

2- The other evidence to Russell's acknowledgement of the existence of metaphysics is his admission of an independent extra-perceptual reality for the objective world as a philosopher who belongs to the realist camp. However, in some other places, to tackle some

---

1- Russell, Bertrand, *Mysticism and Logic.*

philosophical difficulties, he says:

> By acknowledging the reality of the external world, we can deny the existence of material objects.[1]

Undoubtedly, by denying the existence of material objects in the outside world, we shall arrive at a metaphysical reality that cannot have a physical appearance.

3- Metaphysics [in one sense] consists of the underlying principles of issues concerning religion. Russell's stance in this regard is confusing, paradoxical and uncertain.

On this side of metaphysics, Russell has contented himself with mere denial without providing any reason. As we have already seen in the issue regarding God's existence, he has not offered any reason for his denial of Divine Essence. By the same token, he does not provide his reader with any kind of reason for his refusal of the soul's immortality; rather, he only says, "We have no reason to demonstrate that the soul will remain there even after the dissolution of body."

Q8: What is the foothold chosen by Russell for humanity and how do you find it?

Ja'fari: I think Russell has not made much effort in this regard; it might not have been in his eyes the first rate problem that needs to be addressed, since the points that Sir Russell has made in this regard, however significant they may be, are nonetheless by no means satisfactory. He believes:

> ... anxiety is somehow necessary for the intellectual cultivation of people; however, if they have scientific information of an acceptable size, this information will serve as ballast that can reduce the discomforts resulted from the sense of doubt.[2]

I don't think there is any intelligible person who would challenge Sir Russell's latter point. Of course, we must struggle and put all of our energy to use in order to mobilize all aspects of life. We Moslems are acquainted with this principle in our literary Islamic culture that:

> Verily the man of the world and indeed her only man/ is he who does not count on any man in the world. (Tughraei)

Which man do you know, however, in history who could have

1- Russell, Bertrand, *Introduction to Philosophy*.

2- Ja'fari, M. T. (2008), *An Analytical Exposition of the Russell-Wyatt Dialogues*, original Persian edition.

unchained himself from all deterministic laws of nature and social life and the like, and found absolute power in all respects without being bothered with any need whatsoever!! And even then, are our mental activities indeed merely restricted to finding the stuffs of natural life which we could consume either individually or collectively? We need education, and unless the goal is fulfilled, we have to rely on our teacher or instructor. We require cultural management, and to benefit from this management, we should certainly lean on righteous cultural authorities. We need political management, and to sustain our "intelligible life", we will have to have trust in honest politicians.

More significantly, our mind seriously asks us, "Who are you? Whither have you come? Why have you come? Where do you go from here?" It is needless to say, to answer these existential questions we will need to rely on supernatural figures known as prophets and saints. The necessity of depending on these figures is being endorsed by common sense and pure conscience. It is surprising that Russell has argued:

> *On the other hand, suppose you were stone-deaf from birth, but lived among musical people. You could understand, if you had learned to speak and to do lip-reading, that the musical scores represented something quite different from themselves in intrinsic quality, though similar in structure. The value of music would be completely unimaginable to you, but you could infer all its mathematical characteristics, since they are the same as those of the score. Now our knowledge of nature is something like this. We can read the scores, and infer just so much as our stone-deaf person could have inferred about music. But we do not possess the advantages which that person derived from his association with musical people. We cannot know whether the music represented by the scores is beautiful or hideous; perhaps, in the final analysis, we cannot be quite sure that the scores represent anything but themselves. But this is a doubt which the physicist, in a professional capacity, cannot entertain.[1]*

According to the abovementioned ideas, Sir Russell ought to have made a distinction between individuals' reliance upon other peoples, and he also should have discerned the dependence that causes one to have a pallid and thin life from that kind of reliance that makes the man conscious of his own power and magnificence and at the same time exposes him to the radiance of the infinite source of power and dignity. Holy Prophets (Peace Be Upon Them) and great figures such

---

1- Russell, Bertrand (1925), *ABC of Relativity*.

as Imam Ali (PBUH) were highly dependent on God. And they would always say that, *"There is neither power nor strength but in God".* Nevertheless, these men were the most active and serious figures throughout the history of mankind; their life was always full of turbulence. Nonetheless, there are some other figures who, despite of less significance as compared to holy prophets, have done unimaginable and brilliant works under the influence of a divine personality. Rumi's acquaintance with Shams of Tabriz is an outstanding example of this kind of dependences that revolutionized the poet to such an extent that Rumi says:

> *I was a respected man of God;*
>
> *You made me the plaything of children in the lane.*
>
> *If you smile, I become a smile as well,*
>
> *And if you rage, I shall become rage.*
>
> *I am happy with you, o' sweet-lipped beloved of mine.*[1]

Nevertheless, it needs to be conceded that we have scarcely seen such brilliant minds as Rumi's during past seven centuries.

In the same letter (September 11, 1963) in which I had asked Sir Russell about the human primordial sense of the search for perfection, I also asked him a mathematical question about "X", the conventional sign for variables. My question inquired whether it is not correct to use "X" as a sign for variables as it is invariably applicable to every number-concept. Russell replied to me in the following words:

From: The Earl Russell, O.M.,F.R.S.,
16 September 1963

Dear Mr. Ja'afari,

Thank you for your letter. "X" denotes no more than variables because the value it represents varies with the problem. These values may be pre-determined but the uses of "X" as a symbol still vary.

The "search for perfection" is rather vague but, in any event, lofty impulses such as the "search for perfection" are not as common as you suggest.

Yours sincerely,

Bertrand Russell
Bertrand Russell.

Dear Mr. Ja'fari,

1- Rumi's *Sonnets of Shams.*

Thank you for your letter. "X" denotes no more than variables because the value it represents varies with the problem. These values may be pre-determined, but the uses of X as a symbol still vary...

Bertrand Russell

8

Dr. Pickett

Subject: The Philosophy and Meaning of Life
Nationality: British/ Major: Educational Sciences
Dialogue Date: 1963

Pickett: Is it indeed necessary for there to be a universal telos and philosophy for life? If it is necessary, what is that telos and philosophy?

Ja'fari: Of course, this is a perennial question that has occupied many brilliant minds since the dawn of the history of mankind. Nevertheless, since it was invariably taken as a self-evident fact in the past times that not only is man a meaningful creature, but he also certainly lives in a logo-centric world, then an independent chapter for discussion on the question of purposefulness of life has never been regarded as necessary.[1]

This is not to say, of course, that this question was never totally skipped over in those times, but I mean that it seems the question of meaning of life was not regarded by them to be as colorful as it is today for us [due to their particular ontological view of life], and thus, the issue was addressed in an implicit manner rather than in the form

---

1- There is here an interesting reverberation of Heideggerian idea of ancient openness to Being that let the ancient people particularly the pre-Socratic thinkers to live in an ontologically conscious fashion. Heidegger believes that modern man is plagued with forgetfulness of Being and this is why s/he is bogged down in the swamp of nihilism. This nihilism is a product of an understanding of self and the nature that has changed the former into the subject whose only task is the epistemic and technical interrogation of the latter to find out of it whatever it pleases even what does not really exist in it. Then we live in an age of the absence of meaning and we find ourselves needful of asking of the meaning and meaningfulness of our life and existence. For more details particularly see for instance: Martin Heidegger (1968), *What Is It Called Thinking?*, Harper and Row Publishers, New York (An English Translation of original German 1954 *Was Heisst Denken?* By Max Niemeyer Verlag, Tubingen). (Translator).

of an independent debate.

Pickett: It would be appreciated if you would give us an example of such implicit encounters with the question of the meaningfulness of life.

Ja'fari: For example, we can here allude to those human beings who have always sought to pursue human values and magnitudes, without having been persuaded by any kind of reward or punishment, hold human life in high regard in all moments of their lives, and believed that life must fulfill values and magnitudes and bring all potentialities into actuality so as it may hit the target in its course of evolution.

Thus, they thought, life will reach its target if they do magnificent works, actualize the potentialities and take advantage of all available means and forces for life, while all these latter affairs happened to be done by the impulse of the philosophy that underlay them; the ultimate telos, however, was still there to be achieved. Then, they turned this time to fresh doctrines, say happiness requires you to get all these done. The ultimate telos of all human efforts and struggles in life is perfection, or to put it otherwise, there is an inherent enthusiasm in human beings that moves them toward perfection. On the other hand, some materialists have introduced well-being and a healthy environment for life as the underlying drive for all such demanding efforts.

Thus, we can extrapolate five or six theories on the telos of life by surveying ancient ideas, but to tell the truth, neither one of these theories can sufficiently address the question of ultimate telos of life.

Of course, we need to search for the taproot of this primordial sense of Telesis inside human beings themselves. We must answer, for instance, the question why man still finds himself unsatisfied with, say, 80 years of a life full of carnal and intellectual pleasures and seeks to unearth its underlying philosophy. If carnal satisfaction were enough for man, why would he still be so tough in his search for the ultimate telos of life? If, in some cases, we behold a kind of distraction and lack of attention, we should trace it back either to the confusing and troubling conditions of modern life pestered with machinist attitudes and lifestyles or to some hedonistic and utilitarianistic intentions that are pushed forward through some cultural, or political, diabolic plots.

Human inattention to such an existential emergency as the search for the telos of life due to his being trammeled within the marsh of carnal pleasures cannot be a sufficient reason for its being baselessness. To state the matter otherwise, the fire of enthusiasm for the quest of the telos of life will always remain alive under the ashes of fondness for corporeal desires. This is to say, if we insulate human individuals against the effects of machine-like life and the diabolic plots of hedonist and utitlitarianist authorities of societies, they will certainly ask, "Then what is our philosophy of life?"

The other issue that needs to be addressed is who has the right to ask of the ultimate telos of life. Of course, this right belongs to the one for whom the life is not merely an issue of everydayness, and at the same time has a reliable grip on life as well as a dependable knowledge of its *origin* and *end* and also its functions and grandeurs; in fact, someone who knows that the universe has emerged out of something below zero and flourished to a degree infinitely removed from that zero and contains potentialities for mind-boggling breakthroughs and some evil wills that can destroy the whole existing beings.

To speak succinctly, this is not a commonplace matter and cannot be taken up by an individual who is pleased and satisfied in his life with broth and sleep; as a matter of fact, it needs a human being who is not stuck with the routines of life. Such a human being knows that it is not intelligible to credulously assume that this is all we can know about life and that there is no way forward. This kind of human being is the one who has enough grips on life and can lead the way to the unknown realm of meaning. As a result, there are two alternative encounters with life. The alternative one is being featured by its satisfaction with the surface meaning of life and finds itself pleased by life *as it is*. Unfortunately, many societies in the world live their lives based on this perspective of life. They say:

> We are uninformed about the origin and end of this world;
>
> The opening and final pages of this ancient book are lost.

(Kalim Kashani)

It is as if someone does not want to read a book and at the same time he knows that book is not a pillow, but he nonetheless uses it as a cushion. As Rumi has eloquently stated:

> Although this book has been written for the sake of a particular technique,
>
> You can, however, use it as a pillow if you will.[1]

Although this latter perspective of life represents the predominant *lebenanschauung* throughout the history of mankind, the currency is by

---

1- Rumi's *Masnavi*, Book 3.

no means a condition of truth. The second alternative, on the other hand, is characterized by nauseating discontents with the surface meaning of life and the quest for a deep meaning of life *as it ought to be*. This is the life-view of brilliant minds and enlightened souls who are open to the true nature of life and owe their fundamental understanding of the imperativeness of the quest for the ultimate telos of life to life itself as they reside within the bosom of life and do not see it as a strange object before themselves that they must overcome by means of scientific encounter.

The telos already lies within life itself, as the latter primordially knows where it *ought to* anchor by. But almost all of us live our lives like a peasant boy that grazes his cattle on the green foothills of his home village, and the question of the meaning of life to him could be no more than the cows he owns, the land where he lives and the family he has. Then we need to culture ourselves to the degree that life could reveal its ultimate telos to us. This cultivation requires to be done after the following brilliant word by Plato, which should not only be a slogan of philosophers but in fact must become the motto for all human individuals:

> *Die by your will (harness your animal instincts by your will), so that you can be alive by your nature – which is the eternal spirit.*[1]

Pickett: How can people sincerely devote themselves to these fundamental issues in the face of today's machine-like life, modern life and technology?

Ja'fari: Of course, this is a difficult task to fulfill, but it is eventually up to reason to decide whether the utilitarianism of the evil authorities of societies should be satisfied or we must have an ultimate telos in our life. If social authorities are righteous and sympathetic individuals, they should order educational centers to introduce people into the true nature of life and social collectivity. We have to be merely active about the problem of the philosophy of life; indeed, it is a task every managing body in any society to is responsible for in order to provide the necessary conditions for practically addressing this problem.

Pickett: Then what is this telos in your view?

Ja'fari: This telos and philosophy cannot be definitely sought for within the contours of natural life and material life, since if the latter form of life were satisfying as such, there would never have been any

---

1- Quoted by Mulla Sadra in his magnum opus, *Asfar*.

quest for a higher telos of life. As a result, the telos must be itself something nobler than natural issues so that it can expose life to a transcendental turn. This expresses a universal law that tells us that the human goal must reside in a position higher than his current situation so as he can have an incentive to take action. Thus, the telos of life must be something more than carnal pleasures. Rumi poetizes this very idea as follows:

The sweetness of honey and milk is a reflection of the heart;

Every joy reveals a delight in the heart.

So the heart is the substance and the universe is its accident;

How can the shadow of the heart be the purpose of the heart?[1]

This is to say that carnal pleasures are shadows of human life and thus cannot be the telos of life. Honey, milk and beauties become one's ultimate goal when one submerges oneself in corporeal affairs up to one's neck. It is not intelligible to ground one's life in such relative phenomena as worldly beauty, since it is merely an image of absolute beauty. In fact, every goal that is adopted in this world is a shadow of a higher telos. Therefore, we should say that the ultimate telos of life is exposing oneself to the radiation of Absolute Perfection that orients our actions in all moments of life.

Pickett: The idea that you have just elaborated is not understandable for the public today. What do you think in this regard?

Ja'fari: I concede that many people are unfortunately blind to this idea, but as you know, the reality of a phenomenon is different from the manner of its acceptance. We must make this point fathomable for the public that by sticking to sour grapes, they cannot taste the sweetness of a ripe grape. Nevertheless, man is not an unconscious entity like a sour grape which does not know anything of the ripeness of a full-blown grape; in fact, he sees the sacrifices and offers that are made by developed minds and enlightened souls who slaughter their natural self in the alter of maturity to reach the station of ripeness.

1- Rumi's *Masnavi*, Book 3.

9

Dr. Klaus

Subject: The Necessity of Religion in Human Life
Nationality: German/Area of Expertise: Psychiatry
Dialogue Date: 1964

Klaus: Before my arrival in Iran, I travelled through Middle Eastern countries and posed my question to the scholars of those countries as well.

Ja'fari: Let us have your question, please.

Klaus: As a professor of psychiatry, it seems necessary to have a thorough knowledge of the function and the impact of spiritual impressions and religious attitudes [in the constitution of the self and society], so my question is as follows: is religion indeed necessary in *menschenleben* and how should this necessity be categorized?

Ja'fari: To answer this question, we must come to grips with the significance of *leben* and religion. If our meaning of life is the ordinary phenomenon that is observable in all living beings, even in human beings albeit with some complexities, not only is religion unnecessary for such a phenomenon, but there would also not be any conceivable telos for it other than its very ordinary coordinates and properties (eating and sleeping and wrath and lust), either. Moreover, if religion represents a shallow and baseless set of creeds and deeds, not only will religion in this sense be unnecessary for human life, it will also prove in fact to create upset in intelligible life. But if we mean by human life a meaningful reality in a *logocentric* world, such a concept will never be possible without answering, both theoretically and practically, these four questions: Who am I? Whence have I come? Whither will I return? Why have I come? As you know, ordinary answers based on limited knowledge have never satisfied humanity and will not do so even in future, either. Thus, the necessity of religion for human life is demonstrated.

Ja'fari now opens a copy of Whitehead's Adventures of

Ideas, puts his finger on an "is" in the book and asks Dr. Klaus:

Is this "is" conscious of its meaning? Does it really have any knowledge of the words and sentences before and after it? Is this "is" aware of the contents and chapters of the book and the basic inspiration of the author?! Doubtlessly, these questions have all the same answer, i.e. no. Now, if man were to be asked whether he preferred such an unconscious life to a *lebenform* within which the human person is thoroughly conscious of all dimensions, phenomena, possibilities and ends of life, what would his answer be? To put the matter more conspicuously, which one of these two forms of life is more desirable for human evolution?

Klaus: Surely, the second one.

Ja'fari: Thus, religion is the last resort for a purposeful life. If you have any alternative trajectory to reach intelligible life, please let us know, too.

Klaus: Today, many people live their life with utmost satisfaction without finding themselves obliged to answer these four questions both theoretically and practically.

Ja'fari: Yes, the majority of people live their life with ultimate gratification without having any sense of obligation to understand the scientific, philosophical, artistic, industrial, cultural and economic rules and propositions, indeed. Most of all, there are only a few exceptions in human societies across the world in which some people are aware of the philosophy behind the ruling law and politics in their communities. Unfortunately, you even find in a sore minority those people who live their life with self-awareness. This is the very reason for human backwardness, not the claim that living with self-awareness is baseless.

Klaus: Would you please express your mind more conspicuously?

Ja'fari: There are, indeed, a few people in human societies who have a sufficient knowledge of their surrounding events. There would also be only one human person among millions of citizens of a society who is actually aware of the background philosophy of the ruling law and politics in his society and has the ability to meaningfully address their issues. Thus, if we see that people in the modern world live their lives with the utmost gratification without having any sense of necessity to answer the aforementioned four basic questions, this is not the reason why their life is thoughtful and logical.

Klaus: As you know, a philosophical school has emerged within the recent two centuries in the West known as humanism, which has also been endorsed and reiterated by many scholars. Could this intellectual school free humanity from the need for religion and make the four questions unnecessary?

Ja'fari: Never. I shall provide a simple example here: let us suppose that we have well trained some people to play music and provided them with all they need to perform. Is it enough for them to just there, or do they in fact need to proceed to show their musical capabilities?

Let us also assume that humanism can afford humanity with a thoroughly prosperous and safe life. Will this prove to be sufficient, or will it have to orchestrate its symphony?

Klaus: Are you implying that humanity has not yet orchestrated its desired symphony?

Ja'fari: The answer is negative, as also goes for nihilism and narcotism that have dominated the pro-humanist West.

If we analyze the situation according to the scientific methods, we will see that self-alienated life is the prime reason for mental depression in the modern world, and humanism has not sorely proposed any principle or law for a meaningful life.

10

Dr. Peter

Subject: The Philosophy of Islamic Articles of Faith
Nationality: British/Area of Expertise: Sociology
Dialogue Date: 1965

Peter: What are the Islamic articles of faith?

Ja'fari: These articles reside in a primordial nature that is inhered in human common sense. The human primordial nature has clearly understood that the world we human beings live in is the manifestation of orderliness from which the humanity extracts his scientific laws. Thus, common sense pitches in and explicitly concludes that since this wonderful order could not have been originated in an unconscious matter, this world has a creator called "God".

Peter: If God's existence is so clear, why do so many people fail to accept it?

Ja'fari: If by "so many people" you are referring to those conscious and well-educated ones who do not accept God, this should be reconsidered as it has not so far been seen in human history for someone to have demonstrated the non-existence of God through self-evident reasons.

The only thing we have in this case is challenging the reasons and arguments of the demonstrators of God's existence. Furthermore, the second backrest of those who either deny or are doubtful of divine existence is His intangibleness. This latter argument is also baseless, since if incorporeality is the reason for the non-existence of a reality, then the universal laws of nature are among the first realities that should be discredited on account of their intangibleness.

To deny divine existence, however, we need to claim to have searched through the world and not found such a reality as God. It is needless to say that this latter claim is baseless as we human beings have limited knowledge of the *magnus cosmos* indeed. Moreover, if we assume that someone has been around the whole universe and gained notable knowledge of the cosmos, he could still not deny the divine existence, since there are some key and indispensible elements in the human body like will, emotions and self that are not visible but they do still exist. As you know, the concept of divine existence does not exclusively belong to Islam, as it is indeed at the heart of all religions and truth-seeking schools of thought.

The second article is the divine intervention through holy prophets in the depiction of possible trajectories of intellectual and spiritual evolution in intelligible life that is called the article of prophecy.

Peter: Are you implying that man is not able to manage his affairs by means of his reason?

Ja'fari: Humanity has not deplorably been prosperous even in managing those of his natural affairs that chiefly belong to the domain that he shares with other animals, let alone being able to be so in the domain of human perfections. We may take into consideration how Whitehead has put it:

> *Human schools of thought are the source of an enlightenment that is in fact merged with more darkness as they are to lead the people to the supernatural without resorting to holy prophets.*[1]

If you mean by humanity in this context a totality of faculties and possibilities – one of which is finding the answers to the quadruple basic questions of "Who am I? Whence have I come? Whither will I return? Why have I come?" – The answer will be negative. That is to say, humanity is not competent enough to manage his affairs, as suicides, despotisms, selfishnesses, and repressions clearly witness it.

The third article is the journey back, or in other words, resurrection. The return is the day when man's deeds during his life in this world are calculated and judged. This article has been demonstrated both based on human primordial nature and his common sense reasons; conscientious and responsible life shall be evaluated in a day. Is it not so that a human being sees himself an eternal being due to his primordial nature's call of eternity? This internal sense of eternity is genuine if not silenced by narcotism. The only path to an intelligible interpretation of our world which is a mixture of beauties, magnificence and magnitudes, on the one hand, and misfortunes and darkness, on the other hand, is the acceptance of article of the return,

---

1- In his *Adventures of Ideas*, Whitehead says that after the emergence of theology in Alexandria, scientism had been taken on the throne again; thus, the world lost its luminosity, since academicians were to surpass the prophets.

indeed. Human primordial nature and common sense both clearly give witness to this article. Nasir Khosrow has indicated the ontological significance of this article as follows:

The whole universe will be but a childish play

Unless this long day is followed by a tomorrow

I don't think that this has only been considered by an Eastern Muslim poet, for there are many scholars in your West that have been sensitive toward this issue, like the great commentator and translator of Aristotle's works, Jules Barthélemy-Saint-Hilaire.

Peter: I'd already come to the same conclusions in regard to these articles when I was in my late teens.

Ja'fari: I would like to quote a sentence that I have heard from many scholars that I have had dialogues with. They unanimously state that when we reflect on religion in isolation from our families and communities, we come to the same conclusions.

Peter: Do you believe that the cultural and intellectual confliction between the East and the West will continue to be heightened?

Ja'fari: We should initially distinguish between "difference" and "confliction". Unbiased cultural and intellectual differences are not harmful for humanity, but they even give rise to the needed dynamicity for human intellectual evolution. I believe that this could uncontroversially be demonstrated through evident reasons. For example, you must have heard about the long story of forged confliction between religion and science; it has been claimed that although they do not represent the same reality, they surely complement each other, as Max Planck has confirmed. Such conflictions are always forged by bias and ignorant people.

We now come to the article of Imamate, which means sound governance upon rational and divine principles and laws, although human secondary issues are to be solved through the secondary prescriptions and rules that are legislated by human beings – those human beings who have a good moral background. This system of governance varies from the theocracy of Western Middle Ages, since human primordial nature and common sense has a striking role in the codification of governing rules and laws of the society in Islamic Imamate.

As you see, this form of governance represents such a democracy that is reliant upon developed minds rather than ordinary minds who are ensnared by their selfishnesses.

Justice and other divine attributes of beauty and majesty are driven from the Exalted Name of Allah.

11

Prof. Montaigne

Subject: Comparative Debates of French and Persian Literatures
Nationality: France / Major : Literature
Dialogue Date: 1966

Ja'fari: Does Victor Hugo's *Les Miserables* still have the same significance and credit that it once had in the West?

Montaigne: Yes, there are still many people who believe that this book is unrivalled in its style and theme. Some literary critics have even called it the "Second Bible". How do you see the value of this book in Islamic and Eastern countries?

Ja'fari: Regardless of the few cases in which this book reflects the culture of society that Hugo has lived in, it depicts the common pains, grieves and needs of humanity as well as their remedies – albeit by means of a metaphorical language – in a beautiful and logical fashion. Accordingly, this book has truly gone beyond the borders of the Occident and impressed most societies around the globe.

To explain man's relationships with his fellow human beings in social life, *Les Miserables* has seemingly indicated several instances of human realities and facts. This book is available in Islamic countries in different translations and editions.

Montaigne: Have you read this book?

Ja'fari: Yes, twice. I found this book both meaningful and sympathetic. I mean, the reader of this book realizes that it has not been written by a capricious author persuaded by material affairs and fame.

Moreover, I have selected almost 150 sentences from this book and discussed them in my preface to the third volume of *Rumi the Man and His Ideas: An Analytical and Critical Interpretation of the Masnavi.*[1]

Montaigne: Could you compare Victor Hugo and his masterpiece *Les Miserables* with other famous literati of the East and the West?

Ja'fari: As for Western literati, I should say that I am not familiar with

---

1- In 15 volumes published by one of iranian publishers.

all of them, but my knowledge of Western literature is confined to such renowned figures as Lamartine, Balzac, Shakespeare, Goethe, Dostoyevsky, Tolstoy, Henry Longfellow and the like. Although each one of these literati has discussed very interesting points regarding human life, *Les Miserables* and some works of Dostoyevsky's have their own particular magnificence and charm and one can say that they have had ideas to communicate with humanity. It seems that other Western writers in comparison with these renowned literati are like modern poetry as compared to classic poetry. Although modern poetry has presented some messages for the modern world, its classic rival is of fundamental magnificence due to its devotion to the poetic articulation of the principles and rules of the quadruple ontological relationships (man's relationship with himself, with God, with the world and with his fellow human beings).

The Audience: You have presented a comparative discussion of *Les Miserables* in your preface to the third volume of *An Analytical and Critical Interpretation of Rumi's Masnavi*. Do you believe that this comparison has addressed all aspects of the issue?

Ja'fari: Of course not, but a careful reading of both books [*Les Miserables* and *Masnavi*] shows that Victor Hugo was mostly concerned with human relationships in social life, particularly in the view of modern developments that have led to the emergence of "civilization". However, the other three fundamental ontological relationships have also been somehow addressed in *Les Miserables,* while in *Masnavi* Rumi has discussed these quadruple issues in an integrative fashion. To state the matter otherwise, man in the world and in association with his other fellowmen, either individually or collectively, has been more intellectually attractive in Hugo's view, but Rumi is interested in a kind of human being whose existence's transphysical and spiritual aspect is more significant and authentic than its natural and social aspects, although these latter aspects have their own respective significance as seen by Rumi.

Moreover, the boundary that separates the physical from the transphysical is the most important of all:

> *You paired together the two ends of the rings of existence thanks to the truth.*

12

Dr. S. Elizabeth

Subject: Some Conditions of Judgment in Islam
Nationality: British/ Major: Law
Dialogue Date: 1967

Elizabeth: Is retaliation a decided form of judgment in Islam that cannot be changed under any condition?

Ja'fari: To begin with, we need to pay more attention to the essence of judgment as such. Before any assessment of this judgment, it must be taken into account that retaliation is one of the judgments of willful homicide rather than all kinds of murder, since if a homicide happens involuntarily due to a misunderstanding, it does not have any reprisal in the form of blood ransom; this is particularly the case with felonious homicide. On the other hand, retaliation is not the only [final] judgment of murder; in fact, retribution is merely one of the three forms of judgment that have been determined for homicide in Islamic Shari'ah Law:

1. Paying blood-money to the family of the murdered person.
2. Remission by the family of the murdered person.
3. Retaliation as the last option on the table that is executed if the family of murdered person does not to accept the blood-money or the remission.

Elizabeth: Although retaliation is one of the forms of legal judgment, do you not see it as against human feelings? When a man has been killed, what advantage or payoff could be obtained by taking another individual's life? Isn't it better to decide a lesser brutal and more cultural judgment for homicide so that it may discipline the individual who has committed murder?

Ja'fari: This question has to be analyzed in a thorough manner. The idea that retaliation is against human sentiments should be precisely appraised, since human sentiments are divided into two major groups:

1- Naïve natural sentiments that are undoubtedly being incited even by killing a python that can threaten many human lives. Moreover, what is supposed then to recompense the emotional and existential loss of the family and relatives of the slain?

2- Transcendental sentiments that insist on the execution of judgment.

Accordingly, retaliation is a kind of judgment that is to be issued for willful murder when there is no mistake, compulsion, mental disorder or slant involved. In such a case, the murderer has encroached upon all human individuals. As the Holy Quran has stated:

> *Whoever slays a soul, unless it be for manslaughter or for mischief in the land, it is as though he slew all men; and whoever keeps it alive, it is as though he kept alive all men.*
> (The Table Spread 5:32)

However, it must be noted that according to an accepted jurisprudential principle which states that *judgments are rescinded by the emergence of doubts,* any form of uncertainty over the murderer's ignorance of the judgment or the probability of any kind of mental and psychological disorder in the murderer could halt the execution of retaliation.

On the other hand, the legal inclusion of retaliation as one of the triple forms of punishment for voluntary homicide is a very significant act toward the recognition of the essential value of human life, since it exposes all human individuals to the grave consequence of encroachment to other peoples' right to life.

Having said these, if we compare the loss of an innocent life with the breaking of a chandelier or setting a wooden table on fire, it will be even more evil and more disgusting than the act of homicide itself. We are humans living in a complicated network of relations. A homicide is not merely a matter of killing one individual; in fact, it involves many other people as well. How one can recompense the possible losses incurred in such a scale?

Elizabeth: As you know, today's human relations are not as tight as the past. As a result, the annulment of the judgment of retaliation does not impose any loss upon anyone. Isn't it so?

Ja'fari: This is merely the reification of the dynamic phenomenon of human life and changing it into an unconscious cog of a machine. Thus conceived, suicide is not more serious than the breaking of a glass. Giving impunity to a willful murderer would not only stigmatize human dignity, but also change homicide into a social paradigm!

13

Allal al-Fassi

Subject: Shi'ah and Asharite Takes on Theological Issues
Nationality: Moroccan/ Major: Theology
Dialogue Date: 1970

Allal al-Fassi: Considering the new questions that are being posed these days by different ideologies, don't you feel that we require a theology more compatible with the modern body of knowledge so as Moslems can lay the groundwork for a new science of Kalam?

Ja'fari: From some aspects, it would not be realistic to expect a new science of Kalam to be established regardless of the past principles and foundations, since the problems of Kalam are still the same even in the face of new developments made in (human or divine) sciences. Among these perennial issues are the necessity of religion, the world's need for a creator, the attributes of the Creator – God – and God's relationship with the universe, God's relationship with man, resurrection, eternity and the like, that were discussed in the past and today, due to the conjunctions engendered between the beliefs and the theology of nations, are debated in a more comprehensive and exhaustive fashion. Establishing a new science of Kalam in isolation from the classic issues is not an intelligible thing to do at all, because Kalam in Islam has unshakable foundations and principles that are still dependable.

One of the perennial questions of Kalam that has been broadly discussed in the past and remains to this day at the center of Kalam debates and needs to be researched from new angles, is the primordial question regarding "liberty and compulsion", for no slight change has ever happened in Divine Knowledge since then; in fact, only the scientific mind-set has evolved into a new shape. To put the matter differently, it was the classic analysis of causality that set the scene for determinism in the past; as it states "until all constitutive parts of the cause have not come together, it is impossible to issue the effect from it". In other words, if a certain cause has, let's say, 100 constituents, there would not be any effect around unless all of these components of the cause have made a whole even if, a half-piece of one of the components is absent. Today determinists understand causality in the same classic sense and accept its existence in the natural world.

Now, the question is whether it is correct to invariably consider the law of causality, in the same inflexible sense that ends up in determinism, both in the domain of nature and human affairs. In divine knowledge, everything is already determined as God is omniscient and knows which action is being issued from which creature and when, and this expresses the supernatural and primordial side of the issue of causation. However, this issue has another aspect that must be handled by science, which varies from time to time. It is in this latter aspect that the privilege of today's debates on causality, which are more systematic and coherent, lies.

Allal al-Fassi: We do not believe in causality in the robust sense that natural sciences impose to the human mind; rather, we say that the law of causality is a divine tradition, i.e. God has decided that causes shoud be followed by effects. As a result, there is no necessity in natural causality (which is the Asharite view).

Ja'fari: Asharites were partially on the right track regarding this issue, but it should be asked that if a certain cause can be followed by a heterogeneous effect, say the issue whether an apple tree can produce watermelons, since it is not *necessary* for an apple tree to produce apples. This latter has not been addressed in the Asharite point of view.

Thus, we (Shi'ah scholars) believe that causality is a necessary law that governs the whole gamut of outside nature. That is to say, it is necessary in the outside world that an apple tree produce apples or a heater produce heat and a particular disease to be engendered by a particular virus and so on and so forth.

Thus, causality is an essential law that is invariably applied to outside nature. However, it is Divine Will that is the primordial source of the causality of all causes.

Although this is not correct as to human affairs, causality in the latter sense is merely applied to the outside world, where every determinate cause must necessarily be followed by its respective effect. Of course, this is something other than the philosophico-thelogical idea that nothing is issued but from the Cause of all causes, as the following verses by Rumi offer:

> *Though stone and iron are the cause,*

You can attempt to look beyond them, noble man.

This cause was prompted by a prior one,

So how can men assume that it has none?[1]

***

Those causes which decide what Prophets do

Are higher than these causes you can view.

Those ones can choose to make these take effect,

Or make them fruitless things we all neglect.

These causes can be grasped with just your mind,

But only Prophets know the other kind.[2]

Or, as we read in many orisons, "O' the Cause of all Causes." Thus, we see that no single cause in the world contains the effect that depends on it in a way that can manage it alone. Theoretical physics also approves of this fact. According to the Heisenberg uncertainty principle, we are not aware of the next moment of a phenomenon as we do not know exactly how and where it has existed previously. However, some scholars have invoked this theory as an excuse to deny causality in general both in the outside surface of the world as well as in its essential side. We are not happy with this view, as we can determine the cause of any particular effect at hand one way or another. Thus, we can keep the search up to the Cause of all causes and this somewhat shows where that effect has effused from.[3]

The fact that by considering one thing as a "cause" we cannot determine its effect by all means does not demonstrate that the law of causality has failed; as a matter of fact, through it we can recognize that the "the world is different from knowing the world"[4] rather than concluding that a universal law of nature has collapsed. This law says that nothing would spring into existence by chance, as the very idea of chance is self-contradictory; however, this does not imply that we can surely determine the exact cause of an effect. Our knowledge is merely confined to the fact that everything cannot emerge from everything.

When Hume reduced causation to the mere association of events and ideas and said that there is no necessary relationship whatsoever

---

1- Rumi's *Masnavi*, Book 1.

2- Ibid.

3- This type of etiology is common both in natural and human sciences.

4- This has been quoted from Albert Einstein.

between the cause and the effect and what we consider as a meaningful relation is no more than an association of two things or a chain of things that follow each other like seasons, one critic came along, as Russell relates, and asked:

> Now that you claim that the alleged necessary causal relation is only the psychological metamorphosis of a mere association of two phenomena, then the question arises why everything is not issued from everything. Hume answered his critic in a clear voice, "I do not know."

The answer to the latter question indeed is that if we assumed that causality is not rooted in the essence of facts but is rather a quality of their outside existence, we would in fact be attempting to provide a platform for man to regulate his relationships with life and its factors. Thus conceived, causality does not offer anything more than the existence of congruity, not of course in its robust classic sense, between two objects that are respectively considered the cause and the effect. Although the origin of movement is transcendental, we have two distinct chains of objects that stand in a causal relation with each other. However, we cannot understand their relationship in purely scientific and mathematical terms.

If we accept the existence of causality in nature in this strict sense, this does not mean that we can apply it to human beings as well, since there is something called "personality" in man – a factor in man that allows him to act even with partial fulfillment of causal conditions.[1] Said differently, the human being is such an agent that acts even when the chain of occasional causes required is not whole. As a result, we must be careful defining liberty, as it astonishingly changes into an analogically graded notion when it comes to considering man as a creature who has an ever-dynamic factor inside called *personality*.

Allal al-Fassi: When seventy percent of the underlying motive for action is provided from outside and only thirty percent is prepared by personality, doesn't this thirty percent merely play an occasional and complementary role?

Ja'fari: We are not denying the complementary role of personality in causation; in fact, our claim is that causality law has a more gentle dynamics inside human beings as compared to the outside world due to the former's existential subtleties. The "self" can render an effect

---

1- This is a route that Max Planck has treaded in his discussions on causation in theoretical physics.

possible even with half of the required occasional causes around through its delicate potencies.

The idea that the self uses these precipitated potencies as its subjective capital to make the causal chain whole needs to be revisited, since we do not have access to sufficient evidence to substantiate the latter idea. In addition, we must have in mind the fact that it could be from other active agents that the self has been in contact with through its course of evolution. There is also another possibility involved according to which this dynamicity of the self can have its origin in its nature.

It is necessary to be noted that this thirty percent has nothing to do with phenomena or conscious activities of the self; as a matter of fact, it is an immanent desire inside man that provokes him to bring about the effect. This immanent desire is not motivated by any extra-subjective compulsory factor, so it does not make an occasion for compulsion and determinism. The intensity of this immanent desire depends on the personality's subjective capital, particularly when the effect is a moral action like the search for perfection or self-fulfillment. Thus, even the least percentage of the presence of the self in causation, say forty percent, nullifies the possibility of the domination of compulsion.

14

Prof. Filippani Ronconi

Subject: Philosophical and Theological Issues
Nationality: Italian/ Major: Eastern philosophy
Dialogue Date: 1970

This dialogue dates back to the conversation that Professor Ronconi had with Allameh Ja'fari at the conference held in Mashhad on the Millennium of Sheikh Tusi, the great Shi'ah Scholar.

Ronconi: I am very happy to have been fortunate enough to attend such a magnificent conference like this. During the past five days, during which I have been part of the panel on "philosophy and heresiology," a large number of philosophical principles and issues were discussed. Fortunately, many of the discussed issues had been researched thoroughly and all managed to find their final answers. Sadly, philosophy is now dead in the West, but it is still alive in your East, unless as Goethe, the German poet, says, "Once again, an Oriental breeze will blow and bring along a universal and coherent philosophy for the West." Here is my question: why is West not able to introduce a universal and systematic philosophy to humanity?

Ja'fari: To be honest, the analytical reflections in the West are very powerful and no one can deny this fact. The mode of thought that is featured by these analytical reflections has mistakenly been termed as "new positivism" under the influence of an excessive objectivism, while it was better if they mentioned that they have given the prominence to analytic method and adopted it as their chosen philosophical method. As Russell replied when he was asked to which school he belonged:

> *The only label that I have accepted is "logical atomism", but I am not so interested in labels and always try to avoid them.*[1]

Then, if the West were aware of its monopolization of the analytic

---

1- Ja'fari, M. T. *An Analytical Exposition of the Russell-Wyatt Dialogues.*

method, it would have recognized this deficiency and tried to clear a room for the synthetic method in its philosophy and *weltanschauung*. If such a consciousness had in fact emerged there, we would have had systematic philosophy in the West today.

The Westerners may have not understood that the excessive objectivism of twentieth century positivism was the swan song of this method. The analytic method cannot depict an integrated picture of the world as it studies all facts in isolation from each other. This insufficiency of the analytic method can be easily felt from the global yearning for universal and systematic philosophies that could only be achieved through the application of the synthetic method.

The example that I once used in a comparative seminar on the Islamic science of the soul and modern psychology in the conference hall at Ruzbeh Hospital – which was then under the direction of Prof. Mirsepasi in Tehran, and two seminars on psychiatry and psychology were held there each month– can also be applied in this case. To construct a good building, we necessarily need not to use such stuffs as unprocessed stones and timbers, and by the same token, it is not allowed in philosophy to use limited knowledge of issues and problems that has not been sufficiently researched. As a result, philosophy must be grounded in well-processed and established knowledge. I think this is the Achilles heel of Western philosophy that – despite the emergence of brilliant developments in such sciences as mathematics, chemistry, physics and the like – was not able to break the bondages of the analytic method and make its contribution to the discipline.

For example, Western scholars have proposed intelligent analyses of various types of time including contractual time, physical time, cosmic time and so on and so forth, but these analyses cannot offer us an integrative knowledge of the nature of time as such. This is a task that needs to be done by means of the synthetic method.

Ronconi: What do you mean by the synthetic method? Can this method be equally applied both in the East and the West in the face of their intellectual differences?

Ja'fari: According to the synthetic method, man is a being who dwells inside the world and is able to know it. Moreover, the knowledge that man obtains of the world determines his situation in world and orients his purposeful movement. Therefore, man needs to acquire a universal knowledge of the universe in view of the fundamental quadruple relationships so that he may achieve answers to his questions. Man's relationship with himself, his relationship with God, his relationship with the world and also his relationship with his fellow human beings, are the four basic relationships that the man must understand so as to have an integrative knowledge of existence and avoid being lost inside dispersed facts.

Thus, we see that man is able to apply the synthetic method as an existential emergency. As to the intellectual differences existing between the West and the East, I should say that these differences do not have any impact on the necessity of the application of this method, since both poles enjoy the same epistemic capabilities and methods, although there may be some scientific and philosophical propositions that they do not share. Of course, we should not forget the influence of the cultural element, which brings about changes in the quality of the application of this method in these regions.

15

Dr. Van Wayek

Subject: Political Philosophy and Mysticism
Nationality: American (originally Dutch) Major : Philosophy
Dialogue Date: 1972

Ja'fari: Regardless of that how extensively Rumi was in touch with realities in his intuitions and intellectual methods, we all – both Easterners and Westerners – need to think and research to a vaster extent about the magnificence and highly varied mental activities of this man. In other words, serious studies and works have to be done on the mind that has left us with such a rich heritage of diverse intellectual principles and moving analytic and synthetic innovations in basic tenets and (philosophical, moral, psychological, religious and mystical) worldviews.

Of course, we do not expect Western thinkers to accept all of what Rumi has said, because they may have their own ideas about him that more suit the particular culture they belong to. However, this cultural consideration does not mean that Western scholars are not able to understand Rumi's ideas or do not accept them at all, since if they are to study the scientific and philosophical character of this man in the perspective of transcendental cultural principles, they will certainly be benefited from Rumi's musings, as not only does he have a universal view of both science and philosophy, but his reflections in these fields as well as in other fields of study like mysticism, theology and even literature are also all established upon rational bases that are invariable for all human individuals. Thus, we need to reflectively analyze these ecstatic meditations to see why there have been so few of such figures as Rumi in history? Surprising is the fact that we cannot find even some diluted versions of such figures around these days.

Van Wayek: It is true, there is still much to be done as to such studies. What is your suggestion in this regard?

Ja'fari: Generally speaking, we can study historical figures in two ways:

I) To study the figure's family background, the social and political circumstances he has lived in as well as his personal achievements and then content oneself with this and proceed no further.

II) To study if this figure's mental state is originated in love. How much of his activities have been of his own, and how much has he owed to others? And even that how much of that have been the result of the association of ideas? What role have these themes played in his self-justification? Has he used these to feign an intellectual posture or a social status? Or were these themes spillovers of his soul? This kind of study of figures in human sciences can be very helpful for us, but unfortunately, such research has not been pursued enough yet.

Van Wayek: This has been truly a brilliant mind that one cannot almost find any equal for in any of the numerous branches of knowledge.

Ja'fari: One of the occasions in which Rumi has spoken of the ultimate magnificence and value of humanity is where he addresses the issue of transcendental unity of human individuals and the value of human souls; as we read:

> *For their plurality is like waves in seas;*
>
> *They seem like separate forms if there's a breeze.*
>
> *Like light in different windows, each man's soul*
>
> *Just seems discrete and not part of one whole.*
>
> *When you look at the sun, you see one sphere,*
>
> *But those still veiled by forms claim that's not clear.*
>
> *Animal spirits have divisions, friend,*
>
> *The human's, though, is one and has no end,*
>
> *Because God's light was sprayed on them,*
>
> *And you can never separate that light in two.*[1]

This is an understanding of the nature of humanity, the depth and magnificence of which is fathomed when compared with such diabolic views as those of Machiavelli and Hobbes.

Van Wayek: Of course, Machiavelli was not saying that a politician must indifferently sacrifice all moral, religious and cultural principles for his goal. Machiavelli does not dictate that we must act either in this or in that way, but he has described and conceptualized an external flow of events and it is politicians indeed that scapegoat everything for

---

1- Rumi's *Masnavi*, Book 2.

their satanic intentions.

Ja'fari: Despite his delicate humanistic approach, Victor Hugo has also made this mistake and said something like what you have just indicated. Machiavelli is not himself a wicked person, but he has in fact merely described the natural course of politics, where means are always being slaughtered in the altar of goals. As Hugo argues:

> The property of right is to remain eternally beautiful and pure. Reality, even when most necessary to all appearances, even when most thoroughly accepted by contemporaries, if it exists only as a fact, and if it contains only too little of right, or none at all, is infallibly destined to become, in the course of time, deformed, impure, perhaps, even monstrous. If one desires to learn, at one blow, to what degree of hideousness the fact can attain, viewed at the distance of centuries, one should look at Machiavelli. Machiavelli is neither an evil genius, nor a demon, or a miserable and cowardly writer; he is nothing but the fact. Furthermore, he is not only the Italian fact; he is the European fact, the fact of the sixteenth century. He seems hideous, and so he is, in the presence of the moral idea of the nineteenth. This conflict of right and reality has been going on ever since the origin of society. To terminate this duel, to amalgamate the pure idea with the humane reality, to cause right to penetrate pacifically into the fact and the fact into right, is truly the task of sages.[1]

It is not fair to ignore existing facts for intellectual purposes. In *The Prince* (1532), Machiavelli recommends quite clearly that you should act this way in politics. Although he shows a partial respect for laws and their independence in *Discourses*, this is not the case with *The Prince* too. Let us read together one example of these diabolic orders:

> As a prince must be able to act just like a beast, he should also learn from the fox and the lion, because the lion does not defend itself against traps, and the fox does not defend itself against wolves. Thus, one has to be a fox in order to recognize traps, and a lion to frighten off wolves.[2]

This sentence does not express a critical view of a scholar who tries to intellectualize a state of affairs, but it is a piece of instruction that is offered for the practitioners of politics.

If we say that Machiavelli has outlined these views in order to help

---

1- Hugo, Victor, *Les Miserables*.
1- *The Prince*, Chapter 18.

Italy to regain its unity, then he should have mentioned his methodic application of "means versus goals" maxim so as to thwart future misunderstandings. This fault is not acceptable from an intellectual who truly cares about humanity and man's values. It is said that Machiavelli's ideas have been criticized even by the most evil politicians.

However, it should be taken into consideration that the methodic adoption of this maxim is itself contingent upon a condition that states that if some realities are being sacrificed as means for some determined goals, the latter must be of a value that could redress the inflicted loss. This needs a precise calculation of the values of the means and the goals, which hardly appears to be a task that can be taken on by politicians who see worthwhile whatever which serves their purposes. On the other hand, Plato says:

> True politicians are those who know that they must evaluate affairs upon a sagaciously acquired knowledge of human nature and then proceed to act.

16

Prof. Charles Adams

Subject: Comparative Debates on Hindu and Islamic Mysticism
Nationality: Canadian/ Major: Mysticism
Dialogue Date: 1977

Adams: What differences are there between Islamic mysticism and Hindu gnosis?

Ja'fari: These differences have their origin in the very essence of the schools that these mysticisms belong to, i.e. Islam and Hinduism. To put the matter otherwise, the spiritual outlook of the Islamic and Hindu gnosis should be understood in terms of the ideological principles of Islam and Hinduism.

Of course, it must be noted that by Islamic mysticism in this context we mean what we have termed as "positive mysticism" and devoted many courses to its vindication, since whenever we discuss Islamic mysticism, it is necessary to distinguish between Islamic mysticism and Moslems' mystical ideas like Islamic philosophy and Moslems' philosophical views.

To state the matter differently, for example, Farabi is an Islamic philosopher and a Moslem, but we cannot say that Farabi is tantamount to Islamic philosophy, although he has made significant contributions into Islamic philosophy as such. By the same token, Avicenna, Averroes, Mullah Sadra and others have all been Islamic philosophers and each one approached the discipline from his point of vantage; however, this does not mean that their philosophical ideas represent Islamic philosophy as a whole.

This is also the case with Islamic mysticism; for example, Muhyaddin Ibn Arabi is a globally appreciated Moslem Gnostic thinker, but we cannot designate the nature of Islamic mysticism by his name alone. Rumi is certainly a significant figure in the whole history of Islamic Gnosticism; however, we do not consider his mystical ideas as a representation of the whole gamut of Islamic mysticism. The only thing that we can say in regard to Rumi is that he has evolved within Islamic culture and moved within the paradigm of the Holy Quran's verse which states "*We are Allah's and to Him we shall surely return*" (Qur'an, The Cow 2: 156); that is, he has moved from "*We are Allah's*" to "*to Him we shall surely return*" and excellently interpreted the holy verses of the Quran based upon authentic Islamic sources. Although as a matter of taste some may criticize Rumi for his substantiation of a particular idea of his own by a determinate verse of the Quran, by and large Rumi has interpreted almost 2200 verses in his magnum opus *Masnavi*. This clearly shows that it is Islam that has given rise to such a magnificent mystical outlook; however, we cannot say that Rumi is the whole fabric of Islamic mysticism.

This is also the case with other mystics who have emerged in the context of Islam, such as Hafez, Suhrewardi and the like, as we cannot regard their ideas an expression of the whole mystical outlook of Islam. It is very likely that say Sheikh Mahmud Shabestari has treaded a path in mysticism that Rumi did not agree with on many occasions.

In any event, Islamic mysticism is an integrated whole whose various embodiments in different mystical outlooks demonstrate that Moslem mystics have paced the path of Islamic mysticism in their own particular way.

Adams: What are the common grounds of Islamic mysticism?

Ja'fari: It can be said that Islamic mysticism, at a higher level, can contain all of these ideas. The core idea of this school, according to positive Islamic mysticism, is a realistic view of existence according to which man and the world are real identities. As the Holy Quran states:

> **And we did not create the heavens and the earth and what is between them two but in truth.** (The Rocky Tract 15:85)

As you see, Hindu mysticism differs from Islamic positive gnosis in respect of its idealistic view of existence. Consequently, we cannot easily interpret these schools in a way as if they are elaborating the same idea in different words. The world has an inalienable reality and the Quran has, in more than ten verses, used the word "*haq*" as regards to the world and *haq*, as it has been demonstrated in its place, is the reality proper of existence. Now we can turn to the world's relationship with God, which is the relationship of an emanation with the All-Emanating, or of a beam of light with the engendering source of light, not that the world of existence is a pure reality of Light (i.e., God). The external world is moving, while God, according to Islamic ontology, is non-moving. As a result, they cannot be various moments of the same continuum. Thus conceived, Hindu mysticism may be comparable with Islamic gnosis in respect of its resort to the notion of emanation for explaining the relationship between God and the world as the sun and the place wherefrom the sun shines. This is the only way we can make comparisons between these two Gnostic schools; otherwise, other Hindu interpretations of this relationship that result in the absolute denial of the existence of the natural world are not acceptable in Islam, as the latter does not consider the world as a hallucination. If some mystics and poets are seen to deny the reality of the world, this can be declared merely as a matter of taste, for they can by no means accept the requirements of such a denial.

The following quatrains by Jami are examples of the abovementioned poetic views:

> When God became uncovered in details and aspects,
> Tthus this world of gain and loss came along.
> When disappear the world and its settlers,
> In the station of integrity God appears alone.

***

> The heavenly witness from the treasury of existence
> Stalked to the wilderness of existence and put up the tent.
> Every knot she tied on her hair from the beauties manifested
> Stole the hearts of a hundred circles.

***

> The existence that emerges in everything
> If you want to understand its status in everything,
> Go and see the bubble on the surface of wine
> How it is a wine in the wine and the wine inside the wine.

Here we want the reader to precisely consider the first quatrain which depicts the world as a differentiated form of God who is in turn the integrated form of the world. This does not suit the ontological outlook of Islam. As a result, they should be understood as the poetic side of these figures' character that does not represent their true religious view in the exact sense of the term. This is what I heard from my master Mirza Mahdi Ashtyani, a truly respected philosopher, in a personal dialogue.

Thus, according to Islamic mysticism, the world is a crystal-like reality that can reflect the divine blaze, and this occurs only to those who have purified themselves of carnal desires and taints.

17

Prof. Najmuddin Bamaat

**Subject: The Philosophy
of the Principles and Foundations of Islam**
Nationality: French/ Major: Islamic Philosophy
Dialogue Date: 1981

Bamaat: In your view, what are the major basic principles of Islam that are not permitted to be violated?

Ja'fari: The principles of Islam are definitely grounded in human primordial nature, i.e. in the human quadruple primordial relationships (with God, the world, himself and with his fellowmen). For example, as regards to existence, whether in knowing its reality "*as it is*" or in the depiction of its reality "*as ought to be*", Islam speaks in terms of the heavenly endowed nature of humanity and realities. This is an essential point that must be taken into consideration by every Islamologist. In fact, Islam, in all of its political, economical, legal, moral and ontological aspects, has avoided the factors outside "the knower" and "the known", and to put the matter in modern theoretical terms concerned in physics, Islam has excluded varied factors, since in Islamic sources, there are two kinds of view of and relationship with the world of existence (pure view and relationship/view and relationship combined with the interference of subjective elements). It is a profound issue how able man is in developing a pure relationship with realities free from the encroachments of subjective perceptual interferences.

The demarcation of the boundary between "I" and "not-I" in knowledge and in various appropriational and impressional relationships may remain unaccomplished forever. This is not to say that it could not be accomplished even partially. Generally speaking, our knowledge is always a product of the coordination of "I" and "not-I" except in two cases – one of which is our grasp and intuition of God, while the other is presential knowledge, where man directly comes in contact with the subject without the interference of senses as well as the appearances, quantities and qualities of the natural world. Except for these two latter cases, according to Chinese Lao Tzu,[1] and as quoted by the Danish physicist Niels Bohr, "in the great drama of existence, we are both the actors and the spectators."

Briefly speaking, the underlying cause for the persistence of Islam and Islamic ideas is that they are grounded in realities and seek to touch the reality as such away from the impressions of perceptual factors; as a matter of fact, we read in some mystical books that:

> O' Lord! Show us in this house of deception
>
> How things are truly, their real state.[2]
>
> We didn't see the hook beneath the bait;
>
> Show us how things are truly, their real state.[3]

Rumi has also stated that:

> This jug's our body, so it must contain
>
> All of our outward senses' bitter rain.
>
> O Lord, accept this water that we've brought
>
> By the grace of their lives the Lord has bought!
>
> This jug has five spouts, for each sense, you see,
>
> To preserve its water from impurity.
>
> So to the sea the jug might find a way
>
> And thus take on its nature too, one day.[4]

1- Also known as Laozi, according to *The Records of History* by Sima Qian, is believed to have been an elder contemporary of Confucius (551–479 BCE) and the author of the *Laozi* (*Daode jing* or *Tao-te-ching*), a work roughly five thousand characters long. This and other traditional accounts of Laozi and the date of his work have been seriously challenged, and various hypotheses about the authorship of the work and its date have been proposed. Nevertheless, three incomplete Guodian bamboo versions of the *Laozi* excavated in 1993 prove that the text was in circulation in the fourth century BCE and may have been composed still earlier. Laozi is believed to be the first person in Chinese intellectual history to develop a brief theory on the source and grounds of the universe, represented by the concept of Dao (also commonly called Tao in Western writings). [Macmillan Encyclopedia of Philosophy, Vol. 5, p. 194] (Translator).

2- Rumi's *Masnavi*, Book 5.

3- Ibid, Book 2.

4- Ibid, Book 1.

Bamaat: I am very interested in Rumi's *Masnavi*, although there is still no complete and precise translation of it available in French. I have only seen Nicholson's English edition of *Masnavi*; nevertheless, I have felt that Rumi has achieved a striking success in the articulation of Islamic views of philosophical, theosophical, moral and mystical issues in a poetic language. Do you believe too that *Masnavi* is a unique book?

Ja'fari: This book is truly a brilliant work of genius, but we should not overstate about its status. There are of course some mistakes in *Masnavi* that we have courteously and cautiously critiqued. As Rumi is a great mind, we have posed our critiques with utmost care, because it is very likely that he may have meant something else by a given verse.

Bamaat: However, we do not have any thinker in his status in the West.

Ja'fari: In a ceremony that was held in celebration of a renowned professor of Persian literature in Sorbonne, the professor said,

> Generally speaking, there is a figure in Persian literature corresponding to every literary thinker in the West. For example, if we have Homer with his Iliad in the West, there is also Ferdowsi with his Shahnameh in Persia. Or if we have Dante Alighieri with his Divine Comedy in the West, there is Nezami in Persian; for Shakespeare, we have Sa'adi, and for Goethe, we have Hafez, and so on and so forth.

Although I do not totally agree with his latter statement, the professor ends with a thoughtful consideration that reads:

> Having said these, there is a figure in Persian literature that stands above all these [Western as well as Persian] literati, and he is Mullana Jalaluddin Muhammad Balkhi Rumi.

Masnavi itself demonstrates this issue; however, we should never carry it to excess. Nevertheless, it is our duty always to hold such brilliant figures as Rumi in highest regard.

Bamaat: To what extent have Moslem scientists and scholars contributed to global knowledge and industry?

Ja'fari: Suffice it to mention the names of such innovative figures as Hassan Ibn Haytham in physics, or Sheikh Musa Khwarizmi, Abu Kamel and Abu al-Hassan Ali Ibn Ahmad Nasawi in mathematics.[1]

Bamaat: Would you please provide me with some more information about Nasawi?

1- Ja'fari, M. T., (2009), *Science and Religion in Intelligible Life.* (Originally in Persian).

Ja'fari: He was a renowned thinker who wrote the first book on logarithms[1] in Arabic and translated it into Persian himself. His name, Nasawi, is a derivative of his hometown village called Nisa, which is the name of several places in Iran, one of which is the hometown of the author of *Sunani Nisaei*, located somewhere near the province of Khurasan.

Of course, his book's name, *A Companion to Indian Arithmetic*, suggests that logarithms had an Indian root, but as a proficient and authoritative mathematician, he has discussed it in an independent essay. The history of logarithms, however, dates way back to Neper and others.

Bamaat: In your view, how could the West be introduced to Islamic philosophy?

Ja'fari: Of course, it is needless to say that scientific, philosophical and cultural interaction between nations is a historical tradition. As you know, science and technical issues completely disappeared from Islamic communities by the late second century A.H., and after a while, Westerners felt that in order to provide their needs, they needed to turn to science and technique. Nevertheless, Western scholars and scientists' efforts during the past two centuries have been beneficial for Wastern nations, including Moslems as well. In fact, true science, as opposed to the science that has been ruined by racism, egotism, utilitarianism and politics, knows no border.

1- In mathematics, the power to which a base must be raised to produce a given number. (Translator).

18

Najmih Zuhreh

**Subject: A Critical Assessment of Imam Hussein's Martyrdom
Nationality: Egyptian/ Major: Sociology
Dialogue Date: 1982**

Najmih Zuhreh: Shi'ah/Sunni relationships in the past have not been in a fashion for us to be able to regard them as analyzable in all respects. Undoubtedly, some prejudices throughout history have led these two sects to horrible contradictions, while they could and still can enjoy a happy religious life together by continuous revisions and a sound intellectual coordination upon basic joint positions.

This issue has numerous sides that cannot all be discussed thoroughly in one or two hours. Thus, I would like to ask your view on the necessity of a logical utilization of the story of Imam Hussein (PBUH) by all Islamic denominations.

Ja'fari: Regarding the depth and significance of this story, as well as its underlying motives and consequences, we must accept that the tragic event of Karbala has lessons for all humanity, not merely for Shi'ah and Sunni people. As historical records demonstrate, Imam Hussein's martyrdom had been motivated by neither wealth nor office, since if he had indeed submitted himself to Yazid, he would easily have reached these both without any further difficulty. By reviewing the Imam's words on his departure from Medina until the last minutes of his life, you will undoubtedly conclude that his only goal and motive was saving the true Islam and the lofty principles of humanity that were then exposed to annihilation.

Najmih Zuhreh: In your view, what has been the main obstacle before the fulfillment of a necessary and sufficient analysis of this event, while the logic of divine religion and the ideal principles of humanity required the tragic event of Karbala to have been frequently analyzed and interpreted by anthropologists and those scholars who carry out research on the evolution of human morality?

Ja'fari: This majestic human movement and uprising should have been thoroughly researched by the members of the Islamic family, and then the outcomes of this research could have been communicated and propagated by other scholars.

Najmih Zuhreh: What has in your view impeded this not to happen until this day?

Ja'fari: It must be taken into consideration that it is not so that Imam Hussein's constructive movement has not been studied by Moslem scholars at all, but as you know, some remarkable works have been authored in this regard by both Shi'ah and Sunni thinkers. However, there is still much that needs to be done. Unfortunately, sectarian prejudices and clashes have not allowed us to reach a serious agreement for scoring a deep understanding of Imam Hussein's figure and his sacrifices. Consequently, we have not succeeded in achieving a dependable knowledge of different political, social, moral and cultural aspects of this great event.

Unfortunately, this very obstacle has gravely hindered non-Moslem scholars from accomplishing an exact study and an understanding of this humane movement; nonetheless, we should not forget the influence of phenomena such as utilitarianism and authoritarianism that have lately lured them.

Now that we [Shi'ah and Sunni Moslems] confess to the vital importance of the tragic event of Karbala, we must take out the facts of this event from the pages written on the history of Islam and discuss them in our historical, political, religious and moral textbooks in a serious way. As you know, amongst other convincing and authorized reasons, by means of holding intellectual debates on this unique sacrificial event, we can simultaneously demonstrate the seriousness of "origin", "return" and "human transcendental commitment" in answering the basic questions, which are: Who am I? Whither have I come? Why have I come? Where shall I return to?

I assume you will agree with me that we will not find any single sacrifice in the total course of human history to have been made in the wake of the lofty motive and goal that caused Imam Hussein (PBUH) to undergo through such tortures and hardships. This truth can be clearly substantiated by the Imam's words and objective deeds for the realization of "the right of a descent life", "the right of inherent dignity", "the right of committed freedom", and "the right of equality before laws".

For example, we can allude to the observation of liberal-mindedness and toleration by Imam Hussein (PBUH) in the hardest times when every human individual sacrifices everything to his life. During this meaningful movement, Imam Hussein did not add anyone to his forces by "compulsion";[1] as a matter of fact, he continuously insisted that no one was obliged to endanger his life for his sake. In some cases, he has explicitly stated:

> *This massive enemy you see does not have any objective but my murder. You are free to go! Since these drunken beasts could not surrender me to the tyrant despot of the time, they have surrounded us, as you see. I regard human dignity higher than a wretched life even if it is an eternal one. These deceived people have targeted your human dignity, so I shall not compel you to stay in this blood-thirsty wilderness.*

As a sociologist, you can study this tragic event from the perspective of human dignity as a social phenomenon. It is not so hard to imagine that when Imam Hussein (PBUH) invites his evil and blood-thirsty enemies in that scorching desert to be open-minded and decent in their lives and persuadingly recommends them, "If you do not believe in any religion and or the truth of eternity and resurrection, at least you can live as a liberal-minded man in the world", he stands on the uppermost point of all ages and promotes the worthiest reformation with utmost seriousness, since liberality and being a liberal man has its own respective rules that should be observed by all individuals.

It seems that, to have a deep understanding of the objectives and ideals of both opposing parties (the Right and the Wrong), we should suffice it to evaluate the claims and arguments of the opposing parties – Imam Hussein (PBUH) and his disciples and Yazid and his followers – from a critical point of view.

The wicked followers of Yazid were to satisfy their animal desires through slaying the highest ideals of humanity; indeed, they believed that their commander Yazid would help them in this path. The disciples of Imam Hussein (PBUH), on the other hand, had a decent claim: "We want to promote human principles and rules, and not only do we not intend to trample on them in order to have an abundant natural life, but we are also ready to sacrifice our lives for their promotion." The necessity of the acquisition of such a lesson for

---

1- It is needless to say that Imam Hussein's ideal uprising is something different than the official defence of a nation's homeland, in which every competent citizen must be mobilized to take part in the defence.

humanity is far too clear to need to be demonstrated by ordinary arguments, only if man is interested in a purposeful life.

19-22

Prof. Gangovsky, Dr. Gennady Avdeyev, Prof. Arapachyan and Dr. Salih Aliyev

Subject: Islam and Materialism
Nationality: Russian/ Major: Philosophy and Oriental Sociology
Dialogue Date: 1982

Gangovsky: Several books have been published on British interferences in Iran as well as books on Iran's contemporary history at the USSR Institute of Oriental Studies. Dr. Aliyev, who studies the history of Iran, has published a book on Iran, for which he has toiled for almost five years. Professor Arapachyan, who is the head of the Iran desk at the Institute, has recently compiled a book about Iran's economic issues that will be published this year. I need to mention that these books all are in Russian. I would like to ask you to tell us about your education and fields of study.

Ja'fari: After finishing my elementary school, I continued my studies in different places like the Tabriz Seminary of Theology, the Qom Seminary of Islamic Studies, Marwi School in Tehran, and finally, I studied at the Najaf Seminary of Religious Sciences for eleven years.

Gangovsky: For several years now, I have been studying the history of Islam. For some time in the past, there were renowned politicians and scholars who tried to revive the Orthodox Caliphs' Islam once again so that people could have a happy life. The question is: how can we implement the dynamic principles of Islam today?

Ja'fari: The ideology of Islam, indeed, accepts both the existential and objective aspects of matter and does not ignore the realities of life; neither does it imagine life in vacuum. In fact, it says that man resides in a real world that should be modified by him so as to fit his purposes. "Reality", according to Islam, has a concrete existence independent of my mind. This reality is the basis of values and relations.

Islam's coexistence with all nations is possible, provided that they do not have any intention to battle Islam and Moslems, since Islam does not exclude any nation and does not declare war upon any nation, either. Islam has many positions in common with other schools and religions, which can serve as a foothold for the fulfillment of various tasks.

It seems that those schools and ideologies that have the uncovering of the logic of life as their target can change their pernicious conflicts into constructive competitions through discovering their common principles. To make this real, we should firstly mobilize all scientists to depict a scientific picture of the world with utmost impartiality without being motivated by their predetermined frames of mind, and then, ask the scholars of humanities to know "man as he is" based on pure reality. Then we must give the results of these studies to a group of neutral ideologists to derive the common grounds in worldview and anthropology and determine the common values of humanity as a whole. As an example, I shall indicate one of these common grounds.

In *Life, Its Nature and Source of Evolution,* Oparin, the renowned Russian biologist, says:

> *Our bodies are flowing like streams and their materials are continuously renewed like the brook's flow.*

This point has also been underlined in Rumi's *Masnavi*:

> *Each breath the world's renewed, though we can't tell,*
>
> *While it's renewed, the world persists as well.*
>
> *Life's constantly renewed just like the stream,*
>
> *A single mass in form though it might seem,*
>
> *Its swift flow makes it seem continuous.*[1]

As you see, Oparin has reached the same conclusion through modern experimental equipments in the twentieth century that Rumi has come to almost seven hundred years ago in Quniyah.

Thus, we can use these common grounds as a basis to change the existing destructive conflict of ideologies into a constructive competition. Unfortunately, even with these common grounds, politics does not allow us to come to terms with each other.

Mr. Avdyev, as a human being, do you have any problem with me as your fellow human being?

1- Rumi's *Masnavi*, Book 1.

Avdyev: No!

Ja'fari: I have no problem with you, either. Then we need to see how policy makers of societies orchestrate such conflicts?!

Avdyev: You argued that intellectual schools must have in the end some common grounds to stand on. What is your idea about Pakistanis?

Ja'fari: I have travelled to Pakistan; I was attending a conference held on Islamic law and jurisprudence, and I found the people there nice and friendly.

Aliyev: I have a question in regard to Rumi. Almost twenty years ago, a scientific symposium was held in our institute, and we had some guests from Iran as well. One of the Iranian participants argued that there had been a strong materialist impulse inside Rumi to the extent that, even five centuries before Hegel, Rumi had fathomed the essence of material subjects. What is your idea in this regard?

Ja'fari: My fifteen years of research on Rumi have proven to me that he was indeed an astonishing man. He has made remarks regarding almost all famous intellectual schools from Buddhism and Hinduism to contemporary pragmatism. Although Rumi did not know anything about modernity and modern life, he still had a dynamic mind that deserves to be studied seriously. I have myself seen the basic principles of many worldviews in Rumi's works, particularly in his *Masnavi*.[1]

Therefore, those who seek to push Rumi into an intellectual school seem to be in fact trying to park a trailer with thirty tons of cargo in a match box and even reserve two seats for passengers!

Gangovsky: Have you compared Rumi with Marx in your book?

Ja'fari: As Marx himself has once said, his philosophy is the reversed version of Hegel's. Thus, since we have already compared Rumi's ideas with some basic principles of Hegel's philosophy, we will no longer need to open an independent chapter for Marx.

Avdyev: How does Islam bring about a balance between the clergy and the laity? Do all organizations of an Islamic state certainly have to be Islamic through and through? Moreover, is there any place for non-clerics in an Islamic Republic?

1- The Allameh then brought a copy of his work *Rumi and World-views* and showed his findings in this book to the audience.

Ja'fari: An Islamic society welcomes all individuals with every intellectual bent, of course as long as they have not crossed the red lines of existing social order, since every human individual has an equal right to live [in peace]. However, if someone tries to disturb the social makeup, it would not be tolerated by law, and this is seen in all human societies.

We merely act upon Islamic laws and do not impose anything intellectually onto anybody since *"there is no compulsion in religion"*[1], according to Islam – unless, as I already have stated, someone tries to interrupt social order.

All human beings have equal rights to life, dignity and committed freedom. There are five types of personality in Islam:

1- A human being as such who has the right to a respected life.
2- Those individuals who believe in a particular set of principles. These people are respected as long as their presence is not harmful for other citizens. The human value of this group lies in the fact that they have distanced themselves from animal life and thus stand in a higher place than the first group.
3- Those individuals who follow the rules of reason and common sense; this group stand in an even higher rank in respect of human value.
4- The people of the Book, like Christians; they have a higher human status than the previous groups, but this does not mean that they have any privilege over the rest in general human rights.
5- Moslems, who have taken a step further than the others in the course of intellectual evolution; thus, they have more human values indeed.

In Islam, a human being is more valuable and in fact *"the most honorable ... with Allah ... [who is] most morally integrated"* [2], i.e. the one who is more faithful to lofty principles of humanity.

Gangovsky: Numerous prophets have been delegated by God, the last one of whom is Prophet Muhammad. What Muhammad brought was the last message of Allah to mankind. If whatever is necessary for human life has already been indicated in the Quran, what role does an "Imam" have to accomplish then?

Ja'fari: There are two issues here that need to be addressed:
Firstly, what is the new thing that Muhammad (PBUH) has brought for

---

1- The Holy Quran, The Cow 2: 256.
2- The Holy Quran, The Apartments 49:13.

us? In a number of places, the Quran indicates that Muhammad (PBUH) has brought the same message that had been brought by Abraham (PBUH) and the former's religion is the same as that of the latter, at least in its general outlines. Moreover, other prophets have also brought the same thing that has been brought by Abraham (PBUH).

Secondly, what does the Imam have to do? The term Imam has two applications, one of which exclusively belongs to Shi'ah and is the designation of twelve brilliant persons. Thus, they have been the continuers of the Prophet Muhammad's eternal path; their task has been the interpretation of the Quran and the ideology of Islam in Moslem communities. They pursued Muhammad's enterprise toward a more extensive and better introduction of people into Islam and its implementation as far as possible.

In the Shi'ah perspective, the Imam has the highest status among all human individuals, and at the same time, he is the leader of the society as well. However, he is not merely a church father, but in fact the personal medium of individuals for connecting themselves to the transphysical.

After these twelve Imams, the leader is the fully qualified jurist. He is to be elected by the votes of experts and people are committed to follow his orders. The leader is spiritually and intellectually purified of all egotisms and carnal desires and cares more than anyone else about his moral and religious duties; indeed, his heart only beats for people. If reason and conscience are cultivated well in human individuals and if people are immunized against impurities and whims and whams, they could accomplish truly great goals.

Gangovsky: Has any new title been published recently on Imamate and its place in the society?

Ja'fari: *Imam: The Identity of the Society* by the scholar Muhammad Reza Hakimi can help you in this regard.

Arapachyan: What is your idea about historical materialism? As you know, our official ideology is Marxism. Earlier in your discussions, you said that Islam recognizes both matter and spiritual factors as facts. What is, in your view, the basic difference between Islam and Marxism?

Ja'fari: Marxism is mostly known through its strong atheistic stance that is hardly acceptable for humanity. Unfortunately, this stance has been persistently defended by Marxists, while if the arguments on the existence of God are not convincing for someone, he must pass them over in silence, since as we know, not even one single [intelligent] argument has been posed against the existence of God to this day. This is a completely clear fact. The one who claims that there is no God is in fact making a truly demanding claim that requires the claimant to have searched the whole gamut of reality and eventually failed to find a being called God! Moreover, we all know that man lives in a small part of the great cosmos and his existence, as compared to the cosmos as such, is lesser than a droplet as compared to the sea. Having said these, how could man claim that, "I have searched the entire world and have not found a being called God!"

Let us suppose that someone or some group of individuals have managed to search the entire gamut of reality. They cannot still make such a baseless claim that, "We have searched the whole world and did not see such reality as God!" Likewise, you can dissect the organs of a human body by various instruments in an anatomy class, but it is impossible to you to see "I", "thought", "emotions", "sentiments", "will" and the like, because they can be seen neither by natural senses nor by other means. Nevertheless, they certainly exist.

Accordingly, if the believers were to say that God stands in the same relation with the world of existence that "I" or "will" have with our physical body, we would have no way to refute or criticize their claim. This must be added to the routine arguments of God's existence.

On the other hand, Islam does not reduce human life into some manual or intellectual works and bottles of narcotic liquors so that, after eighty years, man were to say, "That was life, and now it is time to leave!"

For Islam, this world is a meaningful thoroughfare where man must put forth his maximum effort to realize his own gifts. As I have mentioned earlier, we cannot empirically demonstrate the existence of will or soul by analyzing the human body; however, this does not mean that they do not exist at all. By the same token, Islam regards the world as a material body which has a soul that is not visible. When you analyze the world into quantum level, you cannot accept the existing causal relations between particles without reason. Islam says that there is a huge management behind this material corpus that you cannot deny.

Professor Gangovsky! In some philosophical works of your thinkers, it is seen that they have accused Islam of being idealist. I must ask these thinkers to show their evidence of the latter claim.

In *Rumi and World-Views*, I have criticized the idealism presented by Berkley,[1] Fichte[2] and Schelling[3] and demonstrated the objective reality of world via three arguments.[4]

The First Argument is based on the unity of perception and the difference of perceived objects. The function proper of the eye is seeing the appearances of figures, colors and the like. This activity is exclusively done by the eye and nothing else can undertake such a function but the eye. On the other hand, when the eye sees a bench as its object, it sees that bench in its particular form. To put the matter otherwise, this particular form of bench is not, say, bread, a flower or a mountain. In fact, this is the case with all other visual objects. Everything appears in its particular form and color. Now we should ask the idealists, "If those objects do not have a concrete reality of their own in the outside world, where has our visual diversity resulted from then?" This diversity cannot have its origin in the mind as it has the same function in all cases, i.e. the representation of the facts of the objective world. Then what is it that causes such visual diversity?

The Second Argument is to be developed upon the fact that no reality can fluctuate between being itself and not being itself. To be sure, everything that has a reality is indeed a determinate entity – even if its demonstration is dependent on my perception – not an identity fluctuating between itself and something else. For example, I see an object in a wilderness from a far distance and I do not know if it is a man or a stone. It is in reality either a man that is not a stone or a stone that is not a man. My perceptual sway does not change the reality of an object as such.

No idealist could say that what he sees is in fact a suspended reality! If an idealist says so, then he is not a true philosopher, but his place is the drunken clam of Greek sophists. It is indeed the idealist who is not able to prove his own "self" as he does not have any picture of it in his mind.

The idealist may invoke the principle of uncertainty to say that no phenomenon has a preestablished determination according

1- Berkeley, George (1685-1753), Irish philosopher and bishop. (Translator).
2- Fichte, Johann Gottlieb (1762-1814), German philosopher. (Translator).
3- Schelling, Friedrich Wilhelm Joseph von (1775-1854), German philosopher.
4- Ja'fari, M. T. (2009), *Rumi and World-views*. (Originally in Persian).

to modern physics and as long as an event has not taken place, we are not able to recognize its identity. Firstly, if we jump from "I don't see it" to "it does not exist" in sciences and other branches of knowledge, we will have to throw away the subject-matters of such disciplines as psychology, psychiatry and psychoanalysis, for no human mental phenomena and activities which constitute the underlying truth of the latter disciplines is visible. Can we say that they do not exist? Secondly, an event that is in the course of coming into being in any point of this course has a particular determination that exclusively belongs to that point, and after departing that point for a new point, it takes a new determination proportionate to the newly reached point, although the beholder believes that this latter determination was implicitly hidden in the former one. I do not see why idealists are reluctant to accept the fact that the reality of the world is a category other than the perception of the world.

The Third Argument grounds itself in the necessity of human reactions to "non-subjective" realities.[1] For example, cold weather compels man to put on warm clothes, he escapes from wild animals, when he sees a hole along his path, he changes his route, he seeks for light in order to see better and so on and so forth. These reactions as such are proofs to the existence of non-subjective facts. Man knows that he is necessarily engaged with realities regardless of his understanding of them.

As you see, idealism does not invoke science to explain the criterion of the essential reality of objects; in fact, science is alien to idealism.

The following is the most explicit verse of Rumi's on the acceptance of "reality in itself":

O' Lord! Show us in this house of deception

How things truly are, what their real state is like.[2]

Rumi alludes here to the following statement that has been quoted from the Prophet Muhammad (PBUH):

O' Lord! Show me things as they are.

If one still refuses to accept the world as an objective reality even after

---

1- One of these three reasons has been quoted from Allameh Tabatabaee; the other two have been theorized by Allameh Ja'fari.

2- Rumi's *Masnavi*, Book 5.

reading the following verse of the Holly Quran that reads:

> *And we did not create the heavens and the earth and what is between them two but in truth.* (The Rocky Tract 15: 85)

Such a person is not a Moslem indeed. Of course, you know that truth in one sense refers to a reality that is higher than objective reality.

Gangovsky: This is my personal view and you can retort. I think there is no unbridgeable gap between Islam and Communism as they have many shared grounds.

For example, after the October Revolution of Russia, in Bukhara there were Islamic circles alongside Communist circles. There were Moslem Communists who believed in the basic principles of Islam and worked for the Communist party.

Ja'fari: You know that God's existence is an uncompromising hypothesis in Islam, like all other revealed religions, while it is challenged by Marxism.

Gangovsky: Let me give you another example. Zulfaqar Ali Bhutto was executed by Zyaulhaq in Pakistan. Bhutto was from a rich family, but he devoted himself to the poor people. In our last meeting in December 1976, he said to me, "I am becoming more and more interested in Islam, but I intend to design a socialist economy for Pakistan." Bhutto was not a dogmatist; he was a Shi'ah and his wife was Iranian. However, he sought to realize socialist economical ideals in Pakistan. This is why I think we can have friendly relations with each other based mutual understanding.

Ja'fari: Nevertheless, what I pointed out earlier still needs to be taken into consideration because the interpretation of man and his place in the world is indispensible in Islam.

Prof. Glary Shirokov, Mr. Nabi Khazari (Babayev)
and Mr. Gennady Avdeyev

Subject: Aesthetics and the Philosophy of Literature
Nationality: Russian/ Major: Orientalism and Literature
Dialogue Date: 1983

Shirakov: I would like to begin with a brief introduction of *The USSR Institute of Oriental Studies.* This institute is an old academic center that has been founded in 1818 and now has a staff of over one thousand employees. The institute majorly studies Asian and North African countries, but it has recently started a series of studies on Oceania, too. Our institute collectively works on ancient and modern economical, philosophical, social and historical issues.

Ja'fari: How does your institute work on philosophical issues?

Shirakov: The issues are mostly studied regionally and per country. However, there are sections [of the institute] that work based on themes, like the branches dealing with language, literature, economy and international relations. Research projects are firstly performed in the scale of the target country, and then they are expanded to the continental level. Although our faculty is a research institute, we also offer some training programs for researchers in the institute. Moreover, we have 91 trainees from foreign countries in the faculty.

Our faculty has two journals, one of which is published monthly and the other is a peer-reviewed journal that is published every two months. We have also a publishing house that annually publishes almost 120 up to 140 titles, all of which are unfortunately in Russian, because of the heavy costs of translation. There, friends such as Proffessor Arapachyan and Dr. Aliyev work on Middle Eastern countries, including Iran.

Ja'fari: Thank you for your excellent report. I think such researches and investigations are rewarding, particularly if all cultural, scientific and philosophical aspects of the issue are addressed and deeply dealt with.

Shirakov: I completely agree, for by considering just one aspect of the issue, it will never come to light.

Ja'fari: You're right! For example, some Orientalists like Edward Brown, who has done research on our culture, have made sincere efforts but failed to examine all aspects of the issue. This is the common mistake made by almost all Orientalists.

Shirakov: I completely agree with Mr. Ja'fari. It is not sane to think merely about money and material issues. If we only concentrate on material aspects, that would not allow us to understand history and culture. Thus, we always need to take every aspect of the issue into consideration.

Ja'fari: I think so, too. For example, some Orientalists have discussed Mullah Sadra, Mirdamad, Suhrewardi, Rumi and Khayyam in a way that is not, in my view, whole. We cannot truly rely on the studies of this group of Orientalists. For instance, in *The Encyclopedia of Philosophy*, we read:

> Mystics have called divinity "absolute nothingness". At the same time, they regard divinity as the origin of everything.

By "non-existence", mystics do not mean "absolute nothingness". As Rumi has stated:

> So when I become nothingness,
>
> I shall say, "Indeed I am returning to God.[1]

Let us consider the following verses of Rumi together:

> I died as a mineral and became a plant,
>
> I died as a plant and rose to an animal,
>
> I died as an animal and I was human.
>
> Why should I fear? When was I less by dying?
>
> Yet once more, I shall die as man, to soarwith angels blest;
>
> But even from angelhood, I must pass on;
>
> All except God doth perish.
>
> When I have sacrificed my angel-soul,
>
> I shall become what no mind e'er conceived.
>
> O, let me not exist! For non-existence proclaims

1- Rumi's *Masnavi*, Book 3.

In organ tones: "To Him we shall return.[1]

"Non-existence" in this context does not imply nothingness; rather, it alludes to "organic non-existence", i.e. the tone that is created by musical instruments.

Shirakov: I can also mention two cases. If we are going to examine philosophy, we should say that philosophy is the science of sciences. To this very reason, philosophy is a very difficult branch of knowledge. Thus, there are few people who seek to become philosophers, but there are many people who want to be mathematicians. This is why many people fail to understand philosophical issues.[2]

Ja'fari: We can call philosophy the "science of sciences" as it is one of the tasks of philosophy to examine the principles, foundations and findings of sciences. Undoubtedly, philosophy can adjust the principles, foundations and findings of sciences one way or another, but philosophy has a much wider prospect than what I just depicted, since the philosophical speculation of sciences will be definitely a synthetic speculation in the sense that it can interpret the existing connections between the subjects of sciences and the relations of their respective laws.

This conception is not applicable to the whole extent of discipline, because philosophy also deals with values, as discussed in ethics, aesthetics and worldviews, which require to be fathomed in an integrated fashion, not in a compartmentalized form of a natural science like physics, biology, chemistry and others. Moreover, we do not have a chain of universal laws by which we can develop a harmony between mathematical issues and such values as beauty and morality. What is your idea in this regard?

Shirakov: I think that universal values have been reflected in philosophy.

Ja'fari: That's right, but have they have become part of philosophy as "science of sciences" or are they independent? I do not know any rule of philosophy as the science of sciences that expresses a law that can objectivistically interpret the power of mathematical sciences for being combined with the intuition of beauty and human morality as

---

1- Ibid.
2- Mr. Shirakov gave no reply to Mr. Ja'fari's point on the problem with the mistakes made by Orientalists.

mutually compatible realities.

Shirakov: We begin with biology and proceed through other empirical sciences, and then we come to mathematical sciences. I think philosophy stands above mathematical sciences. This is why every science grounds itself in some particular set of laws. Philosophy should bestow universality upon these laws.

Ja'fari: This is an issue that needs to be discussed here. It is true that there should be a particular set of laws in every science so that philosophy can universalize them, a fact that has frequently been underlined by Western thinkers. The significant issue is how one can interpret these artistic, aesthetic and moral values based on the scientific laws that are merely concerned with numbers and quantities. Like mathematics that, in your view, is inferior to philosophy.

Shirakov: I concede that this is a hard task. Let us suppose that reality is an extended whole which has not been thoroughly studied yet and everyone seeks to understand part of it. Thus, every science has to cast light on part of this whole so as to decrease the domain of unknowns.

Ja'fari: Yes, all branches of knowledge are required to uncover part of this whole for us so that to decrease the domain of unknowns.

Shirakov: That is it! We want to lessen the unknown part of reality.

Ja'fari: Let us to beauty as an example. This orange is beautiful, but we cannot analyze its beauty in terms of quantums. In other words, there is no place here for the particles of Democritus.[1] Of course, you know that the atomic theory was firstly developed by an Indian thinker called Mox Sidonyi in 1500 B. C. and Democritus had indeed inherited this theory from Leucippus, who lived 30 years before Democritus. Later on, Moslem philosophers and theologians worked on this theory.

Shirakov: Democritus says that there was a group of people with lame limbs who approached a musical instrument to explain it. This anecdote is other than that of water. I am very glad that Ja'fari mentioned Democritus, for it reminded me of these anecdotes. Although Ja'fari knows these parables, I would like to mention them for the audience. Someone approached water and said, "It is wet." Another came and said, "It is cold." The third one said, "It will not run dry." Everyone spoke of one property of water, but nobody had a universal definition of water.

1- Ancient Greek scientist and philosopher, and precursor of the atomic theory (ca. 400 B.C.) (Translator).

Ja'fari: This anecdote is more similar to Rumi's story of the blind folks' encounter with the elephant. This epistemic method of ours has a universal result which, if observed in the East and the West, could resolve many difficulties concerning worldview. If I work, say, on mathematics, I should not underestimate the efforts of someone who works on aesthetics, as the latter should not undervalue epistemologist's toils and so on and so forth. The thinkers must be asked not to build a Great Wall of China[1] between that aspect of reality on which they work and its other aspects.

Shirakov: I concur.

Avdyev: You just mentioned an interesting example about the orange, but you forgot to say that it is me who has chosen its color. This brings us to the notion of class values. The class value of beauty varies from one class to another. That is to say, there are various notions of beauty by different classes of society. For example, a rural man may prefer a brownish woman who works on the farm, while a patrician may not find any beauty in the same woman. According to Marxist philosophy, every class has its own particular understanding of facts. Thus, when we come to life affairs, we should say this is good for this class and is bad for that class. This is what our philosopher says.

Ja'fari: You mean Chernyshevsky?[2]

Avdyev: Yes.

Ja'fari: He has written a book called "What Is To Be Done?", which I have worked on. Anyway, there are many counterexamples to your latter claim of beauty. The beauty of moonlight is invariably sensible for me and for you and also for an African as well as for all social classes.

This is also the case with the beauty of a flower. It does not matter if you like this or that kind of flower; what is important is that flower, whether it be a rose or an orchid, has been always beautiful as seen by all human individuals.

Of course, one can have a different perspective of beauties and relativity in this sense even for good and evil, as Rumi has eloquently indicated in his *Masnavi*:

1- The Great Wall of China, a 200-mile long wall that was built to protect northern China during the 3rd century. (Translator).

2- Chernyshevsky, Nikolay Gavrilovich(1828-1889) was a Russian revolutionary democrat, materialist philosopher, critic, and socialist. (Translator).

Then there is no absolute evil in this world;

Evil is relative, you must know it.[1]

As I have discussed it at length in *Aesthetics and Art from an Islamic Point of View*, many extensions of beauty, like those of good and evil, are directly dependent on mental conditions. Nevertheless, we have still countless common feelings of beauty. Motherly love is a universal beauty. The mother hugs her baby and kisses him and presses him to her bosom. These are invariably beautiful as seen by all human individuals, classes and groups.

One day, when I was in Mecca for pilgrimage, I saw an African mother holding a baby in her arms and kissing him. I approached her and asked her to let me to hug her baby, but the mother pressed the baby in her bosom lest I may want to harm him. That woman's relation with her child was so beautiful that it aroused the aesthetic sense inside me.

Shirakov: I agree with your argument! There are cases that do not have anything to do with class and nationality.

Ja'fari: Chernyshevsky has turned a blind eye on these common notions of beauty. Thus, his ideas need to be revisited in this respect.

Shirakov: The beauty of moonlight and a flower is unvarying for all as you said, but there are still some cases that vary from one land to the other, like sunlight. For example, for us who live in ice-cold lands, the sunlight is more pleasurable than those who live in the tropics. We construct our houses in a way that more sunlight can be available, while they prefer to have a cool residence.

Ja'fari: As I mentioned earlier, there are always some cases that vary upon mental conditions and perspectives, but this does not change the fact that we have common grounds that are shared by all nations and classes.

Babayev: Let us turn now to poetry. You already read some verses of Rumi.

Ja'fari: In a conference which was held on Farabius, we were discussing Farabius' philosophical ideas and had some poets as part of the panel. Our debates got somewhat extended and delayed the scheduled poetical discussions. Suddenly one of the poets stood up and shouted, "Damn philosophers! Poetry becomes important when you hit a locked door."

1- Rumi's *Masnavi*, Book 4.

Babayev: I am very glad to see you. It is as if I am visiting my ancestors and mentors. They have done research in the same conditions. It is an honor for me to meet you on the first day of my visit of Iran. Today is a historical day for me and my friends and it is happily coincident with another historical occasion, i.e. the 60th anniversary of the establishment of the Union of Soviet Socialist Republics.

There is an assembly of writers in the Soviet Union which has fifty members whose healthcare, food and books are supplied by the government. A literary foundation is working together with this assembly. We also have magazines for youth, children and teenagers which are published in Azerbaijan. Besides being a poet, I am also the head of the Azerbaijan Society, the mission of which is developing relations with other countries. It currently has good relations with almost 120 countries around the globe. For example, we held several festivals on Azerbaijan's literature and culture with delegates from Mozambique, Australia, Switzerland, Italy, Ireland, Spain, West Germany, India, Guinea, Algeria and Vietnam. Mr. Avdyev is the director of the USSR-Iran Friendship Association. It is friendship that makes people strong. The closer people become, the more unbeatable they shall be, as a tree needs a stump to stand on. We have a proverb that says: *The neighbor is better than the brother*. We are good neighbors; we share the same history and culture, and during your Revolution, our hearts were with you. When your Revolution succeeded, we were also as happy as you were. Many poems have been composed about the Islamic Revolution of Iran. I shall now recite one of these, which I have written myself in fact.[1]

Ja'fari: As you mentioned, there is also philosophy in Persian literature. Even Ferdowsi, who is regarded as an epic poet, has put many sagacious themes in the *Shahnameh*. Even such lyric poets as Khajuyi Kermani, who was much interested in the literary and aesthetic aspects of poetry, has discussed many sapiential issues in his works.

Shirakov: It is because of these very beauties that our institute works on them.

1- The poem, which was in Turkish, said that, "Martyrs are like tulips. A teacher reads in the paper that one of his students had been martyred. The student's seat in the classroom is empty, and tulips have replaced the students there..."

Ja'fari: Are you working on their beauties or their contents?

Shirakov: It is indeed the beauty of these works that has helped them to survive; otherwise, if they had a deep content without beauty, they would never be able outlast to this day.

Ja'fari: Beauties cannot survive without content, either.

Shirakov: When we decide to translate these verses into Russian, we feel their beauty is lost in translation. Last year we published a book called *Benevolent Fruits,* a bouquet of the works of 25 poets from the 10th century until now, but the translations were disappointing.

Ja'fari: Who were these poets?

Shirakov: Rudaki, Khayyam and so on and so forth, who all belonged to Central Asia, since it was the Persian language that determined the previous geography of this region as its scientific and diplomatic language.

Ja'fari: As to Khayyam, I should say that Orientalists have committed a big mistake. They ascribe almost two hundred and fifty and sometimes three hundred quatrains to him while is not clear if they belong to the same Khayyam of whom we are speaking, since Khayyam, considering his scientific and philosophical works, had been definitely a theosopher. Now a question arises: how could a theosopher be a nihilist in his poems?

Shirakov: Of course, your studies are much deeper than mine, but as you know, Khayyam was firstly introduced to non- Persian readers through Fitzgerald's English translation of quatrains. In those days, Orientalists did not know any other Persian poet but Khayyam.

Ja'fari: The following verse is Khayyam's:

> *Alike to no such aureate Earth are turn'd*
>
> *As, buried once, Men want dug up again*

This is the Khayyam who is known as "Imam" and "Hujat al-Haq [The Sign of God]" in Islamic books. Then, it is not intelligible to ascribe such nihilistic quatrains to a theosopher in Khayyam's status. Either we should say that Khayyam suffered from multiple personality disorder and was a theosopher who was also a nihilist poet, or we will have to say that these quatrains have been wrongly ascribed to Khayyam.

Shirakov: This is an interesting issue and I think that the Allameh is right.

Ja'fari: Khayyam has numerous philosophical ideas that bear witness to the fact that Khayyam could not have had a pessimistic view of the world.

Shirakov: I agree. He had been a philanthropist thinker and couldn't be a nihilist.

Ja'fari: All books of Khayyam that have been published in Moscow are on science and philosophy.[1] These essays are *The Clarification of Difficulties of Axioms of Euclidean Geometry* and *is and Ought*. Khayyam starts these books with by praising God and says:

> To demonstrate God's existence, we should resort to scientific reasons and arguments, and to fulfill our divine duties, we must follow scientific methods.

These words show that all quatrains that have been ascribed to Khayyam are questionable. What is certain is three Arabic plus some twenty Persian quatrains that are about the undependability of this world and the restrictions of science. Thus, it seems that there are two or even three Khayyams, one of whom is Khayyam the poet and the other is Khayyam the philosopher and mathematician, who has also written some dozens of quatrains.

Shirakov: Which poet of the middle ages has drawn your attention and impressed you more than others?

Ja'fari: Jalaluddin Muhammad Rumi; not of course because he had been a dexterous poet, but rather since he has expressed his thoughts and ideas in poetical form.

Babayev: What about Nezami?

Ja'fari: Nezami Ganjavi is a truly admirable poet with respect to his poetical and aesthetic subtleties as well as the ideas that he has developed in the exordiums of his works concerning the issues of worldview and supreme human ideals. However, Rumi's merit is that he has approached the issues of wisdom, ethics and worldview from the vantage point of psychology, psychoanalysis and human sciences. Said differently, although Nezami's poems are beautiful, they are not as much sapiential as those of Rumi's.

Babayev: Last year we celebrated the 840th anniversary of Nezami's birthday. We have decided to hold festivities on this occasion in the

---

1- Mr. Ja'fari then showed Mr. Shirakov books written by Khayyam that had been printed in Moscow.

country every year.

Ja'fari: We need to take it into earnest attention that when it comes to a figure in Rumi and Khayyam's size, the judgment becomes more difficult as there are many factors that should be considered.

Shirakov: I agree. I think it is indeed a disaster to live a one-sided life. It ends up in egotism and selfishness.

Babayev: Have you ever traveled to the Soviet Union?

Ja'fari: No.

Babayev: I hope you can come to Soviet Azerbaijan in the future and visit the tomb of Nezami as well as the faculty that has been constructed beside it in his name. There a state commission comprised of many scientists – including me – who study his works. Every year we hold a festival on Nezami that kicks off beside his tomb and then continues in Baku by his memorial monument, that is eighteen meters in height.

Ja'fari: There are also some festivals held annually in Turkey in Rumi's honor, but unfortunately they are mostly limited to Whirling Dervish dances and are less devoted to the contents of Rumi's couplets. They say that Rumi was a Turk and not a Persian, while he in fact hailed from Balkh.
Some years ago, I traveled to Turkey. I visited Professor Abdulbaqi Gulpinarli in Istanbul; he has also worked on Rumi's *Masnavi*. He said, "People here believe that Rumi had composed the *Masnawi* in Turkish and you Iranians translated it into Persian"!
In one of his verses, Rumi says that he hailed from Khurasan. However, it is futile indeed to squabble about the nationality of such figures as Rumi. Although they are brought up in a particular cultural and social context, they are global characters and belong to all humanity. This is no longer a matter of me and you!

Shirakov: I think so, too.

Babayev: Was Khaqani a Turkish poet?

Ja'fari: He was born in Shirvan, but he lived and died in Tabriz.

Babayev: I wish we could visit his tomb. I visited Nasimi's tomb and shed some tears there. On his gravestone, it was written, "I was Nasimi, for whom this world was a small place and now I have been buried under a fist of soil." We proposed Syrian officials to construct a mausoleum for Nasimi in collaboration with the Soviet Union.

Shirakov: A theory that had been developed in Central Europe by the

5th century proposed that we should translate the works of Eastern thinkers and engage with their ideas. This is why the terms have lost their meanings. Thus, we need to see how they have rendered the terms. During the past 23 years, we have translated 25 works from Saudi Arabia, China, Iran and India into Russian. We have also established an office for research on these works. Unfortunately many of these works are in manuscript and have not been published yet. Sometimes there is more than one manuscript of the same work and this demands a serious examination of the available manuscripts so as to recognize the original document. We have already done the same as to *Shahnameh*.

Ja'fari: Yes. I have a copy of your edition of *Shahnameh*.

Shirakov: We have published this edition only one time. I think the new edition would take almost 10 up to 15 years of research to be published.

Ja'fari: Have you ever encountered in these works with themes that are discussed even today? I mean, have you ever encountered original ideas and truths in these works? Have you dug up the thick streaks of diamonds buried under the embers of their ideas?

Shirakov: Yes, I think so.

Ja'fari: For example, as I mentioned earlier, two thousand and five hundred years before Christ, a Phoenician thinker composed a piece on the atomic structure of physical objects. One thousand years later, this idea is being revived in India. Then in Greece, thirty years before Democritus, someone called Leucippus has rediscovered it and thirty years later Democritus discovers the same idea, by the same token that Moslems discovered it before Europeans and began to research on it.

By means of this example, I want to pull your attention towards the fact that although the past is mostly considered as outdated and fictional, under this heavy dust of ember, there are thick streaks of diamond. My question is: have your friends drawn these streaks out or not?

Shirakov: I think Mr. Ja'fari agrees with me that in the same spirit, Toynbee has divided people into two groups: those nations who have history and those who do not have history. According to Toynbee, there were nations who created history and there were also nations who just got impressed by it and there is nothing of them in the history to be proud of. This is very significant indeed, firstly in respect of universal and theoretic anthropology and secondly because it has been less a thousand years since science was introduced into Eastern countries.

Ja'fari: No! It is now almost three thousand years since there have been scientific ideas, although every so often and not in a systematic form in some points of the East.

Shirakov: In the eighteenth century, when scientific progress occurred in Europe, all Eastern countries crossed it out as worthless. When we study the works of Easterners, we seek to discern their underlying research goals. For example, in the case of Avicenna's works, we strive to spot the treatment methods and medical procedures that he has put into work.

Ja'fari: The taxonomies and classifications that are drawn by Westerners require some more precision since epistemic evolution has not directly begun from an environment.

Shirakov: I concur.

Ja'fari: For example, some fragments of mathematics have survived from the era of the Pharaohs in Egypt, showing their geometrical calculations of the Nile and its surroundings.

Shirakov: I am going to ask a question that is more philosophical. You already spoke of scientific classifications. You also made some remarks of atomism. When we read the works of past masters and thinkers, we come across several points that draw our attention, but when we approach them more closely, they appear to be odd and irrelevant. It seems as if some parts of their words have been lost during their oral communication. It is indeed much easier to understand the ideas of a thinker who lived in 6 B.C. than to fathom the ideas of a philosopher who lived in 3 A.D. What is your idea in this regard?

Ja'fari: The reason why the ideas of ancient thinkers as well as Islamic weltanschauung are not understandable for us lies in the fact that since the eighteenth century, some European philosophers have theorized empiricism[1] as the right mode of philosophization.

Shirakov: Then it brings us to the conclusion that if we do not know history, we cannot understand the issue.

Ja'fari: This radical empiricism was the outcome of fundamental ideas of rationalists. I think it was that fundamentalism that led to this

---

1- A doctrine that states that all knowledge is based on observation and experience. (Translator)

radicalism. We need to understand both the reality of reason and sense.

Shirakov: It is surely so.

Babayev: Thank you very much for time giving and taking part in the dialogue.

Shirakov: Would you allow our faculty members to visit you once in a while to hold dialogues with you?

Ja'fari: You're most welcome.

26*

Ved Pratap Vaidic

Subject: Islamic Mysticism and Hinduism on Human Being
Nationality: Indian/ Major: Sociology and Mysticism
Dialogue Date: 1984

Vaidic: What status does the human being have in Islam and Islamic mysticism?

Ja'fari: Man has different characters according to Islam, with respect to morality, law, culture, social relations and values:

First: Man's natural character, which is not bound to any principle and belief, and has its origin in human nature as such. For the nonce, we baptize this as "natural man".

The character of natural man, according to Islam, has inherent value, dignity and honor only because he is human. Man has the rights to life, dignity and engaged freedom. Although he is not still bound to any principle and law, he does not violate any principle or law, either.

This latter condition must be taken into consideration through our discussions of all human values. That is to say, generally speaking, man in Islam's view has inherent dignity insofar as he does not violate others' dignity and life.

Man, by nature, has the right of life even if he does not believe in any religion, belief, principle and law. Man has this basic right only because he is human, providing that he does not trespass other humans' rights. To put the matter otherwise, according to Islam, natural man, who features the first type of human character, has inalienable rights and respects as long as he has not crossed the consecrated limits of life, has not ruined his own life and insofar as he knows the value of his own and other peoples' lives.

Vaidic: You know that human life has a significant place in Hindu philosophy. Thus, in this respect, we have much in common with you.

Ja'fari: The second type of human character shows itself up when man accepts and believes in certain principles and rules for life. Whether these principles are divine or not. This kind of man has taken a step forward and chosen some particular cultural and moral principles for her life and thus, he is more developed than the first type. It is indeed natural if we give more value to this kind of human being's rights of life, dignity and committed freedom than those of the first type. The man who follows certain rules and principles in his life shows that he is not pestered with egotism and selfishness and respects other peoples' rights and lives and cooperates with them in social life. Whoever puts these two types of man in the same sclae has betrayed humanity indeed. The second type has certain rights that are higher than those of the first type.

Vaidic: What kind of rights are these?

Ja'fari: For example, if we are supposed to give someone the right of management, there are two candidates: one of them lives a purely natural life without any principle or belief, while the other has his own moral principles and rules in life. There is no doubt that the second candidate is the right choice due to his existential merits.

Generally speaking, if we come across difficulties in our social life that require certainty and knowledge as well as commitment, the second group is undoubtedly prior. If someone says that the two are equal, he has certainly overlooked human values and majesties.

The third type of human character is featured by man's belief in religious creeds. In other words, besides having the inherent human dignity of the first group as well as the cultural and moral privileges of the second group, this third type of character has reached the point that makes him able to interpret his existence and say, "Whence have I come? Where have I come? Why have I come? Whither am I heading to?"

Since this station is higher than the previous stations, it is surely more valuable than them.

This type of human character is owned by those who restructure their lives upon spiritual and religious truths and believe that the whole gamut of existence is under the supervision of Divine Essence. Thus, it is for sure that these people have a more developed, perfect and mature character. If we are supposed to live an ever-dynamic and intelligible life, this type of human character is its pioneer. The masters of religions belong to this class.

This type of character is chiefly represented today by the followers of three great Abrahamic Religions, i.e. Judaism, Christianity and Islam, around the globe. Of course, some claim that Zoroastrians consider themselves the sons of Abraham. Some argue that Zoroaster is the name of Abraham in ancient Persian. In any event, they do also see themselves the believers of a revealed religion.

There might have been some other religions led by Prophets that were either not lucky enough to survive to this day or history has failed to carry out its task as to them in terms of providing a platform for them to communicate their ideas with the next generations so that you could see whether they are among the revealed religions or not. Such religions have existed particularly in southeastern Asia and the Mediterranean region and we give the priority to them in respect of the fullness of life.

The fourth group hosts those people who have adopted Islam as their religion and form of life. Islam is a religion that originates from Abraham's primordial religion, and as it is frequently indicated in the Quran, it has been immune from any type of distortion. This can be even endorsed by other revealed religions, as it is a matter of primordial nature shared by all human individuals.

Then as the youngest of all revealed religions on the planet, Islam is more primordial, rational and demonstrable than its fellow religions in terms of its rules and beliefs as well as its philosophical, ideological and moral standpoint. This is also held by all Moslems, as they lean on a religion that has not been distorted at all. Thus, these peoples are potentially higher than others in respect of their human character and system of beliefs and values. They are called Moslems.

The fifth type of human character is featured by *taqwā* [1]. As the Holy Quran states:

> **Verily the most honored of you in the sight of Allah is he who is the most righteous of you.** (The Apartments 49:13)

This type of character is owned by those who possess acquired dignity besides their inherent dignity, which is shared even by those who only have natural character. This group of human individuals is higher than all previous types of human characters, as they are both spiritually and morally more evolved than their fellow human beings. They have indeed all of the merits of the previous types of human character as well.

If we suppose that the first type of human character, i.e. natural man,

---

1- For more details see: Ja'fari, M. T., (2014): *Human Universal Rights: A Comparative Research in Islam and the West*. This book has also been translated into English by Allameh Jafari's Institute.

is someone who acts more conscientiously. He is not conscious of his mode of action, but rather only listens to the primordial repercussions of heavens inside; for example, he does not kill or commit rape or steal not because he knows they are evil acts, but because he merely does not do them upon natural reasons.

Moral integrity in this sense causes a new subdivision in first type of human character: a righteous natural character and an unrighteous natural character.

This is also the case with the second group of human individuals who follow certain moral and cultural principles and codes, even if their beliefs and principles are irrational from our point of view. They are respectful as such. Here again, those individuals who act in terms of righteousness and moral integrity are more valuable and respected by us.

By the same token, there is such a normative assessment as to the third type of human character which is represented by the followers of the revealed religions. For example, two Christians or two Jews or one Christian and one Jew quarrel with each other over an issue and decide to call on a Moslem to set justice between them. Now if there is an occasion for a witness in the court, the witness who is just should necessarily be preferred to the other witnesses.

To state the matter differently, a just person is reasonably preferred to an unjust one as a witness in all courts. This rule is to be met even when it comes to determining a leader for the society. Thus, it is understandably necessary that a just, honest and noble person be elected as the leader. This is completely logical.

There might be Moslems who claim to be adherents of Islam but do not have any share of moral integrity and acquired dignity. In other words, they are only Moslems in their identity cards and with respect to the country they live in. Such being the case, we need to prefer the righteous individuals of the previous types of human character to these identity card Moslems.

This is the hierarchy of human character or identity according to Islam. Needless to say, all steps of human character in this hierarchy equally enjoy some inalienable rights, i.e. the right of life, the right of dignity, the right of committed freedom as well as the right of education and the right of decent life.

Islam does not speak of the right of life in form of the modern proponents of human rights, but in fact struggles for "the right of a decent life", for life can be lived either in an indecent form with tortures and agonies or in a decent form with respect and honor. All types of human character have an equal right to live a decent life. This is what Islam offers about human identity. Now this brings us to the issue of Islamic and Hindu mystical stance on human identity.

Vaidic: Man can ascend to the threshold of pure incorporeality through spiritual practice, piety and moral integrity and submerge himself in eternal bliss.

Ja'fari: Of course, as far as my studies allow me to speak, there are various notions such as "Nirvana[1]" and "annihilation in absolute truth" and the like, which have been coined to explain the destination of spiritual ascension, but we have at least five interpretations of Nirvana in Buddhism that some thinkers have tried to complete. For instance, Rumi says:

> O, let me not exist! for non-existence
>
> Proclaims in organ tones: "To Him we shall return." [2]

This nonexistence is the same Nirvanian annihilation. Thus conceived, Nirvana is believed to be the gate of eternal tranquility, but it is not still clear whether Nirvana connects man to divinity like a droplet to sea or not, or whether this existence then continues to be in other form or it merely disappears in nothingness.

Vaidic: It is through self-discipline and following the principles of Hinduism and being inspired by evolutionary ideals that the man becomes united with Divine Essence.

Ja'fari: If by mysticism we mean positive gnosis that originates in common sense, immediate intuition and a state beyond intuition, no doubt would ever challenge us. Intuition as the taproot of gnosis itself has its origin in reason and the heart. If by mysticism we mean the intuitive grasp of reality, however, then human beings can be studied from two perspectives according to Islamic mysticism:

1- Every human being has a material aspect that becomes manifested in his "natural self". In this respect, man is a living thing that has a small share of heavens inside him due to the great capital that has been conferred upon him, but this does not score any value for him as it has not originated in free will. Thus, we can say that since human life is a breath of Divine Essence – **and breathed into him of**

1- A heavenly state that exists beyond the cycle of reincarnation, freedom from karmic suffering in Hinduism and Buddhism. (Translator).

2- Rumi's *Masnavi*, Book 3.

his spirit,[1] as the Holy Quran has said – but it does not bring forth any acquired value for us; rather, it is indeed a capital of magnificence. To state the matter otherwise, man is existentially higher than other creatures with respect to this capital, but this comparative advantage is an inherent value not an acquired one.

2- The second aspect of human existence is man's spiritual side that has the capacity to become united with Divine Essence. As a corporeal entity, man contains a magnificent capital that, if realized, can afford man the status that Sa'di describes in the following words:

> *Man reaches a point where he sees nothing but God;*
>
> *See how glorious the status of humanity is!*

This is the leitmotif of Islamic mysticism as a whole. However, this generic status does not make man an uncreated entity. Everything depends on human choice and action that makes him either Ali (PBUH) or his assassin Ibn Muljam.

In any event, Islamic gnosis does go to extremes as to human beings. Of course, as we know:

> **By the soul and the proportion and order given to it...**

(The Holy Qur'an, the Sun 91:7)

What has been endowed upon the soul can be realized, and as a result, the "ego" can be exposed to Existence. The soul is so great that has it turned into an object of swear: *by the soul and the proportion and order given to it*. The verse does not read: *by the soul and God who made it perfect*, rather it refers to the basis of the soul's proportion and order. The soul's existential capital allows it to ascend through the hierarchy of perfection by possessing divine morals; as Rumi says:

> *I died as a mineral and became a plant,*
>
> *I died as a plant and rose to an animal,*
>
> *I died as an animal and I was man.*
>
> *Why should I fear? When was I less by dying?*
>
> *Yet once more I shall die as man, to soar*
>
> *With angels blest; but even from angelhood*
>
> *I must pass on; all except God doth perish.*
>
> *When I have sacrificed my angel-soul,*

1- The Holy Quran, Luqman 32:9.

I shall become what no mind e'er conceived.

O, let me not exist! For non-existence

Proclaims in organ tones: "To Him we shall return."[1]

These verses depict the spiritual ascension of such noble souls as Meytham Tammar, whose body was mutilated and he still refused to withdraw from the mystic ideal of humanity that he had found in Ali (PBUH).

The history of mankind has indeed witnessed numerous examples of this mystical evolution, although these examples have always been in a minority, as such evolution is a delicate course and needs unbearable sacrifices. This is why Moslems recite the statement *"keep us in the right path"* at least ten times a day in their daily prayers. This is our understanding of humanity based on man's spiritual capital.

Vedic: Don't these verses of Rumi's you just mentioned allude to the theory of transmigration of souls?

Ja'fari: Certainly not! As a matter of fact, through these verses Rumi depicts the steps of intellectual and spiritual evolution of human beings. It is indeed based on this ever-dynamic nature of humanity that Islam describes man as a macrocosm, a radiation of Divine Essence. As some mystics have said:[2]

> *Do you what "the one who is equal to a thousand" means? It refers to great men of God, who are equivalent to a thousand centuries worth of endeavor.*

Through being exposed to Divine Attraction, a true adherent of Allah becomes the total sum of all ages and times.

> *Pass through the garden of world thou the spring's beloved*
>
> *So that fall's custom may be removed from the rosary of world ...[3]*

Islamic mysticism reserves a unique place for human beings in the universe, but this should not be overstated against the Quran, which reads:

> **And man's love for wealth is something serious...**

(The hargers 100:8)

It has also been stated that:

1- Rumi's *Masnavi*, Book 3.

1- Rumi's *Masnavi*, Book 6.

2- Rumi's *Sonnets of Shams*.

> *Most surely man is in loss, except those who believe and do good and enjoin on each other truth, and enjoin on each other patience.* (Time 103: 2-3)

If you leave man to his own, he will always hasten downward and hold the matter fast; history has also proven this to us. Thus, there is no reason to exaggerate about human beings; rather, we must embrace man "as he is" and concede that he has a huge existential capital that should be realized. Two theories have been proposed by Moslem mystics concerning the aftermath of the actualization of the latter human primordial capital. Some believe that man becomes annihilated in Divine Essence like a droplet which disappears inside the sea. On the other hand, some others argue that we are not here for annihilation. The authentic Islamic sources say:

> *You have been created to live, not to leave.*

Otherwise, God would have said: I am the Absolute Everlasting. This is not right. You humans are also everlasting, but via being exposed to divine radiation. If you ascend to the sphere of the Absolute, there you could be exposed to divine radiation and thus the self becomes immortal. Be careful, please! It is indeed very significant whether the "I" dies out or not. No, even the droplet does not fade away in the sea, but it in fact joins the sea. Said differently, the sea only takes off the identity of the droplet and makes it the sea's own.

This brings us to another significant question: how can the droplet which departed the sea join the sea again? According to Islamic mysticism,

> *You can't be Him, but if thou make your best,*
>
> *Thou shall embark upon a path that purges you of selfishness.*

Then you enter Divine Presence and reside in God's paradise; you come to be exposed to divine radiation, the imagination of which is hard for us in our material body. Now what does it mean to be exposed to divine radiation? This cannot be discussed here at length; we can only answer this question in short. It is like telling a sour that it is going to become a ripe grape! It cannot surely understand the notion of becoming a ripe grape. By the same token, a ripe grape cannot understand what it may look like to be a cup of grape juice. However, man is not as unconscious as the grape, for he can cultivate his cognitive faculties and qualify for such a primordial piece of knowledge.

Vaidic: You are not just the master of Moslems; you are in fact the master of Hindus as well!

27-31*

Professors. Mayer, Von Ess, Hans Kung, Wanderant and Daiber

Subject: Philosophy, Mysticism, Islam and Christianity
Nationality: German/ Major: Philosophy and Christian Theology
Dialogue Date: 1984

In 1984, the Institute for Cultural Studies and Researches held a conference on Allameh Muhammad Hussein Tabatabaei (RA), hosting a number of western Islamologists. This occasion brought about an opportunity for Iranian scholars to exchange their ideas with their Western colleagues.

This chapter embodies the debates that these Western scholars had with Ja'fari in their meeting with him in his house on Saturday, November 17, 1984. The meeting lasted about two hours and a half.

The first question asked by Proffessor Daiber was, "Does the story of Joseph (PBUH) as depicted in the Quran fall in line with the existing historical facts or is it purely symbolic, serving only as a parable, as some Western interpreters suggest?"

Ja'fari: The stories that have been related in the Quran are other than the parables that God has offered in the Book to explain truths for people. The stories express the events that have happened in the past and are considered as historical facts. For example, the stories of Moses, the Pharaoh and the Israelites are real historical events that more or less have been recounted in the ancient works and sometimes have also been distorted and deformed by other writers. This is indeed why the Quran states:

> *And thus will thy Lord choose thee and teach thee the interpretation of stories [and events].* (Joseph 12:6)

"The interpretation of stories" in this verse connotes the intelligible interpretation of events that have once happened and been distorted by the ignorant and greedy people as the following suggests:

We relate to thee their story in truth. (The Cave 18:13)

That is to say, this story had been distorted in the past and I shall relate to you the truth. The clearest reason for this claim has also been recited in the same chapter as follows:

Some say they were three, the dog being the fourth among them; some others say that they were five, the dog being the sixth, doubtfully guessing at the unknown;

Yet others say they were seven, the dog being the eighth. Say thou: my Lord knoweth best their number; it is but few who know their real case. Enter not, therefore, controversies concerning them, except on a matter that is clear, nor consult any of them about the affairs of the sleepers. (Ibid: 22)

But as to the story of Joseph (PBUH), we read:

Verily in Joseph and his brethren are signs (or symbols) for seekers of the truth. (Joseph 12:7)

There is no doubt that signs become visible in real facts, not in abstract and symbolic examples.

The Quran is not a historical book; it is in fact a sacred scripture that contains beliefs, rules, wisdom, morals as well as the stories that bespeaks of real events that have once happened and are intended to inform all of humanity of governing principles and rules of the world of existence. It is needless to say that these Quranic stories, which primarily serve as a vehicle to communicate the primordial rules and laws ordained by the Lord to believers, can also be considered from a symbolic point of view.

You Germans' philosophy had been somewhat deeper and more systematic than those of other Europeans. Even in many perennial philosophical issues, you had been in line with Easterners. Unfortunately, in contemporary times, German philosophy has also shown illogical fondness toward positivism, which disqualified it for addressing such critical issues as human knowledge – as a product of "I" and "not-I" – beauty and values and caused it to lose its efficiency. Have you ever thought of saving philosophy from this impasse and reintroducing it into the perennial issues of ontology?

Mayer: The philosophical thinkers in Germany today are the employees of philosophy not philosophers![1]

Ja'fari: You need to seek a remedy for this grave condition.

Van Ess.: This seems almost impossible with the technological development which has haunted Europe today.

Mayer: Heidegger has been quoted as saying, "We have to travel back two hundred years in time so as to reintroduce our philosophy into the higher philosophical notions we have lost already."

1- The reader needs to pay earnest attention to this remark made by Professor Mayer, which is interestingly an explicit confession of the lack of serious and deep philosophical thought in the contemporary West. Philosophy has been reduced to an academic profession that has nothing to do with serious ontological and ideological meditations. I remember the Italian Philippani Ronconi, whom I met at the ceremony held for the Millennium of Sheikh ⇨ Tusi in Mashhad University back in 1970, making a more grievous and deplorable remark than this of the current state of philosophy in the West. "During the past five days that I have been part of the panel on philosophy and heresiology," he said, "a large number of philosophical principles and issues have been discussed. Fortunately, many discussed issues had been researched thoroughly and all yielded final conclusions. Sadly, philosophy is now dead in the West, but it is still alive in your East, unless as the German poet Goethe says, once again an Oriental breeze blows and brings along with itself a universal and coherent philosophy for the West."
These thoughtful remarks of Professor Mayer and Professor Ronconi's bear witness to the fact that contrary to the stereotypical view held by most of students in Eastern academia, Western philosophy is no longer the ideal paragon of philosophical thinking. Such an immature view has its origin in the lack of sufficient knowledge of the current state of philosophy in the West and ignorance in regard to Eastern philosophical ideas. The paradoxes which have haunted the lectures and papers presented by these Westoxificated academics clearly show that they have failed to understand the paradoxical bases of contemporary Western philosophy.
We should never forget Maurice Maeterlinck's brilliant remark that states, "I know that I speak paradoxically. I have chosen this paradoxical jargon not to slip into superstitions." Of course, we are not here to overlook the groundbreaking steps taken in the West since Renaissance onward in philosophy, particularly as far as the analytic methodology is concerned. We do not even agree with Professor Ronconi and Professor Mayer about the death of philosophy in the contemporary West. Instead, we believe that philosophy in the West is not dynamic and systematic now. There are a number of esteemed philosophers in the West who pursue the field in its perennial form. The target of our objections are those radical writers and thinkers who are blind to the fundamentals and bases of both Western and Eastern philosophies.

Ja'fari: To have a philosophy that can meaningfully address the fundamental issues and engage with other philosophical systems today, not only is it not necessary to travel back two hundred years in time, but in fact it is irrational to ignore the scientific progress that has happened during these two centuries and to insist on an illogical regression. What we need to do today is to revive the transcendent sense of ontology which is centered on the human being and has supreme perfection as its goal in contemporary peoples' minds and to prove them the emergency of activity of that sense which has been quelled due to the conflicts over pleasure and power. Needless to say, by "peoples" here I mean those human beings who believe that it is necessary to devote oneself to ontological and philosophical meditations or struggle to engage in such meditations.

Van Ess.: It has been quoted from a contemporary German philosopher as saying, "We should draw a sharp line between metaphysical and theological truths and approach each one from its respective point of vantage."

Ja'fari: This theory once again imposes such malapropos demarcations in ontology upon us that have always led to numerous difficulties. If we are to have an integrated view of the truth, we should necessarily distinguish the truth as such from its particular and context-bounded extensions. Accordingly, if we take the applications of the truth in various domains into account, not only will the truth in metaphysics be other than the truth in theology, but we shall also have countless types of truths, each one of which will fit only to its respective field. Every given principle and law in different domains of sciences refers to a particular truth. Generally speaking, any conformity between the percipient subject and the perceived object gives rise to a truth, the identity of which is dependant merely on these two poles and does not have anything to do with say metaphysics, theology, physics, physiology, biology, psychology and values.

If we understand the "truth" as the "reality of existence", then there is no doubt that we have only one truth in this sense as compared to which the particular truths are mere manifestations. Of course, the reality of existence here is not tantamount to God, but it in fact refers to existence in general, which has the highest unity. Succinctly speaking, we should not mistake the diversity of individual takings with the diversity of truths.

***

In 1985, a meeting was held at the Tehran Islamic Society of Philosophy, which hosted Professors Van Ess, Kung, Wanderant and Daiber as well as a number of renowned Moslem scholars including Ja'fari. The meeting was supposed to focus on the common grounds and beliefs between Islam and Christianity and their conceptions of happiness. Ja'fari had chosen this session to communicate an idea to German and Iranian thinkers. The idea was that Judaism, Christianity and Islam are one in their Abrahamic origin and that if the believers of these revealed religions reach a consensus over the primordial Abrahamic bases shared by their religions, we can hopefully have an intelligible coexistence with each other, as Ja'fari argued.

Allameh Ja'fari has articulated this idea at length in an independent paper that has been published in his voluminous *Translation and Interpretation of the Nahjulbalaghah*.[1]

The M. T. Ja'fari's idea of Abrahamic integrity was embraced by his collocutors in that meeting. It was also later appreciated by two Italian pastors – Rev. Marconavi and Rev. Antonio – and by Italy's cultural attaché in Tehran, Angelo Michelle Pie Montse as well as by two members of UN Committee of Human Rights, Mr. Galindo Paul and Mr. Stephen Paul Marx.

Two years later, on Tuesday, July 1, 1986, the Cultural Relations Bureau of Iran's Ministry of Foreign Affairs sent a letter to M. T. Ja'fari as follows:

Following your sagacious remarks on the Islamic world's relations with other revealed religions and their consensus based on Abrahamic integrity, we call your attention to the Ministry of Islamic Guidance bulletin's brief report of *Le Nouvelle Observateure*'s interview with Michel Louni, the former Secretary General of French Pontifical Committee for Dialogue with Islam (1975-1980) and Vatican's counselor on Christian-Moslem ties:

1- See M. T. Ja'fari's *Translation and Interpretation of Nahjulbalaghah*, Vol. 17. (Originally in Persian). Many issues have been discussed through these pages, including "the history of theology and theism", "Abraham in the Quran", "Abraham in the Quran and the Torah", "Abraham in the Quran and the Bible", "Three Abrahamic Religions Revisited", "Abraham the Forefather of the Revealed Religion" and so on and so forth.

Le Nouvelle Observateure: Today Islam has gained a momentum even in France. Isn't the Catholic Church's assessment of Islamic World somewhat immature?

Michel Louni: It is not fair to blame the Quran for fundamental actions of political and religious groups; likewise, Christianity should not be taken to task for the massacre of Protestants and the radicalism displayed by some Christian militia. Islam is not a religion of violence.

For the first time, the Church has solicited its followers to respect the beliefs and differences of Moslems and seek after the common grounds of two religions and struggle for global peace and justice. It is continuously propagated that Islam threatens the Judaeo-Christian civilization of France. This is totally nonsense. We must leave aside our Judaeo-Christian bigotry and stick to Abraham's tradition, which is the basis of all three revealed religions of Judaism, Christianity and Islam. I think with more mosques, we shall have more good Moslems in France.

I am happy that I live beside good Moslems, as they believe in the same human values that we believe in, too. I think Islam, Moslems and their mosques can bring happiness to our multicultural society.

32

Prof. Roger Garaudy[1]

Subject: Women's Character
Nationality: French/ Major: Social Sciences
Dialogue Date: 1983

Garaudy: As you know, today women are taken more seriously in the West and due to the partial and shallow readings of Islamic sources, some incorrect clichés are in the air concerning Islam's view of women and their character. What is your assessment of these deficient understandings of the Islamic view of women?

Ja'fari: To begin with, we need to take this issue into consideration that today, not only is the Western view of women basically different from that of Islam's, but even the understanding that Islam offers of human beings in general – be it woman or man – is not sensible for the West at all. However, I do not mean that the Western notion of human beings has always been alien to the Islamic concept of man, since in the past there were lofty religious and moral ideas in the West and one can say that these ideas have not yet completely withered away in that part of the globe, although a deplorably small minority of people still believe in them.

Accordingly, our objections target the contemporary worldview of Western societies, which is plagued with utilitarianism and hedonism and has reduced human individuals to unconscious cogs of a machine, and not only has this devalued human "life", "character", "self" and

---

1- Roger Garaudy or Ragaa Garaudy (17 July 1913 – 13 June 2012) was a French philosopher, French resistance fighter and a prominent communist author. He converted to Islam in 1982. Many of his books and ideas particularly his 1996 *Les mythes fondateurs de la politique israelienne* have been deemed controversial and he suffered accordingly in academic circles as well as in the law system of his homeland, France. (Translator).

Professor Garaudy visited Allameh Ja'fari at his house in company with Dr. Khaliji, the Chancellor of Allameh Tabatabaei University at the time.

"soul", but in fact it denies them.

As you know, one of the devastating results of this view of man is the debacle of family and the destruction of lofty human sentiments and emotions that has led to the fall of morality and the occultation of human entity. This occultation gave rise to such books as Alexis Carell's *Man the Unknown* (1935) and others. Above all, this obscuration also caused almost every new title published on human sciences to be fraught with many unknowns concerning human nature and its coordinates.

Then, if the West is to make remarks about women, it firstly needs to depict the existential coordinates of humanity according to man's essential peculiarities.

The second objection is that the contemporary Occident knows little about mankind in general and woman in particular, let alone about Islamic notions of man. It is a general principle that the more someone is ecologically, culturally and ideologically alien to the issue that he handles, the more he becomes exposed to misunderstandings of it.[1]

Men and women are equal in the domain of values, according to Islam, as they are equally capable of receiving noble human virtues. This fact has been explicitly underlined in the following two verses of the Quran:

1- *O' Mankind! We created you from a single pair of a male and a female, and made you into nations and tribes, that ye may know each other (not that ye may despise each other). Verily the most honored of you in the sight of Allah is he who is the most righteous of you.* (The Apartments 49: 13)

2- *For Muslim men and women, for believing men and women, for devout men and women, for true men and women, for men and women who are patient and constant, for men and women who humble themselves, for men and women who give in charity, for men and women who fast, for men and women who guard their chastity, and for men and women who much engage in Allah's*

1- For example, in the sixteenth book of his *De L' espirit de Lois,* Montesquieu writes, " In his biography of Muhammad, Prideaux says, 'He married Khadijeh when he was barely 25 years old and slept with her' (Persian translation)." This is certainly both against reality and reason; the reality is that the Prophet Muhammad (PBUH) married the forty-year-old Khadijeh when he was 25. Even if we assume that Prideaux was speaking of Ayesheh, who was younger than Khadijeh, this does not change the fact that Muhammad was twenty five years old when he got married.

praise, for them has Allah prepared forgiveness and great reward.

(The Confederates 33: 35)

It is indeed the faith, righteous deed and acquired virtues that make someone, be it man or woman, more respectable in Allah's sight as the following verse attests:

> *And in no wise covet those things in which Allah hath bestowed his gifts more freely on some of you than on others: to men is allotted what they earn, and to women what they earn: but ask Allah of his bounty. For Allah hath full knowledge of all things.* (Women 4:32)

Garaudy: If Moslem women have played an effective role in Islamic civilization?

Ja'fari: It seems that women's role in Islamic civilization has been immense both directly and indirectly. Women have sometimes wielded their civilizational influence indirectly, that is, through the efforts and sacrifices that they have made to raise good children upon Islamic beliefs. This was considered a religious obligation for which a woman could be praised or blamed. But as to the women's direct role we should say that they have chiefly contributed to Islamic civilization via knowledge, literature and culture in general sense.

In his voluminous *The Women's Index in Arab and Islamic Worlds*, Omar Reza Kahhalah names more than three thousand women who have made contributions to Islamic civilization through different elements of Islamic culture. Furthermore, such books as *The Woman's Communiqués* and *The Story of Righteous Believing Women* by Abu Bakr Al-Hosni and others, endorse this reality.

Abdul Rahman Jami states:

> *Having indicated the names of some men of Allah, the author of Meccan Revelations says, "Sheikh Abu Abdul Rahman Selmi, the writer of Biographies of Sufi Elders, has authored an independent book on the biographies of female mystics and sufis."* [1]

If we go through all of the works written on women and their influence on Islamic culture and civilization, we can point out more than tens of thousands women who have contributed to this dynamic, profound heritage.

It needs to be mentioned that women's passionate engagement in family and children's affairs has always overshadowed their

---

1- Nuriddin Abdurrahman, Jami, *Nafahat al-Uns ("Breaths of Fellowship")*.

indispensible role in cultural and civilization progresses in the Islamic world, although their contributions have been recorded in books.

Garaudy: Do you think that the existing affection and love between men and women is genuine, or are they merely some means for satisfaction of the sexual instinct which outbursts in the beginning of reproduction?

Ja'fari: This question must be analyzed into a chain of significant issues such as:

1- We have to distinguish here between two concepts: affection and love. The notion that is envisaged of affection in the mind is clearer and more comprehensible than that of love. Therefore, we might say that affection does not need any logical definition, since it is a self-evident notion, while love, due to its extreme complexity, is indefinable. This complexity arises from the uniqueness of love as a product of boundless eagerness toward the beloved. This eagerness takes all relations, ideas, images, wills and thoughts into its service, as if these factors are its servants. The intensity of this eagerness is sometimes so great that the lover considers the beloved as part of his/her own self, as the lover does not find anything more important than the beloved. Thus, he seeks to become united with the beloved or even to annihilate himself into the beloved.

2- The God-given fondness that man and woman have for each other is a unique quality which they cannot experience but through this relationship. This eagerness might have its origin in the necessity of the survival of mankind through reproduction upon divine providence. God has described this wonderful fondness as a divine sign:

> *And among His signs is this, that he created for you mates from among yourselves, that ye may dwell in tranquility with them, and he has put love and mercy between your (hearts): verily in that are signs for those who reflect.* (The Roman Empire 30:21)

3- As the basic drive of the natural process of reproduction, this affection is a predetermined phenomenon that lies outside the domain of values. To state the matter otherwise, since it is free will or voluntary decision that makes human phenomena and activities worth of value, natural affection in its naïve and one-dimensional form, which is equally seen both in human individuals and willless animals, cannot be an evaluative phenomenon. Thus, a man's love and affection for a woman and vice versa gets heightened and escalated when it transcends the necessities of reproduction and grounds itself in the beloved's noble moral and cultural excellencies. Although beauty plays an indispensible role in a man's attraction toward a woman and a woman's fondness for a man, since this latter kind of attraction and fondness is rooted in necessity, one can nonetheless say that though beauty based affection could give rise to values, it is yet not as such an evolved value.

It is true that the pleasure and joy resulted from the perception of a sensible [i.e. phenomenal] beauty can endorse the fact that the perception of beauty and the sense of pleasure which results from it is an independent and substantive and not a secondary and instrumental reality. That is to say, human pleasure of the perception of beauty is resulted from beauty itself.

To put it otherwise, the aesthetic sense of pleasure and joy is not a purely reflexive phenomenon which is mirrored in humans inside via their outer senses; as a matter of fact, this sense is the effect of higher activities of the "brain" or "subject" which goes beyond mere mirror-like reflection. Accordingly, the aesthetic sense of pleasure is an exclusively human phenomenon. The etiological reason of this pleasure seems to be the fact that every beauty, whether directly or indirectly, conveys a sense of perfection to the human mind. This is why we define sensible beauty as,

> An aesthetic and glossy appearance which is put on the face of perfection.

It is said that the more harmoniously the elements of an aesthetic collection can portray themselves to each other, the more beautiful that collection will become. Thus, it becomes clear that if a beautiful scene is to be pleasant for the beholder, it needs to recall a truth or some truths of the desired reality of existence. Consequently, any slight psychic or mental disorder caused by a beautiful object can reduce its aesthetic pleasure.

If a beholder finds any sign of arrogance or contempt even in the most beautiful eyes of the world, he will never experience any sense of pleasure from beholding them. Moreover, if a handsome man proves to be the murderer of innocent people, no one would ever find him pleasant or attractive for his handsome features. Therefore, we need to know that the particular extensions of beauty are not absolute. Remember handsome Nero,[1] the cruel emperor of Rome?

4- When a woman or man succeeds to perceive rational beauty via beholding the sensible beauty the man or woman could have value-based affection for their counterpart. This is the ultimate ideal of humanity that, if fulfilled, can afford the required platform for human intellectual evolution. Sadly, however, since this is against the interests of the slaves of lust and despots we have become today. Even in the most developed countries around the globe, we witness the metamorphosis of genuine love and beauty into a number of banal notions. If we trace this evil process of the trivialization of love back to 1830, when Balzac described love affairs as "hired coaches" in a time when the fundamental notions of human culture had not been yet banalized to this degree, then we can estimate how far these human ideals have been poisoned nowadays.

Garaudy: In your view, could women reach the heights of gnosis as well as men?

Ja'fari: Yes, they can. We have had many female mystics throughout the history of Islam. In his *Nafahat al-Uns* ("Breaths of Fellowship"), Abdul Rahman Jami writes:

> Having indicated the names of some men of Allah, the author of Meccan Revelations says, "Sheikh Abu Abdul Rahman, Selmi the writer of Biographies of Sufi Elders, has authored an independent book on the biographies of female mystics and sufis. One mystic was asked how many saints there were. Forty, he retorted. He was asked again why he had not said forty men. He answered, 'Because there are also some women among them." [2]

Then Jami recounts the names of these female mystics, whose number tallies to more than thirty:

> 1- Rab'eh Adwyah 2- Lubabah al-Muta'bedih 3- Maryam al-Basryah 4- Rayhanah Walihah 5- Ma'azat al-Adwayah 6- Al-Abidah 7- Sha'ranah 8- Kurdyah Hafseh 9- Rab'eh Shamyah 10- Halimah 11- Hafseh Ukhti Sirin 12- Ummi Hasan 13- Fatimah Nayshaburyah 14- Zeytunah 15- Fatimah al-Bard'yah 16- Ummi Ali Zujayi Ahmad Ibn

---

1- Nero Claudius Caesar (37-68, born Lucius Domitius Ahenobarbus), Roman emperor in the years 54-68 A.D. (Translator).

2- Jami: *Nafahat al-Uns* ("Breaths of Fellowship").

Khizruyah 17- Ummi Muhammad Walidyi Sheikh Abu Abdullah Ibn Khafif 18- Fatimah Binti Abi Bakr 19- Fizzih 20- Telmizeh Sarra Saqti 21- Tuhfeh 22- Ummi Muhammad 23- Bibik Marwyah 24- Dukhtari Ka'b 25- Fatimah Binti Al-Muthana 26- Jaryah Sevda 27- Amra'tah Al-Majhulah 28- Jaryah Majhulah 29- Amra'tah Al-Misryah 30- Amra'tah Al-Misryat Al-Ukhra 31- Amra'tah Al-Kharazmyah 32- Jaryatah Al-Habashyah 33- Amra'tah Al-Esfahanyah 34- Amra'tah Al-Farsyah.[1]

As you know, Abdul al-Rahman Jami was born in 817 A.H. in Jam, which is located near the province of Khurasan. If we suppose that he has written this book when he was 40, i.e. in the year 857 A. H., there is no doubt that from that date until now there have been many female mystics in the Islamic world, the names of whom either have been individually indicated in books or buried under the heavy dust of historical forgetfulness.

Muhyiddin Ibn Arabi has also cited the names of some of these female mystics:

1- Maryam Binti Muhammad, who was married to Ibn Arabi 2- Shmas Umm ul-Fuqara 3- Umm ul-Zahra Drashbilyah 4- Gulbahar, known as Setteh Ghazaleh 5- Ruhul Qudus.

Thus, women have been engaged in gnosis and mysticism both theoretically and practically, and there are many historical documents that substantiate this fact. Even in contemporary times, we have seen distinguished female mystics like Mrs. Amin Esfahani and her disciples, who have reached the great heights of both theoretical and practical mysticism. In my sessions on mysticism, I always have a number of ladies among my audience; this shows women's true eagerness for mystical truths as much as the men.

It is noteworthy that family affairs and motherly obligations quite often hinder women from reaching mystical heights. However, there have also been women who used the family as a platform to fulfill their mystical commitments, both theoretically and practically.

Garaudy: Hasn't Islam ignored women's rights in the issue of inheritance?

Ja'fari: Since the major burden of the economy is upon the shoulders of men, both in intellectual and manual levels, and it is the man who runs the family; even under heavy social and economic pressures, the man's

---

1- Ibid.

share of inheritance is more than that of woman in some and not all cases.

On the other hand, the woman, due to her sexual limitations like menstruation and pregnancy, as well as her emotional commitments as a mother, cannot unconditionally take part in economic affairs, and this is why Islam has ordered men to pay their wives monthly allowance.

Garaudy: I have a personal question. I've prayed in community with my wife as the Imam; is that all right?

Ja'fari: No, a man is not permitted to say his prayers behind a woman as the Imam due to the would-be sexual arousals when the woman bows and prostrates.

33

Prof. Herbert

Subject: Islam on Human Beings
Nationality: French/ Major: Theology
Dialogue Date: 1984

Herbert: Could the interpretation that Islam proposes of human beings prove to be acceptable for other societies and nations?

Ja'fari: This is certainly an easy question. To begin with, we need to take it into earnest consideration that when we turn to articulate Islam's view of man "as he is" and "as he ought to be", this does not necessarily mean that we are going to touch a perspective that is diametrically different from other alternatives. There are indeed some primordial and universal moral and cultural values and notions that are accepted by all nations either in the past or today or in future. Among others are the issues of existential dimensions of human beings.

It is needless to say that material needs, even mental necessities, are to a large extent in common among all nations. All human societies, regardless of their respective cultures and civilizations, equally require food, clothing, house, health, and peace. Even the so called underdeveloped countries endorse the necessity of these primary needs; this is also the case with human beings' need for thinking, the enjoyment of beauties and cultural relations.

Islam is not indeed an exception to this reality either, and its description of human beings fits the natural coordinates and limitations of human existence and regards them as necessary for reaching an intelligible understanding of human entity.

Thus, when we compare the Islamic notion of man with other cultures, nations and societies' alternatives, we need to take the fact into account that there are numerous shared points. Moreover, there are still other issues which both schools, i.e. Islamic and non-Islamic, are agreed upon. Such issues as hope, aspiration, enthusiasm for perfection, development and decent life are equally pursued by these schools.

Herbert: I would like to ask you to kindly outline the differences between Islam and other contemporary schools on human beings, as today we are witness to heavy attacks to Islamic anthropology in the West.

Ja'fari: As we mentioned earlier, there are no serious difference between Islam and its rival schools on the basic material and spiritual needs of human beings, which are all rooted in the human primordial nature. The differences and divides arise from cultures and lands otherwise; as Islam suggests, man is a creature that cannot survive without laws, rules, culture and economical principles. Other schools also accept this point, as the latter are necessary both in man's individual and social life.

To state the matter differently, there are many common grounds in the level of general rules as they lie beyond all personal ideals and interests and have an intelligible unity. However, when we seek to apply these rules to the objective reality, countless contradictions and paradoxes are unleashed.

Needless to say, we are not to say that all anthropological schools including Islam are one in their particular intellectual peculiarities. Nowise, since every one of these schools contains some ideas that are not welcomed by other schools, and even in some cases, these ideas contradict the real state of affairs. What we are to say is that these schools, whether secular or religious, have many common grounds in higher horizons. Although they may sound different in respect of their particular cultural and historical backgrounds as well as their respective geographical context, they are united on the higher issues of humanity. Thus, Islam shares numerous points with those anthropological schools which are founded upon firm ontological bases despite their trivial differences.

On the other hand, the Islamic concept of the human being is "*totally other*" as compared to the Western post-industrial nihilistic notion of man. Here is where we split our paths. To put it otherwise, Islam considers man as a "meaningful creature" living in a "meaningful world" and believes that human life is not like the sudden slide of a stone from the top of a mountain to its foot, which lacks any calculation save the causal necessities that have triggered its fall. The human being is never such a thing. They say that "man is a creature that has been pumped out of unconscious nature". This is not the case at all. Man is an intelligent product of Divine Providence, which works upon wisdom and prudence. Let us not forget to note that this meaningful journey of humanity is not supposed to come to its end in this dark, transitory world with eating, drinking, laughing and sleeping. Man is by no means such an absurd creature.

This is the very point that I discussed at length in a dialogue with Professor Gangovsky from the USSR. Having emerged out of a transcendent reality, man paces after a sublime purpose. The denial of this purposefulness does not have anything to do with anthropological schools. These schools, whether secular or religious, are somehow agreed upon the purposefulness of human existence even if one takes the worldly happiness as the ultimate telos of human life while the other seeks for the latter somewhere higher and nobler than this world. Then where does contemporary predicament originate from? What entrapped man in the swamp of hedonism? Why, instead of being contented with his rights and commitments has he turned to utilitarianism? Which factors led to the metamorphasis of man into a slave of machine and its unconscious cogs?

You might say that contemporary industrial societies are happy with their mechanistic life, which is not concerned with the ultimate telos of life, and they do not even find it absurd, either! The answer is that if you purge human life from the factors of narcotization and unconsciousness and provide the individuals with an opportunity to think of their existential capital, then will man still be willing to continue his life as unconscious cogs of a machine without knowing whence he has come? Why he has come? Where is he heading to? And above all, what is the meaning his existence? Can he still be happy? This point must be considered well. We need to pursue these issues through intangible phenomena of human life so as to see if these pleasures and joys are like sea foams or something other. As Islamic moral, legal, economic and ideological principles suggest, Islam has a logo-centric notion of man that is essentially irreconcilable with transitory pleasures. We know that carnal pleasures are both limited and associated with pains. You could never come across on this planet a person who can actually get through a day with conscious joy without narcotism and still be ignorant of his surroundings!

Islam says that such an individual is not a happy man, but in fact a selfish narcissist who has mistakenly confused promiscuity with freedom. Freedom as understood by Islam is one's ability to conduct both the positive and negative aspects of one's tasks in light of goodness and perfection. Genuine freedom is to be found in commitment, which is the particular function of the "higher self" as compared to the "natural self",[1] which is occupied with carnal pleasures.

1- The natural self is in charge of the conduction of creatures' bodily affairs, including man. This self for man is known as a "virtual self". In other words, it is the human "higher self", which is directed toward goodness and perfection and is responsible for the preservation of man in the course of evolution, that stands for man's "true self".

34

Dr. Koroda

Subject: The Principles of Islam
and the Unity of the Islamic Community
Nationality: Japanese / Major : Religions
Dialogue Date: 1985

Koroda: First of all, I would like to express my gratitude to you for giving me this unique opportunity. I'd like to ask you to speak your mind about the "unity of Islamic community", which is today time and again being discussed.

Ja'fari: To discuss the unity of Islamic community, we need at first to handle two basic issues:

Firstly, since the Islamic community has a religious identity, we have to offer a clear definition of religion in general.

Secondly, we must study the taproot of the Islamic community.

The Definition of Religion in General [1]

There are disagreements over the definition of religion, like other truths focused on human intelligible values, which have their origin in the intellectual and cultural backgrounds of the definers. There is no room for further discussion of the roots of these disagreements. Therefore, we shall suffice here to mention the universally accepted notion of religion.

Religion is the belief in the existence of a Unique, Omnipotent, Omniscient, Omnipresent, All-Just God, the Totality of all perfect attributes who has created the world upon wisdom and justice and engaged man in a universal movement toward perfection. The point of departure and destination of this universal movement, as the human common sense attests, is depicted by the Holy Quran as:

1- For more details see: Ja'fari, M. T., *A Translation and Interpretation of Nahjulbalaghah*, Vol. 22.

Surely we are Allah's and to Him we shall surely return.

(The Cow 2: 156)

Reason, conscience and divine prophets are the leaders and regulators of this movement, and after prophets, this task is assigned to saint scholars to continue this divine journey.

The first prophet is Adam (PBUH), the father of mankind and the last prophet is Muhammad (PBUH). Muhammad's book is the Quran, which remains intact to this day.

It is indeed religion in this sense that can give a meaningful purpose to human life in this world.[1] In other words, regarding all existential aspects of human beings and the ideas that have been developed of the philosophy and purpose of man's life, no thinker or school of thought could ever determine an intelligible and convincing goal for human life without addressing the following basic quadruple issues:

1. Man's relationship with himself,
2. Man's relationship with God,
3. Man's relationship with the universe, and
4. Man's relationship with his fellow men.

In our [i.e., Moslems'] definition of religion, the boundaries of these four existential relationships have been intelligently delineated and the telos and philosophy of human life has been convincingly determined.

Koroda: Do you think that your definition of religion is accepted by all scholars? As you know, we find other definitions of this notion in other relevant works.

Ja'fari: You're right. It is not so that all scholars understand religion in the same way that we do. However, my lifelong research of the issue has proven to me that this definition is the total sum of all other definitions and is also more coherent and plausible than other alternatives.

Koroda: Thank you. As I mentioned in the beginning of the interview, my prime concern is the unity of the Islamic community. Let us now turn to that issue.

Ja'fari: The Islamic community in this context refers to those human

---

1- Allameh Iqbal has described religion in the following words:

What is religion? Rising up out of the soil

So that the soul becomes conscious of his/her own.

societies that have accepted Islam as their road to physical and spiritual happiness. Thus, we need to study the basic factors of the public fondness of Islam as well as its underpinnings.

The Basic Factors leading to the Public Fondness of Islam

Various factors have caused a number of societies around the globe to convert to Islam. These factors can be divided into two general groups:

1- The disturbing factors of a desirable life like social, political and cultural corruption, the oppression of cruel dictators, economic inequalities and so on and so forth.[1]

Many societies indeed, having been grappled with these disturbing

---

1- In *The Political History of Islam* by Dr. Hassan Ibrahim Hassan, Vol. 1, some examples of social, moral, cultural and economic corruption have been indicated as the reasons for Bedouins' conversion to Islam. Some of these examples are as follow:

- The abduction of women: One of the hideous customs of Arabs in the pre-Islamic age of pagandom was that when a man confronted a stranger from a non-allied tribe who had a woman in his company, he would combat the stranger to win the woman. If the stranger defeated him, his woman was taken away from him and the winner declared her his own wife.

- Burying girls alive: Bedouins believed that a woman is a useless creature whose upbringing yields no reward. In his magnum opus *The Muqddimah* (Franz Rosenthal's edition), Ibn Khaldun has stated, "The reason for this is that (the Arabs) are a savage nation, fully accustomed to savagery and whatever causes savagery. Savagery has become their character and nature. They enjoy it, because it means freedom from authority and no subservience to leadership. Such a natural disposition is the negation and antithesis of civilization... They recognizes no limit when it comes to taking the possessions of other people. Whenever their eyes fall upon some property, furnishings, or utensils, they take it. When they acquire superiority and royal authority, they have complete power to plunder (as they please). There no longer exists any political (power) to protect property, and civilization is ruined... they use force to make craftsmen and professional workers do their work, whereas they do not see any value in it and do not pay them for it. Now, as we shall mention, labor is the real basis of profit. When labor is not appreciated and work is done for nothing, the hope for profit vanishes, and no (productive) work is done. The sedentary population disperses, and civilization decays....(the Arabs) are not concerned with laws. (They are not concerned) about deterring people from misdeeds or protecting some against the others."

This does not mean, however, that Arabs had no moral advantages at all. In fact, we are not concerned with these advantages here; rather, we are to inform the reader of the Bedouin Arabs' habits.

factors, became fond of conversion to Islam. For example, the widespread bloody quarrels and hostilities in pre-Islamic communities, particularly among Arabs and the inhabitants of the Arabian Peninsula,[1] as well as the imposed long and wearying wars turned peoples' hearts toward Islam. This inhuman and continuous violence not only had deprived people from a purposeful life, but in fact blood had blurred life in their eyes to the extent that an inherent antagonism was cultured inside individuals toward natural course of life.

It is needless to say that sequential battles left no room for the society's cultural, social, legal, religious and economic flourishing, since these matters are all based on respect for life, human dignity and intelligible freedom. Such corruptions as the abduction of women, burying girls alive, plundering other nations and slavery are examples of disturbance in the desirable course of life. This is why people so warmly embraced Islam, as it introduced them into their basic rights of life, dignity and intelligible freedom. Thus, they left antagonisms behind and worked together to reach the ideal unity.[2]

1- Durayd Ibn Semmah, one of the renowned pagan poets, describes these conflicts as follows:

⇨

And verily we are the sword's meat, and this is undeniable

and we engage in war now and then, and it is not a matter of surprise.

Sometimes our enemies attack us to retaliate their loss;

if they defeat us, this will redress their wounds.

And sometimes, we fall upon the enemy for revenge;

then we have share our life with the enemy.

Our life is thus plunged in struggle, either against ourselves or against the enemy.   (*Shoqi Zeif,* The History of Arabic Literature)

In the same book, Dr. Zeif argues that the most significant featuring characteristic of Arab life in the age of pagandom had been this very martial state of life insofar as this continuous struggle has changed into a social tradition. They always either killed or got killed. In his book, Abu Ubaydah (211 A. D.) has documented almost 1200 wars between pagan Arab tribes.

2- One might ask, "How then do you justify the battles that were frequently fought during the Prophet Muhammad's time?" To begin with, we need to note that homicide is absolutely forbidden in Islam. As the Holy Quran reads:

"For this reason did we prescribe to the children of Israel that whoever slays a soul, unless it be for manslaughter or for mischief in the land, it is as though he

The Quran has articulated this truth in the following words:

> *And hold fast by the covenant of Allah all together and be not*
> *disunited, and remember the favor of Allah on you when you*
> *were enemies, then he united your hearts so by his favor you*
> *became brethren; and you were on the brink of a pit of fire, then*
> *he saved you from it, thus does Allah make clear to you his*
> *communications that you may follow the right way.*

(The Family of Imran 3: 103)

2- The driving motives that were inhered in Islam. It is beyond all doubts that it was Islam that, for the first time, delineated the basic triple rights (the right of life, the right of dignity and the right of intelligible freedom) in a serious fashion. These rights have gradually become an inseparable part of the very fabric of the Islamic worldview.[1] Furthermore, Islam continuously invites its

---

slew all men; and whoever keeps it alive, it is as though he kept alive all men; and certainly our messengers came to them with clear arguments, but even after that many of them certainly act extravagantly in the land." (Women 4:32) Moreover, regarding such verses as "It may be that Allah will bring about friendship between you and those whom you hold to be your enemies among them; and Allah is powerful; and Allah is forgiving, merciful." (The One To Be Examined 60:7) as well as such orders as Imam Ali's historic letter to Malik Ashtar, where he advises Malik to treat people in the spirit of justice, kindness and brotherhood, "since they are either your religious brothers or your fellow men," we can conclude quite quickly that Islam prioritizes the right of life, dignity and intelligible freedom. The battles that were fought in the Holy ⇨ Prophet's time were to vanquish the factors that threatened these rights and ideals. When the Prophet started to preach the primordial and liberating message of Islam, the selfish despots decided to sabotage his divine mission, as it endangered their authority. Therefore, the Prophet had to resist their disruptions and battle them. Thus, word has always come before the sword. It is indeed unfair to say that Islam overcame by means of the force of the sword, since the sword was only used against ruthless despots who interrupted the Islamic movement, and people embraced it with open arms. On the other hand, has even a single Moslem soldier ever crossed the borders of Indonesia, Eastern Asia, Africa or India? Was the sword not in Mongols' hands? When Mongols invaded Islamic lands, they found themselves attracted to Islam. Having said this, how can one believe that two great empires, Iran and Rome, were conquered by a dozens of rotten swords of Arabs unless we accept the power of the message which touched the hearts before the swords?

1- For more details on the Islamic view of human basic rights versus the Western perspective, see M. T. Ja'fari (2014): *Human Universal Rights: A Comparative Research in Islam and the West.*

believers to surpass each other in learning. These persuasions have influenced the development of scientific and industrial ideals insofar as Moslems, according to the renowned historians of science, not only have promoted science from purely philosophical and abstractive views to observations and experiments but in fact have sustained and safeguarded science in the face of lethal threats of extinction. Let us read together some examples of Western authors' appreciation of Moslem contribution to science:[1]

In his seminal *Biographical Encyclopedia of Science and Technology* (1972), Isaac Asimov has stated:

> *The Arabs occupied Syria in the 630s and Egypt in the 640s. In so doing, they fell heir to much of Greek science, and this proved of importance and even benefit to the history of science and even to the survival of civilized world from the onslaughts of barbers.*

> *During the whole era of the Eastern Roman Empire, science had no opportunity to flourish, since there was no scientific circle around to sustain the ideas. For a thousand years of Byzantine history, the only name worth mentioning is Callinicus. Western Europe was in darkness. It was the Arabs alone who were in a position to preserve and transit human scientific heritage. Not only through the translation of Greek scientific and philosophical works did Arabs help human knowledge to survive, but they also produced some brilliant works in certain fields of science and enriched the scientific heritage. Alchemy[2] was one of the branches of science that was taken seriously by Moslems and built into great heights.*

Bertrand Russell confesses that:

> *In scientific discoveries – particularly in chemistry – Moslems were more experimental than the Greeks. They sought to transmute the metals into gold, to uncover the mystery of alchemy and to acquire the elixir of life. These were indeed their chief motives to devote themselves to chemistry, Russell argues.*

> *Throughout the dark ages of the Christian world, it was in fact Moslems, according to Russell, who sustained human civilization and those scientific ideas, which were later developed by such medieval*

1- See Ja'fari, M. T. (2008): *Science and Religion in Intelligible Life.*(Originally in Persian).
2- A medieval form of chemistry which focused on the transmutation of base metals into gold. (Translator).

thinkers, as Roger Bacon was mainly drawn on Muslim intellectual heritage.[1]

Geoge Sarton has also appreciated Moslems' contribution in the following words:

Perhaps the main, as well as the least obvious, achievement of the middle ages was the creation of the experimental spirit, or more exactly, its slow incubation. This was primarily due to Muslims down to the end of the twelfth century, then to the Christians.[2]

He continues his appraisal as follows:

The briefest enumeration of the Arabic [Islamic] contributions to knowledge would be too long to be inserted here, but I must insist on the fact that, though a major part of the activity of Arabic-writing scholars consisted in the translation of Greek works and their assimilation, they in fact did far more than that. They did not simply transmit ancient knowledge, they created a new one. To be sure, none of them attained the highest peaks of the Greek genius. No Arabic mathematician can begin to compare with Archimedes or Apollonius. Avicenna makes one think of Galen, but no Arabic physician had the wisdom of Hippocrates. However, such comparisons are hardly fair, for a few Greeks had reached, almost suddenly, extraordinary heights. That is what we call the Greek miracle. But one might speak also, though in a different sense, of an Arabic [i.e., Islamic] miracle. The creation of a new civilization of international and encyclopedic magnitude within less than two centuries is something that we can describe, but not completely explain.[3]

On the other hand, the ideas offered by Islam were primordial, simple, logical and rational. To understand these ideas, the human brain not only had no need to suffer any stress or tension, but rather since they bespoke human primordial nature they were found enthralling by conscious people. It is needless to say that the emergence of such brilliant figures as Nezami, Nasir Khusrow, Rumi, Sanaei, Attar, Sa'di, Hafez, Faryabi, Abu Rayhan Biruni, Avicenna, Zakarya Razi, Mulla Sadra, Sheikh Bahaei and the like demanded a society with a rich and eternal culture that Islam had provided.

1- Russell, Bertrand, *The Scientific Outlook* (1931).
2- Sarton, George, *The Life of Science: Essays in the History of Civilization* (1948).
3- Ibid.

The rules and obligations that Islam has drawn up for humanity are based on "intelligible life,"[1] which is equally accessible to every human collectivity upon the primordial principle of unity and human equality by the Lord regardless of one's race, color and social background as well as the maxim of conditionality of obligations.

Koroda: I should confess that [in Japan] we have not yet achieved enough documentation of research in Islam. Only in recent years have some considerable studies been conducted by such distinguished thinkers as Professor Toshihiko Izutsu.

Ja'fari: Anyway, you need to ground your knowledge mostly in the original sources of Islam, not in some shallow and biased researches that have been done by a number of Orientalists for mean reasons.

The Taproot of Islam

If we accept the definition that was broached in the beginning, we can easily reach the taproot of Islam by considering the knowledge that man has garnered of his basic needs to this day. The taproot of Islam stands on two pillars, i.e. subjective and objective elements.

1- The subjective element consists of "sane thinking" and "conscience", which are two basic elements of human primordial nature.

Not only is neither one of Islamic rules and beliefs objected to by sane sense and conscience, but they are in fact wholly embraced by these two basic factors of human knowledge and practice. This fact is indeed demonstrated by three proofs:

The first proof resides in the fact that Islamic rules and beliefs, if expounded in clear terms, are indeed the very universal principles that have been accepted one way or another as the groundwork of belief by human societies throughout the history. On the other hand, if we deeply analyze the other societies' belief systems, we can discern the universal principles of Islam in them in a delicate fashion.

The second proof is the emphatic orders and recommendations depicted by original sources of Islam, i.e. the Quran, Sunnah[2] and

---

1- For more details on Allameh's seminal theory of Intelligible Life see: Ja'fari, Muhammad Taghi, *Intelligible Life* (2011), translated into English by Beytollah Naderlew, The Allameh Jafari Institute.

2- The body of Islamic religious law which is based upon the words and actions of the Prophet Muhammad (PBUH). (Translator).

the Prophet and his progene (PBUH), about the strengthening and cultivation of reason, thought, heart and conscience and following them. There are huge numbers of verses in the Quran which are concerned with the necessity of rational and sapiential activities. The following list embodies a concise categorical itemization of such verses:

1. The strengthening of reason and following it: 40 verses
2. Exact deliberation: 15 verses
3. Contemplation: 17 verses
4. Reflection: 4 verses
5. The necessity of being considered among the sages: 15 verses
6. The acquisition of intelligence and consciousness: 21 verses
7. The pursuit of knowledge and escaping ignorance: 21 verses
8. The necessity of the acquisition of wisdom, which is among the underlying goals of the delegation of prophets: 20 verses
9. Speculation in regard to the cosmos: 20 verses
10. Adherence to substantiated facts: 18 verses
11. The heart: 35 verses

Regarding these recommendations and persuasions concerning the necessity of engaging oneself with realities through all perceptual means, one can concede that there is nothing against reason and conscience in Islamic rules and beliefs.

Eventually, the third proof is indeed the appointment of reason as a substantiator of Islamic rules and beliefs. Undoubtedly, if we ignore some occasional verbal quarrels, we shall see that as Shi'ism grounds the articles of faith in reason and regards the latter one of the main quadruple sources (the Book, Sunnah, Juristic consensus and reason), Sunnism in one sense also considers human reason as one of the main sources.

2- The objective element comprises of Divine Prophets, who have been delegated by the Lord to guide people toward the Supreme Telos of Life through religious rules and beliefs as well as the successors of the prophets and that group of scholars whose knowledge of religious truths is in such degree that they can take on people's guidance.

To demonstrate the necessity of both elements in Islam, i.e. the necessity of sane sense and conscience as well as prophetic guidance, we need to add that sane sense and conscience should act in two significant domains:

The first domain is concerned with the demonstration of the general requirements of "intelligible life" as articulated in Islam. For example, the appreciation of purposefully-built-ness of human beings and the universe in the wake of the Ultimate Telos of creation; appreciation of the fact that man, with so many glories and gifts, could not be an irrelevant and deserted creature like animals that manage themselves through their animal instincts. To put it otherwise, besides eating, sleeping, mating and struggling as well as other animal activities, the human being is committed to meet some obligations which set him on the path of evolution. Moreover, we should have in mind the idea that the regulation of the quadruple existential relationships (man's relationship with himself, with God, with the world and his fellow men) is one of human beings' obligations; in addition, appreciation of the necessity of self-knowledge and the unity and harmony of all human individuals in intelligible life is also necessary. All of these requirements belong to the first domain of the activity of sane sense and conscience.

The second activity domain of the human conscience consists of the issuance of universal prescriptions on the aspects and quality of individual and social life such as enjoining people to justice and distancing oneself from lies, wile, treason, fornication and every evil which is in conflict with sane human character. The issuance of such injunctions, which are considered significant by Islam, is up to the sane intellect and conscience. As a result, these injunctions are called *ratified prescripts* versus positive prescripts.

But what renders necessary the delegation and guidance of Divine Prophets, their successors and well-versed scholars is the very course of human history which is fraught with blood, deviation, selfishness and ignorance toward human beings' true interests and torts. Man is plunged in a natural life that attests to his unawareness of the reality of an intelligible life that can interpret all aspects of his existence. The laws and rules which have been ordained by man are in fact merely for the regulation of this very natural life, which he has been unconsciously thrown into.

This is why Jean-Jacques Rousseau says:

> *In order to discover the rules of association that are most suitable to nations, a superior intelligence would be necessary. A being who could see all the passions of men without experiencing any of them; one who would have no affinity with our nature and yet know it thoroughly; a being whose happiness would not depend on us, and who would nevertheless be quite willing to interest himself in ours; and, lastly, one who, storing up for himself with the progress of time a far-off glory in the future, could labor in one age and enjoy in another. Gods would be necessary to give laws to men.*[1]

There is no doubt that by "Gods", the monist Rousseau means Divine Prophets, who represent the Lord on earth.

Moreover, regarding so many errors that continuously occur in people's individual reasoning, this concern is always with those who seek to find due answers for the questions posed by life, particularly those concerning the quadruple relationships. Such concerns over human lapses will never fade away without resorting to revelation, since everyone knows that man cannot easily touch on all aspects of his existence.

Koroda: You just declared the human conscience as being one of the underlying factors of the reception of religion as well as its principles and obligations while there is no intellectual consensus whatsoever on both the meaning and applications of conscience. I would like to hear your point of view on this issue.

Ja'fari: We all know that philosophers and psychologists are profoundly divided on the nature of human reason, thought and deep sentiments both in respect of the judgments that are issued by reason and the reverberations of those deep sentiments inside man. Nevertheless, this does not mean that we can turn a blind eye to the very existence of these elements in human beings. But the discords that are felt on the judgments of conscience as well as the consequences of reflections and thoughts are related to occasional perceptions and preliminary recognitions which stand for the raw materials of thinking and conscience.

Koroda: Are the principles of unity in the Islamic community abstract notions and ideals that may not conform to the realities of life, or are

---

1- Rousseau, Jean-Jacques, *On the Social Contract* (2002) [translated by Susan Dunn, Yale University Press, New Heaven and London].

they genuine and fundamental principles which can answer all issues of life?

Ja'fari: I think it is much better to answer this question via the general articulation of the basis of unity in the Islamic community, which is grounded in deep-rooted primordial principles that, in my view, can meaningfully address the contemporary human condition.

The Basis of Unity in the Islamic Community

The true source of unity in the Islamic community is Islam itself indeed. This source has its root in the God-given human primordial nature. This heavenly informed nature is shared by all human individuals, regardless of their cultural and social discrepancies. The modifications and changes that this primordial religion has undergone in history have merely been concerned with secondary details of prescripts that have their origin in the diversity of the conditions of human life in various societies. The general foundations which the religion is built upon, however, have been always the same throughout history. Thus, the basis of unity in the Moslem community, in my view, lies in *the* humanistic primordial religion which has been preached by divine prophets and whose principles were articulated by Abraham, whom Judaism and Christianity see as their forefather.

The Demonstration of the Basic Elements of Primordial Religion

The basic elements of primordial religion, which must be lived according to by the Moslem community, could be demonstrated in a number of ways:

1- The Holy Quran as the manifest of pure monotheism, which consists of the belief in the uniqueness of God, the idea that *Non is like him* and the necessity of the ascription of the attributes of perfection to Divine Essence as well as the negation of the attributes of imperfection from him.

2- Resurrection and eternity, without which human life is not convincingly interpretable in this world. Some may argue that there are people who live their lives without believing in resurrection, like Buddhists and others. We can respond to such a critic as follows:

   I) It is not intelligible indeed to acknowledge every commonplace routine of ordinary people. We are still witness to the dominance of destructive egotistic ideas and corruption in all scenes of human life. For instance, slavery was once a justified social phenomenon in many societies around the globe, but today it has proven to be wrong; likewise, many justifications may be found as being baseless in future.

II) No single one of moral principles and virtues is defendable forever upon social rules, since one cannot regard the morality and virtue only as a means for the "amendment of the mundane order of life" after utilitarianism, for that will make them arbitrary and relative that disappoints such great figures as Kant, who has a categorical understanding of these issues and believes that it is conscience that justifies obligation.

III) Those schools which do not speak of eternity in a clear voice, though satisfying the human primordial tendency toward the Absolute, they in fact approach eternity from their own respective vantage point. For example, the concept of Nirvana in Buddhism, which refers to a heavenly state that exists beyond the cycle of reincarnation and denotes human freedom from karmic suffering, does indeed feature the Buddhist notion of eternity. Even modern thinkers' impression of such concepts as human beings, development and progress is sometimes so imbued with the transcendent presence of the Absolute that not only does it temporarily satisfy the human sense of eternity, but at the same time it also promotes that [secular] absolute to some kind of deity.

IV) The observation of the rational connections of the elements and the relationships between the universe and man can lead to the conclusion that if there is no real eternity for the cosmos, these connections will not be understandable. It must be taken into consideration that every man who believes in God will certainly accept the idea of resurrection and eternity, since God, as an All-Wise Creator, would not create this world wantonly.

V) So many gifts that have been conferred upon man cannot be all for nothing and having occurred merely by chance, as no one of these gifts and their realization is conceivable without a law or a higher purpose. Furthermore, since only a poor number of these gifts can be realized in the short span of earthly life, an eternal life is thus needed so that all of these natural talents to be realized.

3- Human beings need Divine Prophets to teach man the super-sensible-rational truths which are necessary for achieving perfection as the goal of life. This need will be tackled only by the delegation of prophets and their successors.

4- Ritual services which are necessary for connecting oneself to Divine Essence like daily prays, fasting and others.

5- Charity services in general, the most significant of which is providing people's intelligible material and spiritual needs.[1]

6- These principles and elements of Primordial Religion have also been demonstrated through common sense and been extensively discussed in philosophical and theological books. These elements together enjoy a transcendent unity in realizing human gifts, which is indeed the very primordial religion that was revealed to Abraham:

> *And strive hard in (the way of) Allah, (such) a striving is due to him; he has chosen you and has not laid upon you hardship in religion; the faith of your father Ibrahim; he named you Muslims before.* (The Pilgrimage 22:78)

There are other verses in the Quran which demonstrate that Abraham's religion is the very primordial religion that has been revealed to all divine prophets:

> *He has made plain to you of the religion which he enjoined upon Noah, and that which we have revealed to you, and that which we enjoined upon Abraham and Moses and Jesus, that keep to obedience and be not divided therein; hard to the unbelievers is that which you call them to; Allah chooses for Himself whom He pleases, and guides to Himself him who turns (to Him), frequently. And they did not become divided until after knowledge had come to them out of envy among themselves; and had not a word gone forth from your Lord till an appointed term, certainly judgment would have been given between them. And those who were made to inherit the book after them are most surely in disquieting doubt concerning it; to this, then go on inviting, and go on steadfastly on the right way*

1- For the Quran's view on these quintuple cases, see: The Cow 2: 26, The Cattle 6: 79, Jonah 10:47, Abraham 14:40, The Bee 16:36, The Night Journey 17:15, The Prophets 21:73, The Pilgrimage 22:76, and Iron 57:26.

as you are commanded, and do not follow their low desires,
and say, "I believe in what Allah has revealed of the book, and
I am commanded to do justice between you: Allah is our Lord
and your Lord; we shall have our deeds and you shall have
your deeds; no plea need there be (now) between us and you:
Allah will gather us together, and to him is the return.[1]

(The Consultation 42: 13-15)

It is certain that the human nature, in a normative sense, is an undeniable reality. It is also a fact that the human nature, in the positive sense, shall reach the threshold of the 'ideal personality' and 'self-actualized ego' as the disintegration of the primordial nature is a clear piece of evidence that one has not been able to emancipate oneself from the chains of determinism. The more a character becomes sublimated, the more integrated it will be.

The Fulfillment of the Human Primordial Nature via Primordial Religion

It was Abraham's earnest attention to the integrity of these noble human truths that made him prone of being characterized by lofty human attributes. The attributes that God has ascribed to Abraham in the Holy Quran definitely show that it was his adherence to the primordial principles and elements of divine religion that made him qualified for the universal leadership of mankind. Thus, his religion has been considered as the building block of all revealed religions, as universal leadership is the highest degree of perfection and features the noblest integrity of human character. This integrity has its origin in such qualities as truthfulness:

> *And mention Abraham in the book; surely he was a truthful*
> *man, a prophet.*   (Mary 19:41)

And determination for providing his people with their needs:

1- Not only has God decided that Abraham's religion be regarded as people's primordial religion, but He also invites the followers of this religion to unity. As the Holy Quran has stated, "And do not dispute with the followers of the book except by what is best, except those of them who act unjustly, and say, 'We believe in that which has been revealed to us and revealed to you, and our Allah and your Allah is one, and to him do we submit.'"   (The Spider 29:46).

And when Abraham said, "My Lord, make it a secure town and provide its people with fruits, such of them as believe in Allah and the last day." (The Cow 2: 126)

This verse reflects Abraham's serious will for providing his people, in that it depicts the prophet's intimate conversation with his Lord. Since a servant's dialogue with his Lord is undoubtedly serious and significant, as it is the greatest moment of a true believer's life, particularly when that believer is a prophet in Abraham's status. "Fruits" in this verse refers to all products that are necessary for human natural life. The Holy Quran also states:

Whoever disbelieves, I will grant him enjoyment for a short while, then I will drive him to the chastisement of the fire; and it is an evil destination. (The Cow 2:126)

As you see, although Abraham only prays for the sustenance of believers due to his extreme avoidance from infidels, God reminds the prophet about the general rule of life in this world – "I even provide for those who do not believe in me but they will taste an evil destiny at last."

Moreover, the same goes for the repentant (The Cow 2:128), the expositor of wisdom (The Cow 2:129), battling with idolatry (The Cattle 6:74 and The Prophets 21:57); the wayfarer and provider of safe route (The Cattle 6:80-83); the fulfiller of covenant (Repentence 9:114); patient and prayer (Hud 11:75); forgiver (Abraham 14: 36); the worshiper (The Bee 16:120); the man of eternal bliss (The Prophets 26:85); relying on God (The One to Be Examined 60:4); conscious of heavens and the earth (The Cattle 6:75); insisting on unity (The Consultation 42:13); enmity with the infidels (The One to Be Examined 60:4).

Every quality of this sort that has been attributed to Abraham represents a perfection that is the result of his struggle in the path of noble human virtues, which have been enjoined either by God or by his conscience, a radiation itself of Divine Essence.

As we mentioned earlier, all virtuous attributes that have been ascribed to Abraham (PBUH) are integrative constituents of his character, which has transcended disintegrating material facts and achieved a transcendent unity. Thus, what Moslems will get through following Abraham's primordial religion is the necessity of making such a character as far as one can, since:

Allah does not impose upon any soul a duty but to the extent of its ability. (The Cow 2:286)

Koroda: Would you please outline the ways of fulfillment of this unity if time allows?

The Unity of the Islamic Community and How to Achieve It

Ja'fari: Regarding the taproot of unity in the Islamic community and the common ground that not only is the integrating factor of unity in the Islamic denominations and factions, but it in fact must bring together all monotheistic religions that belong to Abrahamic tradition in an intelligible fashion.

In the Holy Quran, regardless of the verses that invite people to Abraham's religion, there are some verses that have been devoted to the stipulation of common grounds of revealed religions such as:

> *Say: O followers of the book! Come to an equitable proposition between us and you that we shall not serve any but Allah and (that) we shall not associate aught with him, and (that) some of us shall not take others for lords besides Allah. But if they turn back, then say, "Bear witness that we are Muslims."*

> (The House of Imran 3:64)

However, as you know, despite these shared bases of revealed religions, they now suffer serious conflicts and antagonisms. Of course, difference of opinion as regards to theoretical issues is a necessary phenomenon, since it guarantees the dynamicity of intellectual debates. The denial of this type of difference is either rooted in ignorance or in one's inability of facing intellectual challenges. This phenomenon is widespread to the extent that no one could ever find two theoreticians in one field who are thoroughly agreed upon all definitions, arguments and methods.

Nevertheless, even in theoretical issues, whether in experimental sciences or in philosophy, ethics, law, economy, politics, art, literature and the like, we have a number of general principles that are taken for granted by all theoreticians.[1] This type of difference of opinion

---

1- Every self-evident proposition is surrounded with a number of theoretical propositions, as every theoretical proposition is preceded by some particular self-evident propositions. For example, "the whole is larger than its parts" is surrounded with the following propositions:
- Can we declare an infinite series as being a "whole"?
- If we can, is this concept a subjective notion or an objective fact?

concerning the applications of universal principles can further our knowledge of reality if delivers itself from biases and pretensions.

The history of Islam has been witness to difference of opinion in every theoretical issue of its own. This difference has even been promoted as a necessary item as far as it has not disordered the common universal principles. Even some debates have been triggered around universal principles like monotheism, prophecy, Imamate, resurrection, divine attributes and the Quran, which not only have not incited Islamic scholars to excommunicate each other, but have in fact expanded and deepened philosophical and theological ideas. Nonetheless, scholarly disagreements on secondary issues like judiciary conundrums which exceed the universal principles in number are too evident to need any further elaboration.[1]

Therefore, we can divide scholarly differences into two general kinds:

I) Intelligible Difference

Intelligible difference is a difference that arises out of data discrepancy of a given issue as well as individual gifts, particularly genius, and covers most of natural opinions of realities like theoretical sciences and philosophical disagreements over the configuration of reality. This is the very "intelligible difference" that not only should not be resisted or denied, but it can in fact expand and deepen our knowledge of issues.[2] The renowned hadith from the Holy Prophet (PBUH) that reads, *"My nation's difference is a divine blessing"*,[3] refers to this intelligible

---

- Will the whole disappear with the disappearance of a part?

On the other hand, when we turn to such a theoretical issue as "Do all human individuals have artistic sense or not?" it is also preceded by self-evident propositions like "Man has particular gifts", "Man enjoys art", and "Some human individuals are artists".

1- Of course, since the general principles of religion and main branches, or in jurisprudential parlance, categorical prescripts, are grounded in human primordial nature, common sense, and revelation in a way that no doubt could ever be casted on them, we can consider them the very essence of Islam, which is accepted by all Moslems regardless of their respective denominations. Thus, any doubt concerning these basic principles can expulse the doubter from Islam.

2- It is self-evident, both philosophically and scientifically, that realities – whatever they may be – cannot be perceived as being independent of the subjective and objective conditions of the perceiver. This is why thinkers have different conceptions of reality and this difference does not result in any conflict.

3- Muhadith Qumi, *Safinat ul-Bihar ("The Ark of Seas")*, Vol. 2.

difference. Thus, we see that the majority of Moslem thinkers, whether in jurisprudence, rational debates of juristic prescripts, philosophy, theology, literature and other fields of study, contently exchange their critical views of different issues without excommunicating each other.

A cursory view of history of Islam shows that there were many distinguished figures that have studied under scholars with different intellectual attitudes and glossed and reviewed their works. For example, *The Book of Catharsis* by Khajeh Nasiruddin Tusi, a famous Shi'ah scholar, has been glossed by Mullah Ali Qushchi, a Sunnite thinker, and Mullah Muhsen Feydh's *Glorious Destination* is an interpretation of Ghazali's magnum opus *The Revival of Religious Sciences*. I have also devoted myself for several years to the interpretation of ideas of Mowlana Jalaluddin Rumi.

II) Unintelligible Difference

Unintelligible difference features a disagreement stemming from unauthorized and aberrant factors like following carnal whims, say via ostentation and reputationism.

There have always been some people throughout history who sought to show off by such pretensions as freedom of thought, freedom of will, freedom of expression and so on and so forth, while their love was power indeed! This love demonstrates the ultimate extent of human weakness. As we see in the founders of fake religions in history, the major motive had been power, even at the expense of social divides.

Not only does this lead to the disintegration of ideas, beliefs and unifying ideals of a society, but it also sometimes triggers devastating conflicts between peoples of one or several societies which have in fact many ideas and beliefs in common. While beliefs and ideals are the interpreters of the goal and philosophy of human life, it is totally inhuman to abuse or scapegoat them for power through creating unintelligible disagreements.

Another example of unintelligible differences is those dissentions that have their origin in mental chess games in theoretical sciences, which are merely to satisfy the imagination and sense of getting the upper hand in intellectual matters.

Thus, one can openly say that the difference in the course of constructive competitions is the most desirable factor of progress in knowledge and practice, without which any single step forward would ever be possible. Islam does not order its believers to think alike. On the other hand, Islam strongly insists on continuous intellectual debate. It is needless to argue that such an engagement will not be possible without difference of opinion.

Therefore, difference of opinion must be accepted as a natural phenomenon which is an effect of the essential dynamism of Islamic teachings. However, this difference should unleash constructive competitions, not destructive conflicts. Of course, sometimes these positive and dynamic engagements and contests are metamorphosed by fanatic votaries of power into fatal conflicts and inertia.

The irrational differences that are provoked for purposes of seeking power and domination are shallow, temporal and mostly recurring, like the books that are written today to create division between Shi'ahs and Sunnis. This kind of works shall either be scorned or regretted by intellectuals and scholars and have a temporary impression on shallow minds.

On the other hand, wherever a fire of division has been triggered, though it has claimed some saplings of the Divine Garden, at the same time it has nonetheless brought about enlightenments for intellectuals which reveal some hidden advantages of religion as well as the diabolic intensions of disuniters. Reality never becomes defeated or chanced by biased attacks, but its potentials find opportunity to show up.

Koroda: May I ask you to express your own taxonomy of unity?

Ja'fari: As you know, this is a very significant issue indeed.

Types of Unity

As we have mentioned earlier, the common ground of Abrahamic religions is the belief in a unique God Who is the Origin and Destination of the human universal movement toward perfection, the Endower of reason and conscience upon human individuals and the Delegator of divine prophets to human communities. This latter belief contains all of the elements of the united identity of the Islamic community, on which stands the total harmony of Islamic character.

However, there are three conceivable types of unity for the Islamic community:

1- **Absolute Unity:** This type of unity comprises a thorough consensus of all basic and secondary doctrines of Islam. The latter utopian kind of unity seems impossible in view of different individual exercises of freedom of thought as to the aforementioned doctrines, intellectual differences, the availability of sources both in terms of the perceiver and the perceived and individual differences regarding genius, intelligence and memory which are undoubtedly determining in one's conception of the doctrines and their respective arguments. As long as these differences are allied with the genuine pursuit of the truth as well as sufficient knowledge of sources and principles, not only will they do no harm to the unity of the Islamic community, but they are in fact necessary for the cultivation of Islamic teachings.

2- **Temporary Pragmatistic Unity:** This type of unity has its roots in the coercion of exogenous factors that do not belong to the very fabric of religion. This unity is necessary when the factors stated before threaten the order of the Islamic community. Generally speaking, when a community is being exposed to malignant and lethal factors, the routine differences and quarrels between factions are temporarily discarded and a kind of harmony or unity takes their place. Since this unity is an effect of extra-religious factors, it fades away when these factors disappear or corresponding to the increase or decrease of the power of the factors, the rhythm of the temporary pragmatistic unity gets either intensified or diminished. As it is irrational to expect an "absolute unity" among the intellectuals and the people of an Islamic community despite so many matters of intelligible difference, by the same token it is also illogical to expect "temporary pragmatistic unity" to sustain the cohesion of Islamic factions and denominations forever.

3- **Intelligible Unity:** Regarding the universal principles of religion, as mentioned earlier, the individual right of freedom of thought and intellectual divisions on the quality and elements of basic and secondary doctrines of Islam, the desirable form of unity among Islamic community will be "intelligible unity".

Therefore, one can define intelligible unity as holding the universal principles of Islam as a pattern for all Moslem societies and leaving all personal, factional, local and regional ideas of the religion.

There is no canonical or rational obstacle in the path of the realization of this type of unity and every thinker who is well introduced into the primordial sources of Islam and Sunnah knows that following the universal principles of Islam along with intellectual effort for understanding the arguments and reason is *necessary*. It is needless to argue that the unity and harmony that has been spotlighted by the primordial sources of Islam (the Quran, *Sunnah*, sane sense and intellectual consensus) as well as ingenious Islamic figures like Ayatollah Hajj Sayyed Hasan Tabatabaei Borujerdi, the jurisprudential authority of Shi'ites worldwide, and Sheikh Muhammad Shaltut, the most respected leader of Sunnites, is neither a temporary pragmatistic unity – as no single one of the Islamic factions chooses it as the ideal form of unity for Islamic community – and nor a utopian comprehensive unity which is not applicable; in fact, it is an intelligible unity based on the universal principles of Islam which govern the social and religious life of all Islamic denominations.

To achieve intelligible unity, the intellectuals and influential figures of the Islamic community must firstly broaden their perspectives. The basic factor in this intellectual broadening is deliverance from narrow and dark frames of illogical bigotries. Due to its majesty and infinity, Islam has succeeded in raising such figures as Muhammad ibn Tarkhan Farabi, Avicenna, Averroes, Ibn Meskawayh, Abu Rayhan Biruni, Hasan ibn Haytham, Jalaluddin Muhammad Rumi, Mir Damad and Sadrulmute'allehin with various range of ideas in different areas of knowledge such as ontology, cosmology and theology as well as hundreds of distinguished Sunnite and Shi'ite jurists who have their own particular jurisprudential frame of reference. They have had both critical and dialogical encounters with each other without getting involved in any counterproductive conflict. As Abu Al-Hasan Ali ibn Ismaeil Asha'ri (died 3 A. H.) notes in his *Believers Discord*, "There are more than a hundred Islamic denominations, including Shi'ite, Mu'tazilite, Ammeh, Bakryyah, Kalbyyah and others, but their differences have never breached the primordial contours of Islam, unless in few cases.

It needs to be mentioned that the existence of various Islamic denominations does not necessary imply that Islam has been really divided into different factions, since if we consider every thinker's view in the history of Islamic doctrines as a denomination, we shall then have thousands of Islamic factions.

On the other hand, no Moslem thinker has ever excommunicated his fellow thinkers. Of course, this is not to say that there were no intellectual engagements whatsoever. Now there are spirited philosophical, theological, literary, juristic and historical debates going on in Islamic countries. If a positive step is taken in a Moslem country, other countries will also benefit from it. For example, today Allameh Tabatabaei's *Al-Mizan* is widely used in Egypt, Lebanon, Syria and other Moslem countries and on the other hand, Sayyed Qutb's *Fi Zelal al-Quran* has been translated into Persian.

35

Elizabeth Gamlin

Subject: The Penalty (Retribution) for Homicide
Nationality: British/ Major: Law
Dialogue Date: 1988

In 1988, two British scholars, Ms. Gamlin and Professor James O'Connell – the Head of the Department of Peace Studies at Bradford University – traveled to Tehran in order to take part in and deliver lectures at a conference. As stated by Ms. Gamlin, Professor O'Connell had to return to the United Kingdom quickly to see to his business engagements. Ms. Gamlin, however, visited Allameh Ja'fari at his home the following day, and had a serious discussion on Islam's points of view on the penalty for murder.

Gamlin: There are two theories regarding the penalty of homicide in Europe:

1- The murderer should not be convicted to death. Accordingly, the mental state of the convict must be taken into consideration.
2- The murderer must understand the moral and cultural consequences of the crime committed, but should not be killed.

Ja'fari: This idea is a variation of a general view that is held by some experts of the philosophy of law who believe now that a man has been killed, why should a second life be claimed?

Although this has an appealing surface, but we cannot accept it as such, since it has to be taken into consideration that human lives are so interconnected that if one's life is claimed the whole *uneasy will remain.*[1]

1- This is a renowned hemistich of a line by Sa'di, Iranian poet of thirteenth century and the author of *Bustan ("The Orchard")* completed in 1257 and *Gulistan ("The Rose Garden")* in 1258. Sa'di sees all human beings as members of

To put it otherwise, murder causes such uneasiness among human individuals that their own lives would seem to have been destroyed.

Of course, you will say that today we no longer see such sentiments among human beings. I have frequently said and still say that the characteristics of machine-stricken contemporary man to human nature are as such. Today's machine-plagued man is one being and the human being who is naturally benefited from all of his gifts and existential capitals is another entity. This divide should not be fallen on deaf ears. It is indeed a logical fact that the more man is dominated by machine, the more his sense of primordial harmony and unity between human souls insofar will decline, as man gradually "vanishes" between the cogs of the machine and turns into a heap of senseless metal scraps that never becomes impressed by the murder of a human individual or even the whole mass. As a Western politician once said, "If an individual dies, it is described as a tragic catastrophe, but if a million people are systematically slaughtered, it is merely considered a matter of statistics!"

As far as machine-stricken man is concerned, this issue is simply conceivable, but it is not tolerable from the human primordial nature's point of view. Accordingly, man – who is the favorite creature of the Lord and has been created for a noble purpose – is like a sea whose waves continually fail to impress the sea, no matter where or when, high or low.

The other significant issue worth mentioning is that retribution is not the only penalty for homicide. When an intentional homicide takes place, three jurisprudential options are raised:

1- **Blood-money and pecuniary punishment:** If the family of the slain accepts the ransom in the spirit of forgiveness, kindness, beneficence and goodness, the murderer will not be executed. Thus, we can spread this spirit of forgiveness among citizens only

---

the same family and invites humanity to be attentive to this primordial existential reality may it extinguishes the fire of conflicts between nations: ⇨

> *Human beings are members of a whole*
>
> *In creation of one essence and soul.*
>
> *If one member is afflicted with pain, other members uneasy will remain.*
>
> *If you have no sympathy for human pain,*
>
> *The name "human" you cannot retain!*

(English translations of lines are by M. Aryanpour). (Translator).

if we are certain that there will be no more homicide or systematic slaughter.

Succinctly speaking, if the family and relatives of the slain have been brought up in accordance with the goodness and beneficence that are at the heart of Islamic ethics, they would not remorselessly narrow their options down to revenge.

2- **Remission:** Such human qualities as compassion, mercy and kindness require us to forgive each other even when one has lost one's most beloved one. We have witnessed numerous examples of remission of the murderer in the Islamic society.

3- **Retribution:** Even the slightest hint of the existence of mental disorder or imbalance in the case of the murderer at the crime scene makes the homicide unintentional and nullifies retribution. Accordingly, the punishment of the murderer is determined based on the degree of intention that has been involved in crime. This judiciary principle is extrapolated from a *hadith* that reads:

> *The slightest doubt nullifies punishments and judgments.*

As you see, retribution is more an interceptive means for social control rather than being a cruel punishment for every form of homicide. There is also another issue that is worth mentioning here. As the major source of Islam, the Quran has stated the philosophy of retribution in the following words:

> *And there is life for you in (the law of) retribution, o' men of understanding, that you may guard yourselves.* (The Cow 2:179)

The verse suggests that retribution insures your life. Many might think that hanging the murderer in public is a guarantee for peaceful life as it is a clear message for all that whoever kills an innocent man shall end up on the gallows. Thus conceived, retribution is merely a mechanic lever to adjust social behaviors. This is the general understanding of the aforementioned verse. Although this is admittedly a necessary working of the law of retribution, it is still supposed to convey a more vital message. Unfortunately, this side of retribution has been sorely neglected in the West and also in many other lands.

To put it otherwise, the law of retribution reveals the true value and significance of human life as it suggests that you should not play with other people's lives since it will cost you your own life. In other words, your life is respected when you respect other lives. This is indeed a sensible equation by both plain and sophisticated minds.

Retribution sheds light on the primordial value of human life and, at the same time, warns people against the consequences of suicide. This is the very indirect implication of the law of retribution which has gone unnoticed by lawyers. Islam regards suicide as an instance of intentional homicide. Said differently, according to Islam, taking one's own life is tantamount to murdering other people. As the intentional murderer is promised to be burnt in the flames of Hell, the suicider has also been cursed to the same degree.

Revealing the primordial significance and value of life, the law of retribution therefore not only guarantees human life against diabolic encroachments from the outside, but it also safeguards it against suicide threats.

Gamlin: Despite this majestic law of retribution, why has the inauspicious phenomenon of homicide not been uprooted yet in Islamic societies, while we are reported today of societies in the world where homicide cases are far fewer than Islamic communities?

Ja'fari: The following issues must be taken into account in this regard:

1- A cursory look at the history of these societies shows that there once were strict penalties for homicide there. This firm stand on murder has led to the emergence of a culture of pacifism and non-violence.

2- The enhancement of education and the internalization of the culture of peaceful coexistence is also one reason for the lower record of homicide in those communities.

3- Social justice and intelligent policy makers have decreased together the fatal conflicts almost down to zero. As a result, it is totally natural to hear of the lower record of homicide in these societies.

But the question why these actions have not been taken in Islamic societies is not indeed a matter of Islam or the Quran, in the same way that the high rates of suicide, regional and world wars in the so-called developed countries have anything to do with their legal system, culture or religion. Moreover, we see many despots throughout the history of Islam who have suspended or abused many Islamic laws to reach their diabolic goals.

36

Yahya Mustafa Imam

Subject: Islam on Governance
Nationality: Egyptian/ Major: Martial Sciences
Dialogue Date: 1988

Mustafa Imam: It is indeed an honor for me to be here and I would like to express my countless thanks for your receiving me so warmly. I would like to ask you to speak about government and ruling in Islam, particularly from the Shi'ite point of view. I am highly interested in hearing your thoughts in regard to Islamic and Shi'ite concepts of governance.

Ja'fari: Government in Islam is one of the fundamental, in fact key, issues on which many books and articles have been written to this day. The great importance that has been attached to this issue by Moslem thinkers, as I mentioned earlier, was due as it is a vital issue. In Islam, governance is of significance both in respect of its principles (in other words, the origin and basis of governance in Islam) as well as its limits. The government is important in view of its principles in Islam as it is a divine activity on earth, particularly according to Shi'ism. Since you are more interested in knowing the Shi'ite perspective of this issue, I will mainly focus on Shi'ite views; nonetheless, the Sunnite views are also worth mentioning here.

Part One: The Foundation of Islamic Government as Seen in Shi'ism
Government is considered as a divine affair by Shi'ism. To put it otherwise, as the rulership of the Prophet Muhammad (PBUH) in the Islamic community was a divine or heavenly endowed status, if Imam Ali (PBUH) and his progeny had the opportunity to rule the Moslem community, their rulership was also divine in essence.

It has been thoroughly debated in Kalam why government is essentially a sacred [i.e. *nonsecular*] issue in Shi'ism. Laconically speaking, social leadership and Imamate is the continuation of prophecy. In other words, it acts in light of and in the wake of prophecy. Those people who want to govern the society must be delivered of the bondages of carnal desires and animal urges and be immaculate; moreover, they could have a right foothold for the articulation of revealed maxims and also for the interpretation of all elements of Islamic worldview. Thus, they should have a divine character; otherwise, there would be no guarantee as to the authenticity of their claims of truth. To state the matter differently, if rulership in Islam is supposed to be undertaken by people themselves, i.e. ordinary folks rather than educated minds and enlightened spirits, it will result in no advantage as compared to other types of governance. A sacred government is led by enlightened minds who know the truths of heavens. In fact, here lies the basic difference between theocracy and democracy. It is indeed true that people can run themselves provided they have a dependable knowledge of the nature, coordinates and requirements of life. This knowledge requires that they be purged of selfishness and carnal desires as these would surely distort their knowledge of life.

If people can meet the requirements just depicted, then they can certainly run their own affairs. However, this is almost impossible. The history of human life has already proven that such an evolution was either not possible as such for humanity or at least it did not have realizable possibility in philosophical parlance. Even if this has had an essential possibility, no occurring possibility has ever been recorded of it, unless we narrow down the case to individual evolutions and leave the ideal of collective evolution aside. As a result, we can say that Islam has not wholly discredited the idea of democracy, but it nonetheless believes that it cannot be realized on the planet earth. As we mentioned earlier, if the man succeeds in achieving a fundamental knowledge of the truths of life, he could then cure all pains, answer all questions and manage his own affairs. Two verses of the Quran have broached the principle of consultation [collective leadership]:

> 1- *And those who respond to their Lord and keep up prayers, and their rule is to take counsel among themselves, and who spend out of what we have given them.* (The Consultation 42:38)

***

> 2- *And take counsel with them in the affair; so when you have decided, then place your trust in Allah; surely Allah loves those who trust.* (The House of Imran 3:159)

These verses clearly show that people's right of participation in the election of the government has not been overlooked. Moreover, in the application of divine laws to one's individual problems, the right of thought and choice has not been ignored, but the fact is that enlightened minds and sane sense always follow the divine laws.

Anyway, the question is whether man can manage his own affairs alone in a way that he can answer all questions and tackle the problems. What history has demonstrated in this regard is that some schools have emerged and established some forms of government, but unfortunately, along with their partial enlightenments, they have added a huge amount of obscurity to the obscurities of social life and this is a very critical issue. Thus, it is not fair to say that Islam is a despotic system of theocracy. On the contrary, when we say that Islam is a sacred system, it implies that it offers a *sane* interpretation of human primordial nature, human instincts and human existence along with all of its all aspects and properties.

Undoubtedly, the Islamic establishment is required to prepare the necessary conditions for the realization of these properties, gifts and aspects. Man is a purpose-built creature who has been brought to this universe by divine providence; moreover, man's destination is eternity. Such a being cannot be managed by these limited senses and material-stricken ideals. This is why some scholars of the humanities argue that had man accepted the divine codes and laws, we would know the true capacity of humanity for perfection and growth!

Unfortunately, since divine codes – whether those which are supposed to manage governmental affairs or those which are concerned with the management of people's collective life as well as divine culture – are in conflict with animal whims and selfishness, man is thus not willing to accept the fact that divine culture and codes can better assist mankind in the path of evolution. To put it otherwise, as man has been so busy with matter and the material aspect for such a long time, he was not able to fathom the fact that if the rules, government system and even civil, criminal and international laws are based on the sacred, man will certainly reach evolution. But since mankind has failed to understand this critical fact, he has been afflicted with so many pains, plights and grieves since the dawn of human history. All of these misfortunes, which exceed fifty cases, have had their roots in human ignorance of "sane life".

As Avicenna writes in his *Al-Isharat wa-'l-tanbihat* (*"Remarks and Admonitions"*):

> He who endures the lack of perfection has no conception of perfection.

Nevertheless, all of these misfortunes have their origin in the reluctance on the part of man to confess that life must be managed by the Heavens as his reason and other senses are driven by the desires of the "natural self" and cannot provide an ideal life for mankind. There are some verses in the Quran that substantiate this truth. One of these verses reads:

> *Surely those who swear allegiance to you do but swear allegiance to Allah; the hand of Allah is above their hands. Therefore, whoever breaks (his faith), he breaks it only to the injury of his own soul, and whoever fulfills what he has covenanted with Allah, he will grant him a mighty reward.*

(Victory 48:10)

This verse announces in a clear voice that the Islamic government is in fact the rule of God. As a result, the approval of this verse implies that Prophet's reign is the manifestation of rule of God. On the other hand, the successors of the Prophet (SAW) must have the divine requirements of rulership. Thus, it is proved that whether during the reign of the Prophet and Imams (PBUH) or their successors, the government must retain its divine aspect. Another verse of the Quran states:

> *O you who believe! Obey Allah and obey the messenger and those in authority from among you; then if you quarrel about anything, refer it to Allah and the messenger, if you believe in Allah and the last day; this is better and very good in the end.*

(Women 4:59)

Aligning *"those in authority from among you"* with the Prophet and his progeny (PBUH), this verse demonstrates the necessity of the continuous presence of divinity in the leadership of the Moslem community as the nation of God.

It is indeed the allegiance to Allah and his Messenger that distinguishes Islamic society from other societies, and this is itself an argument of the necessity of the divine factor in Islamic leadership.

I have elaborated this necessity in a chapter that I contributed to a book on philosophy of law. There I explained that the recognition of this necessity could enhance human culture into great heights in terms of man's mental and spiritual capacities.

Part Two: Shi'ism on the Limits of Government

As the basic beliefs of Shi'ism suggest, the government has a very wide domain of activity. According to the Shi'ite political doctrine, religion embraces all aspects of human life. The government must take serious actions for the correction of morals in society; it should manage and adjust the society upon these morals; it has to take pragmatic measures to reduce crime rate, to protect people's rights and even to make the citizens ready for the acceptance of noble governmental and legal codes. Imam Ali (PBUH) describes the goals underlying the order he sent to Malik Ashtar in the following words:

> *I have issued this order for the regulation of economic affairs, the prosperity of the country, resistance toward the enemies and the correction of the people of that society.*[1]

In some Islamic sources, we read that the government is to be held accountable for every event that happens in the society. It has been quoted that Ali ibn Musa Reza (PBUH) was in Ma'mun Al-Rashid's court one day when a thief was brought in. Ma'mun ordered his soldiers to cut his hand. "They should first cut your hand and then cut my hand," the thief said. Ma'mun retorted, "I shall not suspend the judgment prescribed by the heavens because of such nonsense. Why are you telling that my hand must be chopped?" "It was your duty to build the economy of society in a way that I would not have to commit theft," the thief replied. Imam Reza (PBUH) turned to Ma'mun and told him, "You must answer the question." Since Ma'mun was unable to answer, he harbored a grudge against the Imam.

This makes it clear whether a government is Islamic or not. The government is accountable before everything in the society from politics to culture, economy, morality and so on and so forth. Thus, the Islamic establishment is the most comprehensive form of governance in the world, for it embraces the whole gamut of human life.[2]

1- *Nahjulbalaghah*, Letter 53.
2- See Ja'fari, M. T., *Translation and Interpretation of the Nahjulbalaghah*, Vol. 9.

37

Shokat Bakir

Subject: The Principles of Sunnite and Shi'ite Jurisprudence
Nationality: Turkish/ Major: Cleric
Dialogue Date: 1988

Bakir: What are the basic principles of Shi'ite jurisprudence and are Shi'ite scholars in fact unanimous on them?

Ja'fari: As you know, any research concerning a school, be it a political, moral, legal, philosophical or religious school, must meet two conditions:

> **The First Condition** regards necessary and sufficient information of the underlying principles, subjects and issues of that school. Unfortunately, due to the inobservance of this condition, most of the research done of schools of ideas has grounded themselves in lies and distortions! We see frequent cases of these distortions in the studies which are published on great figures of the history of science and philosophy. For example, Heraclitus, the Greek pre-Socratic philosopher, and Muhammad ibn Zakarya Razi, the Iranian scientist and the discoverer of alcohol, are labeled as materialist atheists, while both figures are among theosophers. Thus, if you are to do a research of Shi'ism and its pioneers, you need to suspend your judgment until you have garnered necessary and sufficient information on it.

> **The Second Condition** involves keeping one's own mental presuppositions out of one's debates on historical figures as well as aesthetic, moral, religious, legal, political and philosophical schools [i.e., the neutrality condition]. This is a truly hard condition to meet, since such neutrality requires an intellectual liberty that is rarely found save in few individuals. It is in the spirit of this very condition that Whitehead says:

> > Gibbon's *The History of the decline and fall of the Roman Empire* [is indeed a brilliant work].... but throughout this history, it is Gibbon

who speaks. He was the incarnation of the dominant spirit of his own times.[1]

Having said these, now we shall turn to the preliminary sources of Shi'ite jurisprudence. Shi'ite jurisprudence is founded upon four pillars, i.e. the Qur'an, *Sunnah*, consensus and reason.

1- **The Qur'an** is the main source of Islamic beliefs, rules and morals which has remained intact in the face of distorting encroachments. Sadly, some poor writers say that "Shi'ites believe that the Qur'an has been distorted." This is a baseless remark that has no support among Shi'ite jurists and theologians; as a matter of fact, it is merely upheld by a small group of traditionalists who are not recognized by any authority.

Sometimes this issue is highlighted either for attracting public attention or for the satisfaction of outsiders! This view does not have anything to do with Shi'ite ideology. All Shi'ite authorities believe that the Quran has not been distorted and is as such the axis of the unity of Moslem societies. This book is in fact the primary source of Islamic jurisprudence. Of course, there are different views concerning the number of verses that deal with jurisprudential issues. This division is also existent among Sunnite scholars. Some jurists believe that there are five hundred and others have other estimations. Anyway, the fact is that Shi'ite regards the Quran as its main source of general jurisprudential rules.

2- *Sunnah* represents the intellectual and moral heritage of the Prophet Muhammad (PBUH) and his progene. Shi'ites seek to substantiate their jurisprudential rules via the traditions of the Immaculate Imams (PBUT) and the Prophet (PBUH) who was the collocutor of revelation:

> *Nor does he speak out of desire; it is naught but revelation that is revealed.* (The Star 53:3-4)

Accordingly, the Prophet's *words* and *deeds* are the embodiment of revelation. It is needless to say that the aforementioned words and deeds do not refer to the Prophet's everyday routines like eating, sleeping or travelling or even say the economic decisions or contracts that Prophet (PBUH) made upon his times' conditions and terms; for example, such land belongs to such tribe to farm on for such time or such things are subject to taxation (e.g. nine things

---

1- Whitehead, Alfred North, *Adventures of Ideas*.

in the Prophet's era were subjected to alms tax). To put it otherwise, the Prophet (PBUH) was in charge of the quantative and qualitative adjustment of the rules that he directly received from revelation.

Therefore, whatever the Prophet (PBUH) stated as a rule or whatever he did as well as his reactions to other peoples' words and deeds are part of the *Sunnah* in our view. For example, if the tradition demonstrates that the Holy Prophet (PBUH) put his hands on his knees during his genuflection or put his seven limbs on the ground during his prostration, we take it as *Sunnah* and act according to it. This is also the case with the "tacit approval" [i.e. *taqrir*] of some ideas and actions that have been stated or conducted before the Prophet (PBUH) and he has not found them against Islamic rules and creeds. This view of the the Prophet (PBUH) is almost shared by all Moslems save some Sunnite scholars who have considered the Prophet a "Mujtahid [qualified jurist]".

Bakir: Would you name some Sunnite scholars who see the Prophet as a "Mujtahid"?

Ja'fari: Of course. In some theological books like *Sharhi Maqasid* by Sa'd Taftazani and *Sharhi Tajrid* by Mullah Ali Qushchi, who are our Sunnite brother scholars, the Prophet (PBUH) has been openly described as a "Mujtahid". This idea needs to be revised in light of such verses as "*Nor does he speak out of desire; it is naught but revelation that is revealed*", since regardless of the openness of divine verses of the fact that whatever the Prophet (PBUH) speaks of rules and obligations are based on revelation, if we accept the idea of "Ijtihad" as to the Prophet, we have tacitly approved the possibility of error in the Prophet's words and deeds. Such a possibility can destroy the whole legitimacy of our jurisprudential principles. Accordingly, it seems that this idea is not shared by all Sunnite scholars and is merely restricted to a small circle of them.

Thus, we can say that the majority of Moslems believe that the edicts issued by the Prophet (PBUH) are documented to revelation. Even if some of these edicts are the products of the Prophets' own reason, since his reason and heart were the locus of divinity, they are also therefore based on revealed laws. As a result, those edicts for us are also as legitimate as the revelation itself.

The Shi'ite stance on *Sunnah* is also the case with the Immaculate Imams (PBUT). As in *Usul Al-Kafi*, some traditions have been recorded according to which the Prophet's Ahl al-Bayt – the immaculate progeny of the Prophet (PBUH) – are regarded as being the interpreters and expositors of the Quran and *Sunnah,* and the rules that have been articulated by them are also drawn on the words and deeds of Prophet (PBUH) himself in one way or the other. In other words, if we see some rules that had not existed in Prophet's time and Imams have presented them, they should also be declared as divine rules upon their existential immaculateness and moral sanctity.

However, much of the aforementioned rules are somehow documented to prophetic traditions. To state the matter differently, these rules have been conveyed chest to chest via the Immaculate Imams (PBUH). For example, Imam Sadeq (PBUH) has quoted it from Imam Baqir (PBUH), Imam Baqir has quoted it from Imam Ali Ibn Hussein (PBUH), Imam Sajjad (PBUH) has quoted it from Imam Hussein or Imam Hassan (AS) and they have quoted it from Imam Ali (PBUH), who has quoted them from the Prophet Muhammad (PBUH). Thus, whatever the Imams have said is drawn on Prophetic traditions.

Bakir: Is [the Imam's] inspiration therefore the very revelation coming from the Prophet that we are agreed on?

Ja'fari: One can say that every revelation is in fact some kind of divine inspiration, but it is not so that every inspiration is necessarily a revelation, since revelation exclusively belongs to the Prophet and essentially differs from the inspirations that dawn on purified hearts and minds.

3- **Consensus,** which accounts for one of the quadruple pillars of jurisprudence, consists of doctrinal agreement in the Islamic community on a rule that has no dependable document, be it a prophetic tradition or a verse of the Quran. Consensus is of two kinds: acquired and transmitted.

   Acquired consensus is more reliable than transmitted consensus, as acquired consensus features the unanimous stance of Islamic intelligentsia on a given issue while transmitted consensus is based on the majority of intellectuals. These two types of consensus are discussed in theoretical jurisprudence.

4- **Reason** represents the fourth source of Shi'ite jurisprudence. By reason in this context we do not mean the sophisticated theoretical rules which are often the matters of quarrels and disputes; rather, we mean the independent and self-evident rational rules whose evidence has either been independently demonstrated, like the immorality of oppression, goodness of justice, the necessity of returning the trust to its owner as well as the immorality of theft and all actions which are condemned by reason itself, or reason finds their truthfulness via a due deliberation.

Besides self-evident propositions, by these rules we mean also necessarily true propositions. We use two types of propositions in the demonstration of scientific issues, i.e. self-evident propositions and necessarily true propositions. Although general scientific rules like mathematical theorems may not be self-evident in their face, when they proceed on right premises, however, they definitely reach their necessary conclusions and we can recognize their essential truthfulness. Of course, the scholars of theoretical jurisprudence have dealt with this issue. They have only discussed rational self-evident truths. There are huge numbers of essentially true propositions in different branches of human knowledge, however, that are not self-evident.

Nevertheless, we share the same stance with our Sunnite brothers on the authority of the Quran and *Sunnah* as the major sources of Islamic jurisprudential rules, obligations and morals. Of course, consensus is also considered as a genuine source of inspiration of jurisprudential musings by Sunnite scholars, however they have their own reason for its authenticity, which is the *hadith* stating that:

> *My nation does not come together wrongly.*

On the other hand, Shi'ites believe that if a consensus takes form, it demonstrates that a divine element of authority exists in that consensus. What this divine element of authority is, however, indeed a matter of dispute. Some Sunnite scholars act on analogy and preference; an example is Abu Hanifa and his disciples. Analogy is not indeed a general method pursued by all Sunnite scholars. For example, the Imamyah does not act on analogy. Analogy is a judgment that is deduced by the jurist upon a judgment on other relevant issue. For example, suppose we have a reason to wash again the urine outlet. If the jurist argues that this twice washing is due to the fluid that is discharged through that outlet, then it will be also the case with semen, which is ejaculated from the same outlet and we should wash the place twice again. This is not a sound analogy. Those who do not regard analogy as a right means for jurisprudential reasoning argue that doubtful reasons cannot be the source of jurisprudential judgment:

> *And most of them do not follow (anything) but conjecture.*
> (Jonah 10:36)

> *O you who believe! Avoid most of suspicion.*

(The Apartments 49:12)

There are numerous verses like these that suggest that conjecture and suspicion cannot be the basis of jurisprudential judgment, since conjecture is always followed by disagreement. We have three alternative arguments to analogy:

1. Definite deduction
2. Causal stipulation
3. Priority deduction

Causal stipulation features an opinion that is proven of a subject upon a causal explanation, for instance, "Wine is unlawful since it dulls human senses." This is a universal judgment that equally applies to all cases that bear the same causal relations. Some may even not accept this causal generalization and say that it is only limited to that particular case. However, this critique does not meet any of the requirements of rational discourse.

Priority deduction consists of the application of the judgment of a given issue to a category that has comparative priority to that issue. For example, in a verse of the Quran, we read:

> ***Say not to them (Your father and mother) "ugh" nor chide them.***
> (The Night Journey 17:23)

When the Quran warns believers not to even say "ugh" to their parents, it is far evident that the holy book certainly demands them not to humiliate, scorn and beat their parents *for a stronger reason*.

Definite deduction is a jurisprudential process through which a jurist determines the reason behind a judgment in a definite fashion. Even if this reason is not expressed openly in the judgment itself, it has been nonetheless so articulated that every sound mind can easily fathom the reason. For example, cornering is illegal; although this precept does not contain any ratiocinative explanation of its reason, it is still sensible for every average mind, for after all, everyone knows that cornering endangers people's sustenance. Some may want to raise exceptions to this precept. For instance, they might say it is not illegal to corner medicine as it is not food. This is totally wrong, as this precept is a definite deduction.

Thus, according to Shi'ism, the jurist cannot rely on analogy in his arguments, for it is imbued with suspicion and conjecture, which are not dependable. There are many other issues that can be dealt with in regard to Sunnite and Shi'ite jurisprudences, but that would demand much time.

Bakir: Then if a jurist were to offer a rationally dependable argument of a precept, would you hold it fast, too?

Ja'fari: Definitely. We must distinguish between the knowledge of a Justice and that of a jurist. Some say that a justice must act upon his own knowledge alone, without relying on any other sources whatsoever. A jurist, on the other hand, has to obtain his knowledge through legitimate paths that are, according to Shari'ah, neither via mere suspicion nor via mere individual taste.

38

Prof. Muhammad Abdus Salam[1]

Subject: Science and Philosophy
Nationality: Pakistani/ Major: Physics
Dialogue Date: 1988

Professor Abdus Salam visited Allameh Ja'fari on Monday, November 21, 1988 in his house in company with Professor Golshani [a distinguished and highly esteemed Iranian physicist who has the chair of philosophy of science at the Sharif University of Technology]. Both Ja'fari and Abdus Salam insisted on the necessity of industrialization and scientific development in Moslem communities.

Abdus Salam: As you know, today Moslem societies are in urgent need of joining the global industrial and scientific movement. We should remember the glorious advent of Islam and renew ourselves. What is your view in this regard?

Ja'fari: That is absolutely right. Near the end of the second century after Hijra, Moslems began a glorious scientific movement that was alive for almost three centuries latter until the early years of the fifth century. According to the historians of science, Moslems created an intellectual movement that was not limited to Caspian shores; in fact, it spread into the Atlantic coasts as they travelled through various lands to widen their knowledge of other cultures and people. They laid the foundation of an original civilization, Whitehead says, the originality of which is praised by all historians of science and civilization. Whitehead opines that:

1- Prof. Muhammad Abdus Salam (29 Jan.1926 – 21 Nov. 1996) was a theoretical physicist who, sharing the 1979 Nobel Prize in physics for his contribution to electroweak unification, became the first and only Pakistani to receive a Nobel Prize and also the first Moslem to win a Nobel Prize in science. (Translator).

The Byzantines and Mahometans were themselves the civilization.[1]

Moslems, Whitehead continues:

Flourished on their own, revolutionized mathematics, made genuine progresses in physics, commerce, chemistry and other branches of knowledge and created an original civilization.[2]

In his voluminous *Science in History*, J. D. Bernal interestingly says:

Since its advent, Islam was seen as the religion of knowledge and literacy... Furthermore, the cities of Islam were not isolated from the rest of the Eastern world as had been those of the Roman Empire. Islam became the focal point of Asian and European knowledge. As a result, there came into the common pool a new series of inventions quite unknown and inaccessible to Greek and Roman technology. These included such manufactures as steel, silk paper and porcelain. In turn, this formed the basis for further advances, which were able to stimulate the West to its great technical and scientific revolution of the seventeenth and eighteenth centuries.[3]

It must be taken into serious account that Moslem progresses were not merely limited to abstract theoretical and philosophical sciences; as a matter of fact, as this book suggests, it was a matter of technology and inventions. In fact, one can say that Moslems were the forefathers of modern industry and science.

In her renowned *"Allahs Sonne über dem Abendland"* (*"Allah's Sun over the Occident"*) (1960), Sigrid Hunke states:

We are not only an heir to Greece and Roma, but we are indeed the inheritor of Islamic intellectual world which the Occident is undoubtedly indebted to.

Moreover, Philipp Frank has openly written:

In the middle ages no nation has as much contributed to the progress and advance of humanity as the Moslems did.

John Bernal has also said:

The Arabs were no stranger to civilization. They had their own cities and had fulfilled an essential function in organizing the Eastern trade

---

1- Whitehead, Alfred North, *Adventures of Ideas*.

2- Since Mr. Abdus Salam was aware of the history of science in Islam, Mr. Ja'fari merely focused on the points that were of interest for both of them.

3- Bernal, J. D. (1954): *Science in History: The Emergence of Science*, Vol. 1, (Penguin Books Ltd, Harmondsworth, Middlesex, England).

of the Roman Empire. The ease of their conquest showed that all they did was to take over the urban civilization of the Mediterranean with the effective consent of the inhabitants.[1]

***

In fact, if we were only to deal with the history of science, it would be more logical for us to have focused on the period which starts from the seventh century, i.e. the first century of Islam, and ends in the fourteenth century.[2]

***

It is interesting to note that the primary subject of Islamic culture was not only material and terrestrial but also objective.[3]

There are countless examples of such intelligent remarks that have been made by impartial Western historians of science of the Moslems' contribution to the advance of science and industry.

Abdus Salam: I think philosophy is no longer working and we need to turn to science and industry.

Ja'fari: I don't exactly think so. To begin with, you must first define what you mean by the term philosophy. If you mean by it a number of hyper-universal and abstract notions that are totally detached from reality, I would also agree with you that not only could such a philosophy fail to have any practical avail for us, but we would not even be able to defend it as a genuine source of knowledge and insight, either.

I have frequently emphasized in my lectures, speeches and essays that we should approach the issue from a phenomenological standpoint regardless of what has been and is conceived of the notion in past and today. As a matter of fact, philosophy takes issue with the truths that belong to the third stage in the hierarchy of human knowledge. Thus, we need to begin with the other two early stages.

The first stage is the stage of science which relies on senses, alternative instruments, reasoning and ideas; it chiefly deals with concrete facts of the external world. We know, however, that our epistemic struggle is not confined to the branches of knowledge that cover limited subjects in a restricted fashion. We have also theoretical discourses of knowledge. These discourses form the second stage of human

---

1- Ibid.
2- Ibid.
3- Ibid.

knowledge. Theoretical physics is an example of this modality of discourse, which is focused on theorems and hypotheses that have not yet been proven or disproven via experimental or discursive methods.

This modality of discourse is discernable almost in all branches of *geisteswissenschaften* as well as in natural sciences, say law, as a discipline versus theoretical law, physics as a discipline versus theoretical physics, anatomy as a discipline versus theoretical anatomy. To put it otherwise, it is not so that our knowledge of the anatomy of the human body is merely scientific. This is also the case with physics or law, for instance. These disciplines contain a set of theoretical issues concerning the premises of scientific problems or their respective axioms and postulates that may be proven or disproven by experience.

This is followed by the third stage, which is called the stage of *universal knowledge* and covers the totality of the human scientific episteme of reality. In this stage we revise the whole body of our theoretical notions of reality from a more universal point of view in order to reach higher cognitions. Man can by no means understand his existential quadruple relationships (i.e. the human relationship with man himself, with God, with the world and with his fellow human beings) only via experiential experiments, observation and external senses. This is truly impossible as scientific knowledge is limited in its nature, methods and consequences.

On the other hand, there is a genuine yearning in man to understand the world in its totality and in an integral fashion rather than by way of mental puppet shows.

As I mentioned earlier, if philosophy is merely supposed to be limited to mental phantoms and delusions which have nothing to do with realities, not only will you have no need for it at all, but you will even have to find a way to keep yourself away from it, as it may have dire epistemological consequences for you. But if it is concerned with universal issues of worldview, as I have just argued, it is as necessary and vital as theoretical hypotheses in sciences.

The modern hegemony of technology and industrialism that has caused many significant truths to be marginalized should not be the compass of intellectual activity. The men of ideas need to listen only to the call of realities. When a reality proves its necessity for recognition to us, we are obliged to devote ourselves to it, whether in the name of philosophy or in the name of theoretical, scientific, spiritual or cultural issues. We are not to bear anymore the damages and losses that man has suffered due to the denial of ideas and ideologies that interpret the existence for us. The past has been a big lesson for us.

39

Fred Red

Subject: The Pathology of Human Sciences and the Influence of Moslem Intelligentsia on Their Societies
Nationality: Canadian/ Major: Cultural Studies
Dialogue Date: 1988

Mr. Fred Red visited Iran and interviewed Mr. Ja'fari twice.
The first occasion occurred on December 3, 1988.

Red: What has triggered the current crisis in human sciences in many societies around the globe?

Ja'fari: Ever since technology came to be known to humanity as the source of profit and domination, it was natural that some brilliant minds would devote themselves to its development and promotion. This diabolic troika of *profit, pleasure* and *domination* has then pestered many societies and generations worldwide and is now in dire need of consideration and management. There are some ways to deliver mankind from the talons of this troika. It is indeed indulgence in these, and not their very existence, that has brought havoc upon the pantheon of humanity.

For example, suppose we have a bountiful resource of water in the hillside of a mountain, a deep water supply. The water gushing out of that fountain provides water needed by humans, animals, plants and farms. It is needless to say that this generous and life-sustaining supply of water can become poisonous due to mountain slides and change into a serious threat to human beings as well as flora and fauna. Logic requires some individuals to be hired to guard the water supply from possible pollutions and threats.

Now let us analogize natural sciences, technology, humanities, *Weltanschauungen,* moral, cultural and spiritual sciences to clear water that gushes out of human brains. Imagine that the gardeners and farmers who use this water in their gardens and farms reap useful products and raise good livestock, and in short, they take numerous benefits from it. Meanwhile, if the sentries of water supply leave their task in hope of benefiting from the profits of the water like other individuals, this would cost them the destruction of water resource itself.

This is the story of sciences in the past two centuries, particularly since technology and industry have turned into the only game in the town and put the pressure on mankind. It is needless to argue that the guardians of the fountain of ideas have abandoned their duties after the temptation of benefiting from the profits and pleasures of technology and modern sciences. This has naturally led to the decline of original thinkers, both in Moslem countries and the West to the extent that today, sadly, we have no longer any human beings in the caliber of Avicenna, Farabius, MirDamad or Mulla Sadra in the Islamic world, as the Westerners do not have any more like Kant, Saint Augustine, Descartes or Hegel.

I remember some years ago I discussed this very issue with Professor Mayer, who was from Germany. He explicitly said, "Today we have no philosophers in Europe; instead, as a matter of fact, we have employees of philosophy." To put it otherwise, there is no longer any true yearning for profundity and insight.

He also added that Heidegger has been quoted as saying, "We have to travel back two hundred years in time so as to reintroduce our philosophy into the higher philosophical notions we have lost already." Of course, I told him that to have a philosophy that can meaningfully address the fundamental issues and engage with other philosophical systems today, not only is it not necessary to travel back two hundred years in time, but it is in fact irrational to ignore the scientific progress that has happened during these two centuries and to insist on an illogical regression. What we need to do today is to revive the transcendent sense of ontology, which is centered on human beings and has the Supreme Perfection as its goal, in contemporary peoples' minds and to prove them the emergency of activity of that sense which has been quelled due to the conflicts over pleasure and power. Needless to say, by peoples here I mean those men who believe that it is necessary to devote oneself to ontological and philosophical meditations or struggle to engage in such meditations.

Today we have great potentials for development in human sciences in universities and academic centers around the globe that can be put into work by conscientious decisions and intelligible measures of the authorities.

Isn't it really embarrassing that after four thousand years of man's struggles in order to kno his own self and the nature which he lives in, we come across such titles as "*Man the Unknown*", "*Civilization and Its Cure*", "*Civilized Man's Eight Deadly Sins*" or "*World Armament and World Hunger: a Call for Action*", that all bear witness to the human failure in man's epistemic enterprise?

Today, human sciences are no longer able to play their vital role. This has two causes:

1- Man still has many questions about his own existence that have been left unanswered. For example, instead of discussing human institutions, gifts, capabilities and faculties that are major causes of human behaviors in general, we turn to behavioral studies that focus on human behaviors, i.e. the effects, while such studies cannot help us to achieve a whole knowledge of the issue at hand. Logically speaking, knowing such an effect can help us to discover and understand the cause, but in a partial fashion. On the other hand, if we take an integrative method, that is, to merge our knowledge of the effect with knowledge of the causes which can be touched through various ways, we shall obtain more dependable knowledge of human beings. Can the numerous moral and spiritual realities, which are unfortunately not taken into consideration as "values" today, truly not open some ways before us for so that we could discover human institutions?

2- The lack of an integrative view of man that has occulted the logo-driven character of human beings. The votaries of power, wealth and fame have gained the momentum due to the absence of an integral notion of human entity.

Anyway, we have no excuse in this regard and will be accountable before future generations as to our negligence concerning *geisteswissenschaften*. They will ask us about our involvement with nature and forgetting ourselves.

Red: Great figures have always wielded a degree of influence upon their societies throughout history. Sometimes their influence and popularity have far exceeded the borders of their own societies and reached other lands. Having said these, I was wondering if Moslem intelligentsias have indeed had a deep influence on their communities. Where does this influence have its origin? Why are some Moslem figures so influential?

Ja'fari: It is needless to argue that an intellectual's influence upon his society, whether Islamic or non-Islamic, is not a matter of power, since there have many men of power in all societies around the globe that have never been considered an acme of perfection, paragon or a leader. The rise of figures who have dominated and changed human collectivities is more like the outbreak of natural disasters such as volcanic eruptions, earthquakes, deluges and the plague. When Genghis Khan[1] invades a land without offering any righteous ideal to its inhabitants, it is as devastating as the eruption of an earthquake, a flood or a volcano.

Therefore, the cultural, moral and spiritual influence of intelligentsia and distinguished figures in their societies is not essentially a matter of power equations, but in fact it has its origin in the quality of one's individuality. To put it otherwise, those individuals have succeeded in wielding an influence in their society; they indeed were not of a whimsy character.

Having said these, we need to add that this influence is of two kinds: positive and negative. Some of these figures are like natural disasters that unconsciously erupt upon mere selfishness and bring irrecoverable havoc upon human societies. On the other hand, there are conscientious figures in human history that have remained as the acme of perfection and one can even regard them as the "dynamic power of history".

These aforementioned figures are those individuals who have a well-grounded identity as well as a genuine knowledge of their society and the universal soul of humanity. It is only these figures who harbor enlightenment to human societies.

The stability, consistency and magnificence of the character of these figures are functions of their loyalty to useful permanent principles for humanity. As the Holy Quran has stated:

> *He sends down water from the cloud, then watercourses flow (with water) according to their measure, and the torrent bears along the swelling foam, and from what they melt in the fire for the sake of making ornaments or apparatus arises a scum like it; thus does Allah compare truth and falsehood; then as for the scum, it passes away as a worthless thing; and as for that which profits the people, it tarries in the earth; thus does Allah set forth parables.* (Thunder 13:17)

Thus, as the Holy Quran suggests, those things remain that profit people. Accordingly, the secret of figures' perpetuity in history must

---

1- Genghis Khan (1162-1227), founder of the Mongolian empire. (Translator).

be sought for in the services that they have offered to humanity. The more a figure is profitable for humanity, the more everlasting that figure's name in history will be. Although it had been a continuous concern that some prejudiced and unconscious individuals would try to manipulate the historical facts of a given figure or figures, we nonetheless see that a truth has been covertly at work in history to present the figures as they are. This intangible truth could be called either "divine providence" or "sensitive conscience" after historical analysts.

As a result, we should accept that there is a factor in history called "sensitive conscience," but whether this conscience is the acute conscience and pure hearts of human individuals or their brains and sane senses is an issue that remains to be discussed. One might say that a divine providence is at work according to which those individuals who are profitable for humanity and have taken positive steps for it must remain in history. There are numerous historical evidences that support this hypothesis. If we page through history, we shall see hundreds of great human beings upon whose wills were contingent the development of history as well as the existence of higher human principles. The influence of these figures in human history is so powerful and deep-seated that it has even caused some to say that the driving force of history and its justifier is great figures who have emerged in periods of history.

The effective cause of the perpetuity of distinguished figures in history is their adherence to such primordial principles of humanity as perfectionism, justice, committed freedom, human dignity, and moral virtues as well as their efforts to establish useful legal codes and reviving economy.

This is not to say indeed that these figures' *individual* adherence to these lofty ideals has caused them to remain in history; rather, it is their sincere efforts for the fulfillment of these primordial ideals in their society that have eternalized their names.

The other factor that guarantees a figure's permanence in history is the discoveries and inventions that further the genuine aspects of human intelligible life. This is the very issue that the following verse of the Holy Quran underlines:

> **And as for that which profits the people, it tarries in the earth.**
> (Ibid.)

The other factor that causes one figure's name to be recorded in human history is individual gifts such as strong will, courage, intensity, taste, ideas, beauty and the like, which are spontaneous and not used for the fulfillment of human ideals. Then why do these names remain in history? For example, the name of Cleopatra, the famous Egyptian queen, has been recorded in history for her beauty, or it is said that Jahiz the Arab poet was very ugly. Moreover, one's name may have been recorded for one's strong will, although one has not used it for the realization of human ideals. These names are like a metal that is discovered with a distinctive feature among other metals and kept only as an evidence of that distinctive feature as a sample.

The most basic condition for a figure's perpetuality in history is that figure's power to harmonize the existing distinctive gifts and forces the figure has inside. This is a very significant point. The figures that have constructive capitals inside are divided into three groups:

1- Those who can prove to be profitable for the society through the actions and measures that are taken by social authorities for the fulfillment and harmonization of their gifts and forces.

2- Those who fulfill and harmonize their own gifts and forces on their own and take positive steps for the society and its management.

3- Those individuals whose gifts and forces are wasted or misused due to the mismanagements of social authorities. These forces would either erupt like volcanic ashes and destroy the society or do not find a way out and ruin the individual's inside.

To understand the true reach of the influence of figures in their societies and the hearts of their fellow citizens, three factors must be taken into consideration:

I)   The individual's power to influence various aspects of human life including cultural, scientific, religious or moral issues.

II) The people's capacity for the reception of these figures' contributions. It is needless to argue that unless the society is ready for renovation, such figures cannot wield any influence. This reveals how important the social and educational authorities' role is in preparing society for benefiting from the God-given gifts of intelligentsia.

III) A constructive figure must only use his charisma for engaging people in the process of intellectual evolution; moreover, after getting them involved in the process, he should take care so that they are not lured by his charisma and forget the lofty ideals that they are supposed to reach. Said differently, not only must the individual prevent being seduced by his attractiveness, but people should also be warned against becoming bogged down in the slump of this charm.

This spirit in history is mostly found in those individuals who have had trans-physical traits; otherwise, how could those who are plunged in their whims, lusts and carnal desires ever be able to lead the society?

40*

Gudmar Aneer

Subject: Islamic and Western Discourses on Human Rights
Nationality: Swedish/ Major: Law
Dialogue Date: 1988

Aneer: How much do Islamic and Western discourses on human rights have in common?

Ja'fari: One can say that these discourses have at least eighty percent in common. Although these two discourses belong to two different regions of the world with their own distinctive cultural coordinates, they surprisingly have a great deal in common.

The Basic Elements of Universal Human Rights

When we consider the basic elements of universal human rights, we see that these rights must naturally be reserved for all human individuals. These elements are as follows:

1. The principle of decent life
2. The principle of human dignity, which is divided into the right of inherent dignity and the transcendent right of acquired dignity;
3. The principle of education;
4. The principle of committed freedom;
5. The principle of equality.

These "quintuple principles" can be considered as the fundamental and eternal principles of human rights.

Aneer: Have these quintuple principles been addressed in the same tone in two Islamic and Western discourses of human rights?

Ja'fari: As each one of these discourses has its own definition of the nature and value of human beings, they will certainly divide on these basic principles. For example, Western discourse only speaks of the right of life without addressing the condition of decency, while this latter condition stands at the heart of Islam's take on the basic right of life. To put it otherwise, every human individual has the right of decent life, i.e. a life free from compulsion and force. There is no such consideration in the occidentially motivated Universal Declaration of Human Rights, which represents the mainstream Western discourse on human rights.

Moreover, in the principle of inherent dignity, the Universal Declaration of Human Rights confines itself to the natural sense of dignity and does not unfortunately speak of the right of acquired dignity that is decided upon individual moral integrity and virtues without which evolution and purposefulness of life are nonsense. The right of acquired dignity belongs to those who have succeeded in correcting and flourishing their morality and virtues in light of the "intelligible life".

To state the matter differently, if we regard man as a creature who is the product of a thousand inexplicable occurrences, believe that no principle whatsoever justifies man's existence and say that man is an animal who eats, drinks, sleeps, smiles, cries, overcomes and is defeated and finally reproduces one or two kinds of itself and then passes away, such a human being does not need any right of acquired and evaluative dignity. But it is needless to argue that if we content ourselves to give up the idea of virtue, moral integrity and acquired dignity, sooner or later our civilized societies will turn into jungle or even into something worse than jungle. I said something "worse than a jungle" because in a jungle, natural instincts are satisfied upon some rules. In other words, animals at least know how to regulate their sexual affairs and keep it in its natural course. They do not systematically ruin their environment, and when they find their food, they do not disturb other animals' privacy. But man, who does not consider necessary the evaluative dignity and virtue, is to take the control of all food supplies of the world, even if millions of people may die of hunger.

Although man lives in a world of information technology, since he has not succeeded in adjusting his own internal selfishness, it can be stated that he lives in a covered jungle. Thus, a system of human rights that has the claim of universality must sooner or later observe the principle of evaluative dignity; otherwise, human beings will uproot themselves by their own hands, as conscientious thinkers have predicted long ago.

The problem humanity is facing in the twenty-first century is no longer food or hygiene, although some countries are under heavy economic pressures. Nonetheless, is man's major problem in this century how mankind should survive?[1] The problem is that virtue, honor and moral integrity, without which no telos is conceivable for human life, have been lost and the man has turned into unconscious cogs of a machine. In other words, humanity is plunged in confusion. Everyday man waits for the night to come, and at night, he waits for the day to dawn; thus, he whiles away his life with the unconscious compulsion of consumerism as well as factors of power.

As "compulsion does not last", in philosophical parlance, compulsory life does not last either; even if the sense of compulsion lasts, it will continue in the form of a fake compulsory life.

As I already mentioned, Islam speaks of the right of a decent life. This is indeed a requirement of the right of inherent dignity. Man should live a decent life, not merely a biological life. Western thinkers need to revise the respective article of this right in the Universal Declaration of Human Rights.

Aneer: Do you see any difference between Islamic and Western discourses of human rights on the principle of freedom?

Ja'fari: This principle is crucial for human decent life and man's future. Thus, we need to interpret freedom. What does it mean when we say that man is free?

Islam has a committed understanding of freedom. There is no doubt that even other non-Islamic alternative systems of human rights say that Western or Eastern discourses do not tolerate unconditional freedom, as it has many paradoxical consequences.

I think they need to add this stipulation, i.e. *committed*, to the article pertaining freedom in order to avoid possible misunderstandings. What a great and magnificent bounty freedom is indeed! It is needless to argue that freedom in this sense cannot be understood as *doing whatever one wants to do,* as this is exactly the natural course of events in outside world that man shares it with other creatures. Then what distinguishes the man from the rest?

It is obvious that the freedom that man achieves through intellectual and spiritual evolution and by which gives a meaning to human life is not unconditional. This is accepted by all insightful scholars. As we have mentioned earlier, if freedom is supposed to be understood as an unconditional property, the question which arises quickly asks whether other individuals have the same unconditional freedom or not. This would end up in fatal confrontations and endanger human

---

1- See Ja'fari, M. T. (2014): *Human Universal Rights: A Comparative Research in Islam and the West.* P. 111, Human Survival in the 21th century.

life itself. As a result, freedom needs to be committed.

On the other hand, human individual freedom is also conditional. This is the very point that distinguishes Islamic discourse on human rights from Western discourse. To put it otherwise, not only should human freedom not violate other people's rights, but it should not ruin the individual, either. Islam sees this world as a transitory pathway for human evolution that leads man to eternity. This pathway has its own laws and rules that have to be observed. Consequently, man should exercise his freedom within the framework of these rules.

Then human freedom, according to Islamic discourse of human rights, is to be committed in two ways:

1. This freedom should not violate other people's rights
2. Moreover, it should not hamper human individual evolution and growth, either.

If I plunge myself in pleasures and use everything around me to reach pleasure, what will happen to intellection then? Shouldn't I use this magnificent bounty to fulfill my intelligible life? What will come of justice, individual growth, love, kindness and humane feelings then? Unconditional freedom destroys moral ideals and also the human potential for perfection.

As a result, what should be taken into consideration is that if we are seeking after an intelligible life for humanity that can be fulfilled in this world, we must make the freedom conditional upon commitment in order to prevent from its possible conflicts with the laws that govern human life in two domains of "isness" and "oughtness".

Aneer: Do you agree with freedom of expression and thought and other freedoms that are promoted by the Western discourse of human rights as inalienable rights of humanity?

Ja'fari: Freedom of thought is as necessary as freedom of expression and propagation. These are basic and inalienable rights of humanity. But the question is that whether these freedoms must be considered unconditional or conditional.

For example, is it to the human society's interest to allow the citizens to have any baseless and nonsense thought regardless of its confliction with principles and values? Is this logical? Nobody will ever give a positive answer to these questions. To have a sane life and character, man needs to have sane thoughts and ideas.

We need to have in mind that despite of their differences, almost all civilized societies have common grounds in principles and ideas. Moreover, there are sufficient common ideas that can be the source of sane thoughts for human individuals. It is only up to social authorities worldwide to leave antagonisms aside and work together for the promotion of human honor and sane ideas. To put it otherwise, there is no doubt that we have common ideas upon which we can have fair coexistence. It must be promoted that as I should respect other people's right of decent life, they also have to respect my right of decent life, as the understanding of these common rights and principles is a primordial issue.

It can turn into a common idea of human individuals that the underestimation of an individual's work could destroy his life and character. The appreciation of this idea does not require us to immerse ourselves in the history of civilization, but suffices it to listen to our conscience. There are numerous examples of such universal principles and ideas that can bring about an intelligible coexistence for us.

Aneer: I think we – Easterners and Westerners – need to gather around a table and discuss these issues and come up with practical solutions for global antagonisms.

Ja'fari: I agree. Such debates are indeed vital for the achievement of global peace and understanding.

41

Rahim Kamil Sulaiman

Subject: Islamic Issues
Nationality: Malaysian/ Major: Cleric
Dialogue Date: 1988

Mr. Rahim Kamel Suleyman held several dialogs with Allameh Ja'fari in 1988. Their conversation mainly focused on various Islamic issues of the times. Rahim Kamel Suleyman began by explaining his Islamic endeavors in Malaysia and the procedures he used for his activities. Then he posed a question he needed elaboration and research on. His question mainly pertained to the attitude societies nowadays have toward Islam.

Sulaiman: How should we preach Islamic ideas in the contemporary world?

Ja'fari: If we had met the condition of honesty in the exposition of other people and schools' ideas and beliefs, many of today's human pains would have been cured. Most people are not able to conduct an independent and thorough research of schools of thoughts due to their numerous engagements in everyday life. They always listen to the "preaches", and unfortunately, the scholars and thinkers who are interpreting other schools of thought for them suffer from serious deficiencies. We saw with our own eyes what fatal mistakes were made during the exposition of the principles of Shi'ism by the scholars of other societies! Ahmad Amin, the author of *The Dawn of Islam*, is an example of such scholars. I was in Najaf when he came over. His essays of Shi'ism contained some irrelevant stuff. The late Ayatollah Sheikh Hussein Kashif ul-Ghitah, a distinguished and popular jurisprudential authority of that era, was still alive. Ahmad Amin visited the Ayatollah. Sheikh Hussein asked him, "Whence have you driven these incorrect stuffs on Shi'ism?" "I have taken them from Orientalists," Amin retorted. The Ayatollah said, "Aren't we children of the same family? Why should you seek to know me and my ideas through strangers who take their knowledge from us and distort it?" It is quoted that the Sheik took Amin to his library and told him, "Here I have some original books on Shi'ism as well as several books on Sunnism. When I decide to write any anything about Sunnism, I use only the original Sunnite sources and never trust the words of those who have no basis in Islam. This is the logic of scientific research." It is said that Amin then apologized for his mistakes.

Everyone who pitches in to know a school of thought must keep this anecdote in mind. How could a researcher put trust in the propagations of international mass media, which are mostly uninformed of matters or even after unrealistic objectives? Accordingly, I believe that if we could provide unbiased inquiries of Islam and other schools of thought based on the existing realities, then man would not resist the truth.

As a result, every plot for the obscuration of Islam and its principles is doomed to failure as the original sources are available to everyone. One day, humanity will eventually understand how mankind has been deceived in regard to the true nature of Islam.

The issue that needs to be addressed today is that if the scholars of non-Islamic societies are to set out general speculations of the spiritual aspect of humanity and come up with intelligible plans, they will undoubtedly need to form professional panels of religious studies. This is a task that must be fulfilled by universities and academic centers, as all psychologists, psychiatrists and scholars of human sciences endorse the fact that it is only religion that can give a meaningful account of the spiritual aspects of human existence. This is a very significant issue as to human life that cannot be made a victim of human whims, pleasures and lusts. The negligence of this vital issue is tantamount to turning a blind eye to human sciences that unanimously approve the authenticity of religious sense in human existence, although they may have different interpretations of it.

Having said these, if social authorities and academicians are to take positive steps for humanity, I don't know anything more urgent and necessary than arranging basic studies of the nature and functions of religion as well as of the historical achievements of religions in a comparative fashion. Unfortunately, the debates held on these issues are today limited to some formal conferences and symposiums. Furthermore, sometimes even these conferences are changed into the maneuver ground for the shallow *despisers of religion*. To avoid such an exhaustion of energy and time, some fundamental and comparative studies must be planned on a global scale of the commonalities and differences of the world's religions under the supervision of leading experts.

I believe that if we successfully manage to arrange such impartial comparative studies on world religions upon logical, philosophical and scientific methods, we will score an unprecedented epoch-making victory in the whole course of the history of mankind. Of course, I am not so optimistic about authorities in this regard. To put it otherwise, one cannot simply imagine that a day will come when politicians will put aside their concerns over their offices and seek to find a solution to human fatal conflicts via arranging a global, fundamental study on the spiritual aspect of human existence.

Such a study can provide a genuine ground for arriving at true universal human rights; otherwise, speaking of the universal codes of human rights in the face of so many conflicting cultures, lands, races and geographical environments would not be a rational talk.

Let us not neglect religion as the genuine manifestation of human spirituality. To achieve their selfish objectives, some have blurred this brilliant side of human existence via the temporary narcotization and metamorphosis of humanity.

To state the matter differently, Islam, Christianity, Judaism, Hinduism, Buddhism, Zoroastrianism and other spiritual schools can come together and find a common ground for coexistence and arrange a joint research program for studying their differences based upon realities. The fact that we see today some shallow minds claiming that human reason has reached a point that it no longer needs religion is merely a consolation before the loss of the life-giving aspect of religion; in fact, it does not basically express any truth. Moreover, no social, moral and even political school can ever fulfill the primordial ideals of human life unless it is somehow informed by religion.

For example, for some time now, democracy has been posed as a scientific and humanistic school, but we know that democratic ideas have their own theoretical and practical paradoxes, as no correct definition has yet been offered of democracy. Then, as an accountable school before all aspects of human life, democracy should turn to religion in order to satisfy deep human senses and transcendent reason. Democracy is indeed the ideal of humanity, but could we successfully lead humanity on the course of intelligible life by giving unconditional and uncommitted freedom to selfish egotists and despots? If someone thinks so, we shall respect his opinion, but we have a different view. We need to search for a more intelligible and consistent notion of freedom through a comparative study of different schools of thought. This task has not yet been undertaken by anyone.

We have to see whether Machiavellianism is useful for humanity; can it be regarded as a politics that respects and justifies human lives? It remains still to be answered by researchers and scholars whether the victimization of valuable truths for transitory ends has been helpful for man or not   pon rational principles ai   we expect to have a peace

42

Messrs. Martinson, Mathner Markov and Daniello Trec

Subject: Islam and the West on Universal Human Rights
Nationality: Swedish and Yugoslavian/ Major: Law
Dialogue Date: 1988

This dialogue was held amid a conference on Human Rights in Manila, the Philippines, with Professor Martinson, who was the chair of the conference, and his colleagues. It was focused on comparative assessments of Western and Islamic discourses on human rights.

Ja'fari: The charter of human rights, which has been prepared in the West, shares many points with the Islamic discourse of human rights. However, there are some points of disagreement that can hopefully be tackled via further discussions and researches.

Martinson: Would you speak of the points of disagreement?

Ja'fari: The issue that is jointly highlighted by both Western and Islamic discourses on human rights is that of human inherent dignity and honor. It does indeed deserve such an attention, but I think the 19th article of the Universal Declaration of Human Rights in fact contradicts human inherent dignity and honor. It reads:

> *Everyone has the right to freedom of opinion and expression; this right includes freedom to hold opinions without interference and to seek, receive and impart information and ideas through any media and regardless of frontiers.*

Thus, if someone or a group uses this article as a resort to ruin the reputation and honor of a group or a society in the mass media, what kind of action should subsequently be taken against that person or group? Do human rights allow people's reputations to be ruined in the name of freedom of opinion and expression?!

Martinson et al: Human dignity and honor should never be violated, and we also insist on this issue.

Ja'fari: I think a condition must be added to the 19th article to the effect that everyone should have the right to freedom of opinion and expression provided that they do not ruin other people's reputation, honor and dignity.

An idea or a theory may once be critically assessed based on scientific methods and scientific outlook. However, sometimes criticisms are directed toward the character and reputation of a writer or theoretician. Where should this innocent individual lodge his complaint then? Does this innocent victim of unconditional right of freedom of expression have the right to lodge a complaint at all? Scientific debates have their own logic. Nobody would be offended by the critiques that are made of his ideas or theories. Of course, we know that scientific criticism has its own etiquettes that must be observed so that nobody feels insulted.[1]

We need to see if human thought has reached that degree of maturity that would enables man to distinguish between good and evil, beautiful and ugly or white and black, so that we may confer upon man an unconditional right of freedom of opinion. Is the human condition indeed so? Are all Easterners Avicenna, Averroes, Suhrewardi, MirDamad and Mullah Sadra, and are all Westerners Descartes, Kant and Hegel so that one could say whatever one wants to? In other words, have these people have reached the point of maturity at which they can easily recognize the truth from the wrong?

We know that such a degree of maturity has not yet ben reached; rather, human understanding has unfortunately been so dulled by the last machine-plagued century that if you ask an average man "Whence have you come?" he will only stare at you! That is, man can not even understand your question. Accordingly, we are currently living in an era of the *occultation* of all ideologies, worldviews and universal outlooks.

The freedom of thought and expression has so vastly expanded that everyone allows themselves to say whatever they want. No doubt, truths are tightly enfolded in wrongs. This is why we see today that not only are youth caught with nihilistic ideas, but the students of human sciences and philosophy are far fewer in number than other disciplines as there are few people who take thinking serious. The whole world is now fraught with various means of narcotization, as people want to dull their senses. If we shut our eyes to these sore

---

1- Sadly, no answer was given in this regard.

realities today, history shall expose us in future to our deplorable past. The freedom of thought and expression is necessary, but we should first prepare the required conditions and enhance the knowledge of societies; when human thought has not been advanced enough s, human beings will hastily pose any theory coming to their minds and then finds themselves surrounded by paradoxes. As a result, under the shower of paradoxes, man will be forced to deny everything. "I should only eat and drink," he will think, "as my death is coming." This is the logic of contemporary world.

As I have frequently indicated in my dialogues and lectures, excessive indulgences have been done as to freedom of expression and thought. Of course, speaking of such issues is pleasurable, like the irrational pleasure of a candle's light in daylight. However, the source of that fake light is limited, and when night comes, man will have to remain in darkness. Sa'di, may he rest in divine peace, has said:

The poor-minded person who sits by a candle in daylight

Very soon you shall see him sitting in the darkness at night.

It is indeed pleasant to chatter on such issues, and one would admit that these issues are good means to deceive simple minds. Nevertheless, when a scholar treads on his scientific and human conscience, not only will his words turn out to be of no avail, but they will also prove to be harmful as well.

I am always filled with wonder when I read the following remark that has been attributed to Voltaire:

I am ready to sacrifice my life for your freedom of expression although I would be against your opinions.

This axiom, when not practiced in its true spirit, represents an uncommitted view on freedom that may result in the outburst of passionate volcanoes of human carnal desires which would subsequently exterminate human life on the earth!! Voltaire was wise enough to create room for his world-view through the above-mentioned statement, but could not create an open space for others.

Thus conceived, the freedom of expression that is used against the social and spiritual interests of humanity is "unintelligible freedom," that is similar to "the sword at the hand of a drunken man"; otherwise, intelligible freedom is surely protected by the rule of natural law. To put the matter in clear terms, unintelligible freedom is a freedom that helps the ego and its baser self to extinguish its carnal lust to any limits. It is ironical that we can spend millions on experiments on different animals to test the effectiveness of a medicine for headache, and then creating havoc for animal rights in the media, but how much time and energy are we really going to expend for the cause of humanity – for intelligible freedom – as the hallmark of human existence? While medical experiments would have few animal fatalities, any negligence in terms of the ultra-significant issues of humanities could result in the annihilation of the whole mankind.

***

In a chapter of his *Human Universal Rights: A Comparative Research in Islam and the West* (2014), Ja'fari writes:

The Freedom of Expression and Speech in Islam

The expression of realities useful for humanity both in material and spiritual domains not only is free, but in fact anyone who knows a reality and has the ability to express it, and yet deprives people from this reality, deserves to be convicted and shall be reproved both in this world and hereafter. The following verses of the Holy Quran eloquently depict this truth:

> *O followers of the book! Why do you confound the truth with the falsehood and hide the truth while you know?*

(The House of Imran 3: 71)

> *Surely those who conceal the clear proofs and the guidance that we revealed after we made it clear in the book for men, these it is whom Allah shall curse, and those who curse shall curse them (too).*

(The Cow 2:159)

Although the addressees of the first verse are the followers of book, the second one is nonetheless more general in its approach; it holds "clear proofs" and "guidance" as the foundations for the true form of life (i.e., intelligible life). This injunction is applicable to all kinds of concealment and concealers of truth, hiding clear proofs and obstructing guidance.

There are numerous narrations from the Holy Prophet (PBUH) and his progeny on the necessity of expression of practical truths. Here we shall suffice to some examples of them:

1- *Imam Al-Sadegh (PBUH) has stated, "I read in the book of Imam Ali (PBUH) that before making the ignorant promise to seek knowledge, God charged the men of knowledge with the duty of the munificence of wisdom and knowledge, since knowledge existed before the ignorance."* [1]

2- *Imam Al-Sadegh (PBUH) was quoted as saying, "Jesus addressed the Israelites by saying, 'O' Israelites! Don't share wisdom with the ignorant, as it would be an injustice to knowledge and wisdom. And do not conceal knowledge from the men of wisdom, as it would be an injustice to these people."* [2]

3- *Anyone who teaches a good shall be awarded like the one who has carried out that good deed.* [3]

4- *Verily, the knower who hides his knowledge shall be resurrected in the Day of Judgment in a state in which no one could bear his putrid smell.* [4]

5- *All people are members of Allah's family, and their most blessed one with the Lord, is the one who is most beneficial for the members of Allah's family.* [5]

The following results could be deduced from the above-mentioned quotations:

I) The expression of realities and truths is an obligatory practice for those who know them, since God has obliged the possessors of knowledge to disseminate their knowledge.

II) These quotations are equally applied to every kind of knowledge without any exception. According to reason and the two previously cited verses of the Holy Quran, this knowledge should be both materially and spiritually useful for humanity.

III) God has made the men of knowledge promise to disseminate their knowledge and teach the ignorant who are in sacred covenant with Him and also to seek ever increase in knowledge.

IV) Knowledge and wisdom should not be shared with those who express estrangement with it or who are declared the enemies of wisdom, since they do not know its value and would stand against it; as Imam Ali (PBUH) has eloquently stated:

People are the enemies of what they do not know. [6]

1- Kolayni, Muhammad ibn Ya'qūb, *Usul Al-Kafi*, Vol. 1.

2- Ibid.

3- Ibid.

4- Sheikh Al-Horre Al-Ameli, *Was'ael Al-Shi'ah*, Vol 6.

5- Ibid.

6- *Nahjulbalaghah*, Aphorisms 172.

V) Wisdom should not be concealed from the people of knowledge, since this is an unforgivable injustice to enlightened souls. The reason for this injustice lies in the fact that these concealed truths could easily lead people to or at least bring them nearer to wisdom.

VI) Everyone who teaches something to people that is gainful for them shall be benefitted from the advantages of it. The teaching material here includes everything that is of avail for the people.

VII) Those who know some useful truths and hide them from the public shall be punished on the Day of Judgment.

VIII) Social profitability is the criterion for existential excellence, i.e. those who are more beneficial for their society and fellow human beings are of more value for God.

Thus, freedom of expression in Islam is the necessary prerequisite of knowledge dissemination which is of vital significance for social life. In addition, those who deprive the public from necessary information should be treated like social agitators.[1]

1- Ja'fari, M. T. (2014): *Human Universal Rights: A Comparative Research in Islam and the West.*

43

Simone Jeanne Zakiri, Ava Sivovic, Fatima Kamara,
Ingrid Kessler, Lara Nasr, Sayyedih Nawwab, Georgina
Wathin, Joon Peep, Ulya Rowa, Jelvisa Lontu, Invara Eso,
Marietta Stepaniants

Subject: Islam on Women & Khayyam Revisited

Countries: France, Sierra Leon, Germany, Lebanon, Pakistan, Hungary, Philippines and USSR

Majors: Various Branches of Science

Dialogue Date: 1988

In this visit, the majority of the audience asked the Allameh to speak of the legal and evaluative status of women in Islam.

Ja'fari: As you know, Islam's stance on women has been largely distorted in books and other cultural mediums. Accordingly, some people have thought that Islam does not observe justice as to women. As a matter of fact, however, as Islamic sources clearly show, Islam has distinguished the equality regarded for men and women and as well as administering justice between them. There is no doubt that if Islam had stated that men and women are equal in their all of their biological, physiological, psychological and mental aspects, this would have been in contradiction with the reality. I don't think we can find anyone in this world who has sufficient knowledge of men and women and says such things.

There is no doubt that each one of these two sexes has been created in their own peculiar way. This issue has already been sufficiently researched. It remains only to ask if this difference in creation makes one of them perfect and the other imperfect. No, never! This is indeed a matter of diversity rather than being an issue of imperfection versus perfection.

To put it otherwise, we have two types of classification: one based on [the normative dichotomy of] perfection versus imperfection and the other based on diversity of existential aspects. In the eightieth sermon of the *Nahjulbalaghah*, where Imam Ali (PBUH) has described women as "inadequate in respect to reason", "inadequate in respect to fortune" and "inadequate in respect to faith", one can say that this is not definitely an issue of women's evaluative identity or their peculiar creation. Rather, it in fact depicts the quality of women's existential determination as compared to men, since if these inadequacies were matters of women's imperfection versus men, it would contradict the verse of the Holy Quran that reads, *"Certainly we created man in the best make"* (The Fig 95:4), to which Imam Ali (PBUH) was loyal more than anyone else.

One cannot say that a pear is imperfect as compared to an apple or vice versa; in fact, they are two different types of fruit. Likewise, one cannot claim that a given metal is more perfect than other metals, as each one of these metals has its own particular substantive identity. On the other hand, the *Nahjulbalaghah* has been born out of the Quran, so how can it contradict the Quran?

These differences have only affected the superstructure of life in general rather than the essential truths and the substance of the generic life of women and men. For example, a man is more competent when it comes to taking up hard economic affairs, defending his country and bearing the hardships and troubles of life. On the other hand, the main burden of reproduction is on a woman's shoulders and this imposes more limitations on her. Man has *naturally* more freedom in this respect. As Simone de Beauvoir[1] has quoted from Nietzsche:

> *A woman's passion, a total renunciation of all rights of her own, postulates precisely that the same feeling, the same desire for renunciation, exists also in the other sex, for if both made this renunciation for love, there would result, on my word I do not know just what, shall we say, perhaps, the horror of nothingness? The woman wishes to be taken ... she demands, therefore, someone to take her, someone who does not give himself, who does not abandon himself, but who wishes, on the contrary, to enrich his ego through love ... The woman gives herself, the man adds to himself by taking her."* [2]

1- (1908-1986) French writer and philosopher, prominent feminist, and author of *The Second Sex* (1949) (Translator).

2- *The Second Sex* (1956), p. 623 [translated into English by H. M. Parshley, Jonathan Cape Publishers, London].

A woman can reach the heights of value and virtue through delivering herself from the bondages of carnal desires and mental decays. The Quran has explicitly announced that piety is the only criterion of value equally regarded for men and women.

It seems that a woman has the privilege to taste the very flavor of life of which a man only has a conceptual notion of. Man can develop arguments, concepts and judgments of life, but he never can taste the flavor of life as woman does. Thus, God has willed the mother to keep her close maternal relations with the child until the maturation of the child's sentiments and emotions. To put the matter in other words, it is indeed the mother who familiarizes the child with the genuine sense of life and its sentiments and emotions. Accordingly, whenever the history of mankind has produced cases in which children's upbringing has been undertaken by men, states or collective managements, we do not see any sign of these genuine sentiments and emotions. In Sir Russell's parlance, "Those children who are reared under collective managements are better for war!"

On the other hand, men, due to their involvement in the tough turbulences of life, have some discursive and rational capabilities which are not seen almost in any woman. If we expect the same muscular strength and involvement in hardships of life from women which we see in men, we would have wrongly set ourselves at loggerheads with reality. A woman's existential delicacy impedes her from getting involved in disagreeable and burdensome affairs. Some might object that a woman's existential solidity before tragic events not only is not lesser but in fact even, in some cases, more than that of a man. These critics need to take it into account that steadiness before shocking occurrences is other than the reconstruction of character after sequential failures.

To put it otherwise, due to her significant mission regarding the continuance of the human generation, a woman has more power for the reconstruction of life and character. In fact, she can either keep herself away from burdensome occurrences or reconstruct her character failure in no time. On the other hand, we should not underestimate a woman's feeling concerning the necessity of her dependence on man. Of course, these differences are legitimate when both sexes live their life in natural way; otherwise, one can neglect them via some machinistic manipulations of the twain. In other words, a man may be metamorphosed into a woman and vice versa.

But as to a woman's existential value, we should say that her value in

Islam is *only and only* dependent on her character and piety – i.e., her moral integrity – as it is also the case with that of a man. God has not prioritized any of the twain in this case. As the Quran explicitly states:

> *O you men! Surely we have created you of a male and a female, and made you tribes and families that you may know each other; surely the most honorable of you with Allah is the one among you most careful (of his duty); surely Allah is knowing, aware.* (The Apartments 49:13)

Moreover, other sources also prove that existential value in Islam is a matter of moral integrity and virtue and those who claim that Islam and other divine schools have degraded women are intentionally defaming religion.

Stepaniants: Do Islamic beliefs and rules change with time?

Ja'fari: We need to take it into account that Islamic worldview is grounded upon five pillars:

The First Pillar is elemental beliefs which are based on human primordial nature, common sense and conscience and thus will never be changed or modified. To put it in different words, regarding man's current existential status, mental structure and quadruple primordial relationships, human beings *must* hold these elementary dogmas which are termed as articles of faith in Islam, as a natural and not a devotional "ought".

For example, Moslems believe that religion is a necessity for man and that religion is not achievable without the hypothesis that God exists, is one, does not tolerate any plurality and has attributes of perfection all are rooted in human primordial nature, sane sense and conscience and have not been imposed on human individuals even by prophets. Even the belief that this world must wrap up on Judgment Day is an issue of primordial conscience.

The Second Pillar involves morals, consisting of a set of principles and propositions the observation of which suits human existence and is necessary for human intellectual evolution. Furthermore, morals are also concerned with human basic needs which are fixed and unchangeable. For example, *"One must do what one expects another to do in a similar situation"* or *"Do not trample human dignity and honor"* are primordial principles of morality that remain intact forever, even if they find different interpretations in various societies and times.

The Third Pillar is principal rules which are consisted of rules that have been preached by the Prophet Muhammad (PBUH) upon human routine needs and people are obliged to observe them like daily pray, fast, pilgrimage to Mecca as well as the prohibition of lying and fornication, homicide and drinking liquors. These rules have been ordained based on human primary needs and never will change. Even myriads of changes in human life cannot change the baseness of homicide. No one would ever say that man's essential yearning for perfection has disappeared due to the changes that have happened in science, industry and art a; such a claim is tantamount to saying that man is no longer a human being! Of course, the applications and extensions of these rules would change from time to time, but such changes do not affect the very existence of these elementary rules.

The Fourth Pillar is secondary rules which are determined by the leaders of the Islamic community for addressing a newly emerged situation. It is needless to argue that these rules are canceled as soon as the situation disappears, like the boycott of tobacco by Mirzayi Shirazi. Thus, secondary rules change as they have their origin in changing situations.

The Fifth Pillar involves everyday life issues that require human individual rational engagements in order to fulfill man's needs. In these two cases (i.e. secondary issues and decress), Islam has a progressive approach, whereas in the case of moral ethics, ideological issues and primary decrees, Islam takes a pioneer stand – they cannot be changed with one's tendencies or desires. Furthermore, no factor or motive aiming to change them should arise wither, for they are based on man's basic needs. Secondary decrees and issues dependent upon various issues, however, are subject to change. For example, once men had to use animals and sometimes ships as their vehicles and means of transport to travel or go to Hajj, but today animals have given their place to airplanes and coaches, which are obviously far superior when it comes to safety and ability. Thus, new issues have emerged along with new forms of transportation that need to be dealt with new methods and visions, and when the arising issues fade away, the decrees pertaining to them will fade away as well. Nevertheless, articles of faith, morals and principal rules are unchangeable and nobody can ever impose their desires on them as they are rooted in human primordial needs.

Joan Peep: What is your idea about Khayyam's character? Can his character be regarded as acceptable?

Ja'fari: I have done some research on the philosophical, scientific, religious and literary aspects of Khayyam's character. Of course, no one can ever regard himself a truly competent authority on such figures as Khayyam. Anyway, I have read and researched Khayyam for some years past and here I can speak my mind of him as follows:

Firstly, many [cynical] quatrains have been attributed to Khayyam, the number of which sometimes exceeds thousand quatrains. Most of these quatrains do not indeed belong to Khayyam. According to my studies, Khayyam has only composed ten or fifteen quatrains on undependability of world. Some scholars believe that the poet has written 147 quatrains. Although here I am not to say the last word on this issue, what one can seemingly attribute to this scientific and philosophical figure is a limited number of quatrains which, as we mentioned earlier, are mostly about the undependability of world, the passing of time, the extermination of beauties, the demolition of habitations and the limitation of human knowledge. These are among the issues that Khayyam scholars are agreed upon.

In these quatrains, Khayyam has not said even a single unrealistic word. What adds to the obscurity is the fact that some nihilistic verses are being attributed to this man. There is no doubt that these quatrains are unique in view of their literary style, but the question is that how can one attribute such cynical verses to a figure in Khayyam's size who is aligned with Avicenna and Abu Ali Bukhari? This is unbelievable.

On the other hand, in the biographical works which I have read of Khayyam, I have seen about eleven cases in which he has been regarded as "Imam," such as al-Imam al-Khayyami and Hujat ul-Haqq Abu al-Fath al-Imam Omar Ibn Ibrahim Khayyami. Even Zamakhshari has said:

> My first meeting with the world's philosopher and man of wisdom, Sheikh Imam Khayyami, had been in Faridi's session.

In no Islamic, literary or philosophical history has this title ever been used for an ordinary poet who has a melancholic notion of reality. Such person is not called "Imam," for this title suggests that its owner has reached the acme of knowledge and wisdom as well as piety and gnosis. Thus, these cynical verses cannot be attributed to Khayyam.

Joan Peep: Then you have a negative view of Khayyam's quatrains?

Ja'fari: No, my point of view is not a negative one. Literarily speaking, these so-called Khayyam quatrains are among the invaluable heritages of Persian literature. But they have not been composed by a philosopher of Khayyam's caliber, for they are communicating a shallow and obscure understanding of reality.

For example, these quatrains just complain about the undependability of life and temporariness of beauties without offering any account of them in the context of the overall scheme of reality. These quatrains owe much of their reputation to the one who they are attributed to, not to their contents, as he is a philosopher who is ranked after Avicenna and has designed an alternative non-Euclidean geometry. We need to examine the contents of these quatrains and to see which one really suits Khayyam's scientific and philosophical stature.

Surprisingly, an Iranian scholar has recently published a sentimental and shallow essay of Khayyam in which he claims that Khayyam's quatrains have solved all philosophical problems! When I read this book, I couldn't help but wonder what the author was saying. These quatrains only express pains and difficulties and do not even solve a single problem. Then what is to be done as to the solutions? Such judgments have their own roots in extremisms that unfortunately afflict us.

Thus, in our critical assessment of the so-called Khayyamesque quatrains, Ms. Joan, we need to take two points into earnest consideration: firstly, these quatrains are truly powerful and intact from a literary point of view and hence have a unique place in Persian literature. Secondly, Khayyamesque quatrains speak of human epistemic limitations, pains and deficiencies. That is all! They contain no solution to human problems. Humanity expects indeed more than this from a thinker of Khayyam's status. Wounds are not redressed via being spotlighted, but they need cures.

Joan Peep: Why do people in the East and the West know Khayyam more with these quatrains rather than through his scientific theories?

Ja'fari: Fitzgerald translated these quatrains into English and published them in the UK wherefrom they were introduced to the whole Europe. They owe their reputation mostly to hedonism,[1] which they preach. According to them, one can easily escape confronting existential questions by saying "*Stick to the moment you have*". Thus, these quatrains were appreciated by hedonist communities in Europe. But in Islamic societies, their literary aspect was taken more seriously than their contents. As a result, we should ask why these quatrains

1- A doctrine which considers pleasure to be the ultimate goal. (Translator).

became so famous despite their stereotypic contents. The answer is because they were attributed to Khayyam. These quatrains couldn't have such a vast audience if they were attributed to an ordinary poet. Now we need to see where Khayyam's importance lies now that his name scores such a reputation for these quatrains? There is no doubt that Khayyam's importance lies in his epistemic aspects (science and philosophy), particularly in mathematics. It is also for sure that he is a Peripatetic philosopher whose philosophy is focused on theological issues. Thus, nihilism does not suit the aforementioned philosophical taste.

44*

Mr. Finn Thiessen

**Subject: The Common Principles of Revealed Religions
Nationality: Danish/ Major: Cultural Studies
Dialogue Date: 1989**

Tiessen: Do you think that we can compare the principles of Islam and Christianity with each other?

Ja'fari: Judaism, Christianity, Islam, Zoroastrianism and Sabians[1] have been cited in the Quran as revealed religions. We have to see what the common grounds of these religions are. Can we have a just, satisfactory coexistence in future upon these common grounds? Of course, it is indeed quite unintelligible today to expect all revealed religions to be in total agreement with each other. However, when we take a closer look at them, we find that all of them are agreed upon some basic principles. One of these principles is that happiness is impossible without religion. It is through religious worldview and religious systems of values and virtues that man can touch happiness. This is a common view held almost by all world religions. Once again, when we study them carefully, we see that all religions embrace the idea that the universe has been created for a higher purpose and it is not a purposeless phenomenon composed of a set of unconscious elements of nature. On the other hand, all of these religions share the idea that this complicated design has an intelligent designer. In other words, all revealed religions believe that God has created all creatures without having any personal interest in them; as a matter of fact, God has put them on the course of evolution and prosperity.

The belief that humanity has a Day of Judgment ahead of him on which he must stand to trial for his actions is another point of communion. This is also the case with the idea that human happiness lies in embracing the call of reason and conscience as well as the preachings of God-sent prophets who have been delegated to show man that a prosperous life requires justice, cooperation and friendship.

1- The followers of the Prophet John (PBUH).

To put it otherwise, true happiness is achieved when all human individuals see themselves as members of the same whole and care for each other.

Some might argue that this is merely a utopian idea that does not match the current states of affairs, as the contemporary world is divided into two parts – rich and poor. The rich part is sorely unaware of the pains and troubles of the poor part. Anyway, this careless unawareness cannot last forever.

Amongst the other points of agreement is the belief that people have the right to a decent life, all people have the right to inherent dignity and honor as well as the right to committed freedom. All human individuals are equal before the law; everyone has the right to have equal access to education, hygiene and proper culture. I do not think any revealed religion would ever challenge these rights. Aren't these enough for us to have a peaceful and intelligible life in history? These principles together embody the primordial religion of Abraham that has been revealed through human history in the form of different religions in the East as well as in the West. We must work together to fulfill these principles.

Thus, we should not allow seditionists to divide human collectivities for their evil purposes and interests.

45

Elizabeth Gamlin
(Second Interview)

Subject: The Sources of Universal Human Rights in Islam
Nationality: British/ Major: Law/ Dialogue Date: 1989

Gamlin: Are there genuine sources for human rights in Islam or have these codes been adopted by jurists and Moslem scholars?

Ja'fari: We need to have in mind that the universal codes of human rights are best understood in the context of revealed religions, as they depict the most universal picture of humanity. As one can readily see in original Islamic sources, these universal rights of humanity have been explicitly underlined.

Among the interesting points that have to be taken into earnest consideration is the fact that Islam has addressed two groups in its discussions of rights and obligations:

The first group consists of believers and Moslems.

The second group includes all human beings. When Islam speaks of "mankind", " children of Adam", "Allah's servants", "the believers", "the seed of Adam" and "humanity," the latter group is intended. In all these cases, the rights and obligations that Islam has spoken of are applicable to all human societies.

A historical piece of evidence in regard to this issue is the fact that when Moslem governments were at the helm, the stronger the Islamic element of those governments was, the happier the people consequently were.

Moreover, they respected the beliefs and ideals of people and their holy places and also paid enough attention to their economic and legal issues. Gustav Le Bon's *La Civilization de Islam et Arab* is quite informing in this regard. This French sociologist has honestly written:

> *Islam treated humen beings living in the lands conquered by Muslims with fairness and affection and in accordance with the basic principles of humanity.*

The agents of Islamic administration were so unflinching in their pact and treated the people so graciously that they chose Islam and Arabic with open arms. I should reiterate again that such achievements cannot be ever obtained by the force of the sword, and the conquerors who have entered Egypt never could have scored such successes.

Moreover, there are other impartial and objective books, such as Jurji Zaydan's 5-volume *Tarikh al-Tamaddun al-Islami ("The History of Islamic Civilization")*, which have endorsed this historical fact.

As the Holy Quran states:

Say: O followers of the book! Come to an equitable proposition between us and you that we shall not serve any but Allah and (that) we shall not associate aught with him, and (that) some of us shall not take others for lords besides Allah; but if they turn back, then say: bear witness that we are Muslims.

(The House of Imran 3:64)

As you see, even when the Prophet (PBUH) was on the verge of a victory, he still sought to distance himself from aggression. In other words, this verse announces in a clear voice that all human beings can come together as a united collectivity based on their belief in God. It also states that all human individuals are equal before the law and the truth and no one is the lord of the other. The only Lord is God. This can be a genuine basis for human rights.

Some might ask that this verse addresses only *the followers of Book*, so what should the rest of humanity do then? The answer is that all verses which have somehow indicated mankind have also determined a set of rights and obligations that apply to all human individuals. Here I shall mention some of them:

I) Surely Allah is affectionate and merciful to all human beings.

(The Cow 2:143)

***

II) Most surely Allah is gracious to people. (The Cow 2:243)

Now some might say that although God is affectionate, merciful and gracious to all human individuals, he still prefers some to others in basic rights! No, never.

1- All human beings' primordial nature is based on purity and divine religion:

Then set your face upright for religion in the right state the nature made by Allah in which he has made men. (Rome 30:30)

2- God has honored all human beings and created them as honorable creatures:

> *And surely we have honored the children of Adam.*

(The Night Journey 17:70)

3- The most honorable as seen by God are those who are most pious and morally integrated:

> *O you men! Surely we have created you of a male and a female, and made you tribes and families that you may know each other; surely the most honorable of you with Allah is the one among you most careful (of his duty).* (The Apartments 49:13)

4- God accepts repentance from all of His servants:

> *Do they not know that Allah accepts repentance from his servants and takes the alms, and that Allah is the oft-returning (to mercy), the merciful?* (Repentence 9:104)

***

5- *God answers the prayer of the suppliant when he calls on Him, so they should answer His call and believe in Him.* (The Cow 2: 186)

***

6- *God has created lawful and good things on earth for all people to eat.* (The Cow 2:168)

***

7- *All means of comfort and profit on earth are signs of Divine Essence.* (The Cow 2:164)

***

8- *God makes his signs clear for all human beings.* (The Cow 2:187)

9- The common obligations for all men are as follows:

> I) *O men! Serve your Lord, who created you and those before you so that you may guard (against evil).* (The Cow 2:21)

***

> II) *Who break the covenant of Allah after its confirmation and cut asunder what Allah has ordered to be joined, and make mischief in the land; these it is that are the losers.* (The Cow 2:27)

> III) For the management and guidance of human beings in the course of intelligible life, God has determined two leaders, directors or teachers:

↓ The first leader is an inner compass that exists in all human individuals, i.e. sane sense or pure conscience. There are several verses in the Holy Quran of sane sense such as,

> *So we said: 'Strike the (dead body) with part of the (sacrificed cow),' thus Allah brings the dead to life, and He shows you his signs so that you may understand.* (The Cow 2:73)

Moreover, there are about forty seven other verses that have expressed the authority of reason for human beings.

But as to pure conscience, which exists in all human individuals, we have also verses in the Quran such as:

> *Nay! Man is evidence against himself.* (Resurrection 75:14)

Also,

> *Now surely by Allah's remembrance are the hearts set at rest.* (Thunder 13:28)

↓ The second teacher or leader is the divine prophets,

> *And certainly we sent before you messengers to their people.* (Rome 30:47)

There is also another verse that reads:

> *And when His lord tried Ibrahim with certain words, he fulfilled them. He said: 'Surely I will make you an Imam of men.' Ibrahim said, 'And of my offspring?' 'My covenant does not include the unjust,' said He.* (The Cow 2: 124)

We also have this verse in regard to the delegation of the Prophet Muhammad (PBUH):

> *Say: O people! Surely I am the messenger of Allah to you all, of Him whose is the kingdom of the heavens and the earth there is no God but He.* (The Heights 7:158)

10- All divine prophets have been delegated for the promotion of unity, justice, intelligible freedom and wisdom:

> I) *Certainly We sent Our messengers with clear arguments, and sent down with them the book and the balance that men may conduct themselves with equity; and We have made the iron, wherein is great violence and advantages to men, and that Allah may know who helps Him and His messengers in the secret; surely Allah is strong, mighty.* (Iron 57:25)

> II) *(All) people are a single nation; so Allah raised prophets as bearers of good news and as warners, and He revealed with*

them the book with truth, that it might judge between people in that in which they differed; and none but the very people who were given it differed about it after clear arguments had come to them, revolting among themselves; so Allah has guided by His will those who believe to the truth about which they differed and Allah guides whom He pleases to the right path.

(The Cow 2: 213)

III) *Those who follow the messenger-prophet, the unlettered, whom they find written down with them in the Torah and the Gospel (who) enjoins them good and forbids them evil, and makes lawful to them the good things and makes unlawful to them impure things, and removes from them their burden and the shackles which were upon them; so (as for) those who believe in him and honor him and help him, and follow the light which has been sent down with him, these it is that are the successful.* (The Heights 7:157)

IV) *Surely Allah commands you to make over trusts to their owners and that when you judge between people you judge with justice; surely Allah admonishes you with what is excellent; surely Allah is seeing, hearing.* (Women 4:58)

V) *Surely (as for) those who disbelieve in the communications of Allah and slay the prophets unjustly and slay those among men who enjoin justice, announce to them a painful chastisement.*

(The House of Imran 3:21)

VI) *Those who spend (benevolently) in ease as well as in straitness, and those who restrain (their) anger and pardon men; and Allah loves the doers of good (to others).* (The House of Imran 3:134)

11- Betraying people is prohibited in all its forms,

I) *And their taking usury though indeed they were forbidden it and their devouring the property of people falsely.*(Women 4:161)

II) *Who, then, is more unjust than he who forges a lie against Allah that he should lead astray men without knowledge? Surely Allah does not guide the unjust people.* (The Cattle 6:144)

III) *Therefore give full measure and weight and do not diminish to men their things, and do not make mischief in the land after its reform; this is better for you if you are believers.*

(The Heights 7:85)

12- The transcendent unity of humanity and equality beyond all laws and rules,

> *For this reason did we prescribe to the children of Israel that whoever slays a soul, unless it be for manslaughter or for mischief in the land, it is as though he slew all men; and whoever keeps it alive, it is as though he kept alive all men; and certainly our messengers came to them with clear arguments, but even after that many of them certainly act extravagantly in the land.* (The Table Spread 5:32)

The same theme has been repeated in another point of the Quran,

> *O people! be careful of (your duty to) your Lord, who created you from a single being and created its mate of the same (kind) and spread from these two, many men and women; and be careful of (your duty to) Allah, by whom you demand one of another (your rights), and (to) the ties of relationship; surely Allah ever watches over you.* (Women 4:1)

13- Universal laws for all people,

> *But when he delivers them, lo! They are unjustly rebellious in the earth. O men! Your rebellion is against your own souls – provision (only) of this world's life – then to us shall be your return, so we will inform you of what you did.* (Jonah 10:23)

***

> *He sends down water from the cloud, then watercourses flow (with water) according to their measure, and the torrent bears along the swelling foam, and from what they melt in the fire for the sake of making ornaments or apparatus arises a scum like it; thus does Allah compare truth and falsehood; then as for the scum, it passes away as a worthless thing; and as for that which profits the people, it tarries in the earth; thus does Allah set forth parables.* (Thunder 13:17)

***

> *Surely Allah does not change the condition of a people until they change their own condition.* (Ibid:11)

***

> *Corruption has appeared in the land and the sea on account of what the hands of men have wrought, that he may make them taste a part of that which they have done, so that they may return.* (Rome 30:41)

***

You shall speak to men good words.   (The Cow 2:83)

Since all human individuals have the rights to inherent dignity, decent life and committed freedom, then they should use the best words and actions in their communications.

There are also two prophetic narrations in Muhammad ibn Yaqub Kulayni's *Usul Al-Kafi* that directly address the human global stature and their universal rights. The first narration reads as follows:

> *All people are members of Allah's family, and their most blessed one with the Lord, is the one who is most beneficial for the members of Allah's family.*

The second narration from the Holy Prophet Muhammad (PBUH) reads:

> *Anyone who hears the shout of a man for help and does not answer it is indeed not a Moslem.*

Having said these, you may ask that if there are such potential foundations for universal human rights in Islam, why I didn't publish them before 1948 when the UN Declaration was adopted and incited the Moslem scholars to pitch in and search for an alternative discourse. This question is often asked by the intellectuals of Moslem communities. They say that there are no human rights in Islam and we have made them ourselves!

Firstly, I have published a book on universal human rights, where I have researched comparatively on the UN and Cairo Declarations of Human Rights. There, I have shown that all the adopted codes of human rights have been extrapolated from the Holy Quran either directly or through jurisprudential efforts.

Secondly, would the tyrant governors of Moslem societies allow them to perform their rules? Would those tyrants ever allow the Islamic law to be performed in their societies? Of course not, for they thought that the application of these rules would cost them their rule. As a result, they boycotted it in a systematic way, let alone allow Moslems to think of universal human rights.

46

Fred Red
(Second Interview)

Subject: A Pathology of East and West Relations
Nationality: Canadian/ Major: Cultural Studies
Dialogue Date: 1989

Red: Why have the relations between Islam and the West become so difficult in recent years? Why are they just rejecting and denouncing one another instead of reaching some form of engagement?

Ja'fari: We can paraphrase this question this way: why have so many problems emerged in the relations between Islam and the West? The necessity of this paraphrase lies in the fact that both the Moslems and their Western fellowmen are human beings. This homogeneity calls for and necessitates a satisfactory, progressive coexistence. Now we should turn to the causes of these problems that have divided two significant parts of the world.

To unearth the aforementioned causes, or at least point out the significant factors involved in these problems, we will need to analyze our question into some issues.

The relations between Islam and the West could be in two levels:

I) The first issue involves ideological and cultural relations in the domain of *weltanschauung*, in general, as well as in the interpretation of the goal and philosophy of life. If this is the case, then one can say that there are no serious problems between the West and Islam. In both cases (religion and the higher principles of humanity), we have innumerable common beliefs upon which both blocks, i.e. Islamic countries and Western nations, can have a constructive coexistence without being involved in fatal conflicts. This communion, however, does not imply that these blocks are united on all issues, since such a unity is not possible even between the world's great religions like Judaism, Christianity, Islam and Zoroastrianism; in fact, one can say that such a unity is not even found among the followers of these religions, as there are numerous sects and factions inside them. These common principles, nevertheless, have maintained constructive cooperation among Moslems, Jews, Christians and Zoroastrians. We have seen that numerous generous people from other religions working in the hospitals and academic centers of the Islamic world and contributing to the emergence of the magnificent Islamic civilization.

There had been continuous and fruitful intellectual engagements in the domain of sciences and philosophies between the followers of these religions. Moslems turned to Greek, Roman, Egyptian and Indian philosophies, not to mention others, worked on them and made new discoveries and shared their philosophical and scientific findings with Westerners. I think no enlightened mind, be it Moslem or Westerner, would ever deny the fact that the more intellectually mature men are, the more constructive and emancipating their intellectual, ideological and diversities will also be, as corrosive hostilities are always brought about from the selfishness and egotisms of conflicting sides. The debates that Moslem leaders had with the scholars and intellectuals of other religions corroborate this fact. There are numerous records of such intellectual and cultural forums involving the Prophet (PBUH), Immaculate Imams and other distinguished Moslem scholars in historical and traditional sources. For example, you can see Tabarsi's *Al-Ihtijaj ("Argumentation")*, a reconstruction of Imam Reza (PBUH)'s debates with his time's philosophers, scholars and thinkers, some of whom even didn't believe in the trans-physical.[1]

Moreover, Moslems and Westerners can reach an agreement on the Ultimate Telos of life providing that egotists, despots, hedonists and oppressors would allow that to occur! If you make a careful study of the history of mankind, you will come closer to the conclusion that the ruinous conflicts, massacres and destructive divisions that took place among religious authorities throughout the world had not been due to religious beliefs; in fact, it was the egotist votaries of power who have resorted to every means, including the exploitation of religious sentiments and deluding the masses through faked conflicts, to reach their evil purposes. We know that these Leviathans, in Hobbesian parlance, or beasts in folk's tongue, misuse and abuse everything, even science, freedom

---

1- See: Ja'fari, M. T. *Divine Gnosis, An Interpretation of the Imam Ali Ibn Musa al-Reza's (PBUH) Discussions with Imran Sabi.* (Originally in Persian).

and the truth to break up people's unities and push their diabolic plans forward. Accordingly, if they leave people alone and clear the obstacles of proper thinking off their path, people will surely reach a consensus on the Ultimate Telos of life, since all human beings have the *self-orientation toward Supreme Perfection* as the Ultimate Telos of life inside them.

On the other hand, you Westerners and we Moslems are almost united on a very divine character called Abraham (PBUH), who is the religious father of we Moslems, you Christians and also the Jews. We all read in our scriptures, i.e. the Quran, the Gospels and the Torah, that Abraham is the paragon of the Perfect Man. By rediscovering this great divine figure and his religion, which is the religion of the human pure primordial nature, we can overcome our problems and divisions in our struggle for a just and intelligible coexistence, and take back history from the egotists who divide people for the sake of their evil purposes and entrust it to the people who care for human being and humanity.

I have already discussed this theory with some distinguished Western thinkers, who fortunately received it warmly. To name a few, I could mention Professors Hans Kung, Van Ess, Mayer and Wundrant from Germany as well as Reynaldo Galindo Pohl and Paul Marx from the UN Commission on Human Rights.

But regarding the higher principles of humanity, it would be sufficient to say that Westerners, like Moslems, are humans. They are the members of the same family of God, to which Moslems belong, too. This is not a sentimental remark indeed; in fact, it has been derived from an authentic quotation from the the Prophet Muhammad (PBUH), which reads:

> *All people are members of Allah's family, and their most blessed one with the Lord, is the one who is most beneficial for the members of Allah's family.*[1]

Moreover, our shared cultural and moral principles, on the one hand, and the basic principles of human rights upon at least eighty percent of which we are agreed on the other, demonstrate that not only these two blocks but in fact all human beings on the planet can enjoy a fair coexistence.

For my part, I believe we can take effective steps toward the fulfillment of this goal by holding constructive and profound

---

1- Sheikh Horr-e Ameli, *Wasa'el Alshi'ah*, Vol. 6 and also Kulayni's *Usul Al-Kafi*.

conferences on the aforementioned points of agreement provided we do not include those figures in the panels who only use such events as a showcase for satisfaction of their selfish sense of fame and trample the purported goals of these seminars only to say "I exist!" and see the participation in such conferences as in fact their *vocation*.

Only this way will we be able to either settle all of our discrepancies or bring about an atmosphere for a fair coexistence with the least confrontation to be estalished.

II) Islam and the West can expand their relations to the field of the objective phenomena of life, which are the products of legal and economical systems and an objective culture. Even at this level of relations, we have enough shared principles to sustain our intelligible coexistence. This consensus requires a realistic understanding of the shared principles and rules and overcoming the dividing whims, however we all know that utilitarianism, racism, hedonism and totalitarianism have not unfortunately yet allowed man to take a positive step for the intelligiblization of them.

There are numerous instances of evidence in people's life today that show that the words "human being" and "humanity" fill individuals with the same horror that the names of predators cause, as these words imply a guaranteed modification of hedonism and utilitarianism and the necessity of observation of laws and rules, while humanism, which has been developed in the West as an emancipating school, says no more than, "someone who is prosperous in life adapts himself with every condition that arises and does not surrender to any law or rule!"

It is indeed totally natural to see the horror caused by the words "human" and "humanity" in the face of those who seek to get the most pleasure and profit in life even if it costs the destruction of whole humanity.

Do you know what it means to say someone dreads human beings and humanity? It is analogous to a man who is afraid of and in fact escapes from himself. According to Rumi,

> Like the beasts gathering around the lake to drink water,
>
> When we saw our picture on the lake we escaped from ourselves.[1]

1- Jalaluddin Muhammad Rumi, *Dīvān-e Shams-e Tabrīzī* (*"The Sonnets of Shams of Tabriz"*).

Now, can a man who escapes from himself ever taste the flavor of prosperity and development? Can such a creature at all enjoy the reality of natural life itself? It is evident that he cannot do so, as such a being is always involved in internal conflict and friction; he in fact denies his own entity. The status quo of human societies shows that we live in the century of the absence of humanity – the century of self-alienation, and strictly speaking, *the century of self-contradiction*.

Red: Would you explain how politics is not separated from religion in Islam?

Ja'fari: Regarding the definition and interpretation that Islam offers of "religion" and "politics", one cannot separate these two realities which are complementary to each other and together guarantee the wholeness and integrity of life that Islam purports to be after.

Let us have a cursory look at the definitions of these two categories. What is religion? Religion consists of participation in the universal cosmic movement toward Supreme Perfection. Exposing oneself to the radiations of divinity is the Ultimate Telos of life, for it connects man with Divine Essence, the Creator of the universe, and helps mankind understand the divine providence and wisdom behind the creation of human beings. Having exposed oneself to these divine radiations, man sees the whole universe as a pantheon of God and finds himself always in the presence of Divinity, whether he is studying nature through a microscope in the laboratory, making the necessary devices for his life in his workshop, teaching in a classroom or fishing to feed his family. A man's relationship with his fellowmen in the mirror of revealed religion is much like the relationship between a member and an integrated whole, as a radiation of Divine Essence, with its other members. Now what is politics? Politics consists of the management of the human society for reaching the best possible goals in a meaningful social life rather than in a life like that of a honey-bee. Thus conceived, politics is not only separated in any means from religion, but in fact religion is not whole without politics, in the sense that we have just articulated.

Generally speaking, not only politics but also law, economy, art, morality and other cultural elements, as constitutive moments of Islam, are involved in the process of evolutionary life (i.e., intelligible life). To understand this vital issue we need to think of the transcendent unity of human life. It is needless to argue that human life in itself – not its constitutive elements and powers – is an irreducible simple reality. If someone or a school is to reduce this integrity, its unique quality would undoubtedly have been destroyed. Although life itself may not collapse with the disappearance of this integrity, say due to the absence of economic aspects, we will nonetheless lose the genuine quality of life that is provided by that integrity. A man whose life has lost its cultural element may still have a pleasant life, but we all know that an uncultured life is not indeed a human life but rather a type of wild life. A man or a woman who continues life without morality, knowledge or intelligible politics may seem to live a normal life – even with a smile – but such a human being will nevertheless fail to enjoy a free and conscious intelligible life.

Today we are witness to an unprecedented industrial progress in the West; no one can ignore this significant event. The wonderful effects of this industrial advancement are too clear for one to cast any doubt upon. However, when we hear the outcries of Western thinkers about the spiritual and ideological vacuum and the absence of higher moral principles, we remember the principle of transcendent unity in human life and express our great regret at it. This is itself evidence to the aforementioned transcendent unity, for we Easterners are regretful of the spiritual situation in the West, even if the Westerners do not pay enough attention to our concerns.

Let us turn now to nihilism, which can be regarded as an effective example in this regard. We know that in Western countries, as well as some other parts of the world, people have been deprived from having a higher goal which can interpret and justify all aspects of their life. Moreover, we know that no ideal or idea have yet been replaced with that Ultimate Telos. This is why we are nowadays beholding the prevalence of hedonistic and utilitarian ideas in human societies and systematic efforts for filling people's brains with meaningless and entertaining TV programs and artistic works which have been produced only for the temporal anesthetization of the viewers. As a matter of fact, these efforts for silencing human existential questions have not only failed to reduce human anxieties and fears, but have exacerbated them as well.

Furthermore, it is indeed a scientific fact that no one can ever separate the cultural aspect of human life from its political, legal and educational aspects, since - as we have mentioned earlier – human life is an irreducible phenomenon. Whenever you see that the political aspect in a society has been separated from its cultural aspect you should know that both aspects have lost their genuine functions in that society.

In any case, politics in the sense of the management of people's "intelligible life" in a society cannot be regarded as anything but religion, and Islam is strongly opposed to any form of politics that seeks only to serve the goals of oppressors via resorting to all types of means available as recommended by Machiavelli.

Red: I think you do not see the Western way of life as being the true ideal. There are indeed many problems in Western societies that have caused your purported Supreme Telos of life to be occulted in the West. Do you have a solution to these problems?

Ja'fari: As you know, my field of research has mainly been in human sciences and philosophy, and I can approach the situation from this point of view. Thus, I can't say how far I can push the matter.

As I see it, contemporary nihilism has its roots in the positivistic movement of the nineteenth century, which was to regain a momentum for scientific outlook. This movement was to promote some scientific theories, which in some cases were indeed anti-scientific.

Red: May I ask you to speak of some of these theories?

Ja'fari: With pleasure; we have, after all, held this meeting to discuss these issues.

Red: Thank you very much indeed.

Ja'fari: Among these so-called scientific theories was that presented by August Comte (1798-1857), a theory concerning the triple stages of the progress of the human mind, which not only had no positive outcome, but also no scientific proof whatsoever. To begin with, let us go through an outline of the theory together.

Comte's positive philosophy emerged from his historical study of the progress of the human mind—the Western European mind. India and China, he claimed, had not contributed to the development of the human mind. Indeed, by "mind" he was in fact implying the sciences – astronomy, physics, chemistry, and physiology (i.e., biology). As seen by Comte, mathematics was a logical tool, not a science.

> THE THREE STAGES. The history of sciences shows that each of them goes through three stages: the theological, the metaphysical, and

the positive. The progress of each field through the three stages is not only inevitable but also irreversible; it is, in addition, asymptotic — that is, we always approach, but never obtain, perfect positive knowledge.

Briefly, Comte's view of each of the three stages is as follows. In the theological stage, man views everything as animated by a will and a life similar to his own. This general view itself goes through three phases; animism, or fetishism, which views each object as having its own will; polytheism, which believes that many divine wills impose themselves on objects; and monotheism, which conceives the will of one God as imposing itself on objects. Metaphysical thought substitutes abstractions for a personal will. Causes and forces replace desires, and one great entity, i.e. Nature, prevails. Only in the positive stage is the vain search for absolute knowledge — a knowledge of a final will or first cause — abandoned and the study of the laws "of relations of succession and resemblance" seen as the correct object of man's research.

Each stage not only exhibits a particular form of mental development, but also has a corresponding material development. In the theological state, military life predominates; in the metaphysical state, legal forms achieve dominance; and the positive stage is the stage of industrial society. Thus, Comte believed, as did G. W. F. Hegel, that historical development shows a matching movement of ideas and institutions.

According to Comte, the first science to have gone through the triadic movement was astronomy, whose phenomena are most general and simple, and that affects all other sciences without itself being affected. (For instance, chemical changes on Earth, while affecting physiological phenomena, do not affect astronomical or physical phenomena.)[1]

The following criticisms could be leveled at Comte's theory:

1- Comte's proposed theory of the triadic stages of the development of the human mind along with their corresponding realities is not consistent with the human routine for mental activity, as human brain normally tends to search for the causes of an event within nature rather than somewhere outside it. Transphysical

1- Mazlish, Bruce (2006), August Comte in the *Encyclopedia of Philosophy*, Second Edition (in 10 volumes), Editor in Chief Donald M. Borchert, Vol. 2, pp. 410-411 (Thomson Gale Inc., USA).

explanation, on the other hand, requires the mental abstraction that is done in mathematical operations.

2- The so-called pre-metaphysical or theological stage, in Comte's parlance, dating back to the time when Hindu Vedas were written, has recorded many philosophical remarks as well. Upanishad truly provides a good example of the fusion of theological and metaphysical horizons upon the universe; one can even say that there are strong cases of evidence of scientific reflections in this book.

3- In each one of the triple stages, we see counterexamples of what August Comte claims. For example, in the stage of the permeation of philosophical ideas through religion, which is the fifth phase of Indian ideology, two groups of philosophers emerged:

   I) Gnostics who believed in God.

   II) Agnostics who did not believe in God. Both groups were then influential in India. Moreover, in Islamic countries in the same period of time, there had been both mystical and philosophical currents as well as direct scientific activities.

4- Such eminent scientists as Euclid and Archimedes also lived in hey days of Greek philosophy.

5- During the Middle Ages, which is classified as the age of philosophy in Comte's taxonomy, i.e. roughly from the late 9th century until the second half of 12th century, Islamic lands, according to leading Western historians of science, were home to serious scientific activities. In fact, it has been said that this point of history was the age of the flourishing of true science. Therefore, we can say that August Comte had not been careful enough in his classification.

6- Even in the so-called positive stage of the development of the human mind, one can easily discern numerous examples of theological, mystical and philosophical ideas. This stage is indeed the total sum of all stages through which Comte has described the evolution of the human mind.

7- As you know, divine and religious attitudes strikingly exist in all Comte's purported stages of development of human mind. Max Planck, the father of quantum physics and winner of the 1918 Noble prize for physics, writes

> *There can never be any real opposition between religion and science, for one is the complement of the other. Every serious and reflective person realizes, I think, that the religious element in the human nature must be recognized and cultivated if all the powers of the*

human soul are to act together in perfect balance and harmony. And indeed it was not by any accident that the greatest thinkers of all ages were also deeply religious souls, even though they made no public show of their religious feelings and beliefs. It is from the cooperation of understanding with the will that the finest fruit of philosophy has arisen, namely, the ethical fruit. Science enhances the moral values of life, because it furthers a love of the truth and reverence – a love of the truth displaying itself in the constant endeavor to arrive at a more exact knowledge of the world of mind and matter around us, and reverence, because every advance in knowledge brings us face to face with the mystery of our own being.[1]

Now we need to ask August Comte and his followers what it is that sustains this religious and spiritual attitude through all of the triadic stages of the development of the human mind.

8- August Comte should have taken this self-evident truth into account that there is no contradiction between the human triple relationships with the universe, as we come across many figures throughout history who have once seen the world a sign of Divine Essence and said,

Everything bears a sign inside it proving that the Lord is one.

At the same time, they have done considerable philosophical and scientific researches of the universe. Anyone who reads the works of Avicenna or Rumi can easily discern such an intellectual comprehensiveness in them.

Avicenna's *Al-Isharat Wa-'l-tanbihat* (*Remarks and Admonitions*) is a brilliant example of the fusion of these three intellectual attitudes. In his *Masnavi* (*"Spiritual Couplets"*), Rumi has frequently pointed out the integrity of these alternative methods, for example, "*The terrestrial wave is our understanding, imagination and thought*".

This is the most objectivistic theory of human mental phenomena available to man. Moreover, the second hemistich of this verse communicates a very delicate mystical idea:

The aquatic wave is consciousness, ecstasy and eternity.[2]

Red: Is the Islamic Revolution for Iran or for the whole world?

Ja'fari: As it was mentioned earlier, Islam is a perfect manifestation of Abraham's primordial religion, which is the universal religion of

---

1- Planck, Max, (1932), *Where is Science Going?*
2- Rumi's *Masnavi*, Book 1.

humanity as a whole. We know that other revealed religions like Judaism and Christianity see themselves the followers of Abraham (PBUH). Thus, it contains in itself Islam's cultural ideology for all humanity. To put it otherwise, Islam in general interprets and justifies human existence in two domains of *isness* and *oughtness* and seeks to put its ideas into practice through scientific and philosophical apparatus, via neither power nor force.

Red: Iranians are living in a tough economic situation now. Doesn't this cause people to lose their faith and belief in Islam?

Ja'fari: Economic issues and people's sustenance are among the basic concerns of Islam. However, one needs to take it into consideration that part of the economic problems in Iran and also other Islamic societies stem from the radical utilitarianism of some insiders as well as some foreign countries that seek to obtain the utmost profit from the least work and commodity and do not like Islamic societies to be independent. This is obvious for those people who are conscious and aware of what is going on.

On the other hand, we have to take into earnest account that the Islamic community has continuously suffered many economic, cultural and social difficulties due to the incursions of savage nations like the Mongols, but nonetheless, people never lost their faith by means of relying upon the primordial principles of Islam.

Red: Western people believe that there are various versions of Islam throughout the Asian continent and regard many of the countries within the continent as Moslem. Is Islam is a unique reality or are in fact all of these Islam?

Ja'fari: The universal principles of Islam are shared by all Moslem countries. The existing differences between them are mostly rooted in jurisprudential or secondary issues and are not concerned with the substance of Islam. Furthermore, each country has its own particular political configuration, and this brings about some differences that again do not have anything to do with the primordial principles of Islam.

47

Reynaldo Galindo Pohl[1]

Subject: Islam and the West on Universal Human Rights
Country: El Salvador/ Major: Human Rights
Dialogue Date: 1990

Mr. Galindo Pohl, an authority on human rights who had also carried out several UN missions pertaining to human rights, came to visit Allameh Ja'fari at the his residence in 1990 and discussed the philosophy of universal human rights as seen in the West and in Islam and also the compatibility of the two systems. In their discussion, Ja'fari pointed out the areas all religious societies in the world have in common – of course, by "religious societies" here we are referring to communities in which people are religious in the general context of the religion of the Holy Prophet Abraham (PBUH) rather than societies in which the consititution has decreed them as being religious – and said, "As the common father of all of us, the Holy Prophet Abraham (PBUH) can bring us all together as one. If human rights are given a religious and divine aspect, and also with a few revisions so as to eliminate the existing differences between the viewpoints of Islam and the West, human rights can function much more comprehensively and effectively."

Pohl: The articles of Universal Declaration of Human Rights must be put into effect and observed in all countries around the globe as its signatories have pledged to promote the universal respect for and observance of human rights.

Ja'fari: The idea of universal human rights has a long history both in

---

1- Member of the UN Commission on Human Rights.

the East and the West. We are happy that this idea is a global concern. I am personally interested in *primordial rights*, i.e. those rights which are conferred upon all human individuals regardless of their racial, cultural and geographical differences and accept their necessity. Western lawyers may have had these rights in mind when they were codifying those thirty articles. Anyway, the primordial or natural rights which are highlighted by philosophers and lawyers have been held in high regard in most parts of history, whether officially or unofficially.

Pohl: All countries around the world should consider the Universal Human Rights their own heritage and embrace it with open arms and cooperate with each other for its promotion.

Ja'fari: It is true that most of the articles of the Universal Declaration of Human Rights are comprehensive, primordial and effective, but the West needs to see whether these articles are consistent with all world's ideologies and cultures or not. If they are not consistent, we then must see how inconsistent they are and in which way one can tackle this inconsistency.

Pohl: These discords must be discussed. Could you mention an example of these inconsistencies?

Ja'fari: The nineteenth article of the Universal Declaration of Human Rights reads, "Everyone has the right to freedom of opinion and expression; this right includes the freedom to hold opinions without interference and to seek, receive and impart information and ideas through any media and regardless of frontiers." I think this article contradicts human inherent dignity and honor, for someone or a group may use this article as a resort to ruin the reputation and honor of a group or a society in the mass media; what kind of action then should be taken against that person or group? Do human rights allow people's reputations to be ruined in the name of freedom of opinion and expression?!

> *Mr. Pohl had no clear answers for these questions; however, he conceded that human inherent dignity must always be observed. Ja'fari then continued:*

Anyway, this article apparently needs to be revisited. We should add a condition to it and state that everyone has the right to freedom of expression and thought providing they do not trespass other people's freedom and dignity. This is one of those cases which require our sympathetic cooperation.

> *Here, Ja'fari and Pohl were in agreement, and Pohl pointed out that further pondering was needed on the issue. Then the issue of the Holy Prophet Abraham (PBUH) was discussed.*

Ja'fari: We can regard the Prophet Abraham as the forefather of all revealed religions and gather around him as one nation.

> *Mr. Pohl embraced this theory very warmly and asked Mr. Ja'fari to elaborate it in an article and send its translation to the UN so that they could dispatch the essay to all member states. The Allameh accepted Mr. Pohl's request and reiterated that he would pursue it quite seriously as well.*

> *At the end of the conversation, Mr. Pohl expressed his sadness in regard to the war that had broken out in El Salvador. On leaving, he asked Ja'fari for his prayers to help save Mr. Pohl's native land from such dire straits.*

48

Hans Corell

Subject: Islam and the West on Universal Human Rights
Nationality: Swedish/ Major: Law
Dialogue Date: 1990

Corell: What is your appraisal of the Universal Declaration of Human Rights, which mainly reflects the Western notion of human rights; is it in fact acceptable as such or does it need particular revisions?

Ja'fari: As you know, both Western and Islamic systems of human rights strongly insist on human dignity, honor, fraternity and equality, but when we compare them with each other, we find that the Western system is not as deep and thoughtful as its Islamic alternative. To put the matter otherwise, the Islamic system of human rights is established upon some certain foundations that the Western system lacks. To demonstrate the principles of dignity, honor, fraternity and equality, Islam resorts to some scientific, divine, intuitive, philosophical and primordial factors and facts that are taken into account in Western philosophies of human rights. Western scholars may argue that they also rely on ancient cultures and religions and that they have also spoken of man in the same way we do. If this is so, I would be glad to announce that we have a genuine ground for unity.

The Foundations of Human Equalities in Islam

According to Islam, there are twelve kinds of equalities between human beings:

1. Equality in Relation to the Creator

All human beings have been created by a transcendental being who is the Creator of all creatures. The existence of a Divine Being has already been demonstrated by several reasons and his being the Creator of all creatures is a self-evident reality. By understanding this equality, all human individuals could recognize that they all are equally subjected to Divine Love unless they deprive themselves from this divine bounty by means of committing evil acts.

2. Equality in the Wisdom, Will and Law of the Creator of All Human Beings

As seen in Islam, the holy prophets and distinguished human beings have been created in accordance with the same law, will and wisdom that other human beings have been created based upon. In the case of holy prophets, who have possessed inherent characteristics and qualities for the endurance and tolerance of their mission, however, it can be stated that God has bestowed them with special features. As for general values and merits, on the other hand, all human beings have been created based on the same basics and fundamentals.

3. Equality in the Original Material Used for Their Creation

All of us human beings have been created out of the same kind of material (earth), as stated in the following verse of the Holy Quran:

> We have created you mankind from the earth and we will return you to the earth, and on Ressurection Day, we will bring you out from it once again. (Taha 20:55)

We must now see what "earth" means here. Does it really imply earthen materials and the elements existing in the earth, or does it in fact refer to a canal for the human self to pass through? Of course, this issue calls for research and debate, and indeed it has been dealt with in various forms of knowledge and philosophies and highly significant theories have also been presented in its regard. Therefore, in the following poem by Sa'di:

> Human beings are members of a whole
>
> In creation of one essence and soul.
>
> If one member is afflicted with pain,
>
> Other members uneasy will remain.

He probably intends to imply that everything in the realm of nature has been created from the same material. In other words, Sa'di may be conveying that all human souls have been secreted out of a single, general one. In any case, there is no doubt that all human beings have been created out of earthen material. As the Holy Prophet of Islam (PBUH) has stated:

> All of you people originate from Adam, and Adam was created out of earth.

As a matter of fact, it has been stated that all human beings are descendents of Adam, and that Adam was created out of earth.

Therefore, no one human being is preferred to another, as reiterated in the following verse of the Holy Quran:

> *O you men! surely we have created you of a male and a female, and made you tribes and families that you may know each other; surely the most honorable of you with Allah is the one among you most careful (of his duty); surely Allah is knowing, aware.* (The Apartments 49:13)

As a result, we see that human beings have no superiority over one another when it comes to their essence and soul except for piety.

4. The Equality in the Origin of Human Generations

The generation of mankind originated from a man and woman called Adam and Eve, may peace be upon them. This origin of generations is the same for all human beings; we cannot find a human being who has been produced by two men, two women or two angels or jinns! These generations have conituned to progress, and now, the birth of human beings is still the result of a man and a woman, and the process of generations still goes on. Therefore, there is no preference in human beings over one another in his aspect, either.

5. Equality in General Nature and Characteristics

This form of unity is of extreme importance, for all human beings possess brains, mental faculties, comprehension, knowledge, powers of association, will, intellect, reason, the ability to discover and hundreds of other characteristics and forces, all of which are points they have in common with one another.

Of course, due to varieties in environments, systems of education, approaches to upbringing and cultural differences, the truths mentioned above may be activated in various ways, but a human being on this side of the world has comprehension, talent, knowledge and all of such crucial truths, as does a human being living in the most remote parts of the world. Therefore, the fact that human beings are equal and like brothers is an extremely original point rather than being an emotional, subjective remark.

6. Equality in the Ultimate Telos

As a matter of fact, God has allowed all of us human beings, regardless of our differences and without any preferences toward any of us, to participate in the progress along the path toward a single, supreme goal, which is no other than being attracted by divine perfection and becoming drawn into the rays of divine light. No human being is regarded as an exception of this progress. As God has stated in the Holy Quran:

> *I did not create Jinns and men with any other goal and ordain for them any other duty but to worship me.*

> (The Scattering Winds 51:56)

The above verse is applicable to both creatures – jinns, who are hidden, and human beings, who are at large and visible to all.

7. Equality in the Path Human Beings Progress along to Reach Their Ultimate Telos

We have already mentioned the supreme goal in the previous section. Now we must discuss what course this goal is taking. If such a supreme goal is to be reached, there is no other way but to progress along the path of intelligible life. It is intelligible life that provides the road needed to be taken in order to achieve the supreme goal. God has shed light upon this path for man by means of reason, conscience as well as holy prophets. The path is quite clear and definite because not only does our common sense and pure conscience confirm it, but also holy prophets sent by God have also showed us what that path is by means of their own enlightened approaches of progress. Progressing along this path is like feeling there is an immense rhythm created by God in the world; in fact, we have become part of the rhythm in the form of moral laws and ethical regulations set for us by God in order to protect us from falling into evils, destructive paths, animal-like contaminations and other filthy perversions. By following these laws and regulations faithfully and sincerely, we will feel closer and closer to the supremem attraction every moment – this indeed is intelligible life.

8. Equality in Inherent Dignity

God has bestowed upon all of us human beings inherent dignity and greatness, as depicted in this verse of the Holy Quran in regard to humanity and the children of Adam:

> *Indeed we honored the Children of Adam and provided them with means of transportation on land and sea; we also provided them with lawful and pure sustenance and bestowed them priority above many of our creatures.*

(The Divine Excursion into the Night 17:70)

In other words, all descendents and offspring of Adam have been "provided"with inherent dignity – unless, of course, as we have already mentioned, human beings eliminate their deserving this dignity and greatness by committing evil or perversive acts such as murder, which may deviate a society toward doom.

9. Equality in Having the Ability to Achieve Perfection and Optional Merited Dignity

In this regard, God has once again seen all human beings as being equal, i.e. the talent for achieving dignity and optional merited value has been instilled in all human beings equally. If one attempts to achieve merited dignity by means of piety, the talent to do so has been provided for him. No matter how much and to what extent human beings progress along this path, they will still achieve dignity and greatness. In other words, once again human beings are regarded as equal from this aspect as well, and they are by no means different from one another in any way.

10. Unity Having Achieved Perfection and Dignity

Such a form of unity will bring about supreme unity among all human beings. This unity can be represented by the formula all=1 and 1= all.

There is no doubt that such a unity will be impossible through any philosophical theory or school of thought. It is in fact a blessing provided by God-given religions and in particular Islam – the completor of all religions and the basic context of the religion of the Holy Prophet Abraham (PBUH) – which states that if human beings progress along the path of perfection and prosperity, they shall achieve supreme unity. In fact, there is a *hadith* that states:

> *Believers are like brothers; they are like the organs of a single body. If one organ moans with pain, the pain will also be felt by other organs as well. The souls of believers are also from the same soul and spirit. A believer's soul is connected to the*

Divine Spirit, and this connection is even stronger than the connection between sunrays and the sun.[1]

11. Equality in Human Beings' Goals in Both Realms (Natural Life and Desirable Life) from the Viewpoint of Preserving Their Souls as Their Main Axis of Progress

All human beings are equal when it comes to natural life and intelligible life, and if we are to progress objectively and purposefully, "the protection and safeguarding of the essence and the soul" will be the main axis of our progress. As human beings, all of us protect our own souls and essences as "the principle of all principles." Of course, our discussion in regard to the different forms of self-protection can be divided into three parts:

1. The self-preservation of the purely natural self
2. The ideal, desirable inherent self-preservation
3. The preservation of the evolutionary self and essence

We shall not go into more detail for the sake of brevity.

12. Equality in All Forms of Laws, Duties and Liabilities

Laws in this context include natural and positive laws that have been legislated for regulating natural and intelligible life.

13. An Equality beyond Natural Diversities and Unities

We now come to a truth which states that human beings regarded as a truth by God – i.e. from a supernatural point of view – as well. As stated in the Holy Quran:

> *For this reason did we prescribe to the children of Israel that whoever slays a soul, unless it be for manslaughter or for mischief in the land, it is as though he slew all men; and whoever keeps it alive, it is as though he kept alive all men; and certainly our messengers came to them with clear arguments, but even after that many of them certainly act extravagantly in the land.* (The Table Spread 5:32)

This verse eloquently describes human beings' transcendent unity. Whoever slays an individual is as if he has slewn all men and whoever tries to culture an individual is as if he has cultured the whole of

---

1- Kolayni, Muhammad ibn Yaqb, *Usul Al-Kafi*, Vol. 2, translated and explained by Seyyed Javad Mustafavi, Vol. 3.

mankind. In other words, we may see the suprificial aspect of nature as involving a large group of human beings, whereas beyond nature, they are all of one single heavenly unity in fact.

14. Equality in Collective Life

All human individuals have equal right to take part in collective life and it is their evaluative dignity that distinguishes them from each other. These are religion's proposed foundations for universal human rights.

49

Messrs. Cooper and Herzik

Subject: The Literary, Philosophical and Scientific Character of Khayyam
Nationality: British/ Major: Law/ Dialogue Date: 1990

Cooper: What is your evaluation of Khayyam's character and which aspect of his character is more important than other aspects?

Ja'fari: Omar Ibn Khayyami Neyshaburi, who is also known as Khayyam although his philosophical and scientific books bear the name of Khayyami, is among the most eminent philosophical and scientific figures in the Moslem world. He had been a peripatetic philosopher and ardent proponent of discursive debates. We have also two other poets with the name of Khayyam, about whom I have discussed at length in my book *Khayyam: the Man and His Ideas*. Among the survived works of Khayyami, there are some concise works that contain great ideas. The following are the titles of Khayyami's works that I have mentioned in my book, too:

His first book is *Hakim Omar Khayyami Neyshaburi's Essay on Algebra*, which – as the title suggests – concerns the mathematical problems and contains Khayyam's ideas in this regard. The second book is *A Treatise on Euclid's Theorems by Al-Sheikh Al-Imam Ul-Ajal Hujjat Ul-Haq Omar Ibn Ibrahim Khayyami*. As you see, Khayyam has been honored with the title of Imam Ul-Ajal in this book. The other book is *The Measure of Wisdom in Genesis and Obligations*. He also has a book that has been devoted to the analysis of three issues. This book contains outstanding ideas. The next work is entitled *The Rational Enlightenment of the Subject of Universal Science*. In addition, he has a Persian book on ontology and the generality of existence. *The Book of Noruz* and *Malekshah's Horoscope* are two other works by Khayyami. This man has indeed presented significant ideas both in philosophy and sciences.

In some ancient biographies, Khayyam has been aligned with Avicenna in Islamic philosophy. This brings us to the conclusion that

Western and Eastern scholars need to pay more attention to the philosophical and scientific ideas of Khayyam rather than his quatrains. For example, when one takes a look at Khayyam's *A Treatise of Euclid's Theorems,* one readily concedes that the authorship of such a treatise must have required a considerable deal of knowledge. Having said these, it is not fair indeed to introduce this man as a nihilist poet. Let me read for you part of Khayyam's prologue to this book:

> *In the Name of God the Merciful the Beneficent. All praise is due to the Lord of all mercy and compassion, and also our praises are due to His chosen servants, particularly Muhammad, the crown of all prophets and his household ...*

> *Research in sciences based on sound rational proofs is among the things that are unavoidable for those who are after eternal happiness and salvation, particularly the recognition of universal rules, the knowledge of which can help one to demonstrate resurrection, the soul and its eternity, the Necessary Being and its attributes, angels and the order of nature and finally the prophecy of Muhammad, the last one of the Divine prophets and conscience, which is in fact the inner prophet.*

As you see, Khayyam delicately discusses in his mathematical work spiritual matters and their scientific relevance.

Some Arab scholars believe that Khayyam was heavily touched by the ideas of Abu Ala Ma'arri. This is not true, as Abu Ala had been a professional literary thinker with a distinguished poetic taste, while Khayyam was a philosopher, scientist and mathematician who had only memorized some verses of Abu Ala's and, according to Jarrullah Zamakhshari, recited them in a gathering. This is not a good reason to think that Khayyam had been under the influence of Abu Ala. As I have mentioned in my book on Khayyam, Abu Ala was not well versed in philosophy, wisdom, natural sciences and mathematics. Of course, there are some similarities between the quatrains that are attributed to Khayyam and Abu Ala's verses concerning the limitation of human knowledge and the agonies of man on the terrestrial.

Said differently, this issue can be explained as follows:

Firstly, the similarities between the notions that are used by great thinkers in their debates do not necessarily imply that there has been an exchange of ideas between the two. The association of ideas among great minds is a quite general law.

Secondly, there are still many doubts around the quatrains that are attributed to Khayyam. It is really hard to accept that they all belong to Khayyam. There are only fourteen or fifteen quatrains by Khayyam on the undependability of the world. In fact, everyone with a sound sense can easily acknowledge the temporality of mundane affairs and impermanence of the beauties around. Thus, we cannot claim that Abu Ala had been Khayyam's master only upon trivial similarities, as there is no scientific evidence of it.

The other significant issue in this regard is Khayyam's view on supernatural matters. Besides the prologue of *A Treatise on Euclid's Theorems* which we quoted parts of it earlier, Khayyami has written in his *Book of Retorts* which answers the questions asked by Qazi Abu Nasr Muhammad Ibn Abdurrahim Nasawi:

> *Thus, the observation of prophetic injunctions has three advantages: firstly, self-discipline and the purification of the soul from carnal desires that darken the rational faculty, i.e. the promotion of the soul from passion to reason. Secondly, accustoming oneself to the reflection of divine affairs and the Day of Judgment and keeping daily based prays and orisons which prepare the soul for understanding of Divine Essence – that is, God, who creates everything, whose majesty is peerless and whose names are divine and there is no God but Him. He has ordered the divine hierarchy of beings and sustained them through his primordial wisdom ...*[1]

These words shed light on Khayyam's spiritual status and his views on divinity and divine matters.

Concisely speaking, it is not fair to reduce Omar Khayyam's great character to some dubious quatrains and it shows that we have not understood Khayyam at all!

1- Khayyam, *Risaleyeh Jawabiyyah ("Book of Retorts")*.

50

Descalzi

Subject: The Relations of Revealed Religions
Nationality: Italian/ Major: Architecture
Dialogue Date: 1990

In 1990, Mr. Descalzi, a distinguished Italian architect, visited Iran and discussed points in common between various God-given religions and the characteristics of Islam with Allameh Ja'fari. Although he had no claim to be an academic authority on the issue, his common sense and pure conscience along with the principles he encountered as the basic fundamentals of God-sent religions allowed him an attitude of acceptance equipped with the ability for expansion. Therefore, despite the fact that he was no authority on religious issues, he had kept his heart and soul intact, free of any contamination and ready to accept pure truths.

In any case, having confirmed the principles he was presented with in a quite simple and straightforward manner, he stated, "I accept these in total agreement." When it came to Islam, he admitted, "Since my youth, I was eager to know Islam but my work and life always hindered me from focusing on this religion."

Ja'fari: During my dialogues with Western scientists and scholars in the past years, I realized that whenever I spoke of the primordial principles of revealed religions and the basic foundations of Islam – which stands for the primordial religion of Abraham – most of my collocutors showed meaningful sympathy.

One of them was a British gentleman called Dr. Peter, who – after our discussion – said, "I had reached the same conclusions when I was thinking of these issues in my late teens."

Thus, psychologists, psychiatrists and even the psychoanalysts as well as other experts of human sciences need to take it into earnest consideration that regardless of existing cultural, racial and historical differences, one can dig out the transcendent principles of just coexistence in human mind.

Let us now turn to Islam.

Descalzi: I have decided to study of Islam in a comprehensive fashion, but my work does not allow me to dedicate myself to professional Islamic studies. I would like to ask you to introduce me to some introductory works of Islam.[1]

Ja'fari: To begin with, you need to know that Islam has its own law, economy, ethics, philosophy, worldview and politics. To put the matter otherwise, Islam has its own understanding of these disciplines corresponding to its integrative notion of human beings. As Islam delineates human relationship with man's Lord through some particular liturgical rites and individual spiritual practices, in the same way, it also speaks of the quality of man's relationship with himself, with the world and with his fellowmen. In other words, it undertakes the rules of these relationships and mobilizes humanity in an ordered and systematic fashion. This is the distinctive characteristic of Islam. Said differently, as a Moslem leans upon religion in his divine affairs, he also counts on religion in political, ethical, economical and even cultural issues. You know that if man really accepts that his life affairs are all under the supervision of God, who is to raise him to the heavens, he will be filled with what a sense of magnificence!

I shall now quote a sentence from Kant which Barthelme Santhiler has also cited in his preface to one of Aristotle's works:

> I wish humanity would know and accept that the Supreme Perfection is watching him from the high and is to raise him to true perfection — the seed of which has been sowed in inside man. Then we would know how far man can progress!

Thus, the most significant outcome of human relationship with God in all aspects of man's life is that the man never finds himself lost in a meaningless world of baseless events; in fact, he knows that he is always surrounded by Divine Essence, Who regulates his quadruple existential relationships. This is the highest ideal that unless man fulfills, he would have not taken any step toward progress in history. Landing on the moon is merely a sign of the expansion of human natural existence, but it does not change his spiritual situation. If man

---

1- Mr. Ja'fari then introduced some useful books to Mr. Descalzi.

still acts upon the brutal principle of "I am the end and others are the means", what difference would make it if we humans are able to travel through the whole galaxy within one minute!

Do you consider this a progress? Such being the case, could we still think that man is on the course of evolution? This is why Islam insists that man should see himself as being *all-dependent on* the Divine Essence, as otherwise, he would get bogged down in the swamp of carnal desires, as we today behold in Western and Eastern countries. We know that this hyper-sensual life will soon or later lead to bloody clashes and conflicts. Although we hear time and again of transcendent unity of humanity and his universal rights in conferences and seminars, I don't think that these scientific gatherings could help the situation at all.

(Then Ja'fari spoke about the necessity and logicality of principles, rules and beliefs of Islam.)

Descalzi: What conditions does one need to meet to be a Moslem?

Ja'fari then explained the concerned conditions and insisted that Mr. Descalzi should not accept Islam under any compulsion.

Ja'fari: Do you want to convert to Islam?

Descalzi: Yes.

Then Mr. Ja'fari spoke of monotheism, prophecy and resurrection as well as justice and Imamate. After these debates, Mr. Descalzi announced that he wanted to live the rest of his life as a Moslem. He followed by stating the testimonies of the oneness of God and the prophethood of Muhammad (PBUH) and the Imamate of Ali (PBUH).

51

Sheikh Hassan Qana'tli, Sheikh Esmaeil and Sheikh Mahmood

Subject: The Foundations of Shi'ism
Nationality: Turkish/ Major: Clerics/ Dialogue Date: 1990

Qana't Ali: Acknowledging the fact that we (Sunnis and Shi'ites) share the same beliefs as to the basic principles of Islam, I would like to ask you to articulate the underlying principles of Shi'ism.

Ja'fari: Shi'ism is established upon the Quran, Sunnah, jurisprudential consensus and reason.

To begin with, I'd like to speak of the sincere efforts that have been done during the past centuries by Shi'ite clerics for the promotion of Islam and Shi'ism. The atmosphere of sincerity that one finds in Shi'ism is quite interesting, as it is endorsed by all theologians, philosophers, jurists and literates who have lived and worked in Shi'ite communities.

Having said this, it is noteworthy that Shi'ite clerics did not confined themselves to Shi'ite sources in their quest for the truth. Thus, we see that they have had masters from Sunni denominations and other sects under whom they researched Islamic issues. For example, Mullah Ali Qushchi wrote a good interpretation of Khajeh Nasiruddin Tusi's *Catharsis of Belief* and Mullah Mohsen Feydh devoted himself to Ghazali's *Revival of Religious Sciences*. Moreover, a Shi'ite cleric can base his argument upon a tradition related by an honest Sunni tranditionist. This is a very significant fact indeed.

Today we see that good relationships have been developed between Shi'ism and Sunnism, and in some universities of Sunni countries, Shi'ite jurisprudence is being taught. Moreover, in Shi'ite academic circles, Sunni traditions are discussed as well. If you take Shi'ite jurisprudential texts into consideration, you shall find many quotations from Sunni scholars' books and ideas. Then we are witness to the formation of an undercover cooperation between these two denominations for the promotion of Islamic jurisprudence.

Another significant issue in this regard is the fact that Shi'ite scholars' contributions to Islam are driven by a primordial inclination. To put it otherwise, Shi'ite scholars' efforts for the promotion of Islamic ideas and ideals should be understood in terms of their innermost love for Islam. You know that the existing diversity of opinions among Shi'ite and Sunni jurists does not make us to ignore fundamental unity of two denominations on the basic principles of Islam. We need to be careful so as to avoid being brainwashed by the partial statements of prejudiced minds about Sunni and Shi'ah divisions.

It has been demonstrated that these two denominations are not divided on the fundamental principles of Islam, i.e. the transcendent unity of God, the prophecy of Muhammad (PBUH) as the Last divine prophet, resurrection and eternity. These three principles, which stand for the most fundamental tenets of Islam, are embraced by both sects. Accordingly, the two (Sunnism and Shi'ism) meet each other in Islam and no one of them can excommunicate the other upon religious grounds. Thus, any act of sectarian excommunication among these denominations is necessarily driven by personal interests and prejudices.

During my numerous discussions with my Sunni colleagues in various seminars and conferences, I have found that there are many grounds for unity between Sunnism and Shi'ism. In a conference, I was once delivering a lecture on "intelligible unity between Sunnism and Shi'ism." In my speech, I touched upon three significant issues on which these two denominations are divided, namely:

> 1- Asharite acquisition regarding the issue of free will and compulsion
> 2- Justice
> 3- The Quran's significations

Thus, I showed that we have many grounds for unity as to these issues. For example, on the Quran's significations, I argued that except for the allegorical verses, the rest of the Quran is equally understandable for us. The Quran has been revealed in eloquent Arabic and contains the fundamental tenets of Islam, upon which we are agreed. Then I turned to Asharite acquisition.[1] Acquisition, as

---

1- The Asharite believe that since all power and authority belong to God, then action is a divine privilege as well. Man is merely the locus of the emergence of the action, while he has all of these from God. Man acquires it and concretizes the action he has been conferred upon by the Lord through his mental and physical organs.

understood by some Asharite theologians, is an equivocal notion. But Abu Bakr Baqlani has offered an interpretation of this notion in his *Tamhid* which is not so far removed from Shi'ite *"Amr bayn ul-amrayn"*, which translates as "the Golden Mean or Middle Ground". Thus, these two denominations can meet each other even in this issue.

It is to be noted that Baqlani was a highly distinguished Sunnite thinker and authority on *kalam*, and in the book I just mentioned, he has interpreted acquisition in a manner no dissimilar at all from "the Golden Mean".

But as to the issue of justice, I should say that in 1970 I delivered a speech entitled "justice and the principle of charity" at the conference of the Millennium of Sheikh Tusi at Mashhad University. After I had finished my speech, the Moroccan chair of the conference, Professor Allal Alfasi, who was an Asharite scholar, told me:

"We also agree with the notion you have just articulated of justice."

There I argued that both Asharites and Mu'tazilites believe that injustice results either from oppression or from ignorance, since oppression and ignorance are signs of deficiency and God is neither an oppressor nor ignorant. Therefore, God is just. On the other hand, the Quran states:

> *And the word of your lord has been accomplished truly and justly; there is none who can change his words, and he is the hearing, the knowing.* (The Cattle 6:115)

There are numerous verses in the Quran that endorse this fact in a wide variety of forms. Thus, there is no doubt that God is just.

Having said these, we need to see whether we understand this divine justice or not. Said differently, is this justice accessible to me or is it in fact beyond my reach? Of course, we see part of this justice in our quadruple existential relationships (i.e. human relationships with God, himself, the world and his fellowmen), but we are not yet able to touch the secrets of the universe, where justice actually originates from. All Islamic denominations confess to this fact. Thus, we have a surface understanding of divine justice corresponding to our daily life conditions. We only know that everything has a heavenly wisdom behind it. This is the utmost of what we can touch of the meaning of justice. As a result, we have once again agreed with each other in this issue.

Such debates and intellectual engagements can minimize our conflicts and help us to come to an agreement with each other in a rational fashion. Then only trivial differences shall remain, the existence of which guarantees our evolution and dynamicity as difference in theoretical sciences always helps the man in his quest for perfection.

52

Messrs. Paul Marx and William Sirlik[1]

Subject: Human Rights
Nationality: American/ Major: Human Rights
Dialogue Date: 1991

Paul Marx: Would you outline the common features of the Islamic and the Western systems of human rights?

Ja'fari: No one of these systems has independently stipulated as their basic principles the common underlying principles that I have mentioned and had been adopted in The Organization of Islamic Conference's meeting in Tehran. It was for the first time that we tried to extrapolate these common principles upon which one can establish the whole edifice of universal human rights. In this regard, one can say that both systems of human rights are unanimous on the codification of articles for supplying the needs of both types of life (natural and ideal).

The Quintuple Principles

The quintuple principles, which are shared by both the Islamic and the Western systems of human rights, are as follows:

1- **The preservation of human life:** Both legal systems have declared necessary the preservation of life against intruding factors and regarded the state and the society asbeing in charge of the serious fulfillment of this fundamental right. Of course, Islam adds a vital condition here, i.e. the right of a decent life. All human beings have an equal right of living a decent life, as no one desires a life fraught with torture, pain and hardship. I think the Western system could include this condition, as the latter happens to be a requirement of human inherent dignity, in which Universal Declaration of Human Rights also believes. Thus, every human individual has the equal right to have a decent life rather than just any available form of life.

1- Members of the UN Commission of Human Rights.

2- **Human inherent dignity:** Both systems underline human inherent dignity and honor as a vital right which at the same time reveals the necessity of decent life.

3- **Principle of freedom:** This principle is also embraced by both systems. Nevertheless, there is a fundamental difference between them in this regard, as Islam does not accept freedom in its unconditional form. Islam determines a particular set of rules for the management of human physical and spiritual affairs in the course of intelligible life. Accordingly, the principles of freedom in the Islamic legal system is associated with the condition of "commitment", while the only condition considered in the Western system of human rights is that of not trespassing other people's right of freedom.

Paul Marx: Do you see any difference here between the two systems?

Ja'fari: I will explain this difference in my elaboration of the fifth principle. To summarize what we have discussed up to this point, we have to say that both legal systems accept the principle of freedom, although Islam adds the vital condition of commitment to this principle, which should also be taken into account by Western scholars. In the Organization of the Islamic Conference summits in Tehran in 1989, I proposed the condition of commitment to be added to the article pertaining to the right of freedom. Of course, my initial proposal was the condition of intelligibility, but after further discussions, I found that commitment has a more legal bearing than intelligibility, which is in turn more philosophical.
Another significant issue that needs to be taken into account here is that in the Western system of human rights, human dignity has not been divided into inherent and acquired dignity, while Islam insists that what really makes man an exception among other creatures in the universe is the dignity that he acquires through self-cultivation. To put it otherwise, it is indeed through this evaluative dignity that human life becomes meaningful.

4- **Education:** Both systems have declared education as being an indispensible right that must be fulfilled by the state and social authorities. Said differently, both systems concede that all human beings have equal right to be cultured and educated for social and individual life. Islam reiterates that a human being who struggles after perfection should never become entrapped in the iron cage of the routines of life; he has to continuously seek to bring variety into his life and attempt to make a difference. This is why Islam does not restrict human rights to the sphere of "isness", but these rights at the same time speak of the perfection that must be touched.

In other words, Islam does not regard human rights a means for a peaceful coexistence like termites and honey-bees. According to Victor Hugo, some rights are needed to be adopted for human souls as they are more significant than the rights of natural life.

5- **The Right of Equality before Laws and Rules:** There seems to be no discord whatsoever between the two systems as to this right, since both of them accepts the equality of human individuals before laws in one way or another.

As you see, both systems are almost united on these quintuple basic rights. Of course, there are some challenges that have to be addressed earnestly. One of these challenges is incited by the 19th article of the Universal Declaration of Human Rights. It reads, "Everyone has the right to freedom of opinion and expression; this right includes freedom to hold opinions without interference and to seek, receive and impart information and ideas through any media and regardless of frontiers." I think this article contradicts human inherent dignity and honor, Since someone or a group may use this article as a resort to ruin the reputation and honor of a group or a society in the mass media. In that case, what kind of action should be taken against that person or group? Do human rights allow people's reputations to be ruined in the name of the freedom of opinion and expression?!

Paul Marx: Of course, the nineteenth article has proven to be very useful in those countries which heavy-handedly repress the dissidents!

Ja'fari: Let us not confuse our legal debates with political issues! It is indeed a political issue that one politician may hold anther politician in contempt or may respects him.

Political issues are temporary in essence and have their origin in transient motives. Moreover, within a short period of time, political views may change due to policy shifts and turn contempt into respect or vice versa. This should not be confused with legal debates, which are of permanent nature. My objection is that the 19th article is in contradiction with human inherent dignity. I discussed this issue with Professor Martinson and Dr. Danilo Türk in Manila, and although they conceded that human dignity must be observed, they nonetheless did not provide me with any answers to my questions in this regard.

These two systems are also divided on the issue of suicide, which has been strongly condemned by Islam, while the Universal Declaration of Human Rights passes it in silence. On the other hand, the right of life, the right of dignity, the right of education and equality before laws are "divine maxims" rather than mere rights that can be ignored. To put it otherwise, no one is allowed, according to Islam, to kill or contempt himself on the pretext of having the individual right of dignity or life!

In fact, these are divine maxims which have been ordained by the Lord and can only be nullified by Him. No one is allowed to breach these heavenly drawn maxims.

The other point of difference lies in the issue of oppression. The right of dignity denies oppression. The Holy Quran states that:

> *Surely (as for) those whom the angels cause to die while they are unjust to their souls, they shall say, 'In what state were you?' They shall say, 'We were weak in the earth.' They shall say, 'Was not Allah's earth spacious, so that you should have migrated therein?' So these it is whose abode is hell, and it is an evil resort.* (Women 4:97)

According to this verse, everyone has the right to defend his dignity, and no one is allowed to surrender to oppression. This point has not been touched upon by the Universal Declaration of Human Rights. It is needless to argue that this is a very significant issue which eclipses one's general orientations.[1]

1- For more details in this regard, see Ja'fari, M. T. (2014): *Human Universal Rights: A Comparative Research in Islam and the West.*

53

Ms. Guillaume

Subject: Islam and the West on Women
Nationality: French/ Major: Sociology/ Dialogue Date: 1991

Guillaume: What is your estimation of women's place in Islamic and Western legal systems?

Ja'fari: The seventh article of the Cairo Declaration reads:

I) Women are equal to men in human dignity, and have rights to enjoy as well as duties to perform; a woman has her own civil entity and financial independence, and the right to retain her name and lineage.

II) The husband is responsible for the support and welfare of the family.

Moreover, as the tenth article states,

I) The family is the foundation of the society, and marriage is the basis of its formation. Men and women have the right to marriage, and no restrictions stemming from race, color or nationality shall prevent them from enjoying this right.

II) Society and the State shall remove all obstacles to marriage and shall facilitate marital procedure. They shall ensure family protection and welfare.

On the other hand, the sixteenth article of the UN Declaration reads:

1- Men and women of full age, without any limitation due to race, nationality or religion, have the right to marry and to found a family. They are entitled to equal rights as to marriage, during marriage and at its dissolution.

2- Marriage shall be entered into only with the free and full consent of the intending spouses.

3- The family is the natural and fundamental group unit of the society and is entitled to protection by the society and the State.

As you see, these two points of views have commonalities and differences. We will need to address here two ultra-significant issues before making comparative remarks on these articles:

I) The fact that "the family is the natural and fundamental group unit of society" is undoubted in the view of ethno-sociology, religion, psychology and other branches of human sciences. But if this fundamental fact of family is documented to human whims and baseless ideas like other human affairs, it shall undergo serious changes in varying situations of human life; today we see that humanity has been reduced to animal lusts and carnal desires due to unrestricted freedoms propagated under the impulse of excessive utilitarianism and overindulgence in sexual desires by some of uncommitted thinkers who are breaking the primordial principles of morality in the name of liberalism so as to prove themselves competent enough to be awarded prizes.

Due to such deviations from the Divine Law, the foundations of family have been uprooted in the present times. These so-called proponents of liberalism are propagating with utmost impudence such sexual deviations as individual freedoms that one would be ashamed of even mentioning their names.

The hegemony of these devilish views in the West is so clear that no further evidence is needed to explain its ferocity. What is worth mentioning here is the fact that the Universal Declaration of Human Rights with its occidental orientation cannot speak of family as a fundamental unit of society because the prevailing cultural symbols and the semi-scientific works in Western countries seem to undermine the building blocks of family.

II) The rights that have been stipulated in the UN Declaration about family and women are based on such freedoms that are neither natural nor logical. Firstly, if they were logical, the family in Western countries and westoxficated eastern countries should not have been so disordered in this regrettable form that has resulted in many physical and mental disorders, most grievously self-alienation, which has engulfed these countries. Secondly, the Universal Declaration of Human Rights with occidental orientation has not unfortunately provided a distinction between equity and justice in a clear fashion. It is not logical indeed to divide humanity into two poles of male and female in the name of equality and reduce women to a uterus and menstruation!! If the Western culture, which is the main source of inspiration for the UN Declaration, does not accept the truth that "the justice based on the rule of law and reality is better than baseless equality", and if it had tried to redress the mistakes done in the past, it shall not succeed in providing a defendable logic for justifying its statements on male and female freedoms.

Guillaume: What are the differences between the Islamic and the Western notions of women and family?

Ja'fari: The Universal Declaration of Human Rights' understanding of women and family is grounded in freedoms that are neither natural nor logical since:

Firstly, if those freedoms were natural and logical, Western countries and their Eastern imitators should not have had such a tragic state today, grappled with so many physical, mental and social problems.

Secondly, the Western codifiers of the Universal Declaration of Human Rights, who are surely well-versed in human sciences, have regretfully replaced justice with equality. This is not a logical preponderance indeed, as it does not match the realities on the ground. Men and women are neither physiologically nor psychologically alike. Thus, they have their own respective rights and commitments.

Shared Characteristics

1- A woman is equal to a man in human dignity, and has rights to enjoy as well as duties to perform.

2- A woman has her civil entity like a man does, and is equally entitled to enjoy all of the necessities of a decent life.

3- A woman is independent in her financial obligations, like a man. In accordance with all Western legal trends, this is also not documented in the UN Declaration.

4- Marriage shall be entered into only with the free and full consent of the intending spouses.

5- The family is the natural and fundamental unit of society and is entitled to protection by society and the State.

Guillaume: Why can't a Moslem man or woman marry a non-Moslem?

Ja'fari: This question has a clear answer. Islam is the religion of primordial nature and whoever has truly chosen it as his religion has fulfilled his primordial nature, and thus can't submit his heart and soul to someone's love whose ideals and nature are not in tune with Islam.

On the other hand, a meaningful life, according to Islam, requires to be founded upon a rightly chosen religion that interprets all aspects of life. Of course, the most important issue in marriage is that of children. Needless to say, Islam sees this world as the hallway to the eternal world; a man needs to flourish his god-given gifts and talents in this world to prepare for the other world that is the locus of eternity. But Western countries see this world as the last destination of human life. This idea is not driven from their religions or philosophies, as we see that the latter discuss eternity and resurrection. Unfortunately, religion and morality in the West have been reduced to library stuffs. In fact, this has caused some shallow minds to speak of the death of religion in the West.

Regretfully, the Universal Declaration of Human Rights has been established upon the ideals of worldly life and is intended to reduce individual and social conflicts in the public sphere. Codified this way, it is not concerned with value and obligation, while Islam sees this world as a meaningful passageway in which human beings must prepare themselves for an eternal life.

It is needless to argue that this self-discipline and spiritual enlightenment requires particular beliefs and practices ignored in the Universal Declaration of Human Rights. This is the most significant difference between these two legal systems. Of course, there are other differences that need to be discussed in other places. When a man and a woman are not from the same religion, the child's upbringing becomes difficult. Moreover, the child finds himself in a paradoxical situation that can eventually cost the child his future. This is why Islam insists that the parents must come from the same religious background.[1]

Differences

1- In Islam, men and women are both equally obliged to observe the condition of religion in their marriage in the sense that they are not allowed to marry non-Muslim women or men. The reason for this injunction is very clear, since Islam is a primordial religion and everyone who has chosen it as faith to follow has decided to flourish their primordial nature; thus, such a person cannot share love with someone who does not believe in Islam.

On the other hand, since Islam regards religious life as the only

---

1- Due to the significance of the issue of the difference among religions when it comes to marriage and wedlock, we have included the details here from Allameh Ja'fari's *Human Universal Rights: A Comparative Research between Islam and the West.*

lebenform that could be meaningfully interpreted, thus the irreligious life in its view is not basically logical at all. Children are an indispensible part of marriage. There is no doubt that Islam sees this world as the passageway that brings us to the eternal life, the locus of perfection, and peace shall not allow its believers to live an animal-like unrestricted and purposeless life and after a while to disappear in nothingness; thus, it strongly orders the believers to rear their children according to an orthodox set of beliefs for a human and divine life. Now, if one of the parents is not a Muslim, it shall result in many insoluble difficulties in child-rearing. This kind of marriage usually causes the children to live without religion and, as we know, an irreligious life has no identity. Moreover, since parents are not able to reach a viable consensus on this matter, they always prefer pass this vital issue in silence.

2- Whereas "men and women are entitled to equal rights as to marriage, during marriage and at its dissolution", a man is therefore not obliged to pay alimony or a dowry to his wife, according to the UN Declaration; on the other hand, Islam has assigned it to the woman – of course, not compulsorily – to manage the internal affairs of the family by her treasury of purely human affections. It is to this very reason that Islam has obliged the man to pay his wife alimony and an intelligible amount of dowry.

3- Whereas the UN Declaration has stipulated that "men and women are entitled to equal rights during marriage and at its dissolution," it becomes clear that it takes men and women equally entitled to the right to divorce.

Islam does not approach this issue with such simple-mindedness that the Universal Declaration of Human Rights with occidental orientation demonstrates. On the other hand, women are more sensitive toward marital problems due to their emotional nature and often apply for divorce without any strong reasons and must be protected of the loss. We shall suffice here to statistics printed in one of daily newspapers that reads:

> Up to 90% of petitions for divorce in France in the year 1890 have been filed by women.[1]

Furthermore, children need to be reared right from their suckling period under their mothers, as hiring a babysitter or sending them to baby farms or nurseries could deprive them of human emotions

---

1- *Keyhan*, No. 6627, Sep 6, 1965.

and affections and cause them to be involved in nihilism and nothingness in their youth. In fact, as it has been claimed by some thinkers in the West, "These youths are only good for the army, not for human purposes".

Precisely speaking, this is the very point that has already been stipulated in the second clause of Article 25 of the UN Declaration, which reads "motherhood and childhood are entitled to special care and assistance." Islam assigns it firstly to the man to provide the needs and take care of the mother and her baby; only when the father is disabled or the mother and baby are deprived of family care for some reason, in that case the society and the state are obliged to perform their duties. Therefore, the Universal Declaration of Human Rights with occidental orientation has to accept that human beings need to be protected in some ways beyond their social and individual rights.

4- There is an extremely significant issue that is always neglected by the West in cultural and legal debates, and that is the fact that young people, regardless of their higher education, do not still understand many colossal truths of life and cannot distinguish between committed and uncommitted lives. The dominance of sexual desires in this season of human life even further worsens the situation.

To state the matter differently, the young people who decide to marry are naturally overwhelmed with their sexual instinct, which overshadows other issues of life. Moreover, as time goes by, the sexual desires leave the scene and the overshadowed issues begin to show themselves. It is due to this very reason that Islam insists on the permission of parents of the maiden as the precondition of marriage, since girls are not conscious of life affairs as much as boys are due to their gender differences and religious considerations. Thus, they are vulnerable and need to consult with their parents (or anyone who functions as her guardian) on the biggest decision of their lives. Nevertheless, the guardian must be a competent person; otherwise, it is incumbent upon the society and the state to decide on this extremely significant issue.[1]

1- We know that such issues as the necessity of the guardian's permission for the marriage of a maiden are not understandable for most Westerners. Likewise, many of the social and cultural phenomena that are seen as regular in the West are not fathomable for us as Muslims, such as:

Explication: Many irrational attacks have been conducted against Islamic jurisprudence by uninformed persons under the plea why Islam has not declared the genders equal. As a general answer to this objection, we need to mention that the legal differences between a man and a woman originate in the physical and psychological differences existing between the two genders. According to the findings of scientific research done by distinguished researchers such as Professor Rigue on the physical and psychological differences between these two sexes, the belief in the equality of the man and the woman is either for the pursuit of fame or due to ignorance toward the existential coordinates of these human beings. These physical and psychological differences existing between these two genders are observed in more than one hundred occasions.[1]

We need here to address a highly significant issue that could serve as the thread of Ariadne in solving other intricate issues around the male/female dilemma. It is the very issue that shows itself in the law of

---

I) The relationship between a man and a woman, which is one of the most sensitive and significant of human relationships, has to be within a legal framework, not like animals whose relationships are only conditioned upon blind desires.

II) In Islam, the human self has a divine aspect which is counted as the source of human inherent dignity. Therefore, for evolving this divine aspect, we humans need not to overindulge with sexual desires in an unrestricted fashion.

III) Islam does not see the woman as the means of pleasure for the man – although pleasure is naturally a necessary item in a successful sexual relationship – since in Islam the man and the woman are equally entitled to the right to inherent dignity, and thus no one is allowed to trespass this divine ordinance and describe the woman as a means of pleasure for the man.

IV) Islam does not take it necessary to arouse sexual consciousness in the society with explicit materials and pornography as it is done now in the West. In fact, it proclaims that we need to cultivate the spirits of human individuals and make them ready for an intelligible and meaningful life. The aggressive hunters of power do not want to confess that many brilliant minds, like Avicenna, Averroes, Razi, Al-Biruni, Rumi and Mulla Sadra, have been cultured in the past without sexual teachings. These aggressive hunters of power seem to claim that, "We have solved all of the problems and there is no pain which needs to be redressed, and we humans have ⇨ read our lessons of the book of existence!!" The reason for such claims could be sought for in such books as Alexis Carrel's *Man the Unknown* (1935).

1- See for instance Mutahhari, Murteza, *Women's Rights in Islam.*

retaliation that states that if the murderer is a woman who has killed a man, then she shall be retaliated on the condition that the avenger of the blood would not accept the blood money and forgive the murderer. However, if a man has murdered a woman, his retaliation shall be conditioned upon paying half of the murderer's blood money by the avengers of the blood. It has been said that this is an explicitly unjust discrimination between the two genders. This objection has a clear answer as the necessity of paying half of the murderer's blood money is essentially an economic issue and does not have anything to do with the inherent dignity and gender discrimination.

It is needless to say that the major burden of earning a living for the family is on the shoulders of the man, thus the absence of a man in a family could expose it to the bitterness of poverty, while the absence of the woman in a family, in spite of being a dear emotional loss, does not have such grievous economic repercussions. This is to say, this jurisprudential judgment is not an insult or discrimination about a woman's inherent dignity as a human being, but it shows that justice is the building block of Islamic jurisprudence.

The objection that "Today, women are participating in major economic activities shoulder to shoulder with men" and this jurisprudential judgment does not have occasion anymore, and despite the fact that it is seemingly attractive, it is not logical with regard to the grievous implications that have been brought upon families due to the participation of women in economic activities. Generally speaking, we need to either leave off the idea of fundamentality of family in the human society believing that man must gratify his sexual instinct at any price or accept this as an indispensible reality that women should return to their homes and revive the lost warmth of their households. It is needless to say that this shall cause the man and the woman to have different rights and obligations without losing their inherent dignities, since human primordial dignity is one thing and the principles governing the natural course of life is another.[1]

1- See Ja'fari, M. T. (2014): *Human Universal Rights: A Comparative Research in Islam and the West.*

54

Abdurrahman Vahid

Subject: Philosophy and Religion
Nationality: Indonesia/ Major: Sociology of Religion
Dialogue Date: 1991

Vahid: Some Indonesian authorities and scholars refuse to engage in philosophical and theological debates as they regard them as being harmful indeed for the religion. It seems that this reluctance has its origin in Ghazali's *Tahafat ul-Falasifah ("The Incoherence of Philosophers")*[1] as well as the criticisms posed by other Moslem figures of philosophy.

Ja'fari: What is the authorities' reason for the prohibition of philosophy and Kalam?

Vahid: No convincing answer has ever been heard from them.

Ja'fari: We are not interested in classic philosophy and theology in its rigid form that would hamper our intellectual quest in the world; as a matter of fact, we are even against it. We are neither interested in every problem which is categorized as philosophical nor enamored of every word of Kalam that is comprised of a set of issues and rules that have preoccupied Moslem communities since the dawn of Islamic culture.
This appears to be the very alibi offered by the despisers of philosophy and theology. However, rational argument is considered as being a vital element in the Islamic worldview.

Vahid: How should then we deal with this wrong approach to philosophy and theology in our country?

Ja'fari: You need to get in touch with Moslem philosophers and ask them whether occupying oneself with philosophy is to the Islamic world's interest or not. If I were asked to answer this question, I'd surely say that getting bogged down in the past terminologies of

---

1- This epoch-making book has been translated into many languages including English. See, for instance, *The Incoherence of Philosophers*, a parallel English-Arabic text translated, introduced and annotated by Michael E. Marmura, 1997, Brigham Young University Press, Provo, Utah. (Translator).

Greece, Alexandria and Rome and also being mesmerized with contemporary Western themes and terms that are philosophical only in name is forbidden *once and for all*; of course, this prohibition is not a matter of faith, since this inertia erodes human intellectual capacity. Instead, philosophy must be understood as a serious engagement with fundamental quadruple existential questions of whence, whereunto, why and whither that address the human quadruple ontological relationships with himself, with God, with the world and with his fellow men. No one is allowed to be an imitator in this *serious* intellectual engagement even if the imitatee is Mulla Sadra or Farabius, let alone a Greek or Roman thinker.

We never accept an idea from such thinkers as Whitehead or Russell without thinking through its reality. This is also the case with distinguished Eastern philosophers like Allameh Tabatabaei, as we do not approach his ideas as "revealed words", but our estimation of them is based on the Allameh's erudition and intellectual originality. Studying and teaching the Allameh's works for example does not imply that they necessarily need to be imitated.

Vahid: What is your proposal for the science of Kalam?

Ja'fari: As the definition of this science suggests, Kalam consists of the demonstration and justification of religious tenets through rational reasons. By rational reasons here we do not mean those theoretical theorems which are always in dispute, but rather we mean self-evident and necessarily-true propositions. The necessarily true propositions are those propositions about which no one can raise any doubt and this may be a matter of agreement among all scholars and thinkers of Islamic world, particularly those of the Shi'ah world who believe that the articles of faith must be demonstrated via rational arguments, not through imitation, although the scientific and discursive power of theologians differs in a diametric fashion.

Of course, it should not be forgotten that philosophy's relationship with theology is of a vital importance and the separation that has been claimed to be existent between theological and philosophical issues is baseless. Khajeh Narsiruddin Tusi's *The Book of Catharsis*, despite being an essay in Kalam, has discussed most of the principles of philosophy. Even some of our philosophical works have been compiled after the arrangement of Tusi's essay. To begin with, for instance, Khajeh Nasir has taken issue with the general principles of ontology and only then did he turn to other rational debates. It needs to be mentioned that Kalam argues for everyone who seeks to have a meaningful and justifiable life based on primordial religion. To put it otherwise, if man has the slightest degree of reason, he can justify his life upon rational arguments. If these arguments are expanded and deepened, they will lead to the emergence of the science of Kalam. Then you have to provide your society with a correct definition of philosophy in terms of human quadruple ontological relationships (i.e., man with himself, with God, with the world and with his fellow men). If we do not fulfill our task in this regard, our society will constantly be a prey to the baseless ideas propagated by cultural media. This is the task of intellectuals and scholars of the Islamic community.

We see that this idea has also been promoted by some distinguished figures of our own society like the late Grand Ayatollah Mirza Mahdi Isfahani. My discussions with the great pupils of Mirza Mahdi, as well as my research on his works, show that not only was he not at odds with theological debates, but like many other scholars, he in fact considered them as being necessary. In fact, Ayatollah Isfahani was against submerging oneself in the archaic Greek terminologies and withered issues which are disconnected with realities. Mirza Mahdi was indeed aware of such verses of the Holy Quran as:

> *And teach them the book and the wisdom.* (The Cow 2:129)

Several verses of the Quran have described wisdom as the goal or one of the supreme goals of delegation of divine prophets. It is needless to say that Mirza Mahdi Isfahani, like other Shi'ah scholars, regarded rational argument as necessary for the acceptance of the articles of faith. I also discussed this issue with the late Hajj Mirza Javad Tehrani in Mashhad, and he endorsed my point, too. When my critical interpretation of the Masnavi was published, Mirza Javad told me that he agreed with the point of view that I had promoted there.

Anyway, these issues force themselves upon every thinker. They need to be dealt with based on realities, not upon mental prejudices. Were Rumi and other thinkers of his status blind votaries of Greek philosophy?! In fact, we see that they were not only against those philosophies, but they also had great philosophical and mystical ideas.

55

A Group of Turkish Students

Subject: Islam on the Human Being
Nationality: Turkey/ Major: Varied/ Dialogue Date: 1991

Question: What is the reality underlying mankind according to Islam in social life, in relation to himself and in relation to the world?

Ja'fari: The integrity of matter and meaning in Islam is the major factor that has guaranteed this religion's perenniality. Most of the thinkers who deeply deal with human beings and their affairs and properties concede that the best anthropological point of departure is the one which sufficiently addresses both the material and the spiritual aspects of human existence.

If someone delves deep into Islamic beliefs, rules and obligations in an impartial spirit, he will find that Islam has seriously addressed both material and spiritual aspects. Even in one sense, we can say that for someone who has a pure inside, i.e. someone who has purified himself through acting upon the rules of religion, reason and conscience, the world is not a meaningless chunk of matter, but it is in fact certainly built upon a meaning.

For a devoted Moslem who has dyed himself with the ethics and etiquettes of Allah, the whole world is the temple. For a blacksmith who toils in his smithy to serve his family and the society, the workshop is not merely a site of ironwork, but a place of worship, although the means used for praying are iron scraps. This also the case with a farmer who works on his land day and night to provide food for the servants of God, as he is surely serving his Lord.

By the same token, universities, laboratories and wherever knowledge is promoted and people, whether as professors, teachers or students, work together to discover the reality are pantheons of God if the people's intention is public welfare and God's pleasure. In some Islamic sources, this process has been described as "*jihad* [which means a 'divine campaign']" as whoever struggles to feed his family through legitimate ways is regarded as a "warrior of God". Is there any service higher than *jihad*?

This is also the case with the tradesman who runs his business according to the principles of Islamic economy, which is essentially collective and based on consultation rather than physiocracy.[1] In an Islamic economy, ownership is not the end but it is a limited means for the regulation of everyday life affairs. It is needless to argue that such men or women are always serving their Lord.

On the other hand, a mosque is a place for worship where man finds himself closer to Divinity, although this sense of closeness could be found in one's own house too, where human beings can also worship their Lord.

Thus, one can say that the material aspect not only is not in contradiction with the spiritual aspect in Islam, but as a matter of fact, as Imam Ali's words suggest, the whole world is a place of worship for man. Of course this notion of the world is only sensible for those who have an enlightened vision. The world is a place for earning an evolved essence that qualifies one to enter the kingdom of eternity. As the Holy Quran says:

> *Surely my prayer and my sacrifice and my life and my death are*
> *(all) for Allah, the lord of the worlds.*   (The Cattle 6:162)

Therefore, Islam regards all human relationships as belonging to God.

To say that my life belongs to God implies that my life is a life all moments, aspects, motions and relations of which are divine. This requires one to presume that one is part of the universal cosmic movement that heads toward Supreme Perfection and that one is always in the presence of God and thus one must never sin. Whatever man takes, be it a manual affair or an intellectual task, is aimed at an aspect of life which in turn *belongs to* God.

Establishing the reality of eternity and resurrection, thus, Islam gets human life flourished and makes it interpretable. No single ancient or scholastic school of thought could ever make all aspects of human life dependent on Divine Essence in this way. Having said these, today we see in many industrialized countries around the globe that people are pleased with a life which is unfortunately hollowed of spirituality. This reminds me the appalling remarks of Dr. Klaus, whom I met in 1954:

1- The economic system that favors free enterprise and views land as the basis of all wealth. (Translator).

Today, many people live their life with utmost satisfaction without finding themselves obliged to answer these four questions (of whence, whereunto, why and whether) both theoretically and practically.

Let me repeat here the answer that I gave to my German interlocutor:

Since God has endowed man with a powerful life, he can adapt himself with all conditions. Man is able to while away his life with narcotization, inebriety, unconsciousness and selfishness, without knowing what is good and bad in this world, or what is lawful and unlawful. To state the matter differently, the engine of human life has been so rigorously devised by the transcendent wisdom of divinity that man can adjust himself with various artificial conditions that are not in harmony with his nature, and in theoretical physics' parlance, he can consider himself as a reliable beholder of knowledge while man is not merely a beholder; in fact, he has also a role to play.

We come across figures in the course of history who have slaughtered hundreds of thousand or even millions of innocent peoples in a systematic fashion and then held feasts without waiting for the vultures to eat the carrions and wipe the signs of crime off the earth. However, man can be otherwise, as we have also had people who toiled for the betterment of human life.

Man has an undeniable power for the creation of artificial illegal life. We all know that the so-called age of "slavery" continued for a very long time and man was completely satisfied with such a mean life; slavery was then a well-authorized social institution insofar as no one ever could cast any doubt about it. However, today we raise sharp criticisms of the brutal conditions of human life in those times.

Then let us not consider human carnal satisfaction the ultimate truth. Moreover, the natural form of life where man lives with the material alone should not be confused with true life. Can twenty-first century man manage to survive and continue life? This is the very issue that was discussed at a conference held in Vancouver in 1989, as is reflected in the title of its final declaration: **The Vancouver Declaration on Human Survival in the 21th Century.**[1]

Such a declaration would imply that the human oblivion of

1- In 1989, a conference was held in Vancouver to study the question whether man would be able to survive the twenty-first century or not? Muhammad Taghi Ja'fari has provided a critique of the declaration issued at the end of the conference in Vancouver in his book *The Human Genome Project*, which has also been translated into English. (Editor).

spirituality, which is a vital element of human life, will result in collective suicide. This declaration calls up the intellectuals and scholars of all human societies to reinstate the spiritual, cultural, religious and moral aspects of human life that was lost through the monopolization of the material.

56

Prof. Peter Frost

Subject: Management and Islamic Mysticism
Nationality: Canadian/ Major: Management
Dialogue Date: 1991

Frost: What distinguishes Islamic mysticism from other non-Islamic alternatives?

Ja'fari: The distinguishing feature of Islamic mysticism is that its aim is not to remove the matter and materials from the world and human vista. Being is being, and whatever which has reality exists. In fact, Islamic mysticism interprets these realities.

Bluntly speaking, Islamic mysticism regards the material world and corporal things as a wave of the invisible world. It makes them transparent and uncovers and sees through the noumenal world behind them. Islam accepts all human instincts, be it natural or animal, but by means of harnessing them, Islam seeks to demonstrate the magnitude of the spirit and its dominion over the instincts that brings the latter into the service of human personality. Islam does not deny the existence of sexual instincts or the instinct of selfishness, which is in fact the most demanding instinct! Islam accepts the existence of these instincts; however, it adjusts the instinct of selfishness to the preservation of evolutionary nature. Thus, the human individual beholds the whole world with one nature, i.e. the conscious self which is opened to existence. This is the characteristic mark of Islamic mysticism. I discussed this issue with Professor Charles Adams from McGill University on the differences of Islamic mysticism and Hinduism.

It is said that Spinoza was once reproached, "With your pantheistic philosophy, you have degraded God and made Him become one with nature." "No, I have not degraded the Lord", he retorted, "in fact, I have upgraded this nature and revealed its concealed value and meaning."

I don't know whether this story is true or not. Anyway, we have a similar discourse in Islamic mysticism according to which whenever man is deemed to be of an evolutionary nature, it reveals the value and magnificence of matter. To put it otherwise, let us quote from Rumi, who has said:

> Truly, it was you who brought together the two ends of two rings of existence.

Tell me who you are, and I will tell you what the matter and the materials mean to you.

An evolved human individual considers the universe as an observatory for beholding infinity and its effusion. But if man is contented with his "natural self", he will not touch the transcendent realm of individuality and will slope into self-alienation and self-brutalization like animals, or maybe even more despicable than animals, for if a man becomes self-alienated, he would brutalize himself as he devours others when he finds them strange.

This point has not been sufficiently observed in the mystical schools that we find in some other societies from old times. This is why we frequently come across the idea that this world is a huge pantheon when studying the literature and culture of Islamic mysticism. This is even a perspective through which one can behold infinity, as Victor Hugo says:

> If one succeeds to behold infinity, one can also expose oneself to it.

This is the idea that underlies Islamic mysticism both in theory and practice.

Frost: What is an ideal for of management in your view?

Ja'fari: If you mean by ideal management the absorption of all available interests through adopting a utilitarian policy, that is not acceptable for us, although it is the best form of management in the eyes of modern technocrats. An ideal management, whether in a small business or in a large firm, or even at a larger scale involving a country, is a management that is more faithful to human principles and considers the human beings as not unconscious cogs or iron bolts and nuts of machines. Thus, the more managers are informed of lofty human emotions, sentiments, activities and phenomena, the more ideal and successful their management will be. To state the matter differently, as management cares about the wages of the workers and the employers or protects the rights of citizens, in the same way it must seriously observe their human rights. We should not separate people's ordinary rights of material life from the rights of their souls. Today we are unfortunately witness to catastrophic competition among managements for the impetuous utilization of their staffs to fulfill their managemental policies and intentions without considering the fact that the staff is not consisted of iron nuts but in fact humans!

This will remain an incurable pain if we do not adopt more humane policies for management, as beautifully depicted by Imam Ali (PBUH) in the following words:

You are responsible for anyone who is ruled by you.

It doesn't matter if you are ruling one man or billions of people; in any event, you are responsible before those whom you rule. Sadly, today we hear that economists argue that "the satisfaction of personnel is enough" without paying any attention to the value of their work and workers' life, which is gradually worn out. To put it in a nutshell, the best form of management is that which satisfies its *human* staff.

Of course, this is a temporary treatment and calmative, for as long as the true rights of the staff have not been fulfilled, their satisfaction will be confined to shallow affairs as everyone naturally seeks to feed his family. Man is forced by a necessity if not compelled. With a cursory look, we will find that most of the staff is forced by the decisions that have been taken by their managers.

Thus, Islam insists that the value of work of every human individual must be recognized regardless of the individual's position, be it permanent or temporary:

Therefore, give full measure and weight and do not diminish to men their things. (The Heights 7:85)

That is to say, everyone deserves to have his own due position in the society. This management needs to be realized one day in human societies; otherwise, more anxieties, fears and dark horizons will inflict humanity.

Having said these, we can now turn to the question of what an form of ideal management is. I think the more humane the motive and aim of management is, the more sublime the management will also be and the deeper the intended motive gets, the more influential and penetrating the management will prove to be among the staff. This motivational evolution proceeds up to the threshold of heavens. In other words, the managers or directorate see their staff and the scientific and practical means of management are in fact the manifestations of divine providence. Of course, I know that this is almost a far-fetched goal for humanity, but there is no other way as intelligible as this when it comes to ideal management.[1]

A Fundamental Inquiry of the Role of Motivation in Managerial Activities in the Islamic Society and a Criticism of the Contemporary Motivational Theory

It is needless to argue that all human activities, be it talking, doing or thinking or even refusing to do something in despite of the existence of the prerequisites of that thing, are always preceded by their appropriate motives.

This necessary and self-evident principle is expressed in an abridged form as follows:

Every conscious human activity requires a serious appetite for obtaining a goal that motivates man.

The constitutive elements of this principle can be explained as follows:

1- The health of mental factors and natural instincts as well as the balance of external conditions, as the first factor in the preparation of the required grounds for a correct motivation play an influential role in human activities, particularly in managerial affairs. This is why one can say that those individuals who lack this condition cannot be prosperous in managerial affairs.

2- A conscious and free action (i.e., voluntary action) requires an understanding of the purported goal and the acceptance of its motivation as a result of which the serious will for the fulfillment of the intended goal is then created. It should be taken into consideration that when the organization under management is composed of human individuals, the manager has to be of a conscious and liberal character. The lack of these two vital items, i.e. consciousness and liberty, results in traumatic depressions in the manager, which will also derange management.

3- The intensity and weakness of one's will for the fulfillment of the intended goal is a function of the intensity and weakness of the motivation of that goal.

4- After understanding the goal and its respective motivational drive and the emergence of serious will for the fulfillment of the

---

1- On the role of motivation in management in Islamic society and criticism of contemporary motivational theory of management, Mr. Ja'fari delivered a lengthy lecture at the International Conference of Motivation in Management in Tehran that can complement the Allameh's debates in this dialogue. , we shall annex this lecture to this dialogue.

intended goal, the work (behavior), whether in regard to intellectual or manual form, begins to proceed, through which one can touch the intended goal.

5- The fulfillment of goal with which work is finished.

The Essential Task of Leaders of Moslem Societies

The essential task of leaders of Moslem societies is to inform their people of the Ultimate Telos of Life – in general – as well as its underlying motives so that they may always make their choices with consciousness and freedom in any given social condition.

The Ultimate Telos of human life consists of participation in the general cosmic movement toward Supreme Perfection via "a conscious journey into life". Every stage of this journey is heightened with the enthusiasm for the next stage due to its motivational goal. This journey is directed by human character; a character which has an eternally Supreme Perfection as its Ultimate Telos. It is in light of this Supreme Perfection that matter and meaning become united and reflect one another.

The most significant feature of a purpose-built life, which is the key to human happiness, is that regardless of the situation in which someone lives, if he is asked about the quality of his life considering the gifts and possibilities he has had access to in past and present, his answer should be, "Regarding the physical and mental gifts and pure reason and conscience with which I have been equipped, I find myself in the best possible situation insofar as if my death arrives at this very moment, I will receive it warmly, as I believe that there is an eternity where people shall be asked of their words, acts, thoughts and intentions." To put it otherwise, every happy human being has an eternal compass inside that shows him the direction in the ocean of existence.

Management in Islam has two basic conditions. Before turning to these two conditions, we will need to fathom the significance and value of management in Islam. To accomplish the latter task, we have to know that a competent manager should spot the existing gifts, ideals and possibilities in the staff and mobilize them in a harmonic fashion for the fulfillment of one or a number of goals; in other word, a manager should be a wise and conscientious man.

The Fundamental Conditions of Management

The First Condition: Having in view the ideal man as depicted in

Islamic sources, we come to the conclusion that a manager who is in charge of a group of people is indeed like a sane and mature individual who manages the organs of his. This is the best possible relationship that can be imagined between the manager and the staff. It is through such a relationship that the staff can devote themselves to the objectives drawn by their manager with a free conscience.

Thus, when the people in the staff consider themselves as members of the same whole, they shall easily understand the underlying motives of the directions given by their leader. This is the only way to overcome the machinistic worldview that has changed human individuals into unconscious cogs and nuts of a machine.

Any other type of managerial relationship than this will reduce management to a purposeless and deterministic process. Moreover, we need to know that although neither one of the human organs has any independent character for itself, an organization's staff have their own individual identity independent of those ones which the organization has given them and the management should cultivate them.

By true observation of this condition, the incumbent manager or directorate will also find life sweet and happy if they change their place with the crew.

The Second Condition: This condition pertains to the acquisition of fresh knowledge and information regarding management. As the bonds between societies, nations and masses grow larger, the vital significance of this condition becomes more evident, for these bonds which connect societies to each other require the principles and issues of management to be continuously revised and relocated in an open system. On the other hand, even if we assume that the machinistic order of life in modern societies forces the management principles and issue to be stipulated in a closed system, these societies are still inflicted with some incalculable natural factors and events that require to be managed in an open system.

Management and Its Domains of Activity

Management usually covers five areas or domains of activity:
1. Planning
2. Organization
3. Control and supervision
4. The creation and promotion of motives
5. Assessing the aforementioned four items

Management in the Islamic Society

According to human conscience, common sense and authentic Islamic sources, mankind is of an inherent dignity and honor that demonstrates his status and value. In other words, man is a type of animal who has been honored by a transcendent creator. All revealed religions and primordial schools of anthropology are unanimous on this inherent dignity of man. Man can promote this potential dignity into the desired honor and dignity –i.e. volitional perfection – through devoting himself to the quest of acquired dignity. The following holy verse of the Quran demonstrates human inherent dignity:

> *And surely we have honored the children of Adam, and we carry them in the land and the sea, and we have given them of the good things, and we have made them excel by an appropriate excellence over most of those whom we have created.* (The Night journey 17:70)

Thus, one can truly say that the most significant task of a manager in an Islamic society is the recognition of the fact that those individuals who work under his management have two material and spiritual aspects, both of which must be equally appreciated by him. However, since the Ultimate Telos of human life is exposing oneself to the radiations of divine unveiling, man needs to pay even more attention to the spiritual aspect.

This task has its origin in the fact that all human individuals share the same ultimate telos of life, i.e. participation in the cosmic movement toward Supreme Perfection, and no one has any preponderance to the other in this regard. To put it otherwise, there is no difference whatsoever between a manager and his employees in benefiting from an "intelligible life", as it is not so that a manager should enjoy a more interpretable life which ends in happiness while an ordinary member of the organization is to be reduced to an "intelligent gorilla" by such thinkers as Taylor! Isn't this an unwarranted insult to human dignity and honor?! Could one ever conceive a harsher humiliation of humanity than this?! This motivation (the equal right of the manager and his staff to have a decent life which requires the spiritual aspect of employees to be taken into an earnest consideration) is the most important factor that distinguishes Islamic management from other alternatives.

Having said these, one can argue that wherever this vital task concerning the spiritual aspect of human existence has not been fulfilled correctly, for "some-ones" have always been metamorphosed into "some-things". More disastrous and shameful than this humiliation is the fact that this regressive movement has been christened as civilization and its originators have been called the "heroes of intellectual evolution"!

Although the managers have found it highly embarrassing to apply "things" to "ones," they have not refused to use such expressions as "intelligent gorilla". I wish they would use "things" as it stands outside the domain of values and vices.

It is only by the fulfillment of this vital task that management can remove the shameful stigma of Machiavellianism from its face. It other words, it is merely through the observation of this task that management can deliver itself from the bondages of oppressive exploitation as it is only the belief in the value of people's souls and behaving according to this belief that can protect them from falling prey to the selfish whims of Leviathans. This vital task has been seriously highlighted by Imam Ali (PBUH) in his historical letter to Malek Ashtar:

> *Acquaint your heart with love, mercy and sympathy for people and do not behave toward them like a bloody predator who tries to devour them, for people are of two groups: they are either your brothers of the same religion or your brothers of the same origin.[1]*

The leader of a society must grasp the necessity of bearing in his heart love, mercy and sympathy for the people who are under his leadership in the same way that he presently grasps the necessity of defending himself before occurring threats. Imam Ali (PBUH) has related the story of Mu'awyah's invasion on the Al-Anbar province in the following words:

> *It has been reported to me that some soldiers of the enemy have attacked women and plundered their jewels while they begged the invaders to spare them. After doing these, the troops of the enemy have returned to their camps with many trophies without having even a scratch on their cheeks. If a Moslem man dies after hearing this story, he would never be blamed for his death, but such a death for a Moslem man due to that event is worthy in my view.[2]*

This worthy death requires an existential sense of belonging to a

---

1- *Nahjulbalaghah*, Letter 53.
2- Ibid: Sermon 27.

society which has poor and oppressed people. To promote such a lofty sense in the members of society, the leader himself needs to have that sense in the fullest fashion. It is in this spirit that Imam Ali (PBUH) has written to his representative in Basra, Othman Ibn Hanif:

> *Should I suffice as myself to state that this is the Prince of Believers and not to be beside them in the hardships of time?* [1]

The Criterion of the Necessity and the Value of Motives

The most basic motivation, according to Islam, i.e. common sense and pure conscience, is that which stems from the most basic needs. Then the more basic and vital something is, the more basic and vital its respective motivation will also be.

The basic needs of humanity, all of which become manifested in the phenomenon of "self-preservation", can be classified under the following three categories:

1- **Natural Self-preservation** involves needs for food, housing, hygiene, reproduction and the defense of one's life before intruding factors.

2- **Mental Self-preservation** pertains to needs for mental peace, the logical regulation of subjective and objective factors, the preservation of unity and harmony among the constitutive elements of personality and protecting it against disorders which can threaten its health, like multiple personality, dissociative identity disorder and so on and so forth.

3- **Evolutionary Self-preservation:** This category contains the most significant needs of humanity which have been highlighted and addressed by revealed religions, ethicists, legal schools and constructive and pioneering rules, as means of human intellectual evolution.

This brings us to a necessary principle which is of a fundamental significance in management despite its simplicity. Mankind requires a sound management in the process of self-preservation in all of the three aforementioned aspects. Of course, this management becomes harder when the targeted aspect entails complicated situations and settings. For example, the management of housing affairs in a village or a small town is much easier than that in a large city, as educational management in underpopulated areas is far simpler than areas with heavy populations. Accordingly, managers must be appointed based

---

1- Ibid: Sermon 47.

on their capabilities and experiences as the management of complicated situations requires enough information of the elementary and secondary motives of the *managee* if the intended plans and decisions are to be realized in a logical fashion.

Different Types of Motivation in Management

The following taxonomy seems to contain almost all of the motives that are involved in management:

1- **Objective Motivations,** like environmental and social factors, which have in turn various types, for instance:

   I) The compulsion of blind forces. This type of management has indeed no natural motivation, but the only motive of a manager in this stage is the preservation of the natural self before destructive factors. It is needless to say that compulsion lies outside the domain of values.

   II) In a motivationally higher stage than the previous stage, management is motivated by the sustaining factors of natural life such as housing, food, clothing, hygiene, and the like. Although these factors are not as much compulsory as the need for the defence of one's life, since they are the necessary requirements of natural life, one can say that this motivation is based on semi-compulsory factors, scientifically speaking.

2- **Subjective Motivations:** This type of motivation is divided into various kinds:

   I) Regarding oneself as being superior to others; this in turn can have two kinds:

   * This is a realistic estimation of oneself in the sense that one's sense of manual or intellectual superiority is rooted in one's individual merits. The activities of a human being with such a sense of superiority can be driven with value-laden motives if he undertakes these activities with the sense of duty; otherwise, man's actions should be understood as spontaneous effects of natural necessities.

   * This egocentric estimation of oneself does not match the realities on the ground. There is no complaint of this man if his wrong estimation of himself does not damage the reality. However, he would be sued if found guilty of a wrongdoing.

   II) The motivation driven by egotism and ostentation, which is against values.

3- **Utility-driven Motivation:** The manager's decisions and actions are based on his personal interests. This motivation and the previous one are two main motivations of management in the contemporary Western world.

4- **Personal Fondness of Management:** Most of the people who have a temperate mental state show a particular enthusiasm for some special vocations like piloting, industrial affairs, scientific works, army, judgment and so on and so forth. This enthusiasm is so deeply rooted in human existence that Rumi says:

> *As it is pleasant for us to live an urban life*
>
> *It is also pleasant for others to have a tribal life,*
>
> *As you love to be a master,*
>
> *Whereas your fellow man prefers to be a blacksmith.*
>
> *Everyone has been made for a vocation,*
>
> *And its love has been put into their heart.*[1]

Now we have to see where these enthusiasms have their roots in. To answer this question, one needs to resort to psychology and other branches of human sciences. Of course, we may not find the ultimate answer, but we can shed some light on it by our researches.

5- **Having professional knowledge and experience** in management is itself one of the significant factors of one's enthusiasm for managerial activities. In other words, someone's profession in one particular field of knowledge as such shows that he has had a driving enthusiasm for the field that helped him obtain the highest degree in it. The difference between the fourth motivation and the present one lies in the fact that in the previous motivation, it is personal fondness that leads to profession while according to the present motivation it is profession and activity that gradually leads to enthusiasm.

6- **The sense of responsibility resulted from transcendent human commitment:** This motivation and the next one certainly lie within the domain of values. Those who act under the motivation of this transcendent sense of responsibility, which has its roots in human inherent dignity, tread the path of perfection.

1- Rumi's *Masnavi*, Book 3.

This is the very authentic and valuable motivation that has been occulted under an insufficient notion of morality like many other nobilities and necessities of human evolutionary nature.[1] In other words, since the outbreak of the fatal disease of "*morality, evolution and values in general must be kept out of the scientific life of human individuals*", the machine-plagued minds escape from morality and spiritual evolution, without which personality is nothing, as a prey escapes from the predator!

To put the matter in a nutshell, the sublime moral motivation, which is more valuable than the shallow and transitory pleasant phenomena, is the very motivation which can lead a society to civilization, happiness and true freedoms.

7- **The sense of divine obligation**: This is indeed the noblest motivation that one can imagine for management. There is no sign of utilitarianism or deterministic factors of society and environment in this motivation. It is neither infected with egotism or ostentation nor is it driven by gratification of personal fondness or profession. This is the very motivation that has incited the divine prophets and saints to reform human societies and individual lives. The primary effect of this motivation is that the manager regards his staffs as organs of his own existence.[2]

1- If you ask a knowledgeable man to list the three basic causes of debacle of human evolutionary nature, one of them will be certainly the occultation of morality due to the blind scientism and egotisms instead of logical promotion of knowledge, which is one of the necessary pillars of human life. To put it otherwise, with the modern compartmentalization of knowledge by blind votaries of science, all fundamental ethical realities like the necessity of truth-seeking, using power as a means for social reformation and justice, the recognition of sacred phenomenon of human life and so on and so forth, have been occulted.

2- This relationship has been already discussed in the first condition of management.

57

Ms. Christine Caruelle

Subject: Aesthetics
Nationality: Swiss/ Major: Cultural Studies
Dialogue Date: 1992

Caruelle: What is your definition of beauty?

Ja'fari: As you know, there are different definitions of beauty. Some thinkers believe that beauty is a self-evident notion like being, light, darkness and others, and thus requires no definition. On the other hand, some other thinkers say that beauty is a phenomenon which fills human beings inside with joy and pleasure.

It seems we need to distinguish two kinds of beauty (sensible and intelligible beauties) from each other and define them separately:

I) **Sensible Beauty** is a tasteful and expressive portrayal of perfection. Perfection is a supreme order that the human soul discovers in the universe, particularly in beautiful phenomena.

II) **Intelligible Beauty** is the cultivation of the human soul by justice, like the sense of the necessity of gratefulness, the transcendent sense of responsibility, the promotion of justice, the application of one's freedom in the path of goodness and perfection and the sense of union with other men.

The difference between these two kinds of beauty lies in the fact that the intelligible beauty is concerned with the human soul and denotes its flourishing through justice and the freedom of personality and this flourishing, joy and pleasure belong to the soul, which are brought about by justice, the sense of the necessity of gratefulness, the transcendent sense of responsibility, the promotion of justice, the application of one's freedom in the path of goodness and perfection and the sense of union with other men. But sensible beauty has two elements, i.e. objective and subjective elements, which constitute every beauty. The objective element is the very tasteful and expressive phenomenon or portrayal that represents perfection (the supreme order of existence) in the outside world. On the other hand, the subjective element is our aesthetic sense, by which we understand and enjoy the beauties.

Caruelle: What does beauty mean in your life?

Ja'fari: Beauty is of vital significance for me from two respects:
The First Respect: The tranquility and joy that beauty provides for the soul in a quantity-plagued material world and makes nature a pleasurable and friendly place. Allegorically speaking, we are like a bird in the cage within a beautiful garden that enjoys beholding the beauties around.
The Second Respect: Since we have been born into this world as beings toward God and the Lord is the Absolute Beauty, beauty is among the objectives of our life.

Caruelle: What kind of relation does beauty have with art?

Ja'fari: Art consists of the sublime product of a constructive human mental activity upon one's rational and intuitive understandings of oneself, God, the world and one's fellowmen for description of realities "as they are" or their exhibition "as they ought to be". Accordingly, a fine art is a sublime activity which devotes itself to the portrayal of perfection through tasteful and expressive depictions. Thus, the relationship between art and beauty is like the relationship existing between the beauty of a body or clothing with the human soul. For example, a devoted and just figure who sacrifices himself for the promotion of human values can be regarded a manifestation of art and beauty. The [relationships between] these two facts can be analyzed as follows:

1- The sensible and intelligible beauties which have not been made by human hands, like the beauty of natural scenes, mountains, rivers, falls, moonlight and the beauty of human appearances as well as the natural beauty of human soul in her pristine form, fall under the definition of beauty, but they are not works of art because they bear no sign of the act of human will, effort or decision.

2- Those works of art in which beauty is not of the first rate of significance, like the appliances that have been devised by geniuses for the betterment of human life conditions, have artistic roots despite their lack of beauty.

3- Some works of art are also beautiful. In such phenomena, art and beauty have come together and built a charming work of art. The beauty and purity of those souls who devote themselves to the promotion of goodness and justice belong to this category.

Caruelle: What is Iranian art?

Ja'fari: It is needless to argue that one cannot ascribe any particular art to a nation on account of their being humans. Thus, if all nations were supposed to live only with their common human ideals, we would not have such varied forms of art today. Of course, the environmental, geographical and cultural elements which cause the natural life forms to vary from one region to the other always become reflected in works of art. The following are some factors which separate the arts of world nations from each other:

1- The historical principles and phenomena that have been internalized in the people of a society.
2- The cultural, moral, religious and literary characteristics of a nation.
3- Particular assessments of the quadruple human ontological relationships with man himself, with God, with the world and with his fellow men.

Now we turn to the peculiarities of Iranian art. To begin with, we need to mention that no one can ever determine the exact artistic coordinates of a nation. This impossibility has two reasons:

1- The longer the history of a nation is, and the more sophisticated the factors which have changed the culture of that nation are, the more difficult it wconsequently be the recognition of genuine art of the nation at stake will be.
2- The other factor which accounts for the accurate determination of the coordinates of a nation's art is the particular glass which a scholar puts when he turns to the interpretation of the cultural heritage of a nation particularly artistic phenomena, which are mainly based on personal sentiments of the artist. Needless to say, the interpretation of the personal sentiments of an artist is not an easy task to undertake.

For example, there are scholars who explain all human mental activities based on economic issues. It is evident that such thinkers will even interpret works of art and cultural phenomena in terms of economic functions. Moreover, some scholars are optimistic about human nature, while some others approach with in a gloomy attitude, and these attitudes of theirs certainly affect their interpretations of artistic and cultural issues.

On the other hand, artistic orientations also eclipse the judgments of art. Those critics who believe in "art for art" have different assessments of the field as compared to those scholars who promote the idea of "art for man".

Furthermore, if the analysis of a given work of art needs some scientific and historical data, this will certainly cast its shadow on the artistic judgments of different scholars of different views of the data at issue.

Anyway, the remnants of Iranian ancient artistic heritage show that this nation has had an indescribable enthusiasm for the creation of works of art, and history testifies it. For example, the art of poetry has scored an unrivalled success in Iran, according to literary experts around the globe. Moreover, the ancient coins, monuments, mansions and other works of art all reflect this burning enthusiasm for artistic creativity.

What is of vital significance in this regard is the groundbreaking revolution that Iranian art has undergone through after the emergence of Islam. Islam gave a spiritual and ideological turn to Iranian art. This intellectual shift has reflected itself in the mansions, mosques, monuments and other works of art that have been crafted in Islamic era. This shift is also reflected in Iranian poetry, insofar as we see that after the emergence of Islam, a large part of poetic works have been devoted to the promotion of spiritual, cultural and ideological ideas.

58

Mr. Morris[1]

Subject: Islamic Mysticism[2]
Nationality: American/ Major: Mysticism
Dialogue Date: 1993

Ja'fari: Mr. Morris! How could Islamic mysticism touch the souls of contemporary technology-plagued men?

Morris: I think this is an easy question to answer. I have devoted my whole academic career to the teaching of the history of Islamic mysticism, Hafez, Rumi, the Quran and prophetic traditions to students who had no acquaintance whatsoever with Islamic culture. Moreover, I think since these students have had no cultural and educational background in this field, they are more eager to learn about it. Today the human condition, in my opinion, is very horrific as experience and experiments also demonstrate it. In this condition, sacred books like the Bible and the Quran and their parables and stories as well as the tales of great Persian literati such as Rumi, Hafez and Attar can have emancipating effects on the human soul.

Ja'fari: So it became clear that this task is not as easy as we imagined at first!

Nadimi: Is Rumi more influential or Hafez?

Morris: Hafez has been translated into English, as has the Quran. When I teach *Oeuvres de Hafez*, I have to deliver a long lecture, as there are numerous difficult terms that need to be clarified, but Rumi's *Masnavi* are easier for students to understand.[3] Attar's *Mantiq-ul-tayr*

1- From University of Ohio.

2- Dr. Nadimi, the Chancellor of the University of Shahid Beheshti at that time, was also part of this dialogue.

3- Of course, Professor Morris should take it into account that although Rumi's verses are of simple wordings, they bear profound ideas of mysticism, philosophy, wisdom and human sciences. However if the reader takes a closer

("The Conference of Birds") has also been translated into English and is helpful in classroom. To make the ideas more accessible for students we use the films which have been produced based on the stories of *Masnavi*, *The Conference of Birds* and other literary works. Some contemporary films are so imbued with literature that can easily touch the audience in a desirable fashion. Here we see the impact of technology, and one can say that only the mediums have changed while the human soul, the human brain and man's power of understanding still remain untouched. Generally speaking, films play an effective role in conveying the message of Iranian symbols and parables to modern audiences. Having this in mind, I always start my class with parables and stories.

Ja'fari: You have pointed out a very significant point. Rumi appropriates the parables and stories in a profound fashion. Of course, sometimes he says that the narratives which he relates are not real parables.

> *This world does not have an identical configuration*
>
> *For me to afford you with two things alike.*
>
> *I am merely to find a defective parable*
>
> *To redeem the reason from wonder.*[1]

That is to say, there are no two identical things in this world for me to be able to convey the truth that I want to convey by means of using a parable. However, I present the reader with a partial allegory just to help the reasons.

As Rumi himself has humbly argued, a parable does not convey the whole truth even though it is a leap forward. As you mentioned, these parables and narratives have reached their climax in the thoughts of Attar and Rumi. Hafez uses short and limited parables but Rumi sometimes relate a story without leaving even a small detail untold.

My question is whether these parables and stories related by Attar and Rumi can help us today to understand mystical truths or not. For example, Rumi states:

> *From yourself, as a single part composed of the wholes,*
>
> *Understand the status of every unfolded one.*[2]

---

look, he will concede that Rumi is intellectually more sophisticated than Hafez though the latter's poetical art surpasses that of the former.

1- Rumi's *Masnavi*, Book 4.

2- Ibid: Book 1.

O' you man, although you are but a single part of a whole, you have all wholes inside you! Understand the Ultimate Simple's nature based on your own existence. Now the question is whether the media-plagued, romantic and technoxicated minds can understand this truth or not.

Since all my veins now pulse with drunkenness,

How can I represent his loftiness?[1]

Morris: My students are not like ordinary people. Many of them do not even watch television; some are musicians who live in a spiritual world of their music, which is in fact a form of mysticism. Your question is concerned with the mystery of the spiritual aptitude which unbelievably varies from one man to the other, all of whom belong to the same society. Mysticism gives this aptitude to those who pursue it. I do not claim that my students are exemplary in this regard, but they have experienced the extremes and have now come after the truth. To put it otherwise, they have garnered enough experience to embark upon the path of truth. Allow me to recite a verse of the Quran:

> **And Allah's is the east and the west, therefore, whither you turn, thither is Allah's presence; surely Allah is amplegiving, knowing.** (The Cow 2:115)

The point of this verse lies in *"whither you turn"*. That is, Abraham's followers always remember God, but this verse states that most people love to turn to the Lord. Attar believes that Satan constantly struggles to distract people and keep them away from the Divine Essence. People do not know that they are getting lost in darkness, but eventually they come to their senses one day and return to the path. In other words, people learn their lessons from this technoxicated society and one day come back to the path of truth.

Ja'fari: I think this day is when the Twelfth Occulted Imam (PBUH) of Shi'ites rises to fill the world with justice.

Nadimi: We need to take account of two points here: firstly, Professor Morris speaks of a small circle of his own students who are not plagued with dominant culture and have devoted themselves to music ever since their childhood and do not have any particular tendency. As a result, when they attend the lectures presented by Professor Morris, they have different states than those of ordinary people. Secondly, extremism, as Professor Morris mentioned, has a particular mechanism that finally leads man to moderation and the path of truth.

1- Ibid.

Ja'fari: This tendency toward the truth, which requires one to tread the path of moderation, is not possible without the divine factor. On the other hand, this *will to the truth* is rooted in the human primordial nature and reflects the human inner purity.

Nadimi: I have two questions for Pro. Morris. Firstly, I would like to hear your view on the fundamental criticisms that have been leveled against the West due to the West's refusal to return to the primordial principles of humanity. Secondly, I am curious to know your estimation of the theories which claim that the only cure for the human contemporary plight is a universal revolution.

Morris: I think I can answer your questions in a number of ways. Firstly, we are always caught with a sense of alienation whenever a new shift takes place in the normal course of our life as if we've lost whatever once we loved. This always happens. For example, when I was a young man, I wished to live in Iran, a society which is fraught with the remembrance of God. Many individuals have impressions of this kind and due to this very reason they become fond of religion and a votary of, say, Orthodox Christianity, Judaism, Islam and so on and so forth. To state the matter differently, one can say that this state is a reaction to the modern condition of human life. However, God's grace, love and affection for people are more than this. It is wrong to think that divine providence has been ceased for a while. God's friends are always among us, and we can also reach them in the other world. The light of divinity glows in every human's heart and we only need to tear the blinds.

On human commitment in this regard, I should say that the world is a school where man learns how to find his way to God. God Himself changes the settings to try us in a fresh way. This modern world is itself another test, but when things change, people think that it is the end of time! Everyone is waiting for the rise of the Occulted Imam here and there. It is in this time that we see the most creativity in literature and mysticism.

When Rumi's *Masnawi* appeared, it was received as a revolutionary work in its time. This was also the case with Attar's *Conference of Birds* or the story of Sheikh San'an. In those times, Moslems required such creativities to understand the ideas, parables and stories of their religion. We live in similar conditions, but we can't work according to ancient stories. We should exercise our creativity and adapt these stories to the conditions of our time. Many thinkers and scholars have devoted themselves to this task, while we do not even know their names, for history shows that people usually do not recognize the saints of their own time. As Hafez states,

From weeping, the pupil of my eye seated in blood is;

Behold how the state of men in search of Thee is.

Ja'fari: It seems that Professor Morris has touched upon some very significant issues. The first issue is the eternal flow of divine light in the human heart. I have pondered upon this issue for a while and come to the conclusion that it is not so that people are born with a gene for mechanization. Everyone is born with this divine light, i.e. with a pure primordial nature. Accordingly, man is not an evil creature in nature. There is no inborn force that pushes him toward a machinelike, unconscious life. This point has also been endorsed by great Moslem men of wisdom and philosophers. A prophetic tradition reads:

Everyone is born with a pure primordial nature.

The other issue is that of uncalculated causes. In his interview with Woodrow Wyatt,[1] Bertrand Russell highlights fear as the chief cause of people's fondness of religion:

> *Wyatt: Are you calling it fear, since people assign their own problems to God, a priest or a religion and refrain from encountering difficulties themselves?*
>
> *Russell: Yes, now you consider all of the dangerous issues which the world is grappled with. I always receive letters from people which read, "God himself will keep us safe", but He has not kept us safe in the past and I cannot realize why they think that He will do so in future.[2]*

Divine Providence does not emerge in history in a physical form, but it acts through a set of uncalculated causes. For example, an uncalculated black cloud comes over the Waterloo Valley[3] and causes Napoleon to be defeated while no one imagined that would happen; the black cloud had not been taken into consideration in Napoleon's war strategy. Accordingly, God does not exert His influence on affairs in a direct fashion; in fact, he changes the course of human life through uncalculated causes.

1- Former member of British parliament and BBC commentator. (Translator).

2- See Ja'fari, M. T., (2008): *An Analytical Exposition of the Russell-Wyatt Dialogue.* (Originally in Persian).

3- A town in central Belgium and the scene of the final defeat of Napoleon in 1815 by Prussian and British forces. (Translator).

The other noteworthy issue is that until the eleventh century A. D. Moslems were the masters of sciences and in the Middle Ages they saved science, philosophy and even industry from decease. Again, in the thirteenth century we see a colossal intellectual revolution that not only includes such mystics as Jalaluddin Muhammad Rumi but also the distinguished scientists of the century comprising almost a hundred and forty scientists, mathematicians and astronomers. This renaissance happened in Khajeh Nasiruddin Tusi's era. He did not expect to have so many scientific figures by himself after that downfall. As a result, we can't find the true causes of the emergence and the fall of civilizations.

It is us who say that after the emergence and the fall of the Roman Empire such and such will happen; this is not for sure. I wrote this to Sir Russell in response to him in one of our correspondences and I mentioned that in twenty one spotted civilizations – plus the Sabeans (the civilization of the Princess of Saba), which is always ignored – the causes of their emergence and fall are not discussed. This is why we say that a hand from heavens had been at work and it is certainly Divine Providence. On the other hand, in sociology, philosophy and history we argue that these have happened "by chance"! Scientists say that uncalculated causes are in action.

As to the first issue, I should reiterate once again that there is no excuse for acquitting oneself from wrongdoings on the pretext that everything has been written in heavens and no one can change it.

Nadimi: The point that Mr. Morris indicated in his discussions was that the ideas of Shams, Rumi and Attar were revolutionary in their own times and also considered as being very innovative then. Moreover, as the years went by, they have found their true places in society, and finally, the pure has been separated from the impure. Said differently, the society has split the true from the untrue. Professor Morris claims that even today there are people who have such original ideas although no one knows the names of these innovative thinkers and these new theories may have some critics but they would sound intact as fundamental solutions.

But as to your question whether we can present these deep themes through modern instruments, I should say that this issue is pursued seriously as these instruments are pretty popular and used everywhere. But before hearing my answer, I would like to ask you a question. Do Rumi's verses address the public or the elite?

Ja'fari: As Rumi has stated:

What I say only matches your understanding;

I died longing for true understanding.[1]

With my own confidant if I'd been paired,

Just like the reed, such stories I'd have shared.[2]

Rumi was bestowed with a daunting truth, but his mind didn't let him stand still.

I am a sculptor and a painter, and I make an idol every moment;

Then I break that idol before your feet.[3]

After visiting Shams, Rumi's mind had become active in an unprecedented fashion. He was not *for himself* so that to teach people in a logical way. We do this task today in academia. Thus Rumi's son says:

My father said, "My words are not under my control and this is annoying, as I can't manage my speech when I want to communicate a moral message with friends, but I am happy that it is from the Lord."

However, I do not know whether then they understood that:

The sea of truths is hidden, but the land is on display;

Our foams are waves or just ocean spray.[4]

Or:

O' Brother! You know why non-existence is in existence,

Since the opposite is concealed in its opposite.[5]

Or:

Then there is no absolute evil in this world;

Evil is relative, you need to know this, too.[6]

They could understand such themes by analogy but they surely couldn't touch the following truths in those times:

From yourself, a single part composed of the wholes;

Understand the status of every unfolded ones.[1]

1- Rumi's *Masnavi*, Book 3.
2- Ibid: Book 1.
3- Rumi's *Sonnets of Shams*.
4- Rumi's *Masnavi*, Book 1.
5- Ibid: Book 5.
6- Ibid: Book 4.

***

You didn't smite when you smote a sedition

Hundred thousands of stacks inside a fist.

A sun is concealed in a grain;

Suddenly that grain opens its mouth.

The heavens and the earth break to pieces

Before that sun when she rises.[2]

If someone like Hatif Isfahani had spoken of such a mystical spark:

> *Dissect the heart of any particle,*
>
> *You will discover a whole sunlight inside...*

It would have been over, but Rumi states it as "Suddenly, the grain opens its mouth and the heavens and the earth break into pieces."

I don't think they understood at that time what Rumi meant by these verses, like many other great books such as *Les Miserables* of which people only know the names of its characters say Marius, Fantine and Cosette! They do not understand the message which Victor Hugo is trying to communicate to the reader. Therefore, our answer to this question is almost negative. Once, in early 80's, I proposed some artists to have sessions together on Rumi so that I could show them the themes in *Masnavi* that can be filmed.

Nadimi: It would be very effective if our cultural authorities today would turn to metaphors, allegories and analogies to explain the realities, as God has addressed the believers in the Quran in a metaphorical language. It seems that we can do this. If we accept that one can explain even the most complicated notions of the world via simple stories and parables, and if we accept that God has done it already, I think modern science and technology can prove to be an apt vehicle for this task. Needless to say, of course, this task requires one to have sufficient knowledge of these notions in advance. Some action seems to have been taken after your proposal, as we see some films and animated features have been produced based on the stories of Rumi and Attar, since they can easily be conveyed in film, contrary to the notions included in *Oeuvres de Hafez*. For example, some films have been produced based on the stories of *The Old Harpist*, *Waxy Doll* and

---

1- Ibid: Book 1.

2- Ibid: Book 6.

some others, however I doubt if the beauty of notions have been conveyed too!

Now this brings me to another question as to our debate. I do also accept that divine light is primordial. However, we approach the world once from that angle and another time from this angle. From that angle, no change has happened at all and the rain of divine mercy is falling, anyway. From this angle, however, in some moments of history man has had a bigger bowl that gradually became smaller, and even in a certain period, it turned upside down. The point is that if we take a closer look at the world, we will soon understand that the spiritual vision of the world has been blurred, and this is not merely confined to the Western culture, but in fact this has begun to happen since four centuries ago on. To put it otherwise, the modern civilization as a whole is founded on the absence of the invisible world. Of course, I do not intend to put the last word, as there is no cessation [in divine mercy], but if you look carefully, you'll see that even in Christianity, in the dark age of the inquisition, there was a trace of spiritual vision. It was the excess of medieval times indeed that gave rise to the negligence of modern age. In other words, the shallow spirituality of the Middle Ages ended up in modern materialism.

Morris: I believe that people can easily connect themselves with their Lord in very plain environments like the wilderness and mountainous areas. It was very interesting for me when I visited the wilderness of the desert areas in central Iran. There, I wonderfully found myself much closer to God. When I teach, I always ask my students, "Where do you find yourselves closer to God?" They say, "By the sea or in mountains and in places which have not been affected by man in general." It is not by accident either, of course, that most divine prophets come from the wilderness or from mountains. It is totally natural for me that Zoroaster, Muhammad (PBUH) and Jesus have spent a while in nature. The remembrance of God is very difficult in technoxicated environments. The true knowledge to which we should devote ourselves blooms in this environment. I think God cultures us step by step in the same way that we rear our children.

For example, my child gets tired of computer games quite quickly, but when he plays in a natural environment, he hardly becomes fatigued and is happy even for weeks and months. This is indeed the secret of time, and if there are big problems in life, it is simultaneously loaded with big opportunities, too. I accept that there are a huge number of distracting problems in our time, much more than the past. My father, for instance, was a farmer and always prayed when he was working. I had then the same state of mind; however, I think that in this moment of human life, if one turns to God, one will be more prosperous instead of frolicking in nature.

Ja'fari: In fact, human character is not so limited that these problems can trammel it, provided the votaries of wealth and fame leave it alone and let man regulate his relations with technology may he reign the latter. In the same way that a packsaddle maker clearly knows how to make a sound packsaddle which does not injure the animal, and at the same time he knows that his profession is a divine examination. In this spirit, Nezami Ganjavi states:

> *In the world creating world,*
> *No better figure than this could be moulded.*
> *My and your business with such length*
> *Is not play let put it in short;*
> *When the natures were taking shape,*
> *Our destiny was written another way*
> *So that to contemplate and search for the mystery*
> *To follow up the scent in right way*
> *To examine this and that one by one,*
> *Search through the earth and heavens one at a time.*
> *What do all these works and lordhood mean?*
> *Who is he? And who is his lord?*

Today we can still existentially confront people with the world. One could even state that if the human mind is not taken captive by economic problems, these issues will not be able to reign human character providing a true opportunity be given to man.

The media can fill the work and pastime hours of people with a series of spiritual programs; it can even provide an understanding of machinery and the world for man. The magnificent technological advances of modern times show us that the human brain can accomplish all of these tasks. Of course, we should not take people to task for everything in this regard, as they easily give themselves up. The question addresses the philosopher in the following words, 'Why have you forgotten the majesty and grandeur of the universe? Why don't you pay attention to the majesty and magnitude of the world? Why have you neglected the sacred side of existence and have instead limited yourself to the matter, form and their rules?"

Having said these, we see characters in the history of mankind that have not surrendered to the pressures and limits of time and pursued their ideals.

For example, when Omar Ibn Husam met Omar Abhari, he asked him, "What do you do?" "It is twenty years now that I have been studying astronomy," Abhari retorted. That is to say, it is twenty years that he has been interpreting the following verse of the Holy Quran:

> *Surely we have adorned the nearest heaven with an adornment,*
> *the stars.* (Those Ranged in Ranks 37:6)

Morris: We imagine that we know what the whole is, but as the life grows further, we perceive that we've known nothing of the whole. In other words, it is not so that we always see the hands of God in the flow of events when we turn to understand human historical and temporal relations and this world's relation with higher spiritual orders of existence. Sometimes, for example, it takes us nearly twenty years to know whether something is wrong or right. Therefore, man should always be humble. As the Holy Quran states:

> *Allah does not impose upon any soul a duty but to the extent of*
> *its ability.* (The Cow 2:286)

I hope our ability may one day become a little bit further if God wills it so.

An astonishing story has been related in the Quran of the divine trust that I shall cite here word for word:

> *We did indeed offer the Trust to the heavens and the earth and*
> *the mountains; but they refused to undertake it, being afraid*
> *thereof: but man undertook it; he was indeed unjust and*
> *foolish.* (The Confederates 33:72)

As you see, the Quran states that man has taken on this trust and continues that, "he was indeed unjust and foolish". Then both are right, but the later part is more acurate with regards to the world. As times go by, man becomes aware of other factors and gets out the realm of ignorance, but the point is that man must know the extent of "his ability".

Ja'fari: Allow me to present an example in regard to holistic viewpoints. As Nasir Khusrow Qubadiani has said:

> *Our wisdom and reason will never be able to find dominance over the*
> *whole universe,*

For reason is merely a part of the whole, and a part can never dominate the whole.

No philosopher could ever issue any holistic judgment in the total course of human history unless he had a grip on the world as a whole. Every human being is indeed born with a primordial notion of the universe in its totality. All Western, Eastern, ancient, medieval, modern and contemporary philosophers could issue general judgments of the world and sometimes of being if they have an overview of it. When a materialist says that the world is consisted of matter and motion, we say, "Which world? Do you mean the limited and small planet on which you live? This earth is only a droplet within the infinite cosmos. Determine your subject first, and then make your judgment! A judgment cannot be made without a subject. To issue a judgment of the world, one needs to have an overview of it in advance. If you now decide to travel to the remotest points of the cosmos, you will soon pitch in to get a grip of the circumstances and requirements of such a journey. This is the correct method which should be inculcated in the children of Adam. The world's universities must teach the students to realize their own rational capability to understand the universe *in its totality* and orient themselves toward God, since every understanding of the whole contains a sense of existence in itself. It is as though if I get a grip of this room as a whole, I'll understand its dependence on the mason, architect, and painter and so on and so forth, too, but the problem is that they do not allow man to be educated and then be managed. What is the use of managing some beasts at all?! Let the man understand his character first, let his brain flourish and get a grip of the total scheme of affairs and then manage him! Having done these, he will follow you with utmost consciousness. It is an utter betrayal to confine the man to a packsaddle called free-will and in a machine, while reason says that he can understand the universe as a whole.

You can make remarks in the philosophy of history as you have stood in a corner of history and have a good deal of information. You turn back and make comparisons and get a grip of the issue and make arguments and compare what you've not seen with what you see. This is also the case with the understanding of the universe as a whole.

To have a thorough knowledge of existence *in general*, one needs to tackle limitations, diminish utilitarian considerations and reduce egotisms. We should say, "O' Man! You are great, and this greatness is reflected in your tendency toward mastering existence. At least in three or four thousand cases, Rumi has spoken of the general scheme of the universe. Almost 6300 verses of his *Sonnets of Shams* deals with the human "soul". The following is an example of these verses:

There is a grassy plain which we wish shall remain

In full bloom forever,

And there is a beloved for the beauty of whom

The two worlds deserve to be sacrificed.

At dawn, the beloved leaves the house of the Greatest of the Great

For a hunting trip;

If only the bullet of the beloved's beauty would hunt down our heart!

What a bride exists in the soul, the picture of whose face has decorated
The Universe like brides' tender, delicate hands!

What does the soul have which so mirrors the world? Let the universities say these to people, and then we shall see what happens. While we see now that these truths are taught in universities as ancient literature. It is my soul that sees the beauty. Where does this lie? Why don't cows and camels see this beauty? This beauty is a reflection of your soul's countenance. Can a termite, an elephant or a cow understand this beauty?

Here Rumi has exceeded Sa'di who says,

I am happy with Him in this world, with whom the world is happy all;

I love the world which comes from Him all.

Rumi says, "You do not need to fly to the heavens; it suffices you to remain on earth. I will show you the source of majesty and beauty of universe right here. You will find it in the human soul."

What a bride exists in the soul, the picture of whose face

Has decorated the Universe like brides' tender, delicate hands!

I personally believe that these truths can be taught to man only if we give up our utilitarian ambitions and egotisms. Man has also the aptitude to learn these truths, but we hide human souls in factories and limit them and do not let them to understand. I think that we have to inquire about man once again.

In a lecture I delivered at a university, I argued that whenever humanity has embarked upon the path of development, he progressed. Wherever he has let everyone do whatever they want to, man has fallen behind. For example, medicine and weaponry have progressed, since no one is allowed to obstruct their process of development even in the name of freedom of expression! Technology has hit the uttermost degree of development to this day. How can one ever compare an ass with a Boeing 747? Since it is industry, then it is pioneering. I don't think one layman would dare to come up with a proposal for Boeing or a professional medical center. But in mysticism and humanities, the story is otherwise. Every unprofessional is allowed to make a remark in the name of freedom of expression!

Since man was kept a mere pursuant in this field, he never succeeded in achieving any flourish, while wherever man became a pioneer, he progressed. Mankind is prosperous in natural sciences and technology, but he has made no advance in humanities.

We have two terms here, i.e. "pursuant [conservative]" and "pioneer [avant-garde]". For example, there is "pursuant law"[1] versus "pioneer law"[2] or "pursuant culture" versus "pioneer culture" and so on and so forth. Wherever man has appeared as a precursor, he prospered. During the recent decades, humanity has progressed in industry more than all of the past centuries. Why? Because it moves forward upon profession and law. Can one remark of something without profession and reason? However, this is not, unfortunately, the case with humanities and literary studies.

Morris: I think this is a very significant issue. You can exercise a good deal of influence in academic circles in this regard, particularly as far as your knowledge of the Western world is concerned.

Ja'fari: The Canadian Fred Red asked me where the solution to the contemporary predicament of the Western world lies. To be honest, I told him, I am a seminary student and speak to you as a cleric indeed. In my opinion, a part of the anthropological ideas that are taught in universities and mainly belong to the eighteenth and nineteenth centuries are false and should be abandoned, like Auguste Comte's triple stages of human intellectual evolution, i.e. the theological, the metaphysical and the positive. This idea must be excluded from academic textbooks, for it is utterly wrong. The theological stage is

---

1- A pursuant or conservative law represents a legal system composed of a series of codes that have been adopted to regulate human natural life. By "natural" life, we are here referring to the normal phenomena of life, such as feelings, motions, will, thoughts, reproduction, attracting pleasures and repelling harmful factors as much as possible.

2- A pioneer or avant-garde law represents a legal system which has been designed based on the ideals of human intelligible life and has the evolution of human identity as its objective.

fraught with philosophical ideas while Comte claimed that this stage represents the theocentric notion of the world without any philosophical inspiration. We see the same paradox in the philosophical stage, which is witness to the emergence of many scientific theories and ideas. The Middle Ages, which represents the latter stage in Comte's view is at the same time, according to Western historians of sciences, the age of scientific advancement of the Islamic world. The modern times are also fraught with philosophers and theologians. This theory must be revised within the academia.

Morris: I feel this answer is of a more theoretical and rational aspect. There is no sign of action yet.

Ja'fari: No action will be of avail for humanity without some epistemic considerations.

Nadimi: Man is free to unconcernedly choose how to accomplish his private and individual responsibilities. But when man is to fulfill his social commitment, he requires a particular critical notion of society. Otherwise, man can't orient the society. Anyway, this is the path that man has to embark upon, but the issue is that we need to know how we can help others. For example, what should we do when a student longing to learn comes to us for an advice? We can easily give the student individual orientations, but it is not that easy with social issues.

Unfortunately, Eastern societies have absorbed many Western social dogmas without examination. These dogmas are not only indispensible parts of the culture of these societies by commoners, but also for the men of science. Having said these, we need to critically examine these dogmas and see if there is any basis for them at all. With such a social criticism, we can easily find our future path. We have to either receive Western technology in this way or make selections. Of course, we can make a selection when we have enough knowledge of the cultural, intellectual, mental and sociological backgrounds of this culture.

Morris: I think man's issue in this world is that of determination and free will. The answer to your question lies in this very scientific aspect of the issue of determination. To put it otherwise, in the university of life we have only one major, i.e. determination. Many students think that they do not have liberty. For example, in chemistry we learn what a solution is and how something different is obtained by adding a catalyzer to it, that is, either its color gets changed or it becomes solid.

There is a divine tradition of *determination* that reads as follows:

> *Why didn't you feed me when I was hungry?*
>
> *Why didn't you cure me when I was ill?*

That is to say, we can attract God's pleasure and find him by visiting a sick person and feeding a hungry man. Of course, this divine tradition is not merely concerned with physical hunger or illness alone, but it speaks in Quranic language. Whoever devotes himself to the pursuit of knowledge can surely find "God" in this way.

This divine tradition underlines another point as well, namely sincerity in action. We can memorize the Quran and many other ethical books provided that we act to them so that the students do not declare us hypocrites. If we apply this divine tradition, many of our problems will be solved. Of course, such traditions are easy to relate to, but they are very hard to be put into action. We may come across many common people who act to these traditions, while many scholars, philosophers and clerics do not. A mother who helps her neighbor or a taxi driver who helps his passenger find an address are examples of such. We often do not pay enough attention to these traditions.

Ja'fari: The grammatical rules of a language, say Arabic, are not products of deliberate musings of grammarians, but they represent the spontaneous structures of language as they reveal themselves in everyday usages of language.

As you mentioned already, it is only after passing through a historical period that man explains the causes and circumstances of past events.

No one can tell us what will happen next year. You cannot even tell what will happen to an individual after a second. What will happen to his memories? What will happen to his consciousness? What will happen to the unconscious? In these cases, neither history, nor any individual or even the both of them together can give the correct answer. Of course, we can decide to improve some aspects of our life in future although there is no guarantee that the planned amendments will be successfully done. The truth is indicated in this piece of poetry:

> *No one but God knows*
>
> *What game will play tomorrow the world.*

No one knows even when and how the Twelfth Occulted Imam of Shi'ites (PBUH) will emerge. All human societies expect a universal salvation for humanity. This universal salvation is not possible without a divine establishment. However, we can demand that people should prepare themselves for the morning that will finally dawn.

*Surely Allah does not change the condition of a people until
they change their own condition.* (Thunder 13:11)

I have listed almost twenty theories of the *motive power* of history in my
researches and studies of philosophy of history during past twenty one
years. Finally, after reading the Quran, I found that I should not look
for one factor, as the Quran states that the motive power of history is
comprised of two elements:

The unconscious element which comprises everything that is useful for
humanity:

> *He sends down water from the cloud, then watercourses flow
> (with water) according to their measure, and the torrent bears
> along the swelling foam, and from what they melt in the fire for
> the sake of making ornaments or apparatus arises a scum like
> it; thus does Allah compare truth and falsehood; then as for the
> scum, it passes away as a worthless thing; and as for that
> which profits the people, it tarries in the earth; thus does Allah
> set forth parables.* (Ibid: 17)

Then what is useful for man will remain in use.

The second element of motive power of history is the conscious
element:

> *Surely Allah does not change the condition of a people until
> they change their own condition.* (Ibid: 11)

Therefore, Islam gives a promising account of the motive power of
history and there is always a hope for change as long as man exists.

Even one can say that these two verses (Thunder 13:11 & 17) are
reasons why the Quran is in fact God's words. When I synthesized
these two verses with each other, I saw that whatever has been said in
the philosophy of history is uncertain. All proposed theories are one-
sided and do not meet all aspects of the reality.

You asked me to speak about Attar. One can say that Attar's direct
initiation in mysticism is very similar to Rumi's orientation in his
Masnavi. However, it is much better to compare Attar with Shabestari
rather than Rumi. Rumi is a man of spiritual ecstasy and emotions,
whereas Attar does not have such a character and directly turns to the
issues of theology and ethics. Of course, sometimes he says, in the
same fashion as Rumi, that:

> *I have seen a very strange world;*
>
> *I have seen everything absent of myself.*

No one is aware of his inside;

No particle is conscious of another particle.

The soul is hidden in the body and you are hidden in the soul.

O' the hidden in the hidden, o' the soul of the soul.

Rumi has the same theme, but he asks why no particle is conscious of another particle.

Since the destination of soul has been hidden,

Everyone has turned to a direction.[1]

Rumi discusses a sea of issues and this shows that he was a viewer of this heavenly screen. For example, when he sees that someone in the audience has fallen asleep during his lecture, he says:

Sleep overcame the audience for a while;

Water then bore his millstones for a mile.[2]

Old mills work with water. Rumi says that the water of knowledge, which gushes out of my mind, has bore the millstones of the audience with itself.

This water comes up beyond the mill,

For your sake it flows down here by God's will.[3]

That is to say, my ideas are beyond your minds.

When you don't need to have mills anymore,

It then flows above you as before

To teach this truthful speech comes to your tongue

Or else to its own course it could have clung.

It smoothly travels, so one wouldn't know

To gardens under which the rivers flow.[4]

Today psychologists believe that no mental event happens in one's mind twice. Rumi states:

That place to my soul, God, won't you disclose

Where speech without a word is born and grows

So that the pure soul headlong then will race

1- Rumi's *Masnavi*, Book 5.

2- Ibid: Book 1.

3- Ibid.

4- Ibid.

To non-existence's vast open space;

A wide and vast realm of magnificence

From which this false world gains its sustenance.[1]

Now Rumi touches upon issues that are less discussed in Eastern and Western works. Western thinkers have compared this world with a dungeon. Since Pythagoras' time onward, this comparison has been invariably used. Pythagoras likens this world to a dungeon and takes numbers as the principles of everything in the world. Rumi depicts this notion of the world in a wonderful fashion.

Tighter than non-existence is thought's realm;

That's why it causes grieves that overwhelm.

Temporal existence is more cramped than thought;

That's why the moon shrinks almost to a dot.

The sensual world is more cramped than this as well;

It is the most restrictive prison cell.[2]

What causes this tightness? Neither Pythagoras nor any other philosopher has answered this question as beautifully as Rumi has:

What makes it narrow? Multiplicity.

Our senses drag us to plurality;

Unity's not what senses can perceive.

If that's your goal, then this realm you must leave.[3]

Pythagoras has spoken of dungeons and numbers separately, but Rumi has made an integrated sense of them. Rumi says that this world's narrowness has its origin in *the reign of quantity.*

As you see, Attar lacks this ecstatic state of mind. Attar's poetical style is more like that of Shabestari.

1- Ibid.
2- Ibid.
3- Ibid.

59

Dr. Nilüfer Göle[1]

Subject: Islamic and Western Thoughts
Nationality: Turkish/ Major: Sociology
Dialogue Date: 1994

Göle: Since I know that you are acquainted with the ideas of Western thinkers and have continuous philosophical and scientific dialogues with them, I'd like to ask you some questions in this regard. As you know, Islamic and Western thoughts have some similarities and dissimilarities. What is your view of these similarities?

Ja'fari: There are some significant common grounds among Eastern, Western, Moslem, Christian and Jewish societies. When we speak of two geographic regions, we always think of the East versus the West. If we talk about Christianity, we put Moslems before them. The former comparison is more scientific and the latter is more accurate, but since your question is about Islamic and Western thoughts, we shall also follow your proposed conceptual scheme.

There are indeed numerous points of commonality between Islamic countries and the West, such as philosophy, religion and human reasons. Our philosophical consensus has its origin in the fact that we are exposed to the same world to which the Westerners are open. This is the very reason why Islamic philosophy was transported to the Western world. The transference of ideas of Averroes, Avicenna, Ibn Khaldun, Rumi and others is a witness to the fact that both sides have approached the worldviews with an open mind.

To put it otherwise, many figures and ideas from the East have been introduced to the West, and say Victor Hugo with his *Les Miserables* from the Occident comes to the West. Moreover, we see in literature that Attar's *Conference of Birds* is frequently translated into Western

---

1- From Boğaziçi University.

languages. If Western readership had no interest in the literary and mystical ideas of *Conference of Birds,* there would be no need for twelve translations of the work. Or the ideas of Rumi enchant such great figures as Nicholson, Winfield and Hegel. By the same token, on the other hand, when works by Lamartine, Victor Hugo and Balzac come to the West, they are received very warmly.

But as to culture, I should say that my researches of this notion through 24 Western and Eastern encyclopedias demonstrate that there are numerous common grounds in proposed definitions. For example, one can find such elements as the realization of human gifts, the art of benefiting from religions and human evolution in general, as constituents of the definition of culture in these works.

According to contemporary Western and Eastern encyclopedias, we share numerous genuine common cultural grounds with Westerners. Therefore, we can easily benefit from these unities.

We Moslems and Westerners are the grandsons of the same grandfather, i.e. Abraham, the forefather of monotheism, and we Moslems, Christians and Jews regard ourselves the disciples of Abraham. This can serve as a common ground for discovering the primordial religion.

The diversity of ideologies, lands, races and cultures to some extent has caused the civil and criminal laws to differ in Western and Islamic countries. Now let us turn to the differences.

According to scholars, the existence of some differences in the categories that we discussed earlier is natural and unavoidable. Isn't it so that medieval philosophy differs from modern Western philosophy? Isn't it so that medieval schools of philosophy differ from each other? Is Hegel's philosophy exactly like Kantian philosophy? Does Descartes approach philosophical issues in the same fashion as Whitehead? Or does Russell share the same intellectual attitude with Carnap? The answer is undoubtedly negative, as there are differences here and this is a natural fact. Since human individuals differ in respect of their environmental, educational and intellectual backgrounds, they will thus have different notions of humanities and worldviews as well. These discrepancies are so customary that they will never lead to deadly clashes.

As Moslem jurists and lawyers hold different jurisprudential and legal views, there are various legal systems in the West. For example, some intellectuals are proponents of natural law, while some others defend the idea of positive law. These differences are not a big deal if they do not interfere in unscientific issues. In other words, Moslems like their Western fellowmen can live in such atmosphere of diversity of opinions without having any trouble.

This is the case with all subjects be it culture, law or literature. For example, in literature we have realism, surrealism, idealism, impressionism and so on and so forth. These differences can be found also in other branches of knowledge. However, we need to make sure that these differences nurture constructive competitions not fatal clashes. Utilitarianism and selfish chasing of power have been always damaging. To have a universally appreciated *humane* religion, culture and literature we need certainly to give up pessimism, utilitarianism and hedonism, as we have to further the common grounds. There is no doubt that this can easily be done as the troubling issues have their own solutions, while no limitation is imposed by the society or God. Such inhumane intellectual approaches as racism, utilitarianism and egotism have ruined humanity and his history, whereas otherwise. human individuals have enough grounds to move hand in hand.

We see that Moslems and Christians have had extensive relationships whether in medical centers, universities and faculties, laboratories or in other scientific centers until the twelfth and thirteenth centuries. They worked together on joint projects, studied by each other and had much cooperation.

This atmosphere of friendship and cooperation was indeed an achievement of Islamic civilization. Suffice it you, for example, to run over the books that have been written of the joint medications of physicians in these centuries. After a while, egotisms and evil purposes gradually poisoned the atmosphere and created the existing situation within which we live in today.

Göle: After the victory of the Islamic Revolution in 1979, a movement has taken form which calls for the return to the genuine and true values of Islam. What is your idea in this regard?

Ja'fari: It is needless to argue that Islamic values have not been thoroughly implemented in Iran so far. Said differently, there are factors and motives that did not allow these values to be put into effect even in the era of the Prophet Muhammad (PBUH) and Immaculate Imams (PBUT) time. I don't think anyone has ever claimed that Islamic values have been entirely realized, but rather this movement has been an effort to promote these genuine values in a cultural fashion not via oppressive actions.

Göle: What do Islamic values imply in this context?

Ja'fari: Before answering your question, let me pose an issue that is very significant in my view: all of the revolutions that have occurred throughout history, including political, scientific, technological, moral and religious revolutions, have all been induced by certain causes. To put it otherwise, every revolution functions upon the law of causality.

Some may argue that Renaissance[1] or the Industrial Revolution, for example, were revolutions that happened by accident. But this is not a correct argument as both revolutions had their own respective causes that brought about certain effects. On the other hand, a revolution's concrete prosperity as such demonstrates that it is essentially purpose-built and driven by certain causes. In the same way that the East can enjoy the achievements of Western Renaissance and Moslems can reap the benefits of the Industrial Revolution, the West can also enjoy the results of religious revolutions. These revolutions hope to enhance the quality of human life and are not based on utilitarian and egotistic ambitions, as they are basically anti-religion.

Renaissance was to found a new culture, not upon oppression, but based on human ideals and interests, and thus it turned to be so useful for humanity. Having said these, what are important in revolutions and developments are their causes. It is indeed the causes that turn a revolution into something useful for humanity.

Göle: What do you mean by culturo-Islamic values? The values that are today promoted in Iran are declared anti-Western in the West. Do you mean by Islamic values the values that have come to power after the revolution, or do you have other values in mind? Which cultural values are more useful for humanity?

Ja'fari: This is a good question. As it became clear through my previous answers, there are three types of values:

1. Substantive values that belong to all human beings and must be preserved from possible encroachments. These values are embedded in all revealed religions, i.e. Judaism, Christianity and Islam. The questions "Who am I? Whence have I come? Whither have I come? Why have I come?" embody these substantive values whose implementation requires collective and individual efforts. These quadruple ontological questions represent the whole philosophy of human life.

1- The period (c. 1350-1600) of the revival of the arts and learning that began in Italy and spread throughout Europe (most often associated with the works of Michelangelo, Machiavelli, Dante, and Da Vinci). (Translator).

2. Moral values, which are noble values and Islam insists on them. These values are universal, like rights and cultural ideals.

3. The exclusive values of Islam: For example, Islam offers an interpretation of family according to which men and women have their own "determinate legal status", while they are both *equal* in terms of human values. Of course, this is not merely a value, but it is in fact a prescription. To secure the foundation of the family, Islam tries to engage women in family affairs to a larger extent, since the family is a fundamental and genuine reality in Islam. If there were no definite system for marriage, neither men nor women would take on their responsibilities and the children would be unfeeling. Accordingly, Islam highlights these values.

Another point which has been emphasized in revealed religions, particularly in Islam, is that this world is not the last station, but in fact a passageway. We are examined in this world; we expand our talents and exercise our reason and feelings so that we can orient ourselves toward eternity through exposing our mundane life to an *intelligible turn*. Being toward eternity is very important since *if we don't accept eternity, the crux of life will remain unsolved forever*. It is only this notion that solves the issue of resurrection and enables revealed religions to go beyond the limitations of humanism.

Göle: You spoke of three types of values, i.e. ontological, moral and Islamic values. The third type of values merely belongs to Moslems. What is the Western worldview's alternative before these values?

Ja'fari: Unfortunately, Western scholars mostly do not propose exact estimations of these values. Their knowledge of these values is mainly based on books and figures, which are not trustable in our view. For example, Hajj (pilgrimage to Mecca) is a value and an act of devotion in Islam, while some Western thinkers regard it a moral taboo. They indeed do not recognize that Hajj represents one of the most noble and respected values of humanity, although it is an Islamic custom on the surface.

In Hajj, people are delivered from the bondages of their corporeal attachments, egotisms, arrogances and materialistic views and spend some time *with* and *for* themselves. What would be more important than such a self-estimation in seclusion? This is an example of Islamic with a grand philosophy.

Moreover, on the law of retaliation, Westerners say, "Why should another individual be killed for murder? The murderer can be punished in prison and via other instructive methods." They dismiss retaliation as a wrong value. Of course, there are some people even in the West who do not regard retribution as an act of ignorance and backwardness.

There are some considerations of the law of retaliation that should be taken into account. Retaliation is the penalty of intentional homicide provided there has been no compulsion or emergence and mental illness, each of which can nullify the sentence. When all of the conditions of an intentional murder are present, three options are put on the table: retaliation, blood money and forgiveness. Social authorities can promote forgiveness in society via cultural programs.

The law of retaliation reveals the true value of human life, as it states that by taking an innocent life, you expose your own life to an appalling danger. Thus, life becomes valuable and nihilism fades away.

Göle: How do Islamic values go beyond humanism?

Ja'fari: Islam says to people, "If you infringe upon other human beings' lives, your own life will be violated, too." It is by these values that we can prevent from the expansion of nihilism.

Göle: I am more interested in social issues and I'd like to ask some particular sociological questions on the modern world, as so far we have only discussed philosophical issues, which are not so interesting for a sociologist.

Ja'fari: Sociology is always concerned with causes and effects. The causes are what we discussed above. Effects are not good subjects for an exact scientific research. Thus, we need to focus on causes. Suppose a society is afflicted with poverty. Now you have to do a research on the roots of this poverty as a social phenomenon. To what extent can you count on poverty as a scientific phenomenon? Is the culture of this society underdeveloped, is it war-torn or does it have moral problems and the like? Thus, we need to study the effects and the causes together.

Göle: This is indeed the definition of science, and we accept it.

Ja'fari: Suppose that a pious, wise Moslem travels to the West and comes across some negative issues that bother him and are not tolerable for him at all. He should suspend his judgment of the West. He first needs to see what the causes of these phenomena are. If he sees such nihilists as Kafka and Camus, he should see also Whitehead, to whom the East and the West are both indebted.

A thief was brought to Ma'mun ul-Rashid, who ordered his soldiers to chop off the thief's hand. The convict turned to Ma'mun and said, "You should punish yourself first, and then punish me." "Why?" Mamun asked. The thief answered, "You have made the society insecure and poor, and forced me to commit crime." As you see, the thief condemns Mamun by an etiological reasoning.

Göle: Of course, the system is indeed responsible before its citizens, but I think the individuals are also responsible for their actions, as it is a Marxist idea that only the system should be blamed, whereas the individuals must be held accountable, too.

Ja'fari: There are two theories in Iran regarding Islam's engagements with the West. According to the first theory, we must ground our relations with the West upon the central ideals of Islam as depicted in original sources. As I mentioned earlier, these ideals do not induce any conflict; on the contrary, they are good bases for coexistence. As a matter of fact, it is the Westerners who throw wrenches into this process.

Anyway, Moslems believe that their ideology, besides leading them toward the eternal bliss, also provides a platform for scientific and technological engagements with the West. To put it otherwise, Islam is not hostile toward Western people; in fact, Islam opposes the Western notion and alcoholic style of life. Since Islam invites the believers to a conscious and conscientious life, such a religion never tolerates self-intoxication and drunkenness that will dull human consciousness. As a result, our quarrel with the Westerners is basically ideological, and we can gather around and discuss our intellectual disagreements. For example, I have had numerous discussions with Western scholars on human rights, and sometimes we have reached agreements as well. In those cases that the intended agreement is not reached, we have decided that the issue has to be discussed more.

Göle: Doesn't it put Moslems in danger if we try to engage with Western political and social systems, i.e. democracy, nationalism and the like, before securing the foundations of Islamic values? On the other hand, I don't think we are powerful enough to prepare for a confrontation with the West.

Ja'fari: I meant cultural *engagement*, not confrontation.

Göle: If we don't have enough power to engage with them upon equal terms, would it not jeopardize the interests of the Islamic world to reach out to them?

Ja'fari: It depends on the West's intention and what they think of us. If they see us as their own "friends, associates and fellowmen", in Rumi's parlance, and like us, we will certainly reach some agreements, but if they have a different point of view, then we should ask them to explain that.

Göle: I mean, should we compromise with Westerners or not? As you know, some Iranian intellectuals believe that we can have constructive dialogues with the West on such issues as democracy, nationalism, laicism and others, what do you think in this regard?

Ja'fari: As I mentioned earlier, if Westerners have the same view as we have of them, namely, if they consider us as humans like themselves who have undeniable rights and share the same human values, then our relations will be very constructive, but if they think that Moslems and Easterners in general are backward and weak, we shall never reach any agreement whatsoever. Of course, laicism and secularism not only are not compatible with Islam, but also with no other Abrahamic religion. However, this does not mean that we cannot enter into dialogue with the West at all, as we can have constructive engagements on other issues. On the other hand, Islam claims to be a non-racial and universal religion and the promoter of the ideals of Abraham's primordial religion, like Christianity and Judaism. We should work together to expand these common grounds. To put it otherwise, we have to guard this primordial religion.

Göle: Do you accept that the West is more powerful than other parts of the globe in every field such as material affairs, art, industry, science, music, and cinema and so on and so forth, save spiritual matters? As you know, it owns giant media corporations that propagate its values and ideals. Having said these, can we preserve our values and ideals from possible infringements in our engagements with the West?

Ja'fari: As I argued earlier, social effects last as long as their causes do. If these effects have their origin in human original needs, they will last longer, but if they are concerned with human egotisms and carnal whims, they will fade away. On the other hand, "man" is the only touchstone of rightness or wrongness of the path. When a Western thinker of Alexis Carrel's caliber writes a book entitled *Man the Unknown* (1935) that shows the crisis of human sciences in the West, why should we accept its effects? This is an important issue that needs to be taken into earnest account.

Göle: Do you think that satellite antennae are harmful for the Moslem society?

Ja'fari: It depends on what these antennae conduct to the TV screen. If they are used as vehicles for the dissemination of knowledge, human sciences, human values and cultural issues, they are certainly good and everyone should have a satellite antenna in their house. Dogmatic encounters with such matters are wrong. The realities on the ground must be the basis of our judgment. If a satellite is used for the propagation of morality and culture, it is useful, but if it is used as a means for the promotion of immorality, adultery, nihilism and despotism, no one would allow it into their house.

60

Dr. Willibald Pahr

Subject: Human Rights
Nationality: Austrian/ Major: Law/ Dialogue
Date: 1994/5/10

Pahr: As I think you are more competent than anyone else to speak [about the Islamic notion] of human rights, I would like to hear your views in this regard.

Ja'fari: I had a lecture course on human rights in 1978. Since then, I've continuously worked on the Islamic and Western notions of human rights in a comparative context.

Pahr: It would be indeed my pleasure to hear your ideas. Have you published these lectures?

Ja'fari: Yes, I also attended the Organization of Islamic Conference's meeting in Tehran in 1969, where Islamic codes of human rights were discussed and I presented the results of my two-month studies of the issue. I put those ideas in the book and continued my studies for four years. My studies show that the Islamic and Western systems of human rights are united on more than 85 percent of issues. As you see, despite so many cultural, geographical and historical differences that the East and the West have as compared to each other, this amount of agreement seems very interesting and brings glad tidings of future agreements on human rights. Meanwhile, I have taken part in several national and international conferences on human rights in the Philippines, in Tehran and other places and had numerous discussions with Western scholars on human rights, such as Professor Martinson, the chair of the Manila Conference on Human Rights, or Paul Marx and Reynaldo Galindo Pohl from the UN Commission of Human Rights.

The questions that need to be discussed carefully are as follows: Can we have a universal system of human rights for all human cultures in despite of their economic, cultural, political and religious differences?

Can we progress in human rights to the degree that all systems find it acceptable? Has any speculation been made so far of the diversity of religions and cultures?

Pahr: No, nothing has been done in this regard yet. Regarding the differences that you just mentioned, such a task is not possible at all. Even in Austria, the present codes of human rights are interpreted in a different way. For example, there was a particular conception of equality in the country before WWII which changed during the postwar years. Thus, the interpretations of human rights are always context-bounded and differ from one society to the other.

The Charter of the United Nations describes human rights in its first paragraph and makes some exceptions in the second paragraph based on cultural and regional considerations. In other words, these issues have been taken into account even in the Charter of the UN. As a result, one can say that there is a common ground on which stand the universal rights of humanity and it is understood in different ways.

Ja'fari: All Eastern and Western scholars concede that human dignity and honor have been among the motives of the codification of human rights. This is very significant point, but there are two other major issues by the resolution of which we can reach to a more profound understanding of human rights:

Firstly, can we reconcile human inherent dignity and honor, which has been cherished by all religions and primordial schools of philosophy, with the ideas of those scholars who give the priority to power and whose thoughts are taught in academia as official philosophy, and regard it as an essential motive for the codification of human rights? Have these motives had philosophical and scientific impacts on the codification of human rights?

Pahr: I think we can codify the universal codes of human rights upon human inherent dignity and honor and the so-called philosophical schools of thought. We can conglomerate these two elements into an integrated whole, according to Western human rights.

Ja'fari: Let me put it otherwise; we have such thinkers as Nietzsche, Hobbes and Machiavelli, whose ideas are being taught in universities without having been examined already in light of the question that I have just posed. If we suppose that only these thinkers are in the right, namely "*homo homoni lupus* and *power is the fundamental reality in the world*", how then we can prove noble motives for human rights?

Pahr: There are also other thinkers in the West who insist on the fundamentality of *right* and human values, Montesquieu to name just one.

Ja'fari: Of course, we have had decent humanists like Montesquieu who criticize the arguments and ideas of the proponents of struggle for existence and Leviathanism, but the latter group of thinkers also takes the humanists' idea to the task. On the other hand, if we turn to religion and seek the answers of our questions in it, we can easily prove human inherent dignity.

Pahr: You're right that human rights are rooted in revealed religions. All great religions of the world, i.e. Judaism, Christianity and Islam, have spoken of human rights. Unless a unique religion arises to power in Europe, the current problems of human rights will remain unsolved. Many of the existing problems date back to the separation of the church and the state in early modern times. Said differently, until the time when human right was a religious matter, it was considered among religious obligations, but since religious and civil affairs were separated, the observation of human obligations became harder.

Ja'fari: Thus, you also believe that human rights are almost impossible without a universal divine religion. If we have a universal religion – which is Abraham's primordial religion in my view, as Abraham is the father of Jews, Christians and Moslems – disagreements will vanish.

Pahr: I personally agree with you. But I know that there are secular human rights that have not been drawn on any divine school of thought and have their own proponents.

Ja'fari: That is correct, but the problem is that despite the great deal of cooperation and the intellectual engagements that Eastern and Western scholars have with each other, we are still deprived of a universal system of human rights.

Pahr: The problem may lie, as you suggest, in the fact that the West has expelled religion from the public sphere. Our discussions today show how important religion is. You said earlier that eighty-five percent of Islamic and Western systems of human rights are the same. Now I would like to know what the remaining fifteen percent differences are.

Ja'fari: For example, the nineteenth article of the United Nations Declaration of Human Rights speaks of the right of unconditional freedom of expression and thought, while some articles in the same declaration explicitly insist on the necessity of observation of human dignity and honor. Now if someone uses this article as an excuse to insult an individual or a group of people, which international authority will be accountable then?

Pahr: I think the nineteenth article has a clause that stipulates the requirements and conditions of this right.

Ja'fari: We have no such clause in this article. The nineteenth article is unconditional.

Pahr: Then it will lead to difficulties. I think all articles of the United Nations Declaration of Human Rights have determinate limits. They are legitimate as far as do not breach other individuals' rights and cause no damage.

Ja'fari: By damage, do you mean only physical damage or the damages that are done to one's reputation and honor as well?

Pahr: Naturally, all types of damages.

Ja'fari: Unfortunately physical damages are mostly considered in law and freedom in its genuine sense is meaningless. Today in the West, everyone is free to write whatever they want. There is no condition that can limit this freedom and this can result in a social chaos.

Pahr: We have never believed in unconditional freedom.

Ja'fari: But today we see that such an unconditional freedom is given to expression and thought.

Pahr: You're right. Unfortunately, after the emergence of newspapers and other mass media, the freedom of expression has been drastically radicalized. I personally agree with you in this regard. This is why we don't have democracy today; in fact, we have *mediacracy*. I believe that human rights must be restricted to the borders of dignity, honor and prestige and this should be our general strategy.

Ja'fari: I am very glad of these sympathetic debates. I wish we had more time to continue our discussions.

Pahr: It was indeed an honor to be here. I hope that one day in future we can discuss these issues together once again.

Ja'fari: I hope so.

61

A Group of Orthodox Christian Thinkers

Subject: Philosophical and Religious Issues
Nationality: Greek / Dialogue Date: 1994

Dr. Moschopoulos: I'd like to ask permission from my dear colleagues and friends and begin with philosophy, as our colleagues are acquainted with theology. I want to speak as a philosopher and feel myself very near to you due to my academic profession in philosophy.

I've done some research on Plato and Aristotle, and I totally agree with you that they are two pillars of Western culture and philosophy. As you know, contemporary philosophers like Whitehead and others have also devoted themselves to the interpretation of the philosophies of Plato and Aristotle. As far as I know, Iranian philosophers have also studied the books of these two philosophers. This scholarship can actually prepare the path for more philosophical and cultural ties between the two worlds. Of course, both Iranian and Western philosophers do not confine themselves only to Plato and Aristotle. In fact, they also study the works of other philosophers like Abu Hamid Ghazali, who is an Iranian philosopher whose work *The Incoherence of Philosophers* I have read and was quite impressed by how he relates faith to theology. Moreover, you've had numerous poets, such as Hafez of Shiraz, who takes man to heavens with his philosophy and method.

Now we are speaking in one language. Although I don't speak Persian, I do speak philosophically. Two thousand years ago, when our philosophers were in trouble and couldn't speak of philosophy inside their own country, they came to Persia and in their return to their homeland, they claimed that they had not been allowed to teach Greek, but I do not accept this story and believe that they studied Greek texts with Iranian students and colleagues and when they couldn't work in their own country, they pursued their studies in Persia.

Thus, today we Greek intellectuals and academicians have come to visit our Iranian colleagues, so that together we may continue your ancestors' way in the promotion of knowledge. I hope that our cooperation will lead to the publication of a joint Platonic work on the traditions of the two countries.

I'd like to express my gratitude for your warm reception. These discussions will surely deepen our understanding of philosophical issues.

Ja'fari: I also concede that we actually need deep and serious cooperation. I believe that technology and academic positivism have led to human self-alienation.

As you just mentioned, we've had commendable philosophical thoughts in the past, which were mainly inspired by Greeks. If we take an intelligent strategy, we can pose them as novel truths in the machinistic world without having any conflict with science. Moreover, we have also adequate theological, philosophical and mystical conceptual apparatus to provide more coherent interpretation of science so as to insure a more prosperous future for humanity.

In an international conference on Avicenna held in New Delhi, I delivered a short lecture on Avicenna. Sixty countries were present in the conference. There I said, "During the seminar, some colleagues spoke of the philosophical career of Avicenna and proved that he is an original and distinguished philosopher. Some speakers focused on his scientific works, particularly Canon in medicine, and demonstrated that he is one of the founders of modern science. Some preferred to speak of his religious outlook, although they couldn't determine whether Avicenna is an Ismaili, Shi'ah or Sunni. Some others proved that Avicenna is a mystic. Of course, we had already worked on this issue and our reason was the three chapters of Avicenna's *Al-Isharat wa-'l-tanbihat* (*"Remarks and Admonitions"*), which bear a very deep mystical vision. I do not intend to boast about an Iranian thinker, but I want to say that a man can simultaneously master all philosophical, scientific, religious and mystical truths in an excellent form. To put it otherwise, science is not against philosophy, as the latter is not against religion, which in turn is not against mysticism, either; this reality has been demonstrated today by the speakers of the conference."

In a national seminar of philosophy, I said, "Is it not Plato who has a highly respected divine character as a mathematician? Has this mathematician and divine man not provided the best words in aesthetics? How can such things gather in one man?" I think that Western and Eastern conscientious scholars like you should pitch in together to show the falsity of the radical claims of positivists and prove that theology, philosophy, religion, science and mysticism are complementary elements of human existence, so as to save humanity from the fatal dangers of the misuses made of technology and positivistic philosophy.

I know Western thinkers like Alfred North Whitehead and Max Planck who, despite being highly esteemed and very sophisticated philosophers and scientists, are spiritual men and respect theological matters. Max Plank writes:

> *There can never be any real opposition between religion and science, for one is the complement of the other. Every serious and reflective person realizes, I think, that the religious element in his nature must be recognized and cultivated if all the powers of the human soul are to act together in perfect balance and harmony. And indeed, it was not by any accident that the greatest thinkers of all ages were also deeply religious souls, even though they made no public show of their religious feeling. It is from the cooperation of understanding with the will that the finest fruit of philosophy has arisen, namely, the ethical fruit. Science enhances the moral values of life, because it furthers a love of truth and reverence – a love of truth displaying itself in the constant endeavor to arrive at a more exact knowledge of the world of mind and matter around us, and reverence, because every advance in knowledge brings us face to face with the mystery of our own being.*[1]

Do you think too that we should overcome this dreadful compartmentalization of knowledge? Isn't this a very urgent and vital issue?

Dr. Agurdides: It is an honor indeed to be here. The discussion that we have begun of Islam and Christianity is in fact based on divine books and the analyses and interpretations that have been prepared upon those books. These are indeed the basis of our debates and represent the field in which we work.

The influences that ancient Greece has exerted on Sufism are recognized both in the West and the East and everyone is aware of the cultural impacts left by Greece on such phenomena. As you mentioned earlier, people are under the spell of modern sciences. I think we should make willy-nilly use of these modern sciences to find the way to our authentic roots, i.e. the ancient history and culture which were

---

1- Planck, Max (1932), *Where Is Science Going?*

based on sacred books. Moreover, we have to introduce our religious backgrounds through these very modern sciences.

I'd like to finish my words with an answer to myself. I believe that the clash that has erupted today between science, religion and philosophy is not basically a war by which one of the sides of conflict is supposed to be vanquished. In past times, some powers sought to build the society upon religious ideals. There were also other forces which tried to pursue their interests through alternative ways. Naturally, this situation gave rise to some clashes and anomalies that sometimes exceeded the expectations of the society.

Our problem today, as an Orthodox or a Moslem, is not a matter of survival in ongoing clashes, but in fact our problem is to show the principles in which we believe.

Ja'fari: As you mentioned, religion can truly preserve its identity before science and philosophy, as its perennial roots lie inside us and the vision that science offers of reality in general shows that religion is an authentic phenomenon. The issue that I have frequently discussed with Western colleagues is that we have one father called the Prophet Abraham (PBUH). Abraham is the forefather of all Christians (Catholics, Protestants and the Orthodox), Moslems and Jews. Let us gather around our heavenly father and make his primordial religion our own common covenant. Although this goal would take very long time to be fulfilled, it is nonetheless worth pursuing, as it is our main problem.

Dimitri Kitsikis: You spoke of the common grounds Iranians and Greeks have. To the best of my knowledge, since the victory of the 1979 revolution, Iran has clearly announced its opposition to the West and Western culture. On the other hand, you're speaking of common philosophical grounds. I think Plato and Aristotle were Eastern in essence and Westerners try to introduce them as Western. I'd like to hear your view on this issue. Of course, we have numerous geographical shared features. We are Orthodox and insist that we are nearer to Easterners.

Ja'fari: Four months ago, I delivered a speech at the Baku Academy of Nezami Ganjavi. After I had finished my speech, one of the members of the Academy asked me if Nezami was Turkish or Persian. "Great thinkers are born into a determinate place and grow with the particular culture and language of that place," I answered. "For example, Nezami Ganjavi was born in Ganja, and his mother language was Turkish, but when he became the renowned Nezami, he no longer belonged to the East or the West; he was no longer Persian or Turkish, and in fact he belonged to humanity." This is also the case with intellectual heritage. When Plato says that, "Children must have a religious education," he speaks to all humanity. It is only cultural differences that separate geographical regions; otherwise, human truths are common.

Kitsikis: We say that the earth is a globe. As a result, a country like Japan is Western as compared to one point, while it is Eastern as compared to another point. Thus, these designations are relative. However, the Islamic Revolution is against Western ideologies. Although geographically speaking we belong to the Western bloc, we are more like Easterners in our ideas. Do you include us within your plan of confrontation with the West?

Ja'fari: Undoubtedly, no. You should take it into account that Phoenicians have their own particular philosophy, and Sumerians have their peculiar worldview as well. Philosophy is a Western word that means "the love of wisdom". If today a front has formed against the West, it has also been said that Greece has many intellectual debts to the East. In other words, Plato was not a purely Western philosopher. If you ponder upon the ideas of Plato and Aristotle, you would easily find the Eastern roots of their thoughts. An elegy of creation has been found in Phoenicia whose themes are very similar to Platonic ideas. Thus, these regions have had intellectual impacts on each other through commercial, geographical and political interactions. Said differently, we have neither pure West nor pure East. As a result, it is hard to draw a line between these two categories.

The resistance front that you mentioned in your remarks is not a matter of race, science or philosophy, but its aim is to fight against imperialistic and corporate ambitions. If these ambitions were pursued by Easterners, they would have also been the target of our objections. Otherwise, many Christians and Jews helped Moslems in the Middle Ages to establish hospitals and medical centers. They have also contributed to the formation of the Islamic civilization. We do not have any problems in these matters. In fact, the problem is imperialism. In other words, the chief concern of this resistance movement is getting to an equal world void of oppressions.

Marius Begzos: Today our problem is the relation of modern sciences and religion. Any stance one takes on this issue would make some his friends and so some others her enemies. Eastern and Western scholars are not exceptions to this reality. In fact, we Greeks today play the role of a bridge between the East and the West.

George Metalinus: Although I hold the same views as to the issues that have been discussed here, I'd like to add that we should not conceal the problem; in fact, we have to seek to find a solution for it. As a historian, I completely understand what Mr. Kitsikis spoke of and I shall express it in my own way.

Plato and Aristotle actually belong to the whole world. Historically speaking, I believe, we belong more to the East than to the West. Our land is a buffer zone which shares many cultural elements with the East and the West and we have continuously attempted to introduce such figures as Plato and Aristotle to the world, for their ideas can bring about a global consensus. This issue is vital in religious matters as the more we know each other, the more we will approach our ideal global unity. I also insist on what Mr. Ja'fari highlighted in his remarks and I hope we can pace toward unity. We are working together to fulfill this significant ideal while there are other coalitions which try to thwart our efforts for their interests. The basic problem lies here. I shall not name these coalitions of counter-forces and ask you to speak in this regard.

Ja'fari: We have three types of unity:

I) **Substantial Unity:** This unity is almost beyond access even among the believers of one faith, let alone among the believers of different religions.

II) **Strategic Unity:** This unity is created by a crisis that unites people with each other and disappears with the fall of crisis.

III) **Intelligible Unity:** This unity denotes a rational unity which is both achievable and justifiable. It is embodied by revealed religions' consensus on Abraham and the notions of "God" and "eternity". We are obliged to fulfill some tasks in the world, which are beyond natural interests and losses. Of course, these obligations may have different forms in various religions. We should observe the inherent dignity and honor of each other. Furthermore, we have to help each other survive in the face of damaging forces of nature. These are the issues with which we can deal together. This is the very intelligible unity. I don't think this unity would embarrass or bother any human individual, including the forces that you just mentioned.

Voulgaris: It is indeed an honor to be the interlocutor of a committed intellectual who believes in God and is concerned about the destiny of humanity. Your deep concerns on these issues show your strong interest in philosophy and the human society. Thus, I propose to dedicate our next symposium to the "pathology of modern technological developments".

Despite the wonderful developments in technology, modern man is confronted with serious challenges concerning his own existence, which have been fueled by the existing problems in human societies. These challenges and questions have occupied the human mind since the dawn of history. These questions are mainly concerned with the meaning of human life and its goal: Whence has man come? Where is he heading to? And where does he stand in the cosmos? And so on and so forth. No doubt, technology and culture cannot answer these questions, for they can only be addressed by religion and philosophy.

Ja'fari: Some years ago, I began systematic research on the telos of human life, which took two or three years. My research shows that religion can certainly determine a "goal or destination" for human life. Natural sciences cannot accomplish this task, however, as they begin and finish in nature, while the equation of human life will be resolved when man's existence is interpreted from *the above*.

During my studies, I have come across some remarks made by Western philosophers, which endorsed the fact that it is only religion that can determine the goal of human life. Sadly, however, man does not hear or accept these remarks. We should not approach man in this issue like a child who refrains from washing his hands, but we must use all academic means to clarify the notion of supreme telos of life for him and prepare him intellectually to be benefitted from this telos.

Dr. Vasili Chakunas:[1] I am very glad to be in the presence of an enlightened and pious intellectual. From the debates that have been made so far, I came to the conclusion that philosophy and religion can cooperate with each other and find solutions for human contemporary problems. Religion and philosophy can move hand in hand, like Plato and Aristotle.

But the issue is that philosophy cannot touch the majority of people, as most men do not read philosophy, while religion has a larger audience and covers almost all individuals in the society. My question is how we Moslems and Orthodox Christians can pace toward modernization without losing our traditions. How much can we trust these efforts and have impacts on other people?

1- Dean of the Athens Faculty of Theology.

Ja'fari: I cannot speak of the political and economic implications of these questions, as they are beyond my knowledge, and the question whether political and economic issues shall allow us to reach our intended conclusion or not is a matter that history will answer. Nonetheless, history has shown that everyone who honestly dedicates himself to the quest for the truth always succeeds.

The important issue here is what the intention on which one decides to dedicate himself to these efforts is. What are our intentions to involve ourselves in such efforts? If our intentions are pure, this unity is an intelligible unity, and as God has promised that it will work, as history has also given witness.

Moschopoulos: Two things have caught my attention – your interesting ideas and your brilliant writings. These show that you are an honest thinker. I hope that one day we might have the opportunity to hear your speech on these issues in one of the magnificent halls of Athens and expand our academic ties.

Chakunas: I'd like to say that we are leaving here with more consciousness and knowledge. I express our gratitude for your giving this opportunity to us to hear your views on the issues we have just debated.

62

Robin Wright[1]

(The Los Angeles Times)

Subject: A Shi'ah Encounter with Modernity and Democracy
Nationality: American/ Major: Journalist/ Dialogue Date: 1994

Wright: I have two questions to ask:

1- How does Islam approach modern political ideas and what is its general view of political thought?

2- What is your view of Islam and democracy? Are these two compatible with each other or not? What is your idea of the theory that says "democracy cannot reach Eastern cultures"?

Ja'fari: To conceptualize Islam's approach to modern political ideas, one firstly needs to have an exact understanding of the ideological features of the religion. Shi'ah Islam is constructed upon five pillars: 1- articles of faith, 2- morals, 3- life affairs and phenomena, 4- elementary prescriptions and 5- secondary prescriptions. Now I shall explain them one by one, as without the articulation of this fundamental structure, we cannot make any remarks in regard to Shi'ah Islam.

Wright: I have already studied some books on the ideological makeup of Islam. If it is possible, kindly put them in a nutshell because of the

---

1- Robin Wright (born 1948 in Ann Arbor, Michigan) is an American foreign affairs analyst, journalist and author. Wright has reported for *The Washington Post*, *The Los Angeles Times*, *The Sunday Times of London*, CBS News and *The Christian Science Monitor*. Her foreign tours include the Middle East, Europe, Africa, and as a roving foreign correspondent in Latin America and Asia. She most recently covered U.S. foreign policy for *The Washington Post*. Wright has also been a fellow at Yale, Duke, Stanford, the U.S. Institute of Peace, the Smithsonian's Woodrow Wilson International Center for Scholars, the Brookings Institution's Saban Center, the Carnegie Endowment for International Peace, the University of California at Santa Barbara, and the University of Southern California. She is the author of *Sacred Rage: The Wrath of Militant Islam* (1985). (Translator).

lack of time.

Ja'fari:

1- **Articles of Faith:** Since these articles are based on human reason and conscience, they never change. Although people are benefited from these articles in proportion to their reason and conscience, in any case they are unalterable, like monotheism, eternity and prophecy.

2- **Morals:** Moral principles are grounded in conscience, human spiritual beauties and *humane* relations of individuals with each other. The moral principles, however they may differ in some cases from one land to the other, are unalterable. For example, we all appreciate gratitude or philanthropy as moral values, although an American or a European may have a different notion of them than that of a Moslem.

3- **Life Affairs and Phenomena:** Islam has assigned all life affairs to Moslems themselves. To put it otherwise, Moslems are free to manage their own life affairs unless one wants to commit prohibited deeds like the production of narcotic drugs, social conflicts and so on and so forth.

    Except for harmful matters, all other life affairs have been assigned to man himself to decide on in the so called democratic spirit. There is no objection here to use the term democracy. For example, the acquisition of knowledge has been underlined as an obligation in Islam, but the structure and shape of universities, schools and laboratories have been totally assigned to people to decide on. Man is free to choose the form of whatever is necessary for him.

Wright: Who recognizes the harmful nature of these activities? Is it the laity or religious authorities?

Ja'fari: This discernment is of two types:

    I) The discernment of subjects, which concerns the professionals and seasoned experts of the society.

    II) The basic needs, which have spiritual and metaphysical aspects, concern religion and embody the fourth pillar that we shall now turn to.

4- **Elementary Prescriptions:** These prescriptions concern human existential needs in the world and man's relationship with God. These prescriptions never change and man has no authority to modify them like daily prayers, fasting, or Hajj and others, which are obligatory and represent human basic needs. The prohibited phenomena that cause material and spiritual corruption are also subjects of these elementary prescriptions. Of course, believers can perform these prescriptions according to their possibilities in emergency situations, but in normal conditions, these principles are unchangeable.

Wright: Isn't this the very act of cautionary dissimulation (i.e., *taqiyyah*)?

Ja'fari: No, these prescriptions are necessary for man for him to pass through the passageway of life – as we regard this world as a passageway that leads us to eternity – and reach spiritual evolution as far as he *can* perform them. In other words, these prescripts are necessary as far as their performance does not cause any loss to the individual and the society.

To state the matter differently, as you know, Islam does not regard this world as being the last station of life, for it has determined a goal for man's life. Thus, Islam has decided a series of obligations for the human soul so that man can fulfill his evolutionary ideal. These obligations, such as abstinence from homicide, gamble, oppression, promiscuity and so on and so forth, are like mathematical axioms that have to be taken for granted in advance. Said otherwise, the individual accepts Islam with these conditions and these prescriptions are unchangeable.

5- **Secondary Prescriptions:** Due to the emergence of new developments in the conditions of human life, there is always the possibility of the appearance of new problems. In such cases, an Islamic judge can issue orders according to his discretion and when conditions return to normal, these orders automatically become irrelevant, such as the Tobacco Fatwa which was issued by Ayatollah Mirza Shirazi.

Every Shi'ah encounter with modernity must be done in light of these five pillars, and as modernity does not change, mathematical truths in the same way it cannot modify our articles of faith, either. It needs to be noticed of morals that, since we consider morality of a heavenly origin not driven from society, morality is thus unchangeable, or in philosophical parlance, pioneer and not pursuant. A pioneer morality has its roots in the primordial principles of faith and humanity.

For example, philanthropy as a pioneer moral attitude originates in a primordial understanding and sense of humanity according to which we must always respect and help each other as human beings without any extra-human consideration. Having said these, now suppose that a Shiah scientist discovers a medication for cancer. This primordial principle of morality requires that he needs to impart it with all human societies without any utilitarian considerations.

Modernity can merely change the forms of the application of these issues, but it cannot change their substance. For example, when a natural disaster occurs, modern appliances can help us perform our philanthropic duties much more easily. If modernity implies the promotion of primordial principles of faith and humanity through new methods and means, we will surely receive it warmly, but the principles are not negotiable.

As living things always dedicate themselves to the preservation of their life, we have the same approach to our primordial principles. In the same way that the defence of life is significant for human beings, intellectual and spiritual evolution also has its own rules, which are regarded as vital. I think I have answered both of your questions.

Wright: I'd like to know the common parameters of Islam, modernity and democracy.

Ja'fari: This issue has been discussed at length by the late Mr. Rashid almost forty-five years ago, and numerous works have been published even in the West on this matter, and thus it is clear enough and does not need to be addressed anymore. The problem of the diversity of opinions, for example, is a notion that has been accepted by all scholars since the past and there is nothing new in it. Anyway, the basic principles of Shi'ism are the five pillars that I mentioned before.

Wright: Is the incumbent system in the Islamic Republic of Iran ideal? Since Islam is a flexible system, is there any room for modifications in future?

Ja'fari: There is no doubt that the Islamic governments that have emerged during the past centuries failed to successfully implement all Islamic rules. The major reason for this failure is the fact that Islam is based on human primordial nature and is against carnal whims. Most people always prefer to pursue their selfish ambitions and carnal desires in this world. As a result, the ideal context for the implementation of Islam's divine and human rules is hardly prepared. As to the future changes, I should say that every change requires to be conducted within the framework of the previously discussed quintuple primordial principles. Islam and the Islamic government are open to technology and communication with other societies as far as they do not harm the primordial harmony of life. To put it otherwise, the system is open as far as it is useful for human life. As history testifies, Islam is always interested in relations with the outside world provided that the principles of just coexistence and committed freedom are observed. There are numerous examples of such relations between Islam and other religions like Christianity and Judaism. According to my research on human rights, there is only a fifteen-percent difference between Islamic and Western notions of human rights. That is to say, *our agreements outweigh our disagreements*. Thus, we are ready to negotiate even these slim differences, too. My studies show that there are many grounds for peaceful coexistence among nations. Meanwhile, every nation has a series of particular rules that are not in conflict with the basic rights of life.

When I attend international symposiums and conferences on human rights in various parts of the world, I see that we can overcome even these minute differences.

Wright: I think it was a good beginning. It is indeed a start from point zero. I hope that in my future visits we can continue our discussions.

Ja'fari: Religiously speaking, we have all one father, i.e. Abraham (PBUH). Abraham is the forefather of Jews, Christians and Moslems. To have a better coexistence, we need to gather around our father and see what his view of life is, since the Torah, the Gospels and the Quran all accept him. I've discussed this with many of my Western colleagues, but I don't see why – despite such a grand common ground for coexistence – things still going wrong.

Wright: I agree with you and believe that Islam is more flexible than what I thought.

Ja'fari: I hope our efforts will be only for the sake of God, God-willing.

63

Members of Iran-Greece Friendship Association

Subject: The Philosophy of Human Rights
Dialogue Date: 1995/ Greece, Athens

Ja'fari: I am very glad to be in Athens among my friends and colleagues. Last year, we were visited by some of you dear colleagues in Tehran, and now I am very happy that we can have another session together.

The right of life is one of the basic and fundamental human rights which has been widely considered by ancient cultures and civilizations particularly by Abrahamic religions that bear a primordial and sapiential understanding of this right and prove it for all human individuals.

Religion adds a sense of sacredness to the ordinary understanding of the right of life. This is a significant step forward taken by religion. We can state that man is a living creature who has life and naturally defends his right of life, reproduces, understands pleasures and pains and struggles to better his life conditions and protect his territory against the intruders. On the other hand, when we say that man is a living being and naturally enjoys a divine sanctity and is directly subjected to the unceasing Divine Favors, it is evident that the right of life is no longer a natural right that can be divested or carelessly treated by the individual.

No one can say that, "I want to kill myself and take away my life." Or, one cannot say that, "I accept humiliation." He cannot do so! Why? Because life is directly concerned with divine providence and man should continue his life and defend his dignity and honor as far as he can.

This issue has its origin in the teachings of revealed religions (Judaism, Christianity and Islam) concerning man and his life in this world. According to these teachings, man cannot disdain his life however he wants. There is no such freedom as a "right of decent life".

It is noteworthy that the issue of "the inherent dignity of human life" has not been sufficiently discussed within human sciences and different schools of philosophy, while religion has taken a leap forward and interpreted life as a primordially sacred phenomenon which even man cannot himself transgress its divine borders.

Keen-sighted scholars throughout history have done humble struggles and efforts to shed light on this great contribution of religion to our knowledge of human life and show that, by the divinization of life, it has succeeded in answering the major questions we have in regard to life and has at the same time offered the last remedy for all human predicaments and injustices. In the Holy Quran, God states:

> *For this reason did we prescribe to the children of Israel that whoever slays a soul, unless it be for manslaughter or for mischief in the land, it is as though he slew all men; and whoever keeps it alive, it is as though he kept alive all men; and certainly our messengers came to them with clear arguments, but even after that many of them certainly act extravagantly in the land.* (The Table Spread 5:32)

Accordingly, the rights of an individual is equal to the rights of all human beings, i.e. 1=all and all=1. What I've discussed so far is regarded as a confirmed reality by human primordial nature and revealed religions.

There are precious thoughts in The Universal Declaration of Human Rights that has been prepared in thirty articles and adopted by the UN General Assembly in 1948. It would have indeed been very appropriate if the codifiers of the The Universal Declaration of Human Rights had discussed human supernatural values as well, since what the history of mankind shows turns to be no more than Hobbesian *"homo homoni lupus"*.

Thomas Hobbes, Machiavelli, Friedreich Nietzsche and others have interpreted humanity in terms of power and force. I wish the codifiers of The Universal Declaration of Human Rights had included debates of this issue in the preamble and convinced mankind that the union and equality of human individuals are primordial truths.

Now I have to cast light on a paradox that should be tackled. Isn't it actually a paradox that Western and Eastern universities and academic centers promote "Leviathanism", "utilitarianism" and "hedonism" on one hand and speak of equality and fraternity on the other hand? This paradox needs to be dealt with by academicians and seasoned scholars if we are to prepare the ground for the realization of human rights.

In the preamble of The Universal Declaration of Human Rights, in seven paragraphs and some of the articles, human dignity and honor have been strongly highlighted and this is a very significant fact. I confess that these articles are legal, not moral. In other words, we should not make normative debates of them. Anyway, human dignity has been underlined in the preamble. This is the highest principle of morality. However, I wish they had added the fact that besides the "inherent dignity" that equally exists in all human individuals, we have also an "acquired dignity". We have divine prophets and decent figures like Socrates. Their teachings can present a goal for life. They have dedicated themselves to humanity. Can we compare these distinguished figures with ordinary people? If this had been taken into account in the Universal Declaration of Human Rights, it would have enormously contributed to human development.

Concisely speaking, I admit that this is a legal covenant and there is no room for moral consideration in it, but it could have been discussed within the philosophy of law, which underlies the document. How could we align a man who has continuously devoted himself to his society with a villain? If this fact had been observed, we would have progressed instead of marking time. I discussed this issue in my lecture at the Manila International Conference on Human Rights and in my private chat with the chair of conference Professor Martinson. I told him that we can persuade the lawyers and philosophers, both in the West and the East, to work on these fundamental issues of philosophy of human rights.

I express once again my happiness of having the opportunity to visit my dear friends in Athens. I am ready to answer any questions that may occur to the minds of my colleagues on the issues just discussed.

Question 1: Our symposium in Tehran was indeed a unique opportunity for me and my colleagues to enhance our spiritual vision. Unfortunately, we were not aware of your unexpected visit of Greece and couldn't plan programs for you as we wished due to the lack of time. Anyway we wish you are satisfied with the session.

Your remarks on the primordial equality of human individuals were actually very interesting for me and I found them very sympathetic. The difference between human legal value, man's natural rights and religious value, as you mentioned, does not lie in religion, as the latter attaches higher values to humanity. How should we understand this difference?

Ja'fari: Life is sacred when it bears divine values inside, and every individual holds himself responsible before the life of his fellow men.

If we only become focused on natural life, the sincere sacrifices that are made for social progress all would prove to be pointless. To put it otherwise, it is divine values that can kindle the sense of responsibility before other people's lives inside the individual and persuade him to dedicate himself to the revival of humanity and the promotion of human dignity, not to avoid an individual loss or for pursuit of a personal interest.

But if we consider life as a merely natural phenomenon, whether in political or scientific activities, we will not succeed in proving that man is "some-one" and not "some-thing". It was indeed due to viewing man as "some-thing" that human relations couldn't go beyond ordinary bargains, while when man recognizes the divine value of life, he will be responsible before other people's lives as well. "The right of life", "the right of dignity" and "the right of committed freedom" are among the rights that have to be exercised upon divine providence. What seculars come up with as "the law" is not in fact a *reality* in a general sense. Said differently, this law does not have a clear reason so as to be able to take a step forward in the path of the evolution of human personality without having political, legal and social forces behind while religion needs no political, legal or social means to create such a sense of responsibility; rather, it only resorts to human spontaneity. If we content ourselves with the idea that law is merely a means for the regulation of human individual and social relations, though this is a great service offered by law, this will cause it not to have a share in human intellectual evolution and remain a prohibitive subject. Thus conceived, law only gets the individual ready not to encroach upon his fellow men's privacy. It is as though a group of experienced musicians are sitting in a music hall without infringing on each other. The hall, the musicians and everything have been prepared for the performance of a symphony orchestra, but if this purpose is not met, whatever has been done will be futile indeed.

Question 2: I was fortunate enough to visit you in Tehran. Today, once again, I have the opportunity to get acquainted with your elevated ideas. As you mentioned, all human individuals have an equal right of life, but all people do not have equal access to necessary living means. African nations, for example, live in a critical condition. If you have not yet traveled to Africa, I hope that you can you visit there and see how people are living in tough conditions! And this is not something new, either; everyone every day reads or hears about the human situation in Africa. There people are dying from hunger and famine.

They eat grasshoppers. Sometimes even there is no grasshopper to eat and people die of hunger. Hunger offers bad proposals to men. You put it very nicely that whoever slays a soul is as though he has slain all men. A hungry man may kill his fellow men to reach access to food supplies.

A president, whose name I do not intend to mention, once said, "One day the hungry world will rise against the satisfied world and this will give rise to a crisis." Somewhere in the Quran, I read that a poor man is the brother of a rich man and the latter should willingly help the former in a way that poor man does not feel humiliated. Hope to visit you again in Tehran.

Ja'fari: There is a reality in humanity which is either not recognized by social authorities or pretended to be unknown to them. The history of philosophy, science and culture shows that humanity is very skilled in words but man's word is not comparable with his actions. There are beautiful words on human rights. Even eighty-five percent of The Universal Declaration of Human Rights is theoretically in harmony with the Islamic notion of human rights, but the practice does not match the theory. There are great works both in the East and in the West which have been dedicated to the perennial issues of mysticism and morality, like *Les Miserables* by Hugo and Rumi's *Masnavi,* but as you mentioned, there is a true shortness of practical measures.

Question 3: You spoke of human rights. Isn't it so that every right creates a responsibility?

Ja'fari: Right and responsibility are like two wings of a bird, or negative and positive charges of electricity. Every right is followed by a responsibility. The fact that I am responsible before your rights as such implies that you should also have an equal sense of responsibility before me.

Question 4: I expect my God to love me and enable me to do whatever I want to do.

Ja'fari: But all human expectations are not necessarily based on right and reality. Human spiritual and moral rights have a makeup other than man's social rights and obligations as the former is indeed a *divine prescript*. When someone claims that he has the right to be exposed to divine grace, he has indeed revealed God's promise that whoever finds himself near to the Lord and decides to embark upon the path of evolution will certainly succeed by God's grace. This is a matter of divine promise like a father's promise to his son which does not impose any commitment unto the father. This promise proves that He is *the Most Compassionate of the compassionate*. But as to your claim that "I can do whatever I want to do", however, you need to know that this claim must be made conditional upon causing no harm to yourself and others. As you know, all human desires are not based on right and reality.

Question 5: It seems that religion is uncompromising on some issues like life and death. For example, in such cases as abortion or euthanasia, when the issue of human rights is looked at and assessed from a natural point of view, it appears to be in contrast with a religious standpoint. The secular notion of human rights has the upper hand on such issues and has marginalized religion to some extent.

Ja'fari: The ban on abortion is one of the noblest reasons of value of life. If we see human life as a natural phenomenon detached from divine wisdom and grace, then life is what Nero, Genghis Khan and Caligula deemed it to be and they are free to do whatever they want to do with life. But if life has a divine value, we have to observe some rules and sanctions; otherwise, we shall experience what once happened to nihilists.

Throughout history, man has contented himself with some things and taken some phenomena as self-evident truths, which turned to be matters of shame and embarrassment as time has gone by. For instance, we've had a period in human history when slavery has been socially, politically, morally and aesthetically justified and legal, but today we are ashamed of that dark age.

If today, as you maintain, secular protagonists of human rights have the upper hand and this intellectual domination as such is deemed to suggest that this logic has been truly accepted and matches the reality indeed only because it has the majority behind itself neither upon logical grounds nor based on wisdom and intellect, it cannot be an unchanging idea for all times and places. We have had majorities in the past who were totally agreed on a given issue, but later we found that this agreement didn't have a logically sound ground like slavery. The more our understanding of life loses its metaphysical value, the closer it brings us to the brink of nihilism. Today, more than any time before, we understand the reality that the more we approach natural life, the more we shall become submerged in contradictions. On the other hand, if life has a divine aspect, human unity will also find a logical basis for itself.

As another example, today we have gathered here. What has pushed us to gather here? Is it profit? No. It is spirituality, knowledge, piety, virtue and the struggle for the betterment of our society that has gathered us together so as to hold this session. It is the metaphysical aspect of life that has brought us together with love, as if we are the children of one family rather than the citizens of two countries insofar as our discussions are being held in a friendly and peaceful form. However, if this session had been held based on the measures of natural life, it would have widened the gaps and proliferated the contradictions. Thus, human rights must be conceptualized in a way that could bring people together upon divine grounds.

Nonetheless, the ban on abortion can be considered as the noblest reason for the value of life, which is supposed to be demonstrated in Islamic human rights. This ban suggests that life needs to be conserved from its very initial steps until the end. Of course, one is free not to allow the sperm to meet the ovum and form the zygote. As to euthanasia, however, we may distinguish between the continuation of the agony and intensification of illness as the former seems to represent a situation that differs from the latter in many respects. This issue, however, requires to be debated by physicians, jurists and legal experts in conferences so as to reach the final solution.

Question 6: Our understanding of natural rights is juristic in its essence. How would these rights turn to be within a divine frame of reference?

Ja'fari: Man is not merely a natural being and a product and effect of material interplays; rather, he has another side. We have a common law which embodies the current patterns of life. Natural rights are parts of these socially adopted patterns that require no proof. However, religion asserts that this is not the whole story. Man cannot be merely a natural synthesis of sperm and ovum! Man is in fact a creature of Divine Essence, and besides his natural rights, he also has a set of inalienable divine rights which guarantee him eternal life.

Question 7: Does a man have the right not to believe in God?

Ja'fari: Yes, he has the right to deny God, as he has the right to challenge and deny himself, but is this struggle and denial is right or not? As Plato says:

Self-alienated is he who does not know where he has come from and what is the perfect and sacred ideal for the fulfillment of which he should prepare himself.[1]

With regard to my acquaintance with Greek philosophy and its great figures, I have always been interested ever since my youth to visit the historical monuments of such great Greek philosophers as Aristotle, Plato, Thales, Democritus, Anaximander, Socrates, Pythagoras, Euclid and others, in Athens, but unfortunately, I didn't see such monuments at all.

Audience: They are dead!

Ja'fari: I have no doubt that Aristotle, Plato, Socrates and others are alive. Even if their corpses are buried under the ground, but their philosophy is still alive. Haven't you heard that Emerson said:

As long as we have Plato's Republic, there is no room for other political book.

Isn't he alive? As you know, Plato has developed the most significant ideas in aesthetics. Surely scientific, philosophical and moral services of Euclid, Aristotle and Socrates will never disappear, though naturally they undergo some modifications.

Audience: What do you mean? Do you mean statues?

Ja'fari: Their memorial monuments, universities, gymnasiums, cultural and scientific centers, streets and so on and so forth.

Audience: Mr. Ja'fari! I was also interested to see the statues of Darius, Cyrus and others in Tehran.

Ja'fari: But power is other than science and philosophy. These men are symbols of power. As you know, if powers are not used for the promotion of the true order of life and values, they can be ignored like natural powers. We have streets in Tehran which have the names of Hafez, Sa'di, Avicenna, Suhrewardi, Zekaria Razi and others.

Audience: What do you have of Omar Khayyam?

Ja'fari: Iranian people respect their literati and scholars by putting their names on schools and universities and streets. There are many streets and schools and gymnasiums throughout Iran which carry the name of Khayyam.

1- Aristotle's *Nichomachean Ethics.*

64

Prof. Athan Delicostopoulos

Subject: The History of Islam, the Unity of Religions,
Compulsion and Free Will
Dialogue Date: 1995/ Greece, Athens

*Professor Delicostopoulos began the dialogue with an
introduction of his academic career and works and
showed a book entitled "The Kremlin Wall" and said:*

*"In 1986, I went to the Soviet embassy in Athens and
asked the ambassador to give a part of this book to
their translators to translate it into Russian and send it
to Mr. Gorbachev. He generously accepted my proposal
and fulfilled it.*

*"In that part of the book, I had written that regarding
the signals that we receive from the USSR concerning
Perestroika[1] as well as the existing economic problems
in the society and politicians' inattention toward the
material and spiritual conditions of the people, I think
we would expect a diametrical change in the political
system of the USSR. If the government does not take
serious actions in this regard, the opportunists will
misuse the existing freedom and poverty of the society
and imperil the life of the country. The other issue was
the necessity of the reintroduction of religion and
conscience into people's life world. Some months later,
the Soviet Embassy sent a letter of invitation for me and
I travelled to Moscow. Meanwhile, they acquired some
translations of my works from the Cultural Attaché of
the Soviet Union in Athens and sent them to Moscow."*

1- The policy of economic liberalization and restructuring in Russia
(implemented by Gorbachev in the 1980s). (Translator).

Ja'fari: I honestly appreciate your sincere efforts for the compilation of effective philosophical and scientific works. Our mission should be first of all finding a path of salvation for modern man, indeed. I remember our meeting in Tehran, when I offered my suggestions on the mechanisms of logical coexistence of world great religions (Judaism, Christianity and Islam), which were also warmly received by our Orthodox colleagues from the University of Athens, you asked me if I am sure we can fulfill this idea. Now I have a question for you: have you discussed this issue in your books?

> *Professor Delicostopolous passed this question in silence and continued to introduce his other books:*
>
> *1- Orthodox Mysticism: the winner of Prize of the Academy of Sciences*
>
> *2- Greek Intellectualism and Orthodox Philosophy: I have demonstrated in this book that Orthodox philosophical worldview has been shaped upon the ideas of Greek philosophers.*
>
> *3- Orthodox Belief: I wrote this book at the request of Greece's Orthodox Church.*
>
> *4- Madonna and the Sword of Islam: This book is intended to show the Ottoman brutalities in Europe. There is a marble statue of Virgin Mary in Poland which has been scratched by the swords of Ottoman soldiers. I intend to use this as a symbol for the Christian suffering during Ottoman Empire.*

Ja'fari: We all know that Islam owes its expansion to its logical bases, intelligible beliefs and simple and practical prescripts. Of course, Islam has had confrontations with tribes and nations who treated Islam and Moslems coarsely. But the story of the sword is merely a libel on Islam. Although public opinion on Islam is still plagued with Islamophobic propaganda, seasoned historians and scholars know that Islam has spread to other parts of the world through its teachings and ideas, not via the force of the sword.

A sword can chop off one's body into pieces, but it cannot touch people's hearts. Thus, Islam has addressed people's hearts so as to lead them toward salvation, peace and friendship. When Islam emerged in the Arabian Peninsula, the sword was at the hands of Iran and Rome, not a group of illiterate, poor Arabs who had no acquaintance whatsoever with martial techniques. Moreover, we see today some thickly peopled Moslem countries where even no single Moslem warrior has ever came to force them to convert to Islam, like most of the Moslem lands such as the Indian subcontinent, Indonesia and China. This is also the case with many parts of Africa and other countries. Furthermore, it was Mongols who invaded Moslem lands and destroyed most of them. Though the sword was at the hands of the Mongols, after a while they turned to Islam and devoted themselves to its promotion. After all, no sword throughout history has ever touched human hearts in the way that religion touched and induced them to embark on the path of intellectual and spiritual evolution.

Delicostopolous: Having heard your historical and logical explanations, I do accept that the sword is a bad charge against Islam. I see Islamic mercy and compassion in your divine face. Certainly, the sword hypothesis of the expansion of Islam is historical fiction and libel.

> *Prof. Delicostopolous here pressed Ja'fari's hands very softly and told him:*

I will not use this title for my book. This title came to my mind after reading three Turkish scholars' interviews on the re-subjugation of Europe by Turkey and by this book, I was meaning to criticize them. For Turkey, Islam means Turkey, while we know that Turkey does not observe the rights of Moslems (Kurds) inside the country. Now, Turkey has expanded its territory within the Mediterranean Sea and meddles in the internal affairs of the Moslems of Cyprus and Greece. We can retaliate, but we do not do that. I should even add that Turkey's war against Iraq is not a matter of human rights, but it in fact seeks to gain access to the intended oil-rich region.

Mohebbali (Iran's Ambassador in Athens): Following your comments on Turkey, I would like to inform you that Greek authorities had already announced their agreement with the construction of a mosque in Athens for numerous Moslems who live in this city and frequently ensured us of providing the land and facilities for obtaining the required justifications from the municipality and the Orthodox Church, but when this issue was pursued by Moslem ambassadors in Athens, we saw that since Saudi Arabia had not allowed an Orthodox chapel to be built in Riyadh, the Athens Orthodox Establishment does not issue the license for the construction of a mosque in Athens. The Greek authorities know that the believers of other religions have their own churches, synagogues and shrines. Thus, Iran can construct a mosque for Moslem citizens in Athens.

Delicostopolous: I am studying the Holy Quran now. In fact, you should not read the mosque construction issue into the Orthodox fundamentalism, as we can understand it otherwise. I am studying the Holy Quran and highlighting the points that can strengthen our unity and taking notes of them so that I may write a book on our commonalities in the near future. I have at least three hundred books on Islam in my computer. I have acquired them from libraries in Lebanon and Syria. I only do not have the experience of living in Iran. Mr. Ambassador may be kind enough to help me travel to Iran and visit Shi'ah scholars and scientists and complement my notes.

Ja'fari: Your intimations of the dialogue between Shi'ah and Orthodox scholars seem to be very substantial and constructive; on the other hand, it can serve as a model for other inter-religious engagements, say between Catholics and Sunnis and the like. I believe that we have only ideological diversity, not religious conflict. I have frequently discussed this idea with my colleagues from other religions and denominations in various conferences. I even remember that once I asked my Sunni colleagues in an assembly to examine our disagreements on two issues of theodicy and compulsion and free will. I hold the same view of the dialogue between Shiah and Orthodox Christians. We must see how we can remove disagreements and differences via history, philosophy and other branches of knowledge.

Delicostopolous: There is a problem in Orthodox philosophy concerning divine justice, which reads why good people only suffer in this world, while bad people always enjoy wealth, pleasure and happiness?

Ja'fari: The manifestation of divine justice lies in order and law, not human individual desires and lusts.

Islam's Response in Regard to Inconveniences, Occurring Evils and Divine Justice

The First Issue: According to Islam, firstly, one's being a virtuous and pious man does not necessarily require that he should be continuously inflicted with grieve and evils as evil people are not necessarily plunged in pleasures and joys.

Secondly, grieves and evils are divided into two groups: the first group hosts those grieve and evils which arise from the faults and wrongs which people commit themselves, like plundering other people's properties and trespassing other people's rights. These evils are done either by individuals or resulted from the mismanagements of social authorities and thus do not have anything to do with divine justice. In such cases, people must take actions themselves either individually or via social authorities. The second group comprises those phenomena which are beyond human will and power like natural disasters such as earthquakes, volcanic eruptions and floods.

These evils are only against human desires not against order and law; moreover, the manifestation of divine justice is law and order, not human desires. Islam describes these evils as means of the examination of mankind in this transitory world and spiritual refinement.

Imagine we are reported that some major changes have happened in celestial bodies, galaxies and constellations though no harm has been done to any living being. We quickly rush into the observatory to see what has caused these changes without having any gloomy presumptions of divine justice. On the other hand, if a brick falls on our toes, we begin to lament of divine justice! We all become philosophers and address God in the following words: "What kind of justice is this?!" This demonstrates that in most cases, our judgments are based on our limited knowledge. All pleasant events are signs of divine justice, while every unpleasant event bespeaks of divine injustice!!

The Second Issue: Accordingly, Islam adopts a middle stance on the issue of compulsion and free will according to which we are neither absolutely determined nor absolutely free. As a matter of fact, numerous elements are at work comprising natural forces, human decisions, common sense and conscience and divine will. As seen by the Holy Prophet and His Progeny (PBUH), this theory is known as *"Amr bayn ul-Amrayn,"* which tanslates as "the Golden Mean".

Prof. Reinhardt, Prof. Schultz and Prof. Thomas[1]

Subject: Mysticism, Illumination and Aesthetics
Dialogue Date: 1995/ Switzerland, Zurich

Reinhardt: I think Persian is a very sweet and beautiful language. Even though I can barely speak Persian, I have read Juneyd Iraqi's verses in Persian.

Ja'fari: Juneyd's poetic heritage is of no account indeed as compared to those of other mystics who have used poetry as a medium for expression of their ideas. His poems do not amount to more than few short pieces. Some of Juneyd's essays have been published in London, entitled *Majma' ul-Rasa'l ("Collected Essays")* which contain remarkable themes.

Juneyd died in 297 or 298 A.H. in Baghdad. There was also a poet called Juneyd Mu'einuddin Abu Al-Ghasem who, besides his collected Persian odes, has compiled a book on the Shiraz cemetery entitled *Shad ul-Azar fi Hati al-Auzar an Zuwari al-Mazar*. This book was written in 791 and edited, glossed and published by Muhammad Qazvini in 1328. Sanaei, Attar and Rumi seem to be the most distinguished mystical and philosophical figures who have articulated their ideas via poetical musings. I have devoted a considerable part of my intellectual career to research on Rumi and his distinguished and global work, i.e. *Masnavi*.

Not only has Rumi discussed many mystical ideas through his spiritual couplets, but he has covered remarkable amount of principles of sciences and philosophies, too. For the last seven centuries now, humanity has enormously benefited from this great man and particularly from his *Masnavi*. I have written fifteen volumes of critical

---

1- Prof. Reinhardt was the head of the Institute for Oriental Studies at the University of Zurich. Prof. Schultz was the director of the Institute of Theology, and Prof. Thomas taught at the Institute for Oriental Studies at the University of Zurich.

expositions and comparative assessments on Rumi's *Masnavi* and believe that the final step has still not been taken yet in this field. Rumi is almost unrivalled in many aspects of his thoughts, both qualitatively and quantatively.

Rumi's monumental work has been equally received and considered by Western and Eastern scholars. In the Indian subcontinent alone, one hundred and twenty volumes of commentary have been written on Rumi's *Masnavi*. Even atheists, who deny spirituality and spiritual realities, bow down before Rumi's marvelous verses. Mirza Fath-Ali Akhundzadeh, who was a renowned materialist, has clearly said:

> *Rumi is an unrivalled scholar and a unique literary thinker.*

But why indeed is Rumi so interesting? I have detected twenty five factors in response to this question that, if you like, I can list a significant number of for you.

Reinhardt: My pleasure.

Ja'fari:

1- Rumi had known the Quran well and I even believe that he had memorized it, for we see that in twenty-five thousand verses, Rumi has referred to 2142 verses of the Quran.[1] When he uses a verse to substantiate a theme, though we may have read that verse ourselves several times befoe, Rumi's application attaches a fresh meaning to it which is novel in our eyes.

2- Rumi's deep knowledge of prophetic traditions. 756 traditions have been cited in Rumi's *Masnavi* most of which are endorsed both by Shiahs and Sunnis.

3- Although Rumi has no claim of philosophy but his ideas cover most of the principles of ancient and modern schools of philosophy in east and west.

4- Rumi puts complex ideas in simple words as if a professor speaks of an issue in an elementary school. For example, Rumi offers a very simple formulation of the ontological problem of part and whole or the creature and the creator which is very significant indeed. He extrapolates highest truths from ordinary folk stories. There is a famous proverb in Persian which reads: a seasoned butcher sells the mutton with its neck. Rumi uses this proverb to explain the place of contraries within the general scheme of things in this world:

1- See: Ja'fari, M. T., (2008): *Why Are Rumi's Words So Charming?* (Originally in Persian).

Wisdom has fastened these contraries together;

O' butcher, this lump of mutton is with neck.[1]

5- Rumi's focus and insight is quite astonishing. When he is speaking of a trivial matter, all at once his mind turns to a vital issue. For example, when he speaks of flower, all of a sudden he extrapolates a very significant cosmological point to which the reader needs to pay attention.

6- Rumi is very humble. He gives no indication whatsoever of himself in his verses, which reflect his wonderful mental activities, but in fact it seems that the realities upon which he shines the light on have been revealed to him from the heavens. Many of the ideas which have been developed in recent centuries have long ago been discussed by Rumi. For example, the mental illnesses which have been diagnosed and listed by Sigmund Freud in the twentieth century have indeed been debated by Rumi seven centuries ago.

7- Rumi has discussed contrariety in his verses almost eighty-five times, such as:

O' Brother! You know why non-existence is in existence

since the opposite is concealed in its opposite.[2]

This verse, in fact, expresses the central theme of Hegel's philosophy.

Stoltz: Do you see any similarity between the intellectual methods of Freud, Hegel and Rumi? Is there any similarity at all between Islam and Western thought?

Ja'fari: Yes, one can easily find numerous examples of such similarities in Rumi's *Masnavi*. If man gives up his prejudices and egotisms, the East and the West can have constructive intellectual engagements with each other.

Stoltz: Do you think that even today people can taste such illuminations?

Ja'fari: Of course they can. The root of intuition and illumination exists in the human nature, but unfortunately, mechanistic life does not allow it to flourish. Civilization and progress are good, but self-indulgence in utilitarianism and inability of management even sears the reason itself.

1- Rumi's *Masnavi*, Book 5.
2- Ibid: Book 5.

Human nature has not undergone major changes, and it is up to universities to breed this aptitude. Although today spiritual initiation is difficult and we have no longer such figures as Rumi, Plato and Avicenna, there are still people in the world who care about their souls.

The manifestations of modern civilization like statues, paintings and even natural beauties, instead of inducing us to begin a journey to our inside world, seem to more likely draw us to the outward.

We no longer think about our inside and have no inner intuition, while such thinkers as Rumi and Plato and others insist that we must depart from external beauties and return to the inside. However, we always move outwardly and immerse ourselves in ever-changing sensibilia.

An animal does not understand and feel the beauty of a painting or a picture of scenery, and it is only man who perceives that beauty. Rumi says that we must delve into the human nature to see what enables man to have such an aesthetic encounter. This issue is the starting point of intuition.

Reinhardt: Watching the portrait of a saint, for instance Imam Ali (PBUH), arouses something in one's inside. Is this your intended intuition?

Ja'fari: Yes, it is. In the story of *Leili and Majnoon*, we read that in the last days of Majnoon's life, Leili goes to him, but Majnoon does not look at her and says, Your beauty was in fact a manifestation of divine beauty, which I intuited it in my inside.

> *I reflected myself on Leili's face;*
>
> *thus I burnt the simple-minded Majnoon.*

In his *Aesthetic as a Science of Expression and General Linguistics*, Croce, the Italian philosopher, writes:

> *By beauty we mean physical beauties, though there are thinkers who regard physical beauties as being the shadow of real beauty. However, we consider such a theory as a moral estimation of beauty.*

Stoltz: Doesn't the prohibition of iconography in Islam imply that we should never trust our visual perceptions and explore the inner sides of facts?

Ja'fari: This is a good analysis, but it does not express everything about the prohibition of iconography in Islam. In fact, if we promote iconography, it would gradually give rise to the idea that man is an icon alone and this would degrade the human status. Moreover, we know that human intellectual and emotional aptitudes cannot be portrayed. Of course, there are some jurists who believe that partial iconography is not prohibited.

Among Rumi's pioneering theories are his metaphoric applications of the term "wave", some of which are regarded today as new ideas in anthropological sciences, like "wave of thought":

> *From knowledge, when there first arouse thought's wave,*
>
> *Through his speech then a form to you it gave.*
>
> *This form was born of speech, then died again;*
>
> *The waves drew back like cattle to their pen.*
>
> *From formlessness comes form originally*
>
> *And we return to him continually.*[1]

This issue has been discussed by scientists in the nineteenth and twentieth centuries. They believe that thought is a type of material wave which pours out of the matter. Rumi says that he knows that thought is a terrestrial wave, but there is also a spiritual wave which is more powerful and is the source of human evolution:

> *The terrestrial wave is our understanding, imagination and thought;*
>
> *The aquatic wave is consciousness, ecstasy and annihilation.*[2]

This issue has also been frequently discussed in other Iranian poets' works:

> *If you split a parcel*
>
> *You would find a sun inside it.*   (Hatif Isfahani)

Rumi does not seemingly imply the latter, but he seems to allude to nuclear explosion:

> *You didn't smite when you smote a sedition,*
>
> *Hundred thousands of stacks inside a fist.*
>
> *A sun is concealed in a grain;*
>
> *Suddenly, that grain opens its mouth;*
>
> *The heavens and earth break to pieces*
>
> *Before that sun when she rises.*[3]

Stoltz: You choose good metaphors which enable you to easily

1- Rumi's *Masnavi*, Book 1.

2- Ibid.

3- Ibid, Book 6.

articulate your ideas. You are very skilled in choosing metaphors. Can't religious truths be expressed but through metaphor?

Ja'fari:

> When you want to deal with a child,
>
> You have to speak in the child's language.[1]

All revealed books have used metaphors, similes and analogies time and again to communicate truths to folks, but in all such cases they have mentioned their metaphoric use of them, whether directly or indirectly.

As Farabi says:

> The concepts and words which we use [to speak of God] are means with which we are familiar, but God is higher than them. However we are forced to use these abstract notions.

Plato believes:

> A flower is beautiful, a statue is beautiful, and a river is beautiful as well, but these are manifestations and means of understanding beauty. What is the absolute truth of beauty which is applied to all beautiful things even to contradictive elements? It is indeed the idea of beauty which makes the flower, the statue and the river beautiful.

Stoltz: There are various scales and criteria for judging a phenomenal encounter. Man sees different phenomena and assesses them upon rational, moral and experimental criteria, and by each one of these criteria, he perceives a particular manifestation of the truth. Then, in the main, there should be a kind of relationship between them so as to serve as a common ground.

Ja'fari: Some philosophers consider Platonic ideas as the purported common ground, while some others believe that this truth is essentially divine and lies somewhere beyond the realm of perceptible objects. I think this is an indigenous human reality which lies on the borderline between the nature and beyond-nature. This is an extension of those things that God has endowed upon human existence and according to the Holy Quran (The Cow 2: 31), which reads: "*and he taught Adam all the names*", every human nature contain those truths.

Stoltz: You say that these all reside in the human inside, but this inside is not accessible without a hand from the outside. What do you exactly mean by this "hand from the outside"?

1- Ibid: Book 4.

Ja'fari: It is divine instruction which comes firstly through prophets and after having realized one's existential gifts, one can receive it directly from the heavens. Thus, the hand from the outside is revelation, inspiration and illumination. We can see the examples of this illumination and intuition in scientific discoveries and inventions. Every scientific discovery is preceded by an intuition of this kind. Psychologists believe that scientific laws emerge from scientific premises, but to demonstrate a scientific law, one needs intuition. There is a vacuum between the premises of discovery and the discovery itself, which is filled by intuition.

Stoltz: In the West, it is said that man understands himself through self-excavation, but contrary to your arguments on mystical vision, this individual effort is believed to be a personal initiation which is not trustable. Thus, the West and the East have different conceptions of self-knowledge, as the former considers it baseless and unreliable, while the latter attaches a remarkable significance to it.

Ja'fari: There are some issues here that need to be taken into earnest consideration:

1- We evaluate individual experiences and knowledge based on other realities, the authenticity of which has been proven already. If they were correct, we accept them; otherwise, we put them aside as imaginations and superstitions.

2- We call "intuition" the direct perception of realities which do not require extra logical premises, but illumination is an ideological method through which one fathoms existential realities without resorting to intellection. The method of illumination has lost its currency in the West, while intuitive perceptions still reign supreme in scientific discoveries.

3- The fact whether one's self-excavation is reliable or not depends on his mental abilities and personality.

   Generally speaking, human beings can be divided into the following groups in respect of their self-knowledge:

   I) Those who not only cannot analyze their own "self" or "ego", but they even cannot have any presential knowledge of themselves, either.

   II) Those who are able to have presential knowledge of themselves, but their self-knowledge is merely restricted to the recognition of the non-physical structure of the self.

   III) Those who succeed in identifying some unphysical features of the self, like knowledge, imagination, intuition, speculation and intellection, and know that however a unique reality the self may be, but it enjoys dozens of unphysical features as well.

IV) Those who have a more comprehensive knowledge of all sides of unphysical features of the self. This group has made numerous contributions to our understanding of human nature.

All of the intuitive and scientific findings of Eastern scholars like Rumi, Attar, and Avicenna – particularly in the eighth, ninth and tenth chapters of Avicenna's *Isharat* – as well as those of such Western thinkers as Victor Hugo, Dostoyevsky and Shakespeare are the achievements of this group of self-knowers.

No one of intuitive and scientific findings has ever been driven from phenomena and realities of the physical world in the same way that no single one of the findings of great psychologists which cast light on unknown aspects of human soul and open new horizons before the scholars of human sciences is the product of laboratorial researches. We should not think that they have reached these findings through studying human behaviors, as the latter does not have a unique cause but it in fact belongs to the group of multi-causal effects, like behaviors which indicate pleasure or pain.

It is needless to argue that there are more than a hundred causes of pleasure and pain. For example, one cannot seek to find a sensible relationship between one's eyes and his internal state unless he has already had personal experiences of such internal affairs.

One should not base one's analyses of mystical intuitions on the current logical considerations and activities of natural sciences and even psychology, since the first condition of mystical intuition is the observation of moral rules which have revealed by God as well as self-refinement which prepares one to be exposed to divine illumination.

68

Dr. J. Christoph Bürgel[1]

Subject: Comparitive Debates of Hafez, Nezami and Rumi
Dialogue Date: 1995/ Switzerland, Bern

Bürgel: I am very glad to see you. My last month's visit of Iran, particularly Mashhad and Isfahan, in company with Swiss and Austrian Iranologists was useful and interesting.

I have translated and published a bouquet of Rumi's verses into German in two literally and poetic forms so as to introduce the reader to the beauty and subtlety of Persian literature. I have been told that you too have done a great deal of research on Rumi.

Ja'fari: I've written a 15-volume critical commentary on Rumi's *Masnavi*. Have German scholars worked on *Masnavi* as well?

Bürgel: Yes, Professor Annemarie Schimmel is a distinguished German scholar on Rumi who has worked on almost all of Rumi's works such as *Sonnets of Shams, Fihi ma Fihi ("Discourses")* and *Masnavi*. I think her book on Rumi is the best work which is available in a European language. Meanwhile, an Austrian professor has prepared an excellent German translation of *Oeuvre de Hafez*, which is quite rare as well.

Ja'fari: In *Sonnets of Shams*, Rumi has expressed most of his personal emotions and inner sentiments. Sometimes he also discusses the general principles of theoretical mysticism, while *Masnavi* is the book on "education" and "human sciences". Of course, German scholars have worked on *Masnavi*, but I do not know someone in the British Nicholson's caliber who has done so much work on Rumi and his *Masnavi*. Germany is known for its philosophical giants and *Masnavi* is itself a brilliant philosophical work, then many works should have been done by German scholars on *Masnavi*. I have done almost twenty

---

1- Prof. Bürgel was Dean of the Faculty of Orientalism and Islamic Studies of the University of Bern.

comparative studies of Hegel and Rumi.

Bürgel: Unfortunately we do not have a complete German translation of Rumi's *Masnavi* – except for Vincent's book, which has been forgotten today and only experts know about it. Apart from that, there is almost no other work. We need a complete translation of *Masnavi*, and even Schimmel's work cannot fill the vacuum. Much work is required to be done in this regard. Is your 15-volume work on Rumi a commentary of *Masnavi*?

Ja'fari: Yes, this 15-volume work is both a commentary of *Masnavi* and also a comparative study of Rumi's basic ideas as well as other great Wastern and Western thinkers.

Although in this work I have been more focused on the mystical dimensions of Rumi's thought, I have nonetheless not overlooked its other scientific aspects, particularly those which concern human sciences, philosophy and wisdom. The Rumi in *Masnavi* is different from the Rumi we see in *Sonnets of Shams*, as in the latter work Rumi speaks as a lovelorn poet, while in *Masnavi* he is more a philosopher and mystic. It seems that *Masnavi* is globally more important than *Sonnets of Shams*. He has discussed many fundamental ideas of Eastern and Western schools of thought, but we see very few examples of such discussions in *Oeuvre*, despite its thick volume. *Masnavi* represents Rumi's efforts for the articulation of the basic principles of human knowledge. Thus, there have been numerous commentaries of *Masnavi* in the East and in the West, while we have comparatively thinner literature on *Oeuvre*. In India, I heard from Mr. Sayyed Fazel Hussein, who is a distinguished Indian scholar, that in the Indian Subcontinent alone, 112 commentaries have been authored on Rumi's *Masnavi*.

Bürgel: I totally agree with you. I am a poet myself, and have published some of my poems. To this very reason, I am fascinated by Rumi.

Ja'fari: As to the comparisons which some scholars make of Rumi and Hafez, one can say that although Hafez is a great poet, his verses are not thematically comparable with Rumi's couplets. On the other hand, Rumi's verses generally have a lower poetic quality as compared to the verses of Hafez, but they nevertheless bear brilliant ideas and themes.

Bürgel: The poetry of Hafez is appealing for me, as it has a multi-layered meaning, while Rumi's verses are always overshadowed by mysticism and Sufism.

Ja'fari: As I mentioned earlier, Hafez has an unrivalled poetic art, while Rumi's verses are fraught with noble mystical, philosophical and social ideas and themes.

Bürgel: I appreciate Nezami's works, and I am the first one who has translated Nezami Ganjavi's *Khusrow and Shirin* and *Eskandarnameh* [into German]. Of course, I have also translated a selection of odes of Hafez, which is very prevalent.

Ja'fari: As you mentioned, Nezami is a distinguished poet with regard to his poetic taste and fluidity of his verses. One can even say that Nezami is the most towering figure in the history of Persian poetry.

It is noteworthy that Nezami starts his poems with a highly mystical prologue which unfortunately has been rarely considered by literary scholars. Whenever I read Nezami's orisons, I always think of Ibn Khaldun's *The Muqaddimah*, which is scientifically more significant than Ibn Khaldun's *History* itself. But Rumi has discussed in his *Masnavi* many of the ideas which are nowadays taught in universities.

For example, you can easily find such notions as "contradiction or universal reason or evolution and authenticity of human understanding" which have been frequently discussed by Hegel, in Rumi's *Masnavi*. Rumi has composed more than a hundred verses on "wave", which is one of the fundamental notions of modern physics. Thus, there is still much to be done concerning *Masnavi*. Now we should ask if these issues have been products of Rumi's individual intuitions and illuminations or his acquired knowledge, since these classic ideas did not exist in those times!

Bürgel: Do you think that Rumi had been under the influence of Suhrewardi?

Ja'fari: We have to distinguish between the association of ideas and "influence" and "imitation". Rumi has a very powerful mind and his knowledge is very extended and deep. There no convincing evidence to show that Rumi has been under the influence of Muhyaddin, Ghazali or Suhrewardi.

Bürgel: Illumination is also an aspect of astrophysics, as we see light and rays almost everywhere.

Ja'fari: The physical interpretation of spiritual findings is of vital significance for making them acceptable by people, but in such cases, we need to see what reality tell us. One of the mental wonders of Rumi's is that in many cases, he says in the *Masnavi*, "This is story has no end!" In other words, I should finish the story here and turn to another narrative, as this one is endless.

Bürgel: Yes, it is wonderful indeed. I hope to have more time to study Rumi's couplets. I wish I could memorize Rumi's verses like you have.

69

Prof. Richard Friedli[1]

Subject: Interreligious Engagements, the Interpretation of the Opening Chapter of the Quran, Women, *Jihad* Dialogue Date: 1995/ Switzerland, Freiburg

Friedli: Welcome to Freiburg. We will discuss important issues with each other in the seminar on "Islam and Christianity" a few days later, including the relations between the East and the West as well as Islamic traditions and Christianity. I also would like to express my gratitude for your accepting to address our students.

Ja'fari: I am also very glad to see you and it is indeed an honor to be here.

Friedli: I would like to begin with giving you a brief introduction of the University of Freiburg and our institute. The University of Freiburg has a hundred-year history and there are now almost nine thousand students studying here. The campus is the home to the faculties of Catholic Theology, Philosophy, Law and Natural Sciences.

It is noteworthy that all courses are offered in German and French languages. You can find more details in the catalogues that I haven provided you with. However, at the Institute of Comparative Studies of Religions, we have undergraduate and graduate programs. Both programs are held in a four-year term. We start with basic courses, which I teach. My name is Friedli, which translates as "little peace". This may not be much irrelevant to tomorrow's seminar, in fact.

The general views of various religions are taught at this institute. I have specialized in African religions. Other professors of the institute teach Chinese religions, Buddhism, Hinduism, Islam and Latin American religions. Every student is obliged to choose three of these religions to study. Many of them choose Islam. There are numerous concerns both in the East and in the West. To tackle these concerns, we

---

1- Prof. Richard Friedli was Director of the Institute of Comparative Studies of Religions and Interreligious Dialogues at the University of Freiburg.

need to reach an understanding, which in turn is only possible via studying.

The institute provides the students with the necessary means for gaining knowledge of the world. There are courses in Hebrew, Greek, Sanskrit and African languages on the Institute's curriculum. The students of this institute, like students of other academic centers, synthesize their major with majors like psychology, sociology, statistics and the like.

What adds to the importance of this kind of studies is the presence of refugees in Switzerland. For example, their children study in our schools, as do those who come to Switzerland for work.

The students who will attend the class today are students of social sciences, psychology and educational sciences.

Ja'fari: In your philosophy courses, do you only teach the ideas of philosophical schools? Is there a philosopher in your faculty who has presented a new philosophy?

Friedli: We have numerous philosophers; some teach the history of philosophy and philosophical schools such as Marxism and Greek schools. We have also philosophers who specialize in methodology.

Ja'fari: Do these students see religion as a mere behavior and a current phenomenon in people's life or do they also show deep cordial sentiment toward it?

Friedli: Those students who study social sciences do not have any concern of sentiment and heart; in fact, they only study. However, the students who study religions are prepared to become teachers of students or to work in churches.

There are two general styles in theology: the German style, which is a modern and critical theology that studies religion in its social context, and the French style, which deals more with the soul, the heart and sentiments. We have both attitudes in our faculty.

Ja'fari: In your research on religions, do you see religion as museum stuff or do students approach it as an existential matter which can cause major changes in their life?

Friedli: This issue depends on the students. Some of them believe in the religion on which they research. Some others have no religious belief and only study it to know how they should deal with religious peoples in their workplace. However, all students respect religions even if they do not believe in them. You will see in the afternoon class that they respect religions. Before your arrival, I will speak of the seminar of "Dialogue of Islam and Christianity" and introduce you to them.

Among the Students of Faculty of Theology of University of Freiburg

Friedli: Mr. Ja'fari! Welcome to our class. My students are ready to hear your speech.

Ja'fari: As Professor Friedli mentioned, there are many grounds for understanding between the East and the West. As history shows, there had been numerous scientific, philosophical, cultural and economic engagements among these two great parts of the world in the past. We have travelled to Switzerland to take part in the conference of "Islam and Christianity" and hope to reach a transcendent understanding in this regard.

For this session, I have decided to speak of the opening chapter of the Holy Quran. To begin with, I would like to read and translate the chapter:

> *In the name of Allah, the Beneficent, the Merciful. (1)*
>
> *All praise is due to Allah, the Lord of the worlds, (2) the Beneficent, the Merciful, (3) Master of the Day of Judgment (4). Thee do we serve and thee do we beseech for help (5).*
>
> *Keep us on the right path, (6) the path of those upon whom Thou hast bestowed favors, not (the path) of those upon whom Thy wrath is brought down, nor of those who go astray (7).*

This chapter has a distinguished place in the Quran. Moslems recite these chapter ten times a day. Three issues are discussed in this chapter: praise, gratitude and eulogy.

Praise is paying obeisance to a majestic being, for two reasons – firstly because He has given us many bounties, and secondly because He is worthy of obeisance.

Gratitude consists of giving thank before his bounties.

Eulogy means the description of the majesty or beauty of a reality although it has no direct relationship with us. Now the question arises whether all praises are due to God or not. There are two theories in this regard:

I) Since all goods belong to God, then all praise is due to Him as well.

II) Since human individuals voluntarily behave toward each other in the spirit of justice, help each other and take generous steps for the betterment of the society, if we praise an individual, we have surely praised the individual himself although eventually all praise is due to Allah.

Allah, the Lord of the worlds: The word Allah has been used in the Quran more frequently than God's other names. This word reveals the nature and attributes of the Lord. There is no equivalent for this word in other languages.

After Allah, "Lord" has more applications in the Quran. To explain this word, we will need to outline two theories:

1- Some philosophical schools believe that God has created the world, set the laws inside it and left it alone! These schools base their arguments on the immutability of the laws which govern the world and announce that there is no need for God's presence, as the world is a closed system and a closed system does not need a management from the outside!

2- God has created the world based on unchangeable laws and no event occurs against the laws of nature unless through a miracle or intimate supplications. Although nature has a permanent appearance, but since all existing elements of nature are dependent upon each other and there is no independent element among them, accordingly, the world needs a lord to manage it.

Moslem theologians and philosophers and some Christian theosophers defend this theory. Alfred North Whitehead offers four definitions of the law, and in the fourth definition he argues:

> The realities of this world are like photons which are poured into this world from the realm of eternity.

This is the very sense which the Quran intends by "Lord".

After defining time, Sir Russell states:

> If we imagine that all realities of the world spring out from an outside world and eternity, it is indeed a good idea of reality.

Thus, "Lord" is a significant term both in Islamic and Christian theologies.

The Beneficent, the Merciful: Although these two words have emerged in the opening of the chapter, they appear again in the main body as well. As I mentioned earlier, "Beneficent", "Merciful", and "All-Loving", as well as other attributes of divine kindness, have been used in the Quran more than other attributes of God.

Then, Allah and the God about Whom other religions speak is a beneficent and merciful God. It is not so that God is only the Creator of hell. Unfortunately, these distorted conceptions of religion have distanced many people from religion.

In one of my correspondences with Sir Russell throughout 1962 and 1963, I wrote to him:

> *Unfortunately, the God who has been depicted by folks and is refuted by Sir Russell is not the real God. If we could provide a real and intelligible picture of God, I think most people would worship God and become theist.*

The Beneficent: This is a comprehensive notion in the sense that divine beneficence covers all human beings, whether they may be believers or not. Thus, this attribute represents God as the Creator of all worlds and the sustainer of life on the planet.

The Merciful represents the mercy which God will show for good deeds in this world and hereafter. For example, the people who have been pious and helped their fellowmen will enjoy this divine attribute.

The Master of the Day of Judgment: God is the Master of the Day of Resurrection. It may be asked that isn't God the Master right now as well? The answer is that in the Day of Judgment, His masterhood will be exercised directly, not via means and mediums. After putting and understanding these attributes, man gradually approaches God and addresses Him. To state the matter otherwise, until now we were engaged in the description of divine attributes, and from this moment on, our mind and soul becomes concentrated on God as a determinate interlocutor. We address the Lord in the following words: **Thee do we serve and Thee do we beseech for help.**

It might be asked, "Is God a physical being that we say 'Thee do we serve and thee do we beseech for help'? Who is our addressee here?" The answer is that when we speak with someone, we do not address his body, but in fact his mind and soul. This has also been stated in the Quran: *"Whither you turn, thither is Allah's countenance"*(The Cow: 115). This issue has been discussed both in Islamic mysticism and in Christian theology.

Friedli: Thank you for your spiritual and scientific intimations. Your message was important and had a high scientific and religious quality. Now let us have the students' questions.

Question 1: Would you explain the meaning of *jihad* in Islam?

Ja'fari: *Jihad* is a battle against social corruption and antihuman factors, and since *jihad* is an effort for the promotion of the evolutionary movement of humanity, it cannot be oppressive. *Jihad* has various kinds. For example, there can be scientific *jihad*, which indicates that I should share my knowledge with my fellow men. If I feel that my scientific research can treat human sores, my *jihad* is that I should devote myself to these studies. If one of you believes that he can discover a cure for cancer, he is obliged, according to Abrahamic religions, to enroll in a faculty of medicine and try his chance. This is a religious obligation, not a purely moral obligation. This is also the cases with financial, cultural *jihads* and the like.

Question 2: When man invokes God, how does the Lord reveal Himself to His servant?

Ja'fari: In the same way that you fathom the reality of beauty, not beautiful manifestations. The reality of beauty resides inside you. It is beyond all qualities and quantities and does not have anything to do with corporeal realities. You first understand the reality of beauty and then apply it to the extensions of beauty.

Question 3: Would you please explain the difference between the Great *Jihad* and the Lesser *Jihad*?

Ja'fari: When the Prophet Muhammad (PBUH) returned from *Jihad* (a battle against infidels), he turned to his disciples and said, "Now the Lesser *Jihad* is over and it is the time of the Great *Jihad* (i.e., self-refinement). The Great *Jihad* involves the modification of human egotisms. If man succeeds in overcoming his egotisms, the love of truth-seeking awakes in him. Victory in the Great *Jihad* is hard as man rises against and targets himself.

Friedli: You spoke of self-refinement. But today we are witness to a sectarian refinement. Doesn't self-refinement result in dangerous sectarian refinements?

Ja'fari: I do not see any clear relationship between the two categories. Nevertheless, most of the wars that have been erupted in human history have their roots in egotism. Islam and other revealed religions condemn war as such, except the time when the enemy invades you and you have to defend yourself.

Question 4: How can we enter into dialogue with the fundamentalist warmongers?

Ja'fari: If all doors are not closed and there is a room for logical dialogue upon equal terms, we can engage with them as even in the cruelest individuals there remains always something of conscience and it never becomes extinct once and for all.

Question 5: What role has been given to women as seen by the Quran and Islam?

Ja'fari: Humanity has two poles in our eyes, i.e. man and woman. On the other hand, piety is the criterion of the assessment of one's character, as God states:

> *O you men! surely we have created you of a male and a female, and made you tribes and families that you may know each other; surely the most honorable of you with Allah is the one among you most careful (of his duty); surely Allah is knowing, aware.* (The Apartments 49:13)

Accordingly, the woman is equal with the man in knowledge acquisition and obtaining economic and social offices. However, Islam has assigned the management of the family as the most important center for the education of humanity to the woman. Thus, the family should be the primary concern of a woman, and only after accomplishing her duties in the family, she can take part in social activities. Otherwise, the family will collapse, as we see the case is today in some developed countries.

70

Rev. Joseph Gandolfi, Dr. Anton Kadotus, Prof. Kissling, Prof. Johan Galtung[1] and Prof. Azlander

Subject: The Transcendent Unity of Religions and Women's Social Role
Dialogue Date: 1995/ Switzerland, Zurich

Ja'fari: I am very happy to see you dear gentlemen. I always take every opportunity to visit Christian intellectuals and scholars to enhance our knowledge and understanding of each other.

Gandolfi: I am glad to see you too. Did you have good dialogues with the theology professors of the University of Zurich and the University of Freiburg?

Ja'fari: Yes, we did. At the Freiburg Faculty of Theology, Professor Friedli suggested that I should briefly interpret the opening chapter of the Quran for the students.

Kissling: What questions did the students have and what was your impression of the class?

Ja'fari: They asked some questions on social and cultural issues, like the Great *Jihad*, the Lesser *Jihad*, women's condition and others. My impression was positive, particularly because I found a collective eagerness for harmony and unity in them. Our serious philosophical,

---

1- He was Chair of the Conference of Islam and Christianity.
Johan Galtung (born October 24, 1930) is a Norwegian sociologist, mathematician and the principal founder of the discipline of peace and conflict studies. He founded the Peace Research Institute in Oslo in 1959, serving as its director until 1970, and established the Journal of Peace Research in 1964. In 1969 he was appointed to the world's first chair in peace and conflict studies, at the University of Oslo. He resigned his professorship in 1977 and has since held professorships at several other universities; since 1993 he has been Distinguished Professor of Peace Studies at the University of Hawaii. He was awarded the Right Livelihood Award in 1987. (Translator).

scientific and theological debates show that we understand each other and such meetings can depict a bright future for us. Such intellectual engagements can also make religious leaders realize that they should not provoke destructive conflicts, but rather they have to tile the path of intellectual evolution for humanity.

My studies in human sciences have led me to the conclusion that if we are to deliver humanity from the bondages of conflicts and the sense of alienation, we have no remedy but resorting to religion and morality, and it is conscious religious figures that can develop friendly relations between individuals and nations. If we succeed today in demonstrating the fact for human societies that there is no conflict between science, religion, philosophy and mysticism, we will indeed have taken the first step toward a bright and constructive future.

At an international conference on Avicenna held in New Delhi, I delivered a short lecture on Avicenna. Sixty countries were present at the conference. There, I said, "During this seminar, some of our dear colleagues spoke of the philosophical career of Avicenna and proved that he is an original and distinguished philosopher. Some speakers focused on his scientific works, particularly Canon in medicine, and demonstrated that he is one of the founders of modern science. Some preferred to speak of his religious outlook, although they couldn't determine whether Avicenna is an Isma'ili, Shi'ah or Sunni. Some others proved that Avicenna is a mystic. Of course, we had already worked on this issue and our reason was the three chapters of Avicenna's *Al-Isharat*, which bear a very deep mystical vision. I do not intend to boast of an Iranian thinker but I want to say that a man can simultaneously master all philosophical, scientific, religious and mystical truths in an excellent form. To put it otherwise, science is not against philosophy, as the latter is not against religion, which in turn is not against mysticism; this reality was demonstrated today by the speakers of conference."

I know Western thinkers like Alfred North Whitehead and Max Planck who, despite being highly esteemed and very sophisticated philosophers and scientists, are also spiritual men who respect theological matters. Max Plank writes:

> There can never be any real opposition between religion and science, for one is the complement of the other. Every serious and reflective person realizes, I think, that the religious element in his nature must be recognized and cultivated if all of the powers of the human soul are to act together in perfect balance and harmony. And indeed it was not

by any accident that the greatest thinkers of all ages were also deeply religious souls, even though they made no public show of their religious feeling. It is from the cooperation of understanding with the will that the finest fruit of philosophy has arisen, namely, the ethical fruit. Science enhances the moral values of life, because it furthers a love of truth and reverence – the love of the truth displaying itself in the constant endeavor to arrive at a more exact knowledge of the world of mind and matter around us, and reverence, because every advance in knowledge brings us face to face with the mystery of our own being.[1]

Now I ask you: could we, the children of Abraham (PBUH), promise a bright future to humanity under the aegis of religion?

Gandolfi: You have touched upon a very vital issue. There is a particular mental and spiritual harmony between the believers of different faiths. You spoke of mysticism, religion and philosophy, but we have still much distance to treat. Many of us have religious sentiments, but when it comes to their expression, we may have various expressions. The deeper our religious experience, the more united we will be, as the shallower we think, the wider the divisions will on the other hand become.

Ja'fari: Absolutely. The deeper religious authorities think, the closer they will become to a transcendent unity.

Galtung: As you rightly mentioned, we are the children of Abraham, but we also have the believers of other non-Abrahamic faiths like Buddhists and Hindus. What should we do with them?

Ja'fari: Abrahamic religions have authorized strong ties. We can also search for such ties in other religions may we find Abrahamic elements in them that can serve as grounds for interreligious harmony. We can even have constructive relations with faiths which are not of an Abrahamic origin.

For example, there are common grounds in moral issues like Nirvana in Buddhism and eternity in Hinduism. Although the transmigration of souls is one of basic beliefs of Hinduism, there is also a sense of eternity and relation with God in it. These themes can make for our common grounds. Unfortunately, some of us have an irrational science phobia, while there is no room for any phobia.

Science has its own tasks to do and always casts light on divine signs

---

1- Planck, Max (1932), *Where is Science Going?*

wherever it delves deep enough into a subject. Some Moslem and Christian scholars have done great works in this regard. Genuine science and authentic religion have never come into conflict with each other; as a matter of fact, it is *professional* religionists and scientists who have had conflictions. Science discovers the laws and religion shows us how to use these laws to orient ourselves toward eternity.

Azlander: Do you think that religious authorities should interfere in scientific research or should scientists comment on religious issues?

Ja'fari: This is a very significant question. Even if we assume that there is a conflict between scientific and religious issues – although there is no conflict in this sense according to Islam – we should have some supervisors. The professional scientific and religious supervisors must not allow such irrelevant interferences to happen from both sides.

Azlander: History shows that such interferences have frequently occurred, and on the other hand, the idea of a supervisor does not seem to be working.

Ja'fari: As I mentioned earlier, irrelevant interferences have been made by professional religionists and scientists, not by religion and science. On the other hand, there is no reason for the impossibility of the presence of just and professional supervisors. Man, who has travelled to the moon, can undoubtedly accomplish this task, too. To put the matter otherwise, he can train skilled supervisors to prevent the adherents of religion and science from systematically sabotaging each other provided that man gives up egotisms.

Azlander: This is also a difficult task. One day people thought scientists and experimental researchers would solve the problems of the society and organize it. After a while, it was demonstrated that they are not the men of such tasks and it is in fact churchmen and religious people have accomplished this task.

Ja'fari: Yes, it is truly hard for one to modify one's egotisms, but when man feels that if he does not undertake this task, he will fall into the vortex of annihilation, he finds out that *something must be done*. We all know that if ten percent of human difficulties arise from his ignorance, the other ninety percent of misfortunes have their origin in human egotisms.

Kissling: You propose that religious authorities should gather around and work together for peace, while it was religious authorities who have kindled the fire of bloody wars!

Ja'fari: If we provide a sound definition of religion according to which all human individuals have an equal right of life, honor and committed freedom, religion would no longer induce any war or conflict, but in fact it is professional religionists and egotist votaries of science who trigger destructive wars. On the other hand, many of the religious conflicts that have arisen in the past had broken out either due to the lack of knowledge of each other or selfish interests and evil egotisms, none of which have anything to do with divine religion. These conflicts should not hamper our quest for understanding.

It might be argued that some religions also offer descriptions of man and the world which may be in conflict with scientific theories and cause more quarrels. As a result, we see that nothing has been contributed to the situation yet!

This problem must be tackled via fresh hermeneutic encounters with religious texts. Moslems have done such works as to their scripture, i.e. the Quran. I hope that our Christian brothers will also use such hermeneutic methods and discuss this issue in other conferences like this.

Gandolfi: As you know, we have numerous Moslem immigrants in Switzerland and we also would like to help them hold their religious rituals, but there are some problems in this regard. For instance, there none of them has enough knowledge of Islam and Islamic philosophy. On the other hand, there is heavy propaganda against Islam in the media.

Some regard us as simpleminded and say that we cannot enter into dialogue with Moslems. They argue that Saudi Arabia does not allow Christians to construct chapels for themselves and then we want to hold dialogues with Moslems! These are problems we are facing.

Ja'fari: The reason why Saudi Arabia does not allow Christians to have their own chapels while the Prophet Muhammad (PBUH) did not demolish the churches should be asked to Saudi officials themselves.

I think you need to discuss this matter with Saudi scientists and scholars, not with politicians. But as you know, in Iran, Catholics, Orthodox and Protestants have their own churches and even independent representatives in the parliament.

Gandolfi: We have the same problem in Greece. Catholics cannot construct Catholic churches as Orthodoxism is the official religion of the country. A hundred and seventy years ago, if someone were to dare to convert to Catholicism, he would have been abolished.

Anyway, I hope these problems will be solved.

Ja'fari: These problems seem to be able to be solved via conducting some fundamental studies of the causes of such conflicts in past and present.

Galtung: There was a similar problem in Norway in 1947, when Jewish families were deported. It seems that issues have to be pursued firstly in a human level in the sense that everyone should have the right to retain their faiths and then enter into dialogue. Moreover, it must be explained for both sides that the dialogue does not necessarily challenge their faith. This is what we call *tolerance*.

Kissling: In Saudi Arabia, and also in many other Moslem countries, population growth is high due to the increase in births. They believe that sustenance is in God's hands and religious leaders support this idea. What is Iranian religious authorities' view as to the issue of population control measures?

Ja'fari: According to Shi'ah jurisprudence, sperm can be controlled before entering the womb, but after the formation of the zygote, no one is allowed to abort it.

Gandolfi: It is unconceivable for us that in the Bundestag and in the French parliament, MPs consult the Bible. This shows the existing difference between mentalities. On the other hand, it also demonstrates the importance of religious communications.

Ja'fari: It must be taken into account that if the slogans of equality, fraternity and liberty are conceived in their original sense, they will never have any conflict with divine religion.

Kissling: The number of female students is on the rise in Iran. Doesn't this cause any problems?

Ja'fari: Since family is of vital significance in Islam, social relations must be fashioned in a way that women's education at university does not lead to any change in the conditions of the family. Nevertheless, there is no impediment before their pursuing their education as knowledge acquisition is an obligation in Islam both for the man and the woman.

Kissling: Is there a female *Mujtahid*? We are now discussing women's priesthood.

Ja'fari: Women can freely learn jurisprudence and obtain the degree of

Ijtihad.[1] Lady Amin Isfahani was a *Mujtahid* woman who had continuous jurisprudential debates with her contemporary *Mujtahid* men. Women cannot be legal authorities, but *Ijtihad* is a higher scientific degree which can be obtained both by men and women. In Islam, the sources of *Ijtihad* consist of the Quran, the *Sunnah*, jurisprudential consensus and reason. Some Islamic denominations also include analogy as a source of jurisprudential reasoning. In Judaism, the sources of *Ijtihad* are the Torah and the Talmud. Are there such sources in Christianity, upon which one can extrapolate divine judgments of life issues?

Gandolfi: Jesus was delegated to execute the Torah's Ten Commandments. But one can say that *today, only a series of moral rules have been remained of them.*

Ja'fari: What was then the source of religious judgments issued in the Middle Ages for permitted and prohibited affairs?

Gandolfi: After the French Revolution,[2] new principles were adopted and today we have only some moral orders.

Galtung: What should we do if we want to issue jurisprudential judgments *a la* you of human events and issues?

Ja'fari: We can take effective steps in this direction if our Christian colleagues provide a clear picture of Christian textual and primordial sources of jurisprudential judgment.

1- Qualification for issuing jurisprudential judgments of life issues. (Translator).
2- The political revolution which occurred in France and lasted from 1789-1799, resulting in the overthrowing of the French monarchy. (Translator).

71

Prof. Francis Lamand

Subject: The East and The West on Religion and Science
Nationality: French/ Major: Islamic Studies
Dialogue Date: July 24, 1996

At the beginning of this meeting, Ms. Fouladvand provided a background of her work and correspondence with Professor Lamand, explaining that Professor Lamand had made a comparison between Rumi and Goethe and admired the thoughts of this Islamic mystic and philosopher at a conference on Rumi held in Quniya in 1995. Allameh Ja'fari then inquired Professor Lamand's views on Victor Hugo as compared to Geothe.

Lamand: Hugo's thought has involved both spiritual and material sides, but there is something unique in Goethe, and that is his tendency toward Islam. He is told to have turned to Islam in the last days of his life and changed his views on many issues. But we see no such thing in Hugo's case, and he was occupied with romantic matters. He was mostly interested in the East, while Goethe was a passionate admirer of Islam. There are many similarities between Goethe and Rumi. He found unity in Islam, and his common ground with Rumi is "love", for Rumi thought that love exists in inanimate bodies, plants and animals. This idea was what Goethe had incredible passion for as well, but Rumi had touched it almost seven centuries before. Isn't that so?

Ja'fari: There are some points here. Rumi has developed novel and valuable ideas of representational and objective loves; divine love, objective love and the passion for phenomenal beauty, which is a bridge toward real beauty. Divine and spiritual love can bring scholars and mystics closer to each other.

Lamand: A man called Charann says that whenever two objects soar, they come closer to each other and finally become united.

Ja'fari: This is a given spiritual principle that the unity of human souls is possible in higher human orders, not in the realm of material objects, which is the domain of conflicts and contradictions. Now the question is whether we can compare Rumi's ideas with the theories of Western thinkers from all respects. One of the major features of Rumi's thought is that due to his broad and profound comprehension of sublime truths; while he soars in the realm of eternity, he does not forget nature. My researches and studies on this excellent and wonderful mind suggest that many of the ideas which Rumi has once focused on later become part of the fundamental conceptual framework of modern and contemporary schools of philosophy. There are unbelievable similarities between the theories of great Western philosophers like Descartes, Kant and Hegel and Rumi's words. In other words, Rumi's words demonstrate that he had an admirable knowledge of the basics of those theories.

I am in awe how a mystic of Rumi's caliber with so much affection for positive mysticism can introduce the natural world as an authorized means for gaining knowledge of the cosmos. For example, you can find some intimations of Cartesian dualism in Rumi, or Rumi has open remarks on the dialectical relationships of "being" and "nonbeing", which stand at the basis of Hegel's philosophy. Rumi states:

> *Since there is being in nonbeing, o' brother,*
>
> *the opposite was hidden in its opposite.*[1]

Did you touch upon these aspects in your lecture of Rumi?

Lamand: Nonbeing or nothingness? Which one?

Ja'fari: Nonbeing in the sense of the absence of being, not nothingness. Did you discuss the relevance of Rumi's verses as compared to the foundations of human sciences and Western and Eastern philosophies?

Lamand: Would you allow me to disagree with you?

Ja'fari: Yes, surely. Reasonably, of course!

Lamand: To begin, with I would like to say that I agree with you that one cannot compare Rumi's corpus with the works of other foreign poets. The West does not know Islam or at least does not know it well enough, and it is less than a century now that Rumi's verses have begun to be introduced to Western people. For many years, the Islamic world and the Western world had been hidden from each other.

1- Rumi's *Masnavi*, Book 5.

However, history is not an impenetrable mass, and one can pass into it. Nothing has been done yet as to the comparison of Rumi's works with the works of Spanish and French poets. We are still at the dawn of the relations of these two worlds and we cannot speak of a comparison of Rumi with Western thinkers as this discourse is just beginning to take shape and we are still at the dawn. An approximation will gradually begin to develop between two world religions, not among works. The West is now in a dead-end, and to renovate itself, the West is in dire need of philosophical and poetic ideas of such universal thinkers as Rumi. The contemporary intellectual crisis of the West has its origin in the ideas of the philosophers you just mentioned. Despite its high humanistic ideas, Cartesian philosophy was a closed circle. Kant claimed that intellectuals belong to a closed area where everyone is not allowed to leap. Hegel is also the founder of dialectical logic.

Therefore, Rumi's ideas open an aperture through these intellectual limits and restrictions. These philosophers have given a definition of social life which has led man to such a deadlock. For example, Hegel was the forerunner of Marx, as he thought that contradictions are the motive force of life. There is no room for such contradictions in Rumi's thought, as he is a true Moslem and proponent of transcendent continuity, which defines all differences. I think Western philosophy would have now another configuration if Western philosophers had been acquainted with Rumi and his ideas.

In the nineteenth century, Westerners knew Hafez, Sa'di and Khayyam, but they had no acquaintance with Rumi. Goethe did not know Rumi either, but he was acquainted with Hafez and Sa'di. One needs to leap somewhere outside of time to see if two theories from two distinct periods of history have trodden the same course or not. Thus, I think you approach Western philosophers with much more tolerance than what one would normally expect.

Ja'fari: I would rather not make any compromise; as a matter of fact, I believe that these philosophers have some ideas of man and the world, however limited they may be, which can be compared with the ideas of Moslem philosophers and mystics in some respects. We just seek to provide a fair assessment of the ideas of philosophers based on realistic grounds regardless of their geographical, ideological and even religious backgrounds. Every philosophical encounter needs continuously to ground itself in such open-mindedness.

We pursue our debates of Eastern philosophers with the same critical attitude which we adopt in our studies of, say, Kant's quadruple

434 / The Exploration of Ideas

antinomies or Cartesian "cogito ergo sum". I personally believe that as we always assert that Moslem philosophers like Farabius, Avicenna, Mullah Sadra and others, have not reached the absolute knowledge in the same way Western philosophers have their own limitations and bounds. As we criticize Farabius or Averroes, we also have critiques of Western philosophers.

This is an essential requirement of an open system of knowledge in Islam as well as any other authentic philosophical discourse. On the other hand, no conscious philosopher, be Western or Eastern, would ever restrict the reality to his philosophy. If someone has such a claim, he is not surely a philosopher.

For example, Kant says that God's existence is one of the antinomies of pure reason that no one can resolve in the sense that if it is God who has created the world, then who has created the world? Unfortunately, this Kantian view has become quite a pandemic among most of the Western philosophers. Kant has become entrapped in this deadlock without recognizing the simple fact that we always ask about the cause of something which is an effect. If something is not an effect, then one cannot ask of its cause. For example, you have the right to ask, "Whence has come this cosmos?" However, God is a causeless cause and we cannot ask about His cause.

We respect modern Western philosophers, since after renaissance they succeeded in modifying some scholastic radical abstractive approaches and helping the philosophy to step out of the world of imagination. Of course, this respect does not imply that we are compromising with them; in fact, we have serious criticisms as to their radical positivism as well. We need to find the knots and untie them so as not to demolish the whole system! To put it otherwise, we have to seek to overcome the limitations of the philosophical schools founded by, for example, Descartes, Kant, Hegel, Whitehead and others both from the East and the West.

One of these intellectual schools is that of Jalaluddin Muhammad Rumi. Although he approaches the quadruple ontological relationships (man's relationship with God, the world, with his own self and with his fellow human beings) more open-mindedly, he is nonetheless a human being in the end and "limitation" is one of his mental features as such.

We can take advantage of the existing intellectual common grounds to bring the Western and Eastern worldviews closer to each other and thus conduct them toward the path of evolution. The most fundamental factor which can assist us in accomplishing this significant task is religion, since no other reality but religion can *open* one's theoretical and practical intellectual attitudes. When you study Rumi's *Masnavi*, you see that he has cited and interpreted almost 2200 verses of the Holy Quran. It is indeed Rumi's due attention to this Abrahamic divine outlook which has helped him to overcome his intellectual limitations and soar freely into an open space.

Lamand: Exactly.

Ja'fari: Is your agreement with me on this total now?

Lamand: God is in fact a total agreement.

Ja'fari: Do you mean that God is the only matter on which we may have a total agreement or that God is the only one who provides the necessary requirements for agreements?

Lamand: When I say that I agree you, I speak as a Westerner who has come closer to Islam. I think that today the West's great illness is its forgetfulness of the sacred and sacredness. The West has truly lost these concepts.

Ja'fari: Sacredness?

Lamand: Yes, the sacredness and sanctity. I express my own ideas. My ideas are, however, scarcely expressed in the West. I've taught the philosophy of law for some thirty years, and found sacredness in law, since laws must be sacred so as to be accepted and followed by all. The only divine source of laws is religion, but sadly, most Western countries have abandoned religion and become laic. In other words, they've already lost the whole laws of their life. Why? Because laws have lost their sanctity.

I think Islam can reintroduce sacredness into the West. To reconsecrate one's life, one needs some sort of spiritual means which have to be taken from religion. Thus, Rumi's works seem to be a source of sanctity from which the West can be benefited from.

Ja'fari: Of course, this is an effect-based talk. In fact, such a thing (sacredness, religion and spirituality), as you mentioned, is quite desirable, as unfortunately the sacred has disappeared from Western life scene and needs to be called upon again; we are also concerned over this issue.[1] The question is who should know the causes of secular

---

1- It is indeed needless to argue that it is not only the West which has been lost in the scathing desert of denial of sacredness, but unfortunately there are also

life and tackle them and reintroduce sanctity into human society. This task should be undertaken by qualified and seasoned scholars and intellectuals like you. We know that there is an ever-growing thirst for spirituality in the West, but the question is whether Western intellectuals have ever thought collectively how to deal with this situation or not.

Lamand: This is an important question indeed. Many in the West celebrate the disappearance of this sanctity, as this gives them more freedoms to satisfy their lusts and destroy others! The absence of spirituality and sanctity leads to the lack of many vital things, like morality.

Some others expect the youth to struggle to sate this genuine thirst for spirituality and sacredness. When a patient refuses to take his medicine due to its bitter taste, it is not good reason to deprive him from the medicine, even if one has to pour it into the patient's meal.

Ja'fari: Apart from the other fields of endeavor I have been involved in, I have been also working on the philosophy of life for almost six years. My studies and researches proved me that as long as man does not accept a rational sanctity for his life, he will not succeed in finding a dependable meaning for his life.

Lamand: The West needs to know that technology is a means, not the end. The problem, particularly for us, is that the technology is imported from the USA.

Ja'fari: Then who is the one with whom we should deal? Who is our counterpart? Recently I was invited to a conference on peace in Europe called "The Conference of Islam and Christianity". The participants and organizers unanimously insisted that we *must* reach a brotherly agreement on a just life.[1] But one question then ceaselessly forced itself to our minds – will this brotherly agreement be taken into consideration by the social authorities worldwide or not?

Let us suppose that we shall eventually reach positive results as to, firstly, what should we do, what you should you do, and how we, as children of Abraham (PBUH), should reach an agreement on his religion so that ignorance can not to divide us. What measures should be taken so that we can know Christianity aright and you can know Islam well? Secondly, how shall the reached agreement be put into

---

some westoxificated Moslem countries which have been victimized by uncalculated developments of western technology and human sciences.

1- This conference was held in Switzerland in November 24-25, 1995.

effect?

Lamand: I fully understand your concerns. Now we need to see what measures we should adopt so as to force them to accept our agreements.

For example, in the first year of our organization's activity, we published a research concerning the picture that is presented of Islam in the textbooks of European schools. We analyzed twelve school textbooks and detected numerous mistakes. Many of these mistakes, which sought to present Islam as a barbarian and cruel religion, were more rooted in ignorance than intention and prejudice, while Islam comprises a series of Abrahamic values. After the publication of our research results, we received warm and positive messages and reviews. The publishers were among the first appreciators. Of course, there is also an active front of antagonism here. For example, two years ago, when my son was twelve years, old his teacher had ordered the class to write a paper either on Judaism, Christianity or Islam within one month. Naturally enough, most of the class had chosen Christianity. Needless to say, the second choice was Judaism. Only one student had chosen Islam, and that was my son. He also chose it to make me happy and paid a heavy price for his choice as well indeed. Unfortunately, he was treated harshly in his class due to his paper on Islam, and he continuously regretted why he had chosen it.

To fight this ignorance, we need to come up with concrete initiatives and measures. In future months, we will be organizing a major conference in France to reconstruct the image of Islam in the West. The subject of the conference will be "*Islam, France and Europe: How will we build the future?*" Through this conference, we intend to say that not only are Islamic values positive values, but they can in fact help Europe to build its future.

God does not help but those who engage in serious intellection. For example, we just have good dialogues here. We must have more intellectual engagements and interactions and Iran can play an effective role in this regard. This is my personal opinion.

Ja'fari: On the second night of my visit to Switzerland, I met some distinguished European scholars. After some debates, Professor Johan Galtung, the Norwegian chair of the Conference on Islam and Christianity, asked me, "How can we Christians have *Ijtihad* through you Moslems?" "You have to provide us," I told him, "with your theological, jurisprudential and legal principles so that we can show you how should Christianity find its *Ijtihad* path today."

I mean, we do also care about the problems of Christianity – which is a variation of Abraham's primordial religion – as Islam offers a universal view of man and the world and this intellectual universality makes us sensitive toward our surrounding.

Lamand: The issue is this very universal face of Islam, and it is indeed in this sense that I insist that Rumi is a universal poet.

Ja'fari: I hope our Western brothers will pitch in again to know Christianity through science, experiment and history.

The manifest which was issued in the Swiss Conference reads, "We Christian and Moslem participants of this conference, who gathered in Switzerland in November 1995, announce the end of the Crusades." However, in my lecture, I pronounced that the Crusades were not religious wars and we've gathered here to prove th at Abrahamic religions can have a just coexistence.

Lamand: Unfortunately, there is a huge obstacle before this common stuff. Twelve years ago, I introduced the Chancellor of "Islamic Global Relations" to the Pope. They met and exchanged positive messages with each other. Of course there, were other meetings and conferences as well.

But who is against such dialogues and communications? Who gets benefitted if these negotiations reach a deadlock? Everyday French, British and German media broadcast programs in which Islam is presented as the dangerous enemy of their society. Who distances Christianity from Islam? There are underground groups and figures, but God is great and these dialogues and engagements sooner or later will bear fruit.

Ja'fari: We have no objection in this regard. The question is that Western democracy has its own problems which are not hidden from even the Western people's own eyes.

Some years ago, a lady called Christine Caruelle conducted an interview with me on aesthetics, which contained no religious comments, let alone political intimations. This interview was supposed to be published in a journal, but surprisingly, it was rescinded. There was no word of politics in that interview and it couldn't still be published. This is the story of double standards in Western democracy! You have good theses and I truly appreciate them, but how should we fulfill these ideas in the outside world? Will organizing conferences worldwide be enough? Do we have a way ahead to overcome the rising wave of Islamophobia in Europe? Could we assume that

Christianity is now purified of the hatreds that provoked Pope Urban II to initiate the Crusades against Moslems? Of course, I believe that Moslems and Christians are brothers who come from the same family, i.e. Abraham's divine family, and it was not Christianity which declared war against Moslems, as it is not Islam that challenges the Christian world.

I devoted a large part of my speech at the Swiss Conference to this issue. There, I argued that two brothers would never put each other to the sword. Religion was merely misused by some corrupt individuals to brainwash the common people and reach their evil purposes. Otherwise, Jerusalem had been the pantheon of all three Abrahamic religions for many centuries,[1] as the Quran states:

> Say: O' followers of the book! Come to an equitable proposition between us and you that we shall not serve any but Allah and (that) we shall not associate aught with him, and (that) some of us shall not take others for lords besides Allah; but if they turn back, then say: bear witness that we are Muslims. (The House of Imran 3:64; and also cf.

(The Cow 2:62 & 2:177)

Now one needs to ask whether Islam had been the religion of war or it sought to unite the followers of all revealed religions to embark upon the path of salvation as the children of Abraham (PBUH). Can one declare a religion which seeks to bring nations to an *equitable proposition* barbarian warmonger?

Lamand: We should not regard peace as a narcotic means. Every effort, be it collective or individual, must be aimed at removing ignorance from Islam. All efforts and endeavors have to be appreciated.

I think we are passing through a very tough time. Although our time has its own difficulties and shortcomings, it has also its own advantages. One of these advantages is the IT developments which facilitate the communications. This information explosion does also thwart the plots of underground groups who seek to sabotage Islam. Thanks to modern technologies of information, Rumi is no longer a stranger in the West. His works are released throughout Europe and the US in various forms. I think these modern forms of equipment will assist us to overcome the existing ignorance toward Islam. I am very

---

1- Almost all historians admit that Arabs always treated the followers of other faiths with tolerance and never prevented them from visiting holy sites.

optimistic indeed that if we can introduce Islam to the West via better and more active mediums, it will surely be respected and loved by all.

At the end, I would like to express my happiness of your acquaintance and hope to see you again.

Ja'fari: So do I.

72

Prof. Hueber

Subject: Philosophy, Religion and Aesthetics
Nationality: Italian/ Major: Christian Philosophy
Dialogue Date: August 16, 1996

Ja'fari: During my visits to a number of European countries such as Greece, the UK and Switzerland in the past years, I have found that some Western philosophers build their discourse upon abstract notions, limited theses and immature reasons, but religious authorities like Christian clerics are noticeably different from philosophers. Their hearts are interconnected, their paths are more direct and their understanding is more powerful.

Hueber: Of course, there are certainly some linguistic problems, since besides empirical tradition, we have also metaphysical tradition and no matter which discourse we choose to engage in, we can only reach a relative agreement. However, this problem does not exist among clerics, as they are in direct contact with ordinary people and have to keep themselves in their level. Then they reach such agreements much more easily.

Ja'fari: The agreements which man reaches through cordial feelings in various fields of philosophy, ideology and religions are more powerful than those which are reached via arguments based on pure reason, since they are always relied on senses and incapable of transcendental apprehensions. This agreement is not merely concerned with one's relationship with other individuals, but it does exist between individuals and other nations.

For example, as Descartes' *necessity-based* argument of God's existence is comprehensible and self-evident for us, it is also self-evident for other nations – of course, provided that they see the world from the same transcendent point of view of Saint Anselm, Descartes and other French theologians who have confirmed necessity-based argument.

Needless to say, "ontological argument", as Hume has mentioned, is wrong and we must say "necessity-based argument" instead. Since we all can comprehend the Absolute Perfection, our sentiments have come closer together even if our words are not comprehendible for each other.

Hueber: Of course Cartesian pure reason is not sufficient for the exchange of views between two individuals; in fact, it needs to be complemented with Pascal's seminal remark that *"The heart has its reasons, of which reason is ignorant"*.

No agreement would ever be reached in the exchange of ideas between two individuals unless a third partner steps in. To put the matter otherwise, agreement is reached when man approaches a category through imploring assistance from the Lord. This necessity is felt more in philosophical debates. Many believe in this idea although they may not express it that straightforwardly. However, if this were not the case, we would never understand each other. Now when we read Hume's stuff, we see that he has asked interesting questions.

Ja'fari: Hume's questions are important, but his answers are not that important!! When Russell is asked about the condition of philosophy in the UK he says,

> If you ask a question, the philosopher repeats your question again, thinking that he has answered your question! [1]

David Hume is one of these philosophers. I've already done a critical research of his thoughts and ideas concerning four problems.

Hueber: Our knowledge represents our impressions and our ideas are drawn upon this chain of impressions. Thus, the abstraction is only a weak replication of a chain of impressions and people have different impressions of Hume. I've also published a book of Hume in German.

Ja'fari: It is not so that all universals and abstractions have been inferred from particular sensibilia. For example, in the case of numbers, we have abstractions which have not been deduced from senses, like 12 and particularly higher numbers. Are numbers among our mental abstractions? No; of course, their well spring may be sensibilia, but it is our brain which adds to them in an infinite manner.

Hueber: I agree. Edmund Husserl is also against arbitrary orders in mathematics, since mathematics only seeks to construct principles upon some basic assumptions, not sensible matters.

1- See: Ja'fari, M. T. (2008): *An Analytical Exposition of the Russell-Wyatt Dialogues.*

Ja'fari: We have also some *a priori* perceptions which are independent of sensory observation. For example, the facts that what time it is and where it comes are not sensible. Nothing about time is measurable but motion, while we abstract it from motion.

Hueber: According to Aristotle's definition of time, motion only exists in our mind, not in the observation of objective motions and changes.

Ja'fari: Of course, time is a mental category, but we do not accept that motion is not "objective". Your remarks confirm our view in one case. Since Plato's time on, many debates have been made on beauty and its extensions, but the main question is what the fundamental reality of beauty is, which is applicable to such various phenomena as flower, fall, moon and the like. You do not find a common word for beauty in world languages, but an abstract truth in your own mind. In other words, this truth does not exist in the outside world. We only see a beautiful flower and the beautiful sky in the outside, while we find the reality of beauty only in our mind.

Hueber: We have four transcendental categories: 1- unity, 2- truth, 3- beauty and 4- goodness, which are interchangeable.

Ja'fari: The question is how we can compare different beauties, say beauties of flower and the moonlight with each other. What kind of relationship exists between a beautiful handwriting and a symphonic voice? What relationship does a beautiful mountain have with a well-designed mathematical operation? Or what relevance does the perception of beauty which a mathematician has when he works on the latter operation have with the beauty of music?

Ja'fari: Then beauty does not have objective aspect, but it exists only inside us.

Hueber: If we have an *a priori notion* of beauty, we can apply it to various things. Kant's solution does not follow the principles of pure reason in this case. We should be somewhat realistic not transcendental, as Kant's solution is not enough.

Ja'fari: We do not accept Kant's solution in this regard, but we have *a priori* notions in mind which do not exist in the outside world, as in the outside world we have only some phenomena of people's actions.

Hueber: We have a pure and abstract notion in mind which does not need sensible and phenomenal realities, and in higher levels and abstractions, it becomes totally severed from phenomena.

We do not have abstract realities in a Cartesian sense, but we have such realities in a Kantian sense, of course not in the form of a set in our mind, but rather in the form of a function, in a way that the limitations of practical experience is more than experience of contingency in empirical reason. Then in practice, we have both empirical rationality and practical rationality. Kant has broached these issues in his *Prolegomena,* which he liked more than his other books, but he does not demonstrate them. Therefore, empirical and theoretical reasons are always separate from each other.

Ja'fari: Do universal and mathematical notions have objective roots or can our mind reach pure truths through them? In other words, do they play the role of a catalyzer?

Hueber: The basis and root of these truths are in our reason and can only be used in relation to the material world; they are not confined merely to sensibilia. Aristotle also has the same view in this regard.

Ja'fari: Isn't better to study Plato through his own ideas not via Aristotle's theory?

Hueber: If someone reads Plato with the view that all beings are independent from each other, he could not reach a desirable result. I have studied Plato otherwise. All beings and ideas are connected with each other and they have a common differentia. The most significant issue in Plato is the way in which intelligibles are individually connected.

Ja'fari: Plato's theory of ideas is more helpful than Aristotle's theories in understanding the nature of abstract realities. Of course, Rumi has also the same view. The criterion of every beauty in objective world is its degree of compatibility with the universal idea of beauty. Plato has articulated this idea in clear words.

Hueber: Of course, Plotinus has more clear intimations of this point as compared to Plato.

I regret that we cannot converse in a common language. Now Iranian students learn English, while fifty years ago French was taught in Iranian universities. French was more powerful. The students must learn also French and German, as English books are limited. You have to forget your political problems with the USA and learn other languages too to overcome these limitations!

Ja'fari: I think it is better to continue our own debates.

Translator: Almost twenty years ago, I taught linguistics and comparative linguistics in Iran's universities and I have recently had a number of lectures too. The readiness that one finds in seminary students for learning international languages is not comparable with university students. They have exceptional talent in comprehension, speaking and speculative affairs in general. My children study in Italy. It is five years now that my daughter has been studying Latin, but her comprehension skills are disappointing. On the other hand, seminary students have brilliant skills in various fields of language, which they have obtained through continuous rehearses. Unfortunately, there is no such thing in Europe.

Hueber: I expected to see a Peripatetic atmosphere in Iran's seminaries, but in fact I found Iranian students more acquainted with Plato and even Plotinus. Is this a modern approach or a traditional one?

Ja'fari: It is traditional, particularly in Mu'tazilite and Shi'ism.[1]

Hueber: I expected a philosophical atmosphere, but not in this form. It is somewhat strange for me that instead of finding a Peripatetic atmosphere, I visited a Platonic thinker. Of course, there had been a strong Platonic tradition in Iran, and it is not so strange if it has survived to this day.

1- Prof. Hueber has published a book on Mu'tazilite in Italian.

73

Prof. Kari Vogt

Subject: Islamic Mysticism and Sufism
Nationality: Norway / Major: Islamic Studies
Dialogue Date: November 7, 1996

Vogt: I have been told that you are an expert on mysticism. I am not myself specialized in this field, but I am very interested in this subject. My question is about mysticism's place in the modern [Moslem] society, as a cursory view of history shows us that there has not been a peaceful coexistence between Sufism, jurisprudence and Shari'ah in the Islamic world.

Ja'fari: The story of Sufism and mysticism in Islamic countries is different from other countries including Eastern lands like India. Moslem scholars, philosophers and jurists had challenged the Sufism which presents itself as a school of thought independent from Islam; otherwise, the mysticism which is built upon the Islamic worldview has been always received warmly in Moslem societies.

Moslem philosophers and jurists have continuously criticized Sufism, of course not mysticism in general, due to its cynicisitic attitudes towards daily life and political and social affairs. They only care about spiritual matters, of course in a deviated fashion, and pay no attention to other aspects of life, while Islam is simultaneously the religion of here and the religion of hereafter as well.

Generally speaking, Moslem philosophers take a tough stance against Sufis in two issues: their cynical view of the worldly life and pantheism, both of which are condemned by Islam and other Abrahamic religions.

Nevertheless, Sufis and mystics have shed light on such precious realities via their spiritual efforts and ecstasies, which are neither resisted by Islam nor by Moslems. Thus, Persian and Arabic literatures are fraught with issues which have been unearthed by mystics. Therefore, we need to separate these two positive and negative points in our assessments of Sufism. If, instead of saying that *there is nothing but Him*, Sufis had formulated their pantheism as "the world is a reflection of God and His divine attributes", no religion would ever defy them and humanity could in fact be more benefitted from their moral and spiritual achievements. Rumi has successfully adopted this strategy in his *Masnavi* and poetized his mystical views based on genuine Islamic sources. According to my researches, Rumi has discussed almost 2200 verses of the Holy Quran and 756 prophetic traditions in his *Masnavi*. One can find the "Hekmat-wise", of course not philosophical in a disciplinary sense of the word, roots of many branches of human sciences in Rumi's *Masnavi*. Thus, we see that Rumi, as a Sufi poet, has no serious defier among Moslem jurists and scholars, although there are also some criticisms of his views, as I have discussed myself some eighty cases of them in my 15-volume *Critical Commentary of Rumi's Masnavi*.

Vogt: One dimension of Sufism is self-discipline. On the other hand, we see the political face of Sufism in Safavid Iran. Even once in Turkey, Rumi's *Masnavi* was banned for a while, as it incited social movements. What is your assessment of these two aspects and their mutual impressions?

Ja'fari: The *Masnavi* ban in Turkey dates back to the Ottomans' reign and it was not a political issue. There is no sign of political debates in Rumi's *Masnavi* in the modern sense of the term, neither in Machiavellian nor in non-Machiavellian modes of discourse. The problem is indeed Rumi's extraordinary intimations of the noble principles of humanity which happen to be against the interests of Machiavellian politicians. The *Masnavi* ban was either due to Rumi's pantheistic theses or debates of determinism or even his brilliant advices for kings. Thus, the *Masnavi* ban in Turkey was not politically motivated, and it was not even so common, either.

In the Safavid period, Sufism and mysticism had been taken into the service of Shi'ism, and the Safavids sought to use the spirituality of Sufism to unite various ethnic groups inside Iranian territory. Said differently, Sufism was not considered as an end as such, and there were great Shiah clerics who did not recognize Sufism as an authentic worldview. Safavid Kings were heavily under the influence of these clerics and couldn't ignore their views.

For example, in Shah Abbas Safavid's time, there was a Shi'ah scholar in Najaf called Sheikh Ahmad Ardabili (also known as Muqaddas Ardabili), who was highly respected by Shah Abbas due to his piety and juristic status. Muqaddas Ardabili was an anti-Sufism cleric. It is related that once one of the commanders of Shah Abbas was convicted to death by the Shah. The commander was told by his companions to travel to Najaf and bring a handwritten from Muqaddas Ardabili, may the Shah spare him. The commander proves to Muqaddas Ardabili that he is not guilty. Muqaddas Ardabili writes to Shah the following letter:

> The Lord of the Kingdom of Earth, Abbas should know that this man is innocent. Spare his fault, may God spare some of your faults. The Servant of Ali, the Prince of Believers, Ahmad Ibn Muhammad Ardabili.

The commander goes to the king with the letter. Shah Abbas takes the letter, kisses it and says, "The Sheikh has sent me good news of intercession". Then he replies the letter as follows:

> To the respected presence of Hujat-tul-Islam Sheikh Ahmad Ardabili: We forgave this man and hope to enjoy the intercession of that man [in Hereafter]. The Dog of Ali's Threshold, Abbas.

Vogt: Sufism has different aspects, whether positive or negative. How can we separate Sufism from mysticism while Sufism has exercised heavy influence on Shi'ah and Shi'ism? On the other hand, how has Sufism managed to enrich and evolve itself through Shi'ism? I have some information of mysticism in Iran and know that Imam Khomeini has held courses on it. Regarding the roots of mysticism and Sufism, as well as mysticism in the past and also present, how do you appraise the developments of mysticism?

Ja'fari: Mysticism in Shi'ism is not tantamount to the denial of realities. Particularly when we take account of Imam Ali's method in the *Nahjulbalaghah* and read the holy verses of the Quran, we find that true mysticism cannot ignore the realities in the world. This mysticism is neither Buddhist mysticism, nor Hinduism, nor the mysticism which only recognizes the "self" and nothing else.

This genuine mysticism does not neglect any aspect of reality; on the contrary, it burnishes the reality and its goal is the expansion of human "self" in this shined reality which reflects Divine Essence. This mysticism does not ignore obligations either, but it does not disregard even the most significant social issues, however mundane they may seem. As a matter of fact, it polishes the reality to make it even *finer*.

Everything is in its proper place in this form of mysticism, and no human instinct is ignored. It does not even deny egotism, but it does advise us to, "Make it milder!" It does not say that you must kill the "self", as "self" has departed the beginning and heads toward eternity. We must only restrain the "natural self" and instincts in the interests of reason and conscience. This mysticism accepts the Shari'ah codes and thus many Moslem clerics and jurists have been mystics as well.

For example, Sheikh Ansari had studied Rumi's *Masnawi* under a renowned mystic in Isfahan for two years. We do not remove anything from the world and the human spirit; as a matter of fact, we interpret and burnish them, while Sufism does not have these features.

Man always acts immoderately. If we do not say that moderate man is exceptional, we can say that he is in the minority. When man is said not to deny being, matter, motion, law and order but to settle with these issues and use them as a vehicle to ascend to the realm of incorporeality and eternity, he holds the matter so tightly that the soul, immortality and spiritual majesties are forgotten! We have such problems with the immoderate man. When man is said to watch himself, he becomes so much immersed in himself that he says, "*I am the truth* (as Mansur Hallaj has been quoted to have said)!" Or he says, "*There is nothing beneath my mantle but God* (attributed to Aba Yazid Bastami)!"

Yes, you are great, but God is not so much small for you to drunkenly say, "I am the truth!" We have such Shi'ah scholars as Allameh Tabatabaei, who was simultaneously a philosopher, a mystic and a mathematician, or Khajeh Nasiruddin Tusi, who was a mathematician, natural scientist and a mystic as well. These issues are being harmonized in Shi'ism in an exemplary way without any act of immoderation. The soul flourishes and can use the world as a platform through which the soul can rise to the heavens. We have such distinguished mystics in the Shi'ah world as Allameh Tabatabaei, Sayyed Ali Qazi Tabatabaei, Seyed Hussein Bakui, Mirza Ali Shirazi, Mirza Abul Hassan Jelwah, Mirza Mahdi Ashtyani and others, who had an integrative view of knowledge and saw no essential conflicts between various branches of knowledge.

At an international conference on Avicenna in New Delhi, I delivered a short lecture on Avicenna. Sixty countries were present at the conference. There, I said, "During the seminar, some of our dear colleagues spoke of the philosophical career of Avicenna and proved that he is an original and distinguished philosopher. Some speakers focused on his scientific works, particularly *Canon* in medicine, and demonstrated that he is one of the founders of modern science. Some preferred to speak of his religious outlook, although they couldn't determine whether Avicenna is an Isma'ili, Shi'ah or Sunni. Some others proved that Avicenna is a mystic. Of course, we had already worked on this issue and our reason was the three chapters of Avicenna's *Isharat*, which bear a very deep mystical vision. I do not intend to boast of an Iranian thinker, but I would like to say that a man can simultaneously master all philosophical, scientific, religious and mystical truths in an excellent form. To put it otherwise, science is not against philosophy, as the latter is not against religion, which in turn is not against mysticism; this reality was demonstrated today by the speakers at this conference."

Vogt: Is mysticism taught in Iran today? If it is, how is it taught? Are there university courses on mysticism, or is it only restricted to private circles of distinguished clerics?

Ja'fari: We have numerous courses in theoretical mysticism in the faculties of theology and Islamic sciences. There is a society in Iran called the Islamic Society of Philosophy and Theosophy, which organizes various series of lectures on mysticism by renowned lecturers. However, practical mysticism is limited to private circles which host some few talented students. When I taught Rumi's *Masnavi* in the 60's and the 70's, even some materialists attended my lectures and said that Rumi disarms us. They only bowed before Rumi.

If one is to teach mysticism, one needs to be as careful as possible, since there are some professional considerations which have to be taken into earnest account. On the other hand, foreigners must firstly learn Islamic morality, as Islamic ethics is imbued with mysticism and can help them prepare for exposing themselves to the intense light of mystical truths. I always recommend beginners to read on Islamic morality before attending my lectures on mysticism.

Vogt: You spoke of "light." Does mysticism provide the man with an experience of enlightenment?

Ja'fari: Yes, when the soul takes the final steps along the path of fulfillment of immateriality. This is why one cannot tread this path in haste, but one needs to move forward very slowly. For example, one should firstly purify oneself of vices and then modify one's lusts. The man must adjust his relationship with the world so as to not get dazzled by divine enlightenment.

Vogt: Is there any occasion for an instructor or a guide here?

Ja'fari: Surely, the instructor knows the spiritual conditions of his pupils and can show them the best shortcut.

Vogt: You have Sufi centers and Dervish monasteries in Iran. What is the relationship between the mysticism which is taught in Qom with these centers?

Ja'fari: The priority is with mosques in Islam. A mosque is the center of spiritual ecstasy in Islam. Mosques have been prayer houses, sermon halls and even discussion rooms since the dawn of Islam up to now. Since there was no mosque in some points of world and some people wanted to live with continuous remembrance of God, some Sufi centers were built. In Islam, a mosque is *enough* for all spiritual activities. Of course, man can speak with his God in every place and at all times. It does not need any particular place, although Sufis prefer to do so in a Dervish monastery.

Now I have some questions to ask you: do you have academic courses on Islamology at your universities? How is the spiritual condition of Scandinavian countries? As you know, Sweden has no good record in this regard. Is Norway like Sweden, or does it have a better record?

Vogt: There is an intense interest in Islamic studies in Norway. Those students who want to obtain experiences in this field firstly take some courses in Arabic. The political situation of Islam has heightened this interest. We have young researchers who are acquainted with Islamic civilization and such intellectual schools as Sufism and Sufi poets like Jalaluddin Rumi, but we have no experts on Rumi. Regarding the rising interest, however, I think we will have such experts in coming generations.

Norway is less developed than Sweden in the study of Islamic traditions, although four or five researchers are working in these fields in universities. We have one Norwegian translation of the Quran, and the Moslem community of Norway is trying to provide other translations, too.

As for the spiritual condition of Norway, I should say that as you know, Scandinavian countries are known as free societies and there is no significant political, economic or spiritual struggle in them. However, some researchers who have recently emerged in these countries systematically devoted themselves to the study of the political issues of the Middle East and Islamic affairs. They have recognized that they should know Islamic traditions, although these studies are majorly used for political analyses of Middle Eastern affairs.

As for the spiritual condition of families, I do not know Iranian families well enough so as to make comparisons between Iran and Norway. It is said that the situation is different in Middle Eastern countries. There are various classes of citizens in every country, which have their own values and norms. As to social issues, every subject has an external and an internal aspect.

For example, many pretend to be faithful to values, but the reality may be otherwise. Social problems are discussed openly in Norway. Young people have numerous problems there. Divorce rates are high – one out of every three marriage ends in divorce. This percentage is on the rise too, and creates difficulties for children.

Moreover, there are also some problems regarding sexual relations between the woman and the man. Of course, the new generation has started to revise these relations and problems through returning to past traditions and values.

Ja'fari: It is never late for reclaiming primordial values, but rather some labor, time giving and honesty are required. May God help you succeed!

74

Prof. Hisae Nakanishi

**Subject: Eastern and Western Civilizations, Islam and the
West on Women's Rights
Nationality: Japanese / Major: The History of Iran
Dialogue Date: August 30, 1998**

Nakanishi: I have a question in regard to the dialogue among civilizations.[1] Following the remarks of President Seyed Muhammad Khatami concerning the combination of parts of Western and Eastern cultures, I would like to ask which parts of Western culture are of avail for Iranians in your view.

Ja'fari: If the notion of culture covers science and industry as well, whatever which is concerned with the necessities of human life and can contribute to the expansion of human knowledge is seriously defended by Islam.

As a historian, you know that Moslems had founded a library in Andalusia by late second century A.H. which contained more than six hundred thousand manuscripts in various fields of science, philosophy and the like. This example as such shows how highly interested Moslems were in culture and its expansion. There are numerous

---

1- The former Iranian president Seyyed Muhammad Khatami introduced the idea of "Dialogue among Civilizations" as a response to Samuel P. Huntington's theory of a Clash of Civilizations. The term was initially used by Austrian philosopher Hans Köchler who, in 1972 and in a letter to the UNESCO, had suggested the idea of an international conference on the "dialogue between different civilizations" (*dialogue entre les différentes civilisations*) and had organized, in 1974, the first international conference on the role of intercultural dialogue ("The Cultural Self-comprehension of Nations") with the support of and under the auspices of Senegalese President Léopold Sédar Senghor. (Translator).

examples of such rich libraries across Egypt, Iran, Iraq, Lebanon and Syria.

By the early third century A. H., some eighty faculties had been established in Andalusia. If culturophilia had not been an essential part of Islam, Moslems would not have left such magnificent works behind. Moslems' discoveries in chemistry, mathematics and medicine are very renowned.

In his *Adventures of Ideas* (1933), Whitehead compares Islamic culture with Greek culture and describes the former as authentic while he categorizes the latter as imitative. He writes:

The Byzantines and Mahometans were themselves the civilization.[1]

Whitehead is one of the founders of modern mathematical logic and I believe that he is the Plato of the contemporary Western world. He has written the best works on the history of civilization. I've widely quoted from him in most of my lectures and works as I have found him very competent. Whitehead is a wise, conscientious and distinguished philosopher.

But what does "civilization" mean in Islam? If we define civilization as material development and prosperity, no harmony and agreement would ever be envisaged among civilizations, as this definition only encompasses personal interests. Thus, giving the priority to man and his economic interests in civilization will only exhaust the energies and powers for the satisfaction of egotisms. But if our discourse on civilization is purified of racial classifications, civilizations will become more harmonizable and can behold constructive competitions and continuous development.

In a meeting with the secretary general of the Soviet embassy in Tehran during the Brezhnev[2] presidency, I asked him, "Do you have any quarrel with me as a human being?" "No," he replied. I said, "I do not have any problem with you, either. If we are after a human

---

1- Whitehead, Alfred North, *Adventures of Ideas*.

2- Leonid Ilyich Brezhnev (December 19, 1900 – 10 November 1982) was the General Secretary of the Central Committee of the Communist Party of the Soviet Union, presiding over the country from 1964 until his death in 1982. His eighteen-year term as General Secretary was second only to that of Joseph Stalin in duration. During Brezhnev's rule, the global influence of the Soviet Union grew dramatically, in part because of the expansion of the Soviet military during this time. However, his tenure as leader has often been criticized for marking the beginning of an era of economic and social stagnation that eventually led to the dissolution of the Soviet Union in 1991.

civilization, we should not have any conflict. All conflicts have their roots in "egotisms". Islam does not accept a civilization which is fraught with contradictions and conflicts. When there is no cooperation, dialogue is meaningless too. Civilizations require some common principles in order to engage with each other in a peaceful manner.

But as to your question about elements of western culture which can be useful for Eastern people, I should say that there are two significant issues in Islam which have been discussed in a theoretical form and we behold them in practice:

The first issue is discipline. Islam believes that life without discipline ends up in nihilism. There are also numerous prophetic traditions regarding the necessity of discipline in life. Imam Ali (PBUH) states:

I strongly recommend you to observe discipline.[1]

We can find this discipline in practical form in Western civilization. The lesson reads: "O' Moslems! What is in your principles of faith is practicable, so put the discipline into practice!"

The second issue, which is even more important, is taking the world seriously. We have not believed yet that the material world is very serious. Therefore, there are some baseless cultures and moral taboos in the East. We think that we can manage our affairs with sentiments and daydreaming, while it needs practical measures and serious decisions. As every medicine has its own particular chemical formula and not every medicine can be prescribed for every patient, such seriousness and precision is necessary in all aspects of material life. Westerners have taken material affairs very seriously. Of course, Islam has also recommended to believers that, "Whoever does not take this world seriously will not take the hereafter serious, either". To put the matter otherwise, we must take this world as seriously as we take the hereafter world.

It is not clear what has caused Easterners to ignore the importance of material affairs. Of course, Japan has been fortunately less infected with this virus, and this can be studied as a turning point in their culture. When Japan underwent striking economic developments, Mirza Taghi Khan Amir Kabir in Iran also started some movements, which were unfortunately thwarted. We do not exactly know when human sentiments and emotions have begun to permeate into the serious issues of life in Eastern lands. The serious issues of material life

---

1- *Nahjulbalaghah*, Letter 47.

have their own particular procedures which do not fit in the structure of human emotions and sentiments, while these two have been combined in the East and have led to our underdevelopment.

One of the reasons for this technological and industrial underdevelopment seems to be radical spiritualism, which has plagued almost all Eastern countries. Extremism in every form is dangerous. Unfortunately, the West is also pestered with material radicalism. During the nineteenth and twentieth centuries, Western people have been *merely* occupied with material affairs. New developments made in industries, war implements and the like, have changed man into a dangerous creature! Therefore, they are unconscious of the universal spirit of the world. They set on wars and trespass the rights of oppressed and poor people. This is itself one of the factors that have dissuaded Eastern people from taking concrete steps toward industrialization and technological developments. On the other hand, if spiritual matters had been considered by Westerners too along with material affairs, a universal movement would have taken form which could have united the East and the West in many aspects.

Victor Cherbuliez,[1] who has widely written on wars and peace treaties argues:

> From 1500 B.C. to 1860 A. D., less than eight thousand peace treaties were signed, each one supposed to provide everlasting peace, but not even one them lasted any more than two years.[2]

If man had turned to spiritual matters, such wars and peace deals would have never occurred. This statistics show that treaties have been mostly signed under the pressures of one powerful side; otherwise, the fire of war would always keep on burning.

Now you may ask how one can reconcile matter with meaning. There is an unbridgeable gap between physics and metaphysics, and yet we speak of reconciliation!

Max Planck, the greatest religious physicist of the twentieth century, has said:

1- Cherbuliez, Charles Victor (b. July 19, 1829 – d. July 1, 1899) was a French novelist and author. He was born in Geneva, Switzerland and died in Combs-la-Ville. He was the eleventh member elected to occupy Seat 3 of the Académie française in 1881. (Translator).
2- For more details see: Ja'fari, M. T., *A Translation and Interpretation of Nahjulbalaghah*, Vol. 12. (Originally in Persian).

There can never be any real opposition between religion and science, for the one is the complement of the other. Every serious and reflective person realizes, I think, that the religious element in his nature must be recognized and cultivated if all the powers of the human soul are to act together in perfect balance and harmony. And indeed it was not by any accident that the greatest thinkers of all ages were also deeply religious souls, even though they made no public show of their religious feeling. It is from the cooperation of understanding and will that the finest fruit of philosophy has arisen, namely, the ethical fruit. Science enhances the moral values of life, because it furthers a love of truth and reverence – the love for the truth displaying itself in the constant endeavor to arrive at a more exact knowledge of the world of mind and matter around us, and reverence, because every advance in knowledge brings us face to face with the mystery of our own being.[1]

Thus, the cooperation of "understanding" and "will" results in the emergence of the finest fruit of philosophy, i.e. ethical fruit. *Undoubtedly, science adds to the moral values of life.*

There are numerous prophetic traditions which urge believers to take the material world seriously. The Prophet Muhammad (PBUH) has been quoted to have said:

If you eat a date and throw its kernel away without having thought of its planting, you have committed dissipation.

In another *hadith*, the Holy Prophet (PBUH) states:

O' Lord! Bless our bread [i.e. economy]. If we had no bread, we would not have prayed, fasted and fulfilled our other religious obligations.[2]

Therefore, Easterners can learn "discipline" and "seriousness in material affairs" from the Westerners, although both issues have been frequently underlined in our religious texts.

As you are working on Islamic sciences and traditions, I propose that you should make also some studies of Shi'ism and encourage your society to pay attention to this divine school as well.

Nakanishi: Last year I read an article in *Tehran Times,* in which you had written, "Europeans must prove, through philosophical arguments, that man has inherent dignity and is not an animal with a brutal nature". Would you please explain your remark and tell me

---

1- Planck, Max (1932), *Where is Science Going?*
2- Muhammad Ibn Koleyni, *Al-Foru' Min Al-Kafi*, Vol. 5.

whether Islam has a different view of this issue than that of Europeans?

Ja'fari: Yes, Islam has its own particular view on this issue. Man has a definite inherent dignity in Islam. The Quran states:

And surely we have honored the children of Adam.

(The Night Journey 17:70)

In other words, Islam considers all human individuals regardless of their religious backgrounds and affiliations as being worthy of honor, but in the West, we do not see such an egalitarian attitude. If we ground our worldview in Hobbesian and Machiavellian ideas, we should say that human interests have honor, not man's nature! If Machiavellian oppressors had believed that man has an inherent dignity, which must be observed without any consideration, so many wars and bloodsheds would never have happened. Are the wretched human conditions in Africa and other points of the world indeed compatible with human rights? If man had been honored, we wouldn't nowadays see such miserable scenes of human crises worldwide.

Nakanishi: It is not so that all Western schools of philosophy are Machiavellian, and Machiavelli's thesis is basically no more than a philosophical idea.

Ja'fari: That is right, but the evidence existing around us shows that most Western governments are established upon such cruel principles. A great European man has said, "Political philosophy is what philosophers expect from politics, while politics is what politicians *do*." Whitehead states that:

> *Human nature is so complex that plans for the society are to statesman not worth even the price of the defect paper.*[1]

Nakanishi: I would like to know your view on the new movements of women's rights in Iran. In European countries, women and men have equal rights, but Islamic Shari'ah has a different view as to this issue and claims that woman always needs men's support. What is your assessment of this issue?

Ja'fari: When we turn to authentic Islamic sources to find the answers of the dilemmas concerning women, we see that all of these sources unanimously announce that men and women have equal existential value. The Quran openly states:

1- Whitehead, Alfred North, *Adventures of Ideas*.

O' men! Surely we have created you of a male and a female, and made you tribes and families that you may know each other; surely the most honorable of you with Allah is the one among you most careful (of his duty); surely Allah is knowing, aware.

(The Apartments 49:13)

But as to the second question, which can be also examined from a legal point of view, I should say that no one would doubt that the man is physically stronger than the woman and is more patient in the face of natural disasters as well. Struggles with nature, splitting mountains, excavating seas and taking part in wars all fits in with the physical features of men, though this does not mean that men are existentially more valuable than women. However, there are some legal considerations which should be taken into account, as Islam strongly insists on the primacy of the family and the importance of its management, which has been assigned to the woman, who is the "mother" of the family. On the other hand, emotions should be sought in the eyes and bosoms of mothers. A man cannot fill the vacant space of a meaningful motherly look. According to Sir Bertrand Russell:

A child who does not grow in his mother's arms is better for war.

Thus, I believe that **"the woman lives the taste of life, while man only conceives it."** If we see nowadays that people are estranged to each other and live alone in the West, it is indeed a result of the destruction of the family's foundations. As Nietzsche says:

A woman's passion, a total renunciation of all rights of her own, postulates precisely that the same feeling, the same desire for renunciation, exists also in the other sex, for if both severally made this renunciation for love, there would result, on my word I do not know just what, shall we say, perhaps, the horror of nothingness. The woman wishes to be taken ... she demands, therefore, someone to take her, someone who does not give himself, who does not abandon himself, but who wishes, on the contrary, to enrich his ego through love ... The woman gives herself, the man adds to himself by taking her.[1]

Nakanishi: Why should the law support women?

Ja'fari: In Islam, the man is obliged to pay for the woman's cost of living and this has an economic reason, since men are more eroded in

---

1- de Beauvoir, Simone, *Le Deuxième Sexe ("The Second Sex")* (1956), p. 623 [translated into English by H. M. Parshley, Jonathan Cape Publishers, London].

economic processes and women have a secondary presence in the economy. It is men who bear the burden of economic activities. Women play a distinguished role in Iranian families. If a woman is pious and intelligent, her man prefers to lean upon her shoulders and choose her as his companion. In fact, the woman gives the orders and the man implements them. There is no objection against women's employment if it does not cause the family any damage. Many books have been written on women's problems throughout history while it is only less than a half century that there have been debates on women's presence in economic affairs in the West. Since the very dawn of Islam, women have successfully worked in such fields as nursing, medicine, jurisprudence, rational debates and philosophy, while they have also fulfilled their duties within the family. Lady Amin Isfahani was a *Mujtahid* woman who had continuous jurisprudential debates with her contemporary *Mujtahid* men.

Islam has frequent recommendations on the observation of women's rights. For example, one of the legal orders as to the woman is that if someone quarrels with a woman and pulls her hair in this quarrel, the judge can fine the puller to pay the whole price of the blood of a man if her pulled hair does not grow again, because her beauty has been damaged and this is as if her life has been taken. Do you have such tough laws in support of woman in the West? The implementation of these laws is

Translator's Note

Si nous ne trouvons pas des choses agrèables, nous trouverons du moins des choses nouvelles.

If we do not find anything pleasant, at least we shall find something new.　　　　　　　　　　　　　(Voltaire 'Candide' (1759) ch. 17)

Although the lights of casinos of Las Vegas in Nevada State is said to be seen from the moon and almost all parts of the world enjoy the power of electricity but we still live in a dark world. This darkness is so strong that no generator could ever overcome it. It is the darkness of stupidity which has permeated into every corner of the globe. Hundreds of innocent women and children are dying every day in Africa due to the ethnic clashes, lack of hygiene, water and food supply, medical cares, education and so on and so forth. Why do we ignore our fellowmen so easily? The answer which Allameh Ja'fari gives to this question is very thought provoking. He argues,

> The status quo of human societies shows that we live in the century of absence of humanity the century of self-alienation, and strictly speaking, the century of self-contradiction.

One of the major causes of this catastrophic occultation of humanity is the lack of constructive engagements between the intellectuals and elites worldwide. Many of human discourses have been sorely marginalized by evil talks of politics and are direly required to be reclaimed by conscientious intelligentsia. Mr. Ja'fari is one of this conscientious and committed intelligentsia who has devoted his whole academic and intellectual career to the revival of these marginalized discourses. This book reconstructs his passionate intellectual engagements with his western and eastern colleagues for reclaiming valuable notions of human discourses which have been buried under evil dusts of politics and militarism.

I would like to express my wholehearted gratitude to The Allameh Ja'fari Institute and its director Ali Ja'fari for their sincere efforts for preparation of M. T. Ja'fari's works for global audience. I am also obliged by my beloved wife who has kindly sustained me during the preparation of this translation. I was enormously benefitted from her scholarship of Greek and Heidegger in some of my footnotes to this book. I dedicate this work to her as a sign of gratitude and love.

Beytollah Naderlew
April, 2014
Sahand Area, Tabriz

Index of Concepts

Index of Names

Bibliographical Index

1. Al-Hosni, Abu Bakr, *The Story of Righteous Believing Women* original Arabic edition.

2. Allameh Helli, *Kashf ul-Murad*.

3. Ameli, Sheikh Horr-e, *Wasa'il Al-Shi'ah*.

4. Amin, Ahmad, *The Dawn of Islam*.

5. Aristotle, *Politics*, translated by William Ellis (1928).

6. Asha'ri, Abu Al-Hasan Ali Ibn Ismaeil, *Believers Discord*, original Arabic version.

7. Asimov, Isaac (1972), *Biographical Encyclopedia of Science and Technology*.

8. Attar Nishaburi, Abu Hamid Ibn Abu Bakr, *Mantiq-ut-Tayr ("Conference of Birds")*, original Persian edition.

9. Avicenna, *Al-Isharat wa-'l-tanbihat ("Remarks and Admonitions")*.

10. Avicenna, *Canon*, original Persian edition.

11. Baqlani, Abu Bakr, *Tamhid*.

12. Bernal, John D., (1954), *Science in History: The Emergence of Science*.

13. Carrel, Alexis (1935): *Man The Unknown*, New York and London, Harper and Brothers.

14. Dante Alighieri, *Divine Comedy*.

15. De Beauvoir, Simone, *Le Deuxième Sexe ("The Second Sex")*.

16. Delicostopoulos, Constantin S., *Greek Intellectualism and Orthodox Philosophy*.

17. Delicostopoulos, Constantin S., *Madonna and the Sword of Islam*.

18. Delicostopoulos, Constantin S., *Orthodox Belief*.

19. Delicostopoulos, Constantin S., *Orthodox Mysticism*.

20. Delicostopoulos, Constantin S., *The Kremlin Wall*.

21. Feydh Kashani, Mullah Muhsen, *Glorious Destination*.

22. Ferdowsi, Hakim Abulqasem, *Shahnameh*, original Persian edition.

23. Frank, Philip (1947): *Einstein: His Life and Times*, translated from a German manuscript by George Rosen, edited and revised by Shuichi Kusaka, New York, Alfred A. Knope.

24. Freud, Sigmund (1930): *Civilization and its Discontents*, The Standard Edition of the Complete Psychological Works of Sigmund Freud, Volume XXI (1927-1931): *The Future of an Illusion, Civilization and its Discontents, and Other Works*, 57-14.

25. Fromm, Erich, *Religion and Psychoanalysis*.

26. Ghazali, Imam Muhammad, *Tahafat ul-Falasifah ("The Incoherence of Philosophers")*, original Persian edition.

27. Ghazali, Imam Muhammad, *The Revival of Religious Sciences*, original Persian edition.

28. Griffin, P. (2008): *On Human Rights*, Oxford, Oxford University Press.

29. Hakimi, Muhammad Reza, *Imam: The Identity of the Society*, original Persian edition.

30. Hassan, Hassan Ibrahim, *The Political History of Islam*, original Persian edition.

31. Homer, *The Iliad*.

32. Hugo, Victor, *Les Miserables*.

33. Hunke, Sigrid (1960), *"Allahs Sonne über dem Abendland"* (*"Allah's Sun over the Occident"*).

34. Ibn Khaldun, *History*.

35. Ibn Khaldun, *The Muqaddimah*.

36. Jaberi, Abu al-Abbas Ahmad Ibn Yahya Ibn (Balazori), *Futuh ul-Buldan*.

37. Ja'fari, M. T., *Aesthetics and Art from an Islamic Point of View* (2008), The Allameh Ja'fari Institute, Tehran.

38. Ja'fari, M. T., (2008), *An Analytical Exposition of the Russell-Wyatt Dialogues*, 4th Persian edition. The Allameh Jafari Institute, Tehran.

39. Ja'fari, M.T., *Divine Gnosis, An Interpretation of Imam Ali Ibn Musa al-Reza's (PBUH)*. The Allameh Jafari Institute, Tehran.

40. Ja'fari, M. T., *A Survey of the Philosophy of Science* (2007). The Allameh Jafari Institute, Tehran.

41. Ja'fari, M. T., *A Translation and Interpretation of Nahjulbalaghah* (in 27 volumes) (2000), The Allameh Jafari Institute, Tehran.

42. Ja'fari, M. T., (2014): *Human Universal Rights: A Comparative Research in Islam and the West,* English translation, The Allameh Jafari Institute, Tehran.

43. Ja'fari, M. T., (2011): *Intelligible Life,* translated into English by Beytollah Naderlew, The Allameh Jafari Institute.

44. Ja'fari, M. T., *Morality and Religion* (2000), The Allameh Jafari Institute, Tehran.

45. Ja'fari, M. T., *On the Philosophy of Science* (2002), The Allameh Jafari Institute, Tehran.

46. Ja'fari, M. T., *Rumi: the Man and His Ideas, an Interpretation, Criticism and Analysis of Rumi's Masnavi* (in 15 volumes) (2002), The Allameh Jafari Institute, Tehran.

47. Ja'fari, M. T., (2009), *Science and Religion in Intelligible Life,* The Allameh Jafari Institute, Tehran.

48. Ja'fari, M. T., *The Conscience* (2002), The Allameh Jafari Institute, Tehran.

49. Ja'fari, M. T., (2013*), The Human Genome Project,* The Allameh Jafari Institute, Tehran.

50. Ja'fari, M. T., *The Message of Reason* (2007), The Allameh Jafari Institute, Tehran.

51. Ja'fari, M. T., *The Philosophy of Religion* (2014), The Allameh Jafari Institute, Tehran, Tehran.

52. Ja'fari, M. T., *The Principles of Education* (2008), The Allameh Jafari Institute, Tehran.

53. Ja'fari, M. T., *The Quran: the Symbol of Intelligible Life* (2005), The Allameh Jafari Institute, Tehran.

54. Jami, Nuriddin Abdul Rahman, *Nafahat al-Uns ("Breaths of Fellowship"),* original Arabic edition.

55. Juneyd Iraqi, *Collected Essays,* original Arabic version.

56. Juneyd Mu'einuddin Abu Al-Ghasem, *Shad ul-Azar fi Hati al-Auzar an Zuwari.*

57. Heidegger, Martin (1968), *What Is It Called Thinking?* Harper and Row Publishers, New York (An English Translation of original German 1954 *Was Heisst Denken*).

58. Imam Ali (PBUH), *Nahj-ul-Balaghah.*

59. Iqbal, Muhammad (1934): *Reconstruction of Religious Thought in Islam*, London, Oxford University Press: Humphrey Milford.

60. Kahhalah, Omar Reza, *The Women's Index in Arab and Islamic Worlds*.

61. Kant, Immanuel, *Prolegomena*.

62. Khayyam Neishaburi, *A Treatise on Euclid's Theorems*.

63. Khayyam Neishaburi, *Essay on Algebra*.

64. Khayyam Neishaburi, *Malekshah's Horoscope*.

65. Khayyam Neishaburi, *The Book of Noruz*.

66. Khayyam Neishaburi, *The Measure of Wisdom in Genesis and Obligations*.

67. Kolayni, Sheikh Muhammad Ibn Yaqub, *Al-Foru' Min Al-Kafi*.

68. Kolayni, Sheikh Muhammad Ibn Yaqub, (2000): *Usul Al-Kafi* (6 Volumes), translated and glossed by Muhammad Bagher Kamarei, Qum, the Research Institute of the History of Islamic Knowledge.

69. Le Bon, Gustav, *La Civilization d'Islam et Arab*.

70. Machiavelli, Niccolo di Bernardo, *Discourses*.

71. Machiavelli, Niccolo (1985): *The Prince*, translation: Harvey C. Mansfield, Jr, Chicago: University of Chicago Press.

72. Mazlish, Bruce (2006), August Comte in the *Encyclopedia of Philosophy*.

73. Montesquieu, Charles Louis de Secondat: (1995), *De L'esprit de Lois*, edited by Tome Quatrieme, Paris, Gallimard.

74. Mulla Ali Qushchi, *Sharhi Tajrid*.

75. Mulla Sadra, *al-Hikmat al-Mutaalyah fi al-Asfar al-Arbati al-Aqlyah*, original Arabic edition.

76. Nasawi, Abu al-Hassan Ali Ibn Ahmad, *Sunani Nisaei*.

77. Nasr, Seyed H. *An Anthology of Philosophy in Persia*.

78. Nezami Ganjavi, *Eskandarnameh*, original Persian edition.

79. Nezami Ganjavi, *Khusrow and Shirin*, original Persian edition.

80. Oparin, Alexander Ivanovich, *Life, Its Nature and Source of Evolution*.

81. Pines, S., *Madhab al-dhurra inda al-muslimīn wa alāqatuhu bi-madhāhib al-Yūnān wa al-Hunūd: : wa-maahu falsafa Muhammad*

ibn Zakarīyā al-Rāzī ("Muslim Takes of Atomism and Its Relationship with Greek and Hindu Schools of Thought along with the Philosophy of Zakariya-ye Razi").

82. Planck, Max (1932), *Where Is Science Going?*

83. Plato, *Republic.*

84. Qumi, Muhadith, *The Ark of Seas.*

85. Qushchi, Mulla Ali, *The Book of Catharsis.*

86. Rumi, Jalaliddin Muhammad, *Fihi ma Fihi ("Discourses"),* original Persian edition.

87. Rumi, M. Jalaluddin (1990): *Masnavi'e Ma'navi ("Spiritual Couplets"),* translated, edited and glossed by Reynold A. Nicholson, London, Cambridge University Press.

88. Rumi, M. Jalaluddin (1893): *Selected Poems from the Dıvani Shamsi Tabrız,* trans. R. A. Nicholson, London, Cambridge University Press.

89. Rousseau, Jean-Jacques, *On the Social Contract (Du contrat social ou Principes du droit politique, 1762),* English translation.

90. Russell, Bertrand Arthur William, *A History of Western Philosophy* (1964), Persian translation.

91. Russell, Betrand Arthur William. *Bertrand Russell Speaks His Mind* (196), Persian edition.

92. Russell, Bertrand Arthur William, *Mysticism and Logic and Other Essays* (1917), Persian translation.

93. Russell, Bertrand Arthur William, *ABC of Relativity* (1925), Persian translation.

94. Sabri, Muhammad Hafiz, *Between Judaism and Islam: A Jurisprudential Encounter.*

95. Sarton, George (1948), *The Life of Science: Essays in the History of Civilization.*

96. Sayyed Qutb, *Fi Zelal al-Quran.*

97. Selmi, Sheikh Abu Abdul Rahman, *Biographies of Sufi Elders.*

98. Shoqi Zeif, *The History of Arabic Literature.*

99. Tabarsi, Sheikh Abu Ali Fadhl ibn Hassan, *Al-Ihtijaj.*

100. Tabatabaei, Muhammad Hussein, *Al-Mizan.*

101. Tabatabaei, Muhammad Hussein, *Shi'ah Islam.*

102. *The Cairo Declaration of Human Rights in Islam,* The

Organization of the Islamic Conference, 1993.

103. *The Holy Quran* (2009): Translation with commentary by Tahereh Saffarzadeh, Tehran, Pars Ketab Publisher.

104. Tusi, Khajeh Nasiruddin, *Tajrid al-Eteqad*.

105. Whitehead, Alfred North, *Adventures of Ideas*, New York, The Free Press.

106. Zaydan, Jurji, *Tarikh al-Tamaddun al-Islami ("The History of Islamic Civilization")*.

Published Books

1) Positive Mysticism (English).

2) The Conscience (English).

3) Pioneer Culture to the rescue of mankind (English).

4) The mystery Of Life (English).

5) Intelligible Life (English & Russian).

6) Human Universal Rights (English).

7) Imam Hossein's prayers at the Arafat Desert (Arabic & Turkish).

8) The Human Genome Project (English).

9) The Coordination between Science and Religion (Arabic).